FORKS OF ELKHORN CHURCH

By

ERMINA JETT DARNELL

With Genealogies of
Early Members

Reprinted with Numerous
Additions and Corrections

CLEARFIELD

Reprinted for
Clearfield Company, Inc. by
Genealogical Publishing Co., Inc.
Baltimore, Maryland
1993, 1995, 2000, 2002

Originally Published: Louisville, Kentucky, 1946
Reprinted, with Additions and Corrections,
by Genealogical Publishing Co., Inc.
Baltimore, 1980
From a volume in the Virginia State Library, Richmond
Library of Congress Catalogue Card Number 79-92437
International Standard Book Number 0-8063-0883-4
Made in the United States of America

Dedicated

To All Who Love
The Forks of Elkhorn Church

FOREWORD

The history of this church has been written many times before, but never, perhaps, by a native of the community. It is in fact a story of the church and of the community, for it would be impossible to write the one without telling of the other.

It is desirable that these records should be preserved in their local setting, for the Forks of Elkhorn Church occupied an important position in the settlement of Kentucky. It was the gateway through which many of the pioneer Baptists came from the great territory that was then embraced in Fayette County, tarried a while for replenishment, and then floated down the river to form new centers of Christianity, or pushed westward, carrying what they had received to the uttermost parts of the earth.

The chief source of information for the historians is the old minute book of the church, the entries beginning in 1788. It is a remarkable record, and worthy of much study.

The quaint spelling in the old book has so often been exploited that the impression is apt to be prevalent that our forefathers were a crude, unlettered lot; but on the contrary some of the entries, from a literary standpoint, would do credit to Washington or Jefferson, for many of the pioneers had better educational opportunities in Virginia and Maryland than did their children in Kentucky. Even if it were otherwise, it would scarcely be respectful to call attention to such unimportant details as spelling or punctuation. Who among us is worthy to undo the latchet of William Hickman's shoe?

Truly, "the letter killeth, but the spirit giveth life."

Moreover, these writers were of our own blood, and there is little to be said for one who would make sport of his own family.

It is with increasing admiration that one perceives through these records the sincerity, zeal, faith, patience, and the real statesmanship of those who were here before us. It is as though we should find in some obscure corner of the attic a trunk in which our dear old grandparents had lovingly placed gifts to await our coming. How carefully we should handle them, and cherish them as heirlooms!

But these treasures are of little value unless they are put to service. If this accumulation of spiritual insights be enriched by the patina of our own religious experiences, then we may feel in some degree worthy of our inheritance.

Where the old meetinghouse stood there is only a cultivated field, with nothing to indicate that it is God's acre.

> "The wind passeth over it, and it is gone,
> And the place thereof shall know it no more."

But now that the last tombstone has disappeared from that hallowed spot, we ourselves, the lineal and spiritual descendants of that early congregation, must be their memorials, and in our own lives honor them by continuing and enlarging their work.

ERMINA JETT DARNELL

Frankfort, Kentucky
October 19, 1939

ADDITIONS AND CORRECTIONS
To Darnell's Forks of Elkhorn Church

Page 5, para. 4, line 1: after parenthesis mark insert *in Woodford County,*

Page 8, para. 5, line 2: for *1808* read *1832*

Page 8, para. 5, line 3: for *said to have been given* read *sold*

Page 8, para. 6, line 1: for *in 1856* read *July 3, 1857*

Page 11, para. 3, line 4: add *Her mother was a descendant of Alexander Campbell.*

Page 11, para. 5, line 7: delete period after *Shipps* and insert *, Steeles, Porters, and McDowells.*

Page 29, para. 1, line 4: after *Holloway,* insert *Jett,*

Page 29, para. 1, line 5: after *Todd,* insert *Vaughan,*

Page 30, para. 5, line 5: after *Davidge* insert *, a licensed preacher,*

Page 30, para. 5, line 13: add *Rev. John, Elizabeth and Ben Taylor joined, 1814.*

Page 51, para. 6, line 3: after *acre* insert *(formerly owned by Walter N. Ayres, in whose memory a tablet was placed in the old church)*

Page 65, para. 4, line 7: after *went to* insert *Cole Co.,*; for *in 1843* read *before 1829.*

Page 67, line 4: after *Fall* insert *(1800-1888)*

Page 67, para. 1, line 8: after *Mary* delete period and insert *; g, Martha.*

Page 73, para. 2, line 2: after *1801,* insert *had a race track at the Scruggs place,*

Page 73, para. 2, line 15: after *William,* insert *killed by Tom Steele,*

Page 74, para. 1, line 7: for *Wilanna* read *Willina*

Page 74, para. 1, line 11: for *Wilanna* read *Willina*

Page 74, para. 1, line 12: for *– – – Marsh* read *Hannah Marsh*

Page 74, para. 1, line 15: for *– – – Herndon* read *Sallie Herndon*

Page 75, after line 5 insert new paragraph: *Mary Weldon South wrote: "Gideon Blackburn was a missionary to the Cherokee Indians in Tennessee. He also established a school in this tribe."*

Page 75, para. 5, line 4: after *William* insert *(collected for wolf heads, 1724)*

Page 77, para. 2, line 5: after *William* insert , *b Owen 1833, d Carroll 1859*

Page 80, para. 2, line 3: after *1812* insert *witnessed by Abraham*

Page 80, para. 2, line 4: after *children,* insert *Rev. Wm. Miller and*

Page 80, para. 2, line 9/10: for *Judith – – –* read *Judith Ward*

Page 81, para. 3, line 9: after *m* insert *first,;* after *Mallory* insert *second, Mrs. Collins?, third, Susanna Grant?*

Page 82, para 1, line 6: after *Elizabeth* insert *(Sarah?)*

Page 85, para. 4, line 5: after *Jenkins* insert *dau of Harry,*

Page 85, para. 4, line 6: after *1808* insert *(1818?)*

Page 85, para. 4, line 7: after *John* insert *m Elizabeth Wilkirson, dau Snelling, had Leland John, m Martha Wheeler, and they had Susan Mary, m Dr. Robert C. Gayle, and they were parents of Dr. J.W. Gayle, Frankfort druggist*

Page 85, para. 4, line 8: after *m* insert *first,*

Page 85, para. 4, line 9: after *1834* insert *m second, Mrs. Strickler;* for *Joseph Leeland* read *Leeland Joseph m Mary Perkins, of Tenn.*

Page 90, para. 2, line 9: for *Benjamin* read *Berry*

Page 91, para. 4, line 1: after *Brown* insert , *son of Jacob and Susanna, Amherst Co., Va.,*

Page 92, para. 3, line 5: after *Laura – – –* insert , *F census 1880 says Albert was 63, wife Eliza 53, son Edward R. 22, dau Laura 20*

Page 92, para. 5, line 6: after *Thomas* insert *(had Robt. W. b 1795, who had R. C. b 1841, m Kate – – – 1878)*

Page 93, line 2: for *m – – –* read *m Walker*

Page 100, para. 2, line 6: for *Mary – – –* read *Mary Campbell (dau Patrick)*

Page 100, para. 2, line 7: after *Lucy* insert *?*

Page 101, para. 1, line 3: add *Wm. was son of Israel, who was nephew of Gilbert I.*

Page 102, para. 1, line 1: after *Hubbard* insert *(1730-1795, Feb. 11)*

Page 103, para. 4, line 1: delete *Robert*

Page 103, para. 4, line 2: for *Sally Lightfoot* read *Lucretia Waggoner*

Page 104, para. 2, line 7: for *m – – –* read *m John McKim*

Page 104, para. 2, line 8: for *Sallie* read *Sarah Lee m Henry Gassaway;* for *Gazaway* read *John Crittenden;* delete *John; h*

Page 104, para. 5, line 4: after *John* delete period and insert *;Ambrose.*

Page 106, para. 5, line 2: add *Jacob Yates in F tax list 1795. No others.*

Page 107, para. 3, line 1: after *Cook* insert *Jones*

Page 108, line 1: after *Johnson* insert *?*

Page 110, para. 3, line 7: add *John and Alcey Harris Cox were in Henry Co., Va., 1791, when son Ancil was born. Came to Woodford, later to Morgan Co., Ill., where John, aged 90, was living with son Harris, 1850. Ancil and Polly had John Bradley, m 1840 Perlina Luttrell, G. & H., Dec. 15, 1946.*

Page 111, para. 2, line 7: for *their* read *Stephen and Lydia's*

Page 112, para. 2, line 1: after *Smith* insert *(m first Mrs. Andrew Gatewood?)*

Page 114, para. 2, line 4: delete parentheses and question mark; after *Holt* insert *(Fannie B. Holt, Spencer, 1841?)*

Page 115, line 2: For *Wakefield* read *Grubbs Wilson, Shelby 1849*; delete *and went to Shelby* and insert *remained in Shelby, and had Laura, m Matthew Wakefield, parents of John M. Wakefield who m − − − Taylor, and had Katherine, m − − − Hogan*

Page 117, para. 2, line 2: after *Shannon* insert *(1789-1869), Reg. Apr. '53, p. 139*

Page 119, para. 1, line 4: after *were* insert *1,*

Page 119, para. 1, line 5: after *May* insert *; 2, Nancy, m Richard Hawes, 1857, and had Willie Davis Hawes, m Ida Church, 1879.*

Page 119, para. 1, line 10: after *1835.* insert *Miss Jane Lewis wrote: "Joel Scott bought it from Joseph Davis, sold it, and bought it again from John Smith in 1831".*

Page 122, para. 1, line 3: after *Phoebe Dillon* insert *(dau Thomas Brown, Fredericksburg, Va.)*

Page 123, para. 5, line 1: after *Darnell* insert *(Darnall)*

Page 123, para. 5, line 4: for *Grey, and* read *Gray, and was*

Page 123, para. 5, line 12: for *m − − − Shelburn* read *m James Shelburne, Shelby, 1849.*

Page 124, para. 3, line 10: for *j, Edward, went to California* read *j, Edward Marlborough, b W 1833, went to California, m Cordelia Adelaide Davis and had Wilford Darneal who m Lelia May Whiting and had Dudley Leroy, m Ida Aloha Crecelius;*

Page 127, para. 3, line 4: for *north* read *south*

Page 129, para. 1, line 4: for *Heaton* read *Keaton*

Page 129, para. 3, line 2: after *James* delete parenthesis

Page 129, para. 3, line 3: after *1801* delete question mark and parenthesis

Page 129, para. 3, line 5: after *James* delete comma and insert parenthesis; after *1829* insert question mark and parenthesis

Page 137, line 2: after *Virginia,* insert *had dau Mary (1771-1854),*

Page 137, para. 3: after line 5 insert new paragraph: *"Peter Montague (1603-1659) Lancaster Co.; son of Peter and Eleanor Montague, of Boveny, Parish of Burnham, Bucks." (From* Montague Genealogy, *pp. 30-31, and chart in* Some Emigrants to Virginia.*)*

Page 137, para. 7, line 1: after *also* insert *de Force,*

Page 138, line 6: after *Stedmantown;* insert *Laura Penn; Frank; – – –(mother of Mrs. Chas. Duvall); Juliette; and Mary, second wife of E. G. Gaines. Their children were: Elbridge Geary Gaines, Jane Preston, and Juliette, who m Arthur T. Bryson of Ashland;*

Page 138, para. 4, line 5: delete *Mitchell* and insert *m Samuel R. Mitchell, sold to Trabue, went to Mo.*

Page 140, para. 2, line 2: after *William A. Gaines* insert *, b Bourbon 1832,*

Page 141, para. 3, line 3: after *died* insert *1794 or*

Page 141, para. 4, line 10/11: for *Elizabeth Stewart* read *Elizabeth Holmes Stuart*

Page 145, para. 1, line 2: after *John* delete S.; after *Daniel* insert *(1758-1853)*

Page 145, para. 1, line 9: after *Hubbell* insert *(1760-1868)*

Page 145, para. 2, line 1: after *John* delete S. and insert *Stites (1766- – – –)*

Page 145, para. 2, line 6: for *Susanna* read *Susannah (1772- – – – –);* after *Eaton* insert *(1770- – – – –)*

Page 145, para. 2, line 9: after *Sarah* insert *(1764- – – –)*

Page 145, para. 2, line 10: after *Hubbell* insert *(Deed Book P, p. 52, F Co.)*

Page 145, para. 3, line 11: after *Texas.* insert *10, Daughter (1768-1770); 11, William (1782-1798).*

Page 151, para. 7, line 1: after *Jackson* insert *(surety John L.)*

Page 152, para. 2, line 4: after *John H.* insert *(1788-1839);* after *David* insert *(1784-1863)*

Page 152, para. 2, line 6: delete *W.* and insert *Washington (1780-1863)*

Page 152, para. 2, line 7: after *Frankfort.* delete rest of the line and insert *John Rowan Graham (s Geo. W. and Susan) m his cousin, Margaret Graham (dau Francis and Mary Finnie) F 1837. Geo. W. m second Marilda Tupper, F*

Page 152, para. 4, line 1: after *Robinson* insert *(1783-1813)*

Page 152, para. 4, line 2: after *Francis* insert *Jr.*

Page 153, line 1: delete *Montgomery* and insert *(1770-1865) m Wm. Montgomery, F 1801;* delete *Peggy* and insert *Margaret (Peggy) (1771- – – –)*

Page 153, line 3: delete *Samuel* and after *1785* insert *m Larkin Samuel, 1810; 12, James (1786-1805).*

Page 162, para. 5, line 3: after *William* insert *, Frankfort doctor and druggist, had wife Caroline, son Eugene, dau Eloise*

Page 167, line 17: for *Munday* read *Monday*

Page 168, line 10: for *m – – –* read *m Dr. Aquila*

Page 168, line 13: after *Switzer* delete period and insert *; g, Julia m Mason Lucas.*

Page 168, para. 1, line 3: after *Benjamin T.* insert *m Elizabeth Bohon, dau Mercer 1827*

Page 168, para. 3, line 7: delete *(m Margaret?)* and insert *, m Nancy Sheridan, F 1813*

Page 168, para. 3, line 8: after *John M.* insert *; i, Nancy, m in Franklin, first Wm. Brydon, second Robert Brydon.*

Page 168, para. 4, line 1/2 and p. 169, line 1: delete *In Franklin, Benjamin T. Head m Nancy Sheridan, 1813; Benjamin T. m Elizabeth Bohon, 1827;*

Page 169, line 3: delete *Nancy m William Brydon;*

Page 169, para. 2, line 3: after *Gilderoy* insert *(Welsh lady who came to America 1758)*

Page 174, para. 3: after line 8 insert new paragraph: *A family record names the children of William Hickman and his second wife, Elizabeth as: 1, Simeon D.; 2, John Gano, died in infancy; 3, Edwin A., b Oct. 10, 1819, Capt. Mo. State Guard. Later joined Confederacy; 4, James R.; 5, Ezra R.*
As the Garr Genealogy *names them: 1, Edwin Alfred (1818-1885) m Catherine Macintree Oldham in Jackson, Mo., 1843, and they had William Zero, 1845; Annie, 1848. 2, James Richard (1821-1881) m Monica Octavia Darst, Platte, Mo., 1850, and they had Mary Waters; Robert Eliot; Annie E.; Jenna Octavia; Cora Chambers; Alverda; Mabel Julia. 3, Ezra Richmond (1823-1887 or 1888) m Anna Eliza Schnetz, Kenton Co., Ky., 1857 and they had Burton Jones; Edwin Alfred; Robert Lee; Eugene Percy; Annie Sloan; Harry Warren. 4, John Gano, died in infancy.*

Page 175, para. 5, line 5: after *Freeman.* insert *Sally Johnson m in Va., Robert Witherspoon. Lived at Bell's Grove (South Trimble place).*

Page 176, para. 3, line 6: delete *2, Margaret* and insert *and children of Ezra Hubbell, bro. of Capt. Wm.; 2, Catherine Hubbell*

Gano; 3, Mary Ann, m Dr. Peter Vander Veer, of Somerville, N.J., 1826.

Page 176, para. 3, line 7: delete entire line

Page 177, line 2: before *Mary Vaughan* insert *1*, and after *Mary Vaughan* delete period and insert *; 2, Sara Hughes, m Rev. Thos. Waller.*

Page 181, para. 2, line 3: after *father* insert *Thomas*

Page 186, para. 2, line 1: after *Joseph Lewis* insert *(m first – – – Beck, m second Sally Bell)*

Page 186, para. 3, line 5: after *Mitchell* insert *(to Texas)*

Page 186, para. 3, line 9: after *b*, insert *Dr.*

Page 186, para. 3, line 11: after *Georgetown* delete period and insert *; c, Dr. Charles C.; d, Mary (?).*

Page 187, para. 3, line 3: delete *(Whitley?)* and insert *Whitley, Lincoln, 1805*

Page 187, para. 4, line 1: after *Scytha* insert *(dau Thomas Brown, Fredericksburg, Spotsylvania Co., Va.)*

Page 189, line 3: after *Cave* insert *(dau Daniel and Mary Holton Cave)*

Page 190, para. 6, line 1: for *Reuben Long* read *Richard Long;* for *s Richard* read *s Reuben*

Page 193, para. 1, line 11: for *forks* read *Forks*

Page 194, para. 1, line 5: after *Gibson* delete period and insert *; 6, Harrison.*

Page 197, para. 7, line 4: add *It was first on Sullivan's Lane, near Peak's Mill, and was moved to its present site on the Owenton Pike.*

Page 198, para. 3, line 6: for *m – – –* read *m Robert*

Page 199, para. 1, line 8: delete *first Elizabeth Taylor, and second*

Page 199, para. 1, line 11: for *Maytie* read *Sue*

Page 199, para. 3, line 7: for *"Weekawkin"* read *"Weehawken"*

Page 202, line 1: after *1823* insert *and had Ann, m – – – Fairburn, and Henrietta. They went to Louisville*

Page 203, para. 2, line 3: for *1766* read *1763*

Page 208, para. 7, line 1: delete *Isaac Miles m first Mary Curtis,* and insert *Samuel Miles m Sarah James, Baltimore, 1760, died Shelby Co., Ky., 1811. They had: 1, John (1760-1843) m Elizabeth Jones, lived at Duckers, Ky., went to Indiana; 2, Hannah m Thos. Prothero, d Shelby Co.; 3, Enos m first Ann Buchanan, second Sarah Troup, Ohio; 4, Sarah m first Ben W. Bristow, second Abel M. Sargent, lived in Shelby Co.; 5, Samuel m first Eunice Cook, second Ann Lewis, third Polly Vardaman, d Shelby; 6, James m Catherine Mikesell, Ohio; 7, Evan m first*

Mary Christie, second Catherine Harris, went to Wisconsin; 8, Ben m Mrs. Celia Lawson, d Shelby; 9, Isaac (1764-1854), m first Mary Jones,

Page 208, para. 7, line 3: after *mill* delete period and insert , *and died in Indiana.*

Page 208, para. 8, line 3: delete *John Evans, m Malinda Brown, W 1818;* and insert *Evan m first Malinda Brown, W 1818, second Ally Laswell, Indiana, 1827;*

Page 208, para. 8, line 4: after *Jesse* insert *(1789-1870);* for *m − − −* read *m Sarah Christie*

Page 209, line 2: after *1808* insert , *to Indiana;* after *Samuel* insert *(1802-1862)*

Page 209, line 5: for *N.* read *Norman;* after *Franklin;* insert *William Wallace (1855-1865); John (1857-1860); Alma;*

Page 209, line 10: after *Samuel* begin new paragraph: *Other children of Isaac and Mary Jones Miles were: 6, Sarah (1788-1806) m Wm. Christie; 7, Milcah m John Tunnell, W 1812; 8, John; 9, Isaac m Eliz. Miles, dau Evan and Mary; 10, Eliza m Thompson Hudson.*

Page 212, line 2: after *Gallatin* insert , *had Elizabeth Harris, b 1830, d in Iowa*

Page 213, para. 5, line 6: after *Tutt* insert W *1812*

Page 213, para. 6, line 5/6: for *Lucy − − −* read *Lucy Finnell*

Page 215, para. 1, line 2: for *Indiana* read *Missouri*

Page 215, para. 1, line 5: after *1830* insert , *had: 1, Charles, in Legislature from Owen Co., Ky.; 2, Simeon, in Legislature in Indiana*

Page 218, para. 2, line 3: for *John W.* read *John C.*

Page 218, para. 2, line 13: for *John W.* read *John C.*

Page 222, para. 2, line 1: after *Partlow* insert , *b 1792 in Va.*

Page 223, line 4: after *went* insert *to Fayette, then*

Page 223, para. 3, line 5: after *1794* insert ; *5, John m Betsy Hunter; 6, dau m Alexander Hunter.*

Page 224, para. 3, line 8/9: after *Mary, m* delete *Peter G. Voorhies, F 1800* and insert *F 1800, Peter G. Voorhies (b N.J. 1772), to Frankfort 1790, to Red River. He d 1851. Reg. Apr. 1953, p. 146*

Page 228, line 7: for *a, John* read *a, James*

Page 228, line 8: delete parentheses and question mark; after *Mills* insert , *and had John Charles, Geo. Madison, Joel Mills, Wm. Blanton, Anne, Robt. Alexander, Mary Agnes, Archer Patteson, and Jas. Devereux*

Page 230, para. 3, line 5: after *second* insert *Margaret*

Page 232, para. 3, line 3: after *Samuel.* add *Dudley Roundtree m Martha Richardson (b Turner) W 1790. John Richardson (1792-1875), F, in Capt. P. Hickman's Regt., escaped at River Raisin (Reg. Apr. 1953, p. 137).*

Page 234, para. 1, line 4: after *Isabella* insert *; 4, John Hickman, and perhaps others*

Page 234, para. 1, line 8: after *Lewis A.* insert *There was also B.F.*

Page 235, para. 7, line 1: for *Rennick (– – –* read *Rennick (of Pa.*

Page 235, para. 7, line 3/4: for *Mary – – –* read *Mary Huston*

Page 239, para. 1, line 1: delete *– – – and Martha Elliott* and insert *Col. Thos., who m Martha Temple, dau Joseph and – – – Arnold Temple*

Page 239, para. 1, line 4: delete *died before 1832, leaving his* and insert *m Elizabeth Brokenborough in Va., ca 1790, but in the settlement of his estate, W 1832, he left a*

Page 239, para. 1, line 6: delete *Cordelia, Benjamin* and insert *a, Cordelia, m Edward H. Hughes; b, Benjamin Temple, m Pauline Ann North; c,*

Page 239, para. 1, line 10: for *f, John* read *e, John*

Page 239, para. 1, line 11: after *James* insert *b 1798 near Richmond, Va.,*

Page 239, para. 1, line 12: delete question mark

Page 239, para. 1, line 13: after *John James* insert *b 1828*

Page 239, para. 1, line 15: for *Lucy C.* read *Lucy Champe*

Page 239, para. 1, line 17: after *Lucy Ann* insert *(m John Roach, Lawrenceburg, Ky.)*

Page 239, para. 1, line 18: add *Some of these went to Hillsboro, Ohio.*

Page 241, para. 3, line 2: after *W 1809* insert *(1838?)*

Page 247, para. 2, line 6: after *Reuben* insert *(grandfather of Irvin S. Cobb)*

Page 247, para. 5, line 3: for *1817* read *1814*

Page 249, para. 1, line 3: add *Gideon and Wm. Scantland were on the tax list, W 1810.*

Page 249, para. 4, line 7: add *Reuben's son, William B. Hawkins, m Mary Crockett (dau Anthony and Mary Robertson Crockett), F 1802. His will, F 1845, names his wife and children: a, Samuel F.; b, Mary Blanton; c, Rebecca, m James G. Wright, F 1825; d, Martha, m John Clark; e, Anthony C.; f, Elisha Obed; g, William Granville; h, Katherine Farmer; i, Sarah, m Samuel McKee; j, Elizabeth, m William H. Wright, F 1823.*

Page 249, para. 5, line 3: for *John Dyer* read *Jehu Dyer*

Page 249, para. 5, line 4: after *William* insert *R.;* delete *It has been suggested that*

Page 249, para. 5, line 13: before *Elisha* insert *not*

Page 249, para. 5, line 15: for *Another* read *One;* for *he* read *Elisha*

Page 250, line 4: for – – – read *Minoah*

Page 250, para. 1, line 1: after *(1776-1854)* insert , *son of William and Mary,*

Page 250, para. 3, line 4: after *vicinity* delete period and insert , *whose estate is now Hawkeegan Park subdivision.*

Page 251, para. 1, line 10: after *Blanton* insert , *grandmother of Gen. Jesse Lindsay*

Page 251, para. 4, line 1: for – – – *Coleman* read *Betty Coleman*

Page 252, para. 3, line 3: delete *1,;* for *whose son* read *who had, 1,*

Page 252, para. 3, line 5: delete *Moses, who came to Clark, and whose descendants intermarried with the Straughans, in Shelby* and insert *Dr. Joseph;*

Page 254, line 12: after *1822,* insert *had 1, Joseph; 2, Ellen m – – – Quarles, and they were grandparents of Corinne Quarles of Frankfort; 3, Wm. m – – – Evans,;* for *grandparents* read *parents*

Page 255, para. 1, line 4: add *Ryland (1794-1864) s Jas. and grandson of John of the Travelling Church went to Clay Co., Mo., 1830, according to Carr.*

Page 258, para. 2, line 13: after *William* delete period and insert *; h, Barbara, m Gabriel Threlkeld.*

Page 262, para. 5, line 5: add *Joseph Smith, from Loudoun Co., Va., to Harrison Co., Ky., m F 1822 Sally Taylor. They went to Sangamon Co., Ill., 1834.*

Page 265, para. 1, line 6: for – – – – – – read *Wm. S. Harris*

Page 265, para. 1, line 14: for *Elizabeth (Crutcher?)* read *Elizabeth Crutcher, dau of Hugh and Frances Coleman Crutcher*

Page 268, para. 1, line 16: after *Cumberland* insert *(1777-1825) Boone Co., Mo., m Elizabeth Emerson ca 1806. 12 children. (G. & H. July 1949, p. 20)*

Page 271, para. 2, line 13: add *Cerella Stapp of Madison Co., Ind., m Rev. B.T. Quinn.*

Page 272, line 4: after *1808.* insert *G. & H. Oct. 1946 says "Elijah Stout m 11/15/1827 Lucy Bennett and lived in Shelby Co., Ky."*

Page 272, para. 3, line 4: after *1820.* insert *"Early Settlers of Sangamon Co.", by Power, says Philemon b N.J. 1785, to Fayette Co., Ky., 1789, to Scott 1810-1820, Fayette 1820, to Sangamon Co., Ill. 1836; had 7 children.*

Page 276, para. 4, line 7: after *Thomas L. Tate* insert *(1787-1852) (Reg. Apr. 1953, p. 143)*

Page 277, para. 4, line 1/2: after *Benjamin,* delete *evidently the one who m* and insert *m first Theodosia Payne and second*

Page 277, para. 4, line 2/3: delete *(dau John and Susanna Adams Cotton?)*

Page 277, para. 4, line 20: add *John Wickliffe, b Boone 1798, m Jemima Gray. To Sangamon Co., Ill. 1833.*

Page 279, para. 1, line 5: for *1806* read *1826*

Page 280, para. 7, line 1: after *Theobald* insert *(1791-1873) (Reg. Apr. 1953, p. 144)*

Page 282, para. 1, line 2: for *Island* read *Ireland*

Page 285, para. 3, line 6/7: delete *1, "Parson John," a Presbyterian minister in Oldham;;* for *2,* read *1.*

Page 285, para. 3, line 9: for *3,* read *2,;* for *4,* read *3,*

Page 304, para. 1, line 1: after *Isaac* insert *b 1774*

Page 304, para. 1, line 2: after *widow* insert *, Martha Wilcox Wilson (G. & H. Oct. 1946),*

Page 304, para. 1, line 3: add *Spencer, "Kentucky Baptists," says John Whitaker had John, Abraham, Elija, Rev. Isaac, Jesse (see Lindsay), Aquilla. Was at Beargrass Church, 6 mi. e of Louisville.*

Page 304, para. 2, line 1: after *Wilson* insert *, s Isaac and Eliza Cook Wilson,*

CONTENTS

Introduction
John R. Sampey, D.D.

It was my privilege to serve the Forks of Elkhorn Baptist Church as pastor during three periods: 1885-91, 1904-15, and 1920-26. The Centennial of the Church was celebrated in 1888, when several old pastors were present. The Sesquicentennial was observed in June, 1938, at which time I delivered the historical address.

Mrs. Darnell has long felt an interest in the Forks of Elkhorn Church and she has made careful research into its early history. She has brought together much valuable genealogical history connected with the early members of this historic Church. Her treatment of the controversy which disturbed the Church about 1830 seems fair and sympathetic. She loves the old Church to which some of her ancestors belonged.

A wide circle in Kentucky and Missouri can be expected to feel an interest in the story which Mrs Darnell recounts, and many of our leading citizens will be glad to have access to the genealogical data she has so laboriously compiled.

It gives me great pleasure to commend the book to all who feel an interest in the religious life of our country churches.

WILLIAM HICKMAN

WILLIAM HICKMAN'S HOME

This was built in 1788, on the old Steele's Ferry Road between the Lexington-Leestown Road and the Forks of Elkhorn. The site is now occupied by the home of W. W. Scruggs.

JOHN MAJOR'S HOME

It was in this house that the first preaching service was held. Located three miles east of Frankfort, on what is now the W. H. May farm on the Versailles Pike, this building is practically unchanged except for an alteration in the roof, due to a fire, and the addition of the outside stairway.

HARMONY CHURCH

On the Lexington-Leestown Road, it was built by the Presbyterians about 1840, and was sold to the Forks of Elkhorn congregation in 1866.

FORKS OF ELKHORN CHURCH AT DUCKERS

This building was erected in 1912. It was destroyed by fire in 1943, but is now being rebuilt.

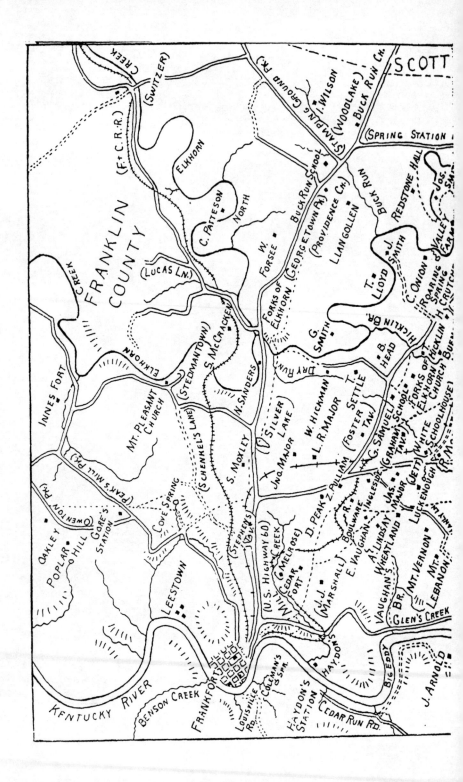

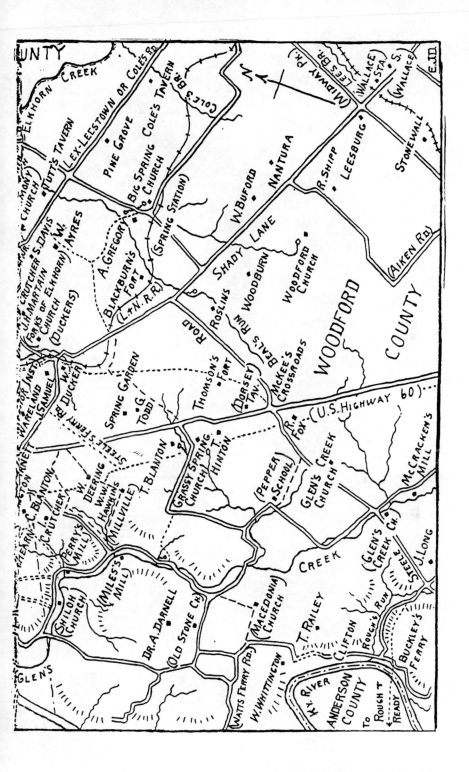

THE SETTING

This accompanying map is fairly accurate. With alterations frequently being made in the old dirt roads, it is impossible on a single map to do more than show the general position of the highways.

When one has grown up with a group of indefatigable picnickers, and has been blessed with a brother who was county surveyor and a husband with a wide country practice, it follows that very few of the old roads and landmarks will remain unexplored. Despite this personal familiarity with the district and its traditions, however, some of the old routes are still elusive, and though they have been put on the map only after prolonged study of court records and consultation with the best informed persons available, they are subject to revision.

This is a compilation of a number of early maps, including Filson's, Munsell's maps of 1818 and 1834, and several others, besides plats made for individuals by Richard Fox, Willis Blanton, and other surveyors. Names of streams and settlements are taken from the maps on which they first appear, though many of the names of homesteads are from the Hewitt map of 1861.

Roundly speaking, this represents the neighborhood about 1800, though many anachronisms are apparent. Names of later sites are put in parentheses, earliest roads are marked by - - - - - - - - - -, later ones by — — — — — —, and county boundaries by — · — · — · —.

This area contains many "sinking springs," in which the water rises, flows for a short distance, and then sinks into the ground. Mr. C. T. Freeman, whose father owned the site of Black's pond ("Silver Lake"), said that it was at first only a sinking spring, but one winter when they fed cattle there the fodder stopped up the sinkhole, and thus the pond was formed. There is a tradition that there was a cave-in, and a building in that tract sank and disappeared. Near Spring Station (originally

Big Spring Station) is a sinking stream which rises as springs in various places and with different names—Lewis's, Peart's, etc., finally reappearing on Miss Georgia Crutcher's place as Roaring Spring—so called because of the sound when it is full.

Elkhorn Creek has been called the aristocrat of Kentucky's streams.

The story is told in an Indian legend. Sweetheart, the Indian maiden, loved the young warrior, Capering Moose, although she was betrothed to the old chief, his father. Capering Moose, determined that Sweetheart should be his own, wrapped her in his blanket, and together they fled, mounted on the back of the friendly elk, Wapiti. For many days they rode, always closely pursued by the angry chief. When they had reached a luxuriant valley in Kentucky, the elk was struck by the last of the old chief's arrows, but in dying he turned his face toward the enemy, and his horns formed an impassable barrier. The frustrated chief gave up the pursuit, and Capering Moose and Sweetheart spent their years in the peaceful valley.

As time went on, Wapiti's horns sank into the ground, but in the hollows they left there appeared an enchantingly beautiful stream of water which the Indians, in memory of their faithful friend, called "Elkhorn."

Buck Run, often written *Buckrun,* was referred to in an old document as "the buck branch," but whether it was named for some of the Buck family living in that vicinity is not known.

Rough's (Rowe's, Rose) Run was named for Nicholas Rough, who raised corn in that region in 1776, but was killed by the Indians in that same year.

Adam Rough (heir of Nicholas), of Washington County, Kentucky, in a deed, W 1795, mentions "Rough's settlement of 400 acres on Rough's Run."

Glen's Creek was named for David and Thomas Glenn, presumably from Virginia, who were in Capt. James Harrod's company of adventurers in 1774. David raised a crop of corn on Glen's Creek in 1775, but was living in Harrodsburg in 1777, and was one of the soldiers sent by George Rogers Clark to bring powder for the defense of Kentucky. Thomas Glenn, whose land was two miles above the forks of Glen's Creek, was probably the father of William and Tyre Glen, of Woodford.

Richard Benson, who was in Harrodsburg in 1775, settled across the river from the Glenns at the mouth of Little Benson, one of the four creeks in Franklin County which bears his name. This land, which was afterward owned by the McKees, was cleared about 1800 by Isaac Johnson and Isaac Hearn. Little Benson marks the boundary between Franklin and Anderson counties.

The buffalo made the first roads, their best known trail being from Scott County through Woodlake, crossing South Elkhorn near the forks. It passed through the present Fairview and across Schenkel's Lane, descending the hill through the Scruggs property. Here it was joined by another trail from the south, and together they passed under the railroad trestle into the Holmes Street valley, following the stream to the crossing at Leestown, and thence to Henry County.

The pioneers explained that the buffalo would congregate near a spring and "stomp around," and for this reason they called those areas "stomping grounds." The most famous of these stamping grounds is the one of that name in Scott County, and court records show that there was another on the Dudley farm, and a "stamping hollow" somewhere in the vicinity of Spring Station.

There was a buffalo trail in the northeast corner of Franklin County, on the line between Franklin and Scott, and another in Woodford between Rough's Run and Glen's Creek, leading to the mouth of Little Benson.

The only road in this section shown on Filson's map of 1784 is the one from Lexington to Leestown, which is thought to occupy its original position as far as the Green Mill, where it continued toward the northwest and came down the hill from what is now Schenkel's Lane to the Fincel house on East Holmes Street. In the vicinity of Cole's Tavern this was known as Cole's Road.

The road from Major William Steele's ferry, above Clifton, to Nathaniel Sanders' mill at the Forks of Elkhorn was established in 1789. John Long was appointed surveyor of the end next to the river, Isaac Wilson had the middle portion, and William Ware the remainder.

The road from Frankfort to Georgetown was established some time before 1791. The late George C. Downing, whose boyhood home was at 326 East Main Street, wrote, "There was a road that left Frankfort just to the north of the old railroad bed. This old road was immediately in the rear of our place. It passed on, and no doubt a road led off to the right about where is does now, joining later both the old Versailles and the old Leestown roads." Though its route up the hill has not been satisfactorily located, it is known that it joined "the Lexington old road" three-quarters of a mile from Frankfort, which would be near the entrance of the Glen's Creek pike. It can be traced from the Green Mill along the north side of the present Georgetown pike and through the bed of Black's pond, crossing Elkhorn south of the Forks, and merging with the present road at Woodlake.

The earliest road from Frankfort to Lexington skirted the East Main Street hill, passing south of it about where the railroad now runs. East of the hill, it can be traced just south of the Daniel Peak (McMillan) farm as it turned sharply to the right and went through the front yard at "Wheatland" and the meadows of "Luckenough." It fell in with the Steele's Ferry road at what is known as the John Morris place, and went on south of Grassy Spring Church. Though its route on to Lexington is not known, it was apparently the same road which continued past "Wild Cat Spring" and joined the road to McCracken's mill on the outskirts of Versailles. A part of this road was embodied in the Frankfort-Versailles road, which was laid out when Versailles was established in 1793.

In that same year, Bennett Pemberton, Nathaniel Sanders, and Daniel Weisiger, being empowered by the Legislature, laid out a new and very steep road which went up the hill where the arsenal now stands, and through the cemetery grounds, merging with the older road at the foot of the hill. The late George A. Lewis wrote that this part of the road was changed to its present location in 1850, in order to obtain a site for the arsenal.

Another road to Lexington separated from the Lexington-Leestown road at the Foster tavern, passing north of the Graham tavern and south of the site of the railroad at Duckers. There it apparently branched, one fork going immediately north of "Thomson's Manor," which faced it, to the vicinity of McKee's Crossroads, and the other branch continuing as the present Shady Lane. Though not shown on the map, there evidently was a connection between this road and the Frankfort-Versailles road nearer Frankfort, as the records frequently speak of "the forks of the Lexington and Woodford roads."

The late Miss Ada May Cromwell used to tell of a large stone which the early settlers found near "Ingleside." It was a tribal guide stone of the Indians, having carved on it an arrow pointing toward the river with the inscription, "Wah-la-ha," meaning, "The way to water."

This suggests that the Indians may have made the road which follows the course of Vaughan's branch to the river, though this road is evidently the one referred to in early deeds as "the old Craig's road."

Leestown, Leesburg (later, Offutt's Crossroads, and now Nugent's), and Lee's Branch were named for three sons of Hancock Lee (1709-1762) who married Mary Willis, of Gloucester County, Virginia, 1733. He was of the same family as Robert E. Lee.

Leestown, where the old buffalo trace crossed the river, was established in 1775 by a group of pioneers, among whom were: Capt. Hancock Lee, Gen. George Rogers Clark who enthusiastically planned to make his home there, Capt. Cyrus McCracken, Willis Lee, and others. Though temporarily abandoned because of Indian attacks, it afterward flourished to such a degree that in 1792 it was one of eight Kentucky towns contesting, with financial inducements, for the honor of being the State capital.

The three Lee brothers were: 1, Capt, Hancock Lee (1740-1819), who returned to Virginia and married Winifred E. Beale in King George County, December, 1776. He had large grants of land in the vicinity of Midway and Woodlake, a part of which he sold in 1794 to Richard Cole, Jr. 2, Major John Lee (1743-1802), one of the founders of Versailles, settled in the neighborhood of Leesburg. He had a large family, including Willis A. Lee of "Glen Willis," and Sarah A. Lee, the first wife of (Governor) John J. Crittenden. 3, Willis Lee (1745-1776), who was in Kentucky with a surveying party in 1774 and was killed in an Indian attack on Leestown. Henry Lee (1750-1804), another brother, settled near Midway, and was the father of Sarah Davis°.

Old documents show that Frankfort was originally called "Franksford" for Stephen Frank, who in 1780 was killed by the Indians while camping where the town now stands. It was founded in 1786 by Gen. James Wilkinson, and in 1792 was selected as the State capital. The first State House was completed in 1794. Of the nine men named as being responsible for securing the capital for Frankfort, five were members of the Forks of Elkhorn Church.

Space permits only a few of the early Frankfort buildings to be shown. Jeremiah Gullion, the first resident, bought from James Wilkinson in January, 1792, two lots on Washington Street and an outlying lot containing four acres, "in consideration of the sum of five Shillings, Current money of Virginia."

The first waterworks system in Kentucky was built in 1804-1805 at Cove Spring, on a hill east of Frankfort, to supply the penitentiary and the town. The pipes were made of cedar logs bored through with an auger, each log being sharpened at one end to fit the reamed end of the one in front.

There is a legend that Cedar Fort was built on the old Frankfort-Versailles road for protection against the Indians, and that during one attack all the settlers reached safety except a lame man who was overtaken and killed. It is possible that this was identical with Haydon's Station.

The old brick building on the slope immediately south of Jett was built in the 1820's by James Major and his son Joseph for a cotton factory. It served later as a manufactory for felt hats, then as a private school conducted by James Major's daughter, and for many years thereafter as a farm building. During the Spanish-American War it was a gathering place for the young men and boys of the neighborhood for military drills under the direction of L. A. Trumbo; and its last public service, in the summer of 1910, was as the setting for an ice cream supper sponsored by the Forks of Elkhorn Church.

Under the leadership of Robert W. Scott, who was instrumental in establishing the common school system, the public school at Jett was the first in the State to be put in operation under the new law. In 1840 a two-room house, called "The White Schoolhouse," was built on a lot given by William Graham, and the first trustees were Thomas Jett, C. H. Trabue, Richard Crutcher, Richard Wiggs, and Henry Crutcher. For almost a hundred years this school continued to benefit the community, but in 1937 it was merged with a consolidated school.

When the Frankfort-Versailles turnpike was built, among the first to take advantage of its possibilities were the family of John Jones, who located their tavern on it. In 1836, as Santa Anna was being taken to Washington for trial, his captors, when they reached this point in their journey, sought to avoid publicity by keeping him overnight at this country tavern instead of in Frankfort. The news leaked out, however, and soon the yard was filled with excited citizens, including the notorious John U. Waring, who vociferously black-dog-dared the prisoner to come out and show his face. But when these overtures met with no response the crowd melted away.

In 1845 William W. Stephens bought this property, which the deed says was then known as "The Brick Tavern," and thereafter it was "The Stephens Tavern."

At the Historical Society are Santa Anna's epaulets, which were taken from him by Gen. William O. Butler and his nephew and aide, Lieut. (Dr.) John Russell Butler, at the capture of the City of Mexico by the American Army in 1847. Dr. Butler, whose home was in Louisville, came to Woodlake about 1857, and lived there several years.

There is a tradition that Santa Anna was a member of the Sanders family of this community who went to Mexico and became President.

Kean O'Hara, the father of the poet, had a school at "Oakley" early in the century when the trees were so thick that he had to blaze a trail for the children to find their way to school. He afterward taught at the Kentucky Seminary in Frankfort, then at the old Ashmore place in what is now Montrose Park, and later at the Downey place on the old Frankfort-Versailles road.

Stedmantown was named for Ebenezer H. and Samuel Stedman, who came in their childhood from Massachusetts. They rebuilt an old mill on Elkhorn and began making paper in 1834. For more than thirty years they furnished paper for newspapers and for State printing, and in 1861 they supplied the Confederate Government with paper for bank notes.

Nathaniel Sanders was given leave to build a mill on North Elkhorn in 1792. He had another mill on South Elkhorn above the mouth of Dry Run, but it was gone in 1809.

One of the oldest school buildings west of the Alleghenies is at Woodlake, where in 1808 the settlers built a stone house on land said to have been given by the Rev. John Taylor, author of *A History of Ten Churches*. It has since been in continuous use, first as a private school, later remodeled as a public school, and now as a community house under the sponsorship of the Homemakers.

Providence Baptist Church was formed in 1856 by a group of members withdrawing, for political reasons, from the Buck Run Church. The Rev. Cadwallader Lewis, who gave the lot on which the building was erected, was the first pastor, and among the early members were Thomas Blackburn, Dr. Churchill Blackburn, Frank Wilson, Alexander Macklin, John Macklin, William Steele, and Nimrod Martin.

The building was wrecked by a storm in 1911, and in 1939 it burned, but it was rebuilt shortly afterward.

An old church at which William Hickman used to preach was at Great Crossings (originally called "Big Crossings"). It was established in 1785 by Lewis Craig and John Taylor, and the congregation met for a time in Col. Robert Johnson's fort. The original members were: William and Susanna Cave; Robert and Jemima Johnson; James and John Suggett; Thomas Ficklin; Julius Gibbs; Robert and Hannah Bradley; Sarah Shipp; Caty Herndon Bohannon; Jane Herndon; Betsy Leemon; Bartlett and Betsy Collins. The first pastor was Elijah Craig, and the second was Joseph Redding.

In 1828 the congregation had not only white and colored members, but seventeen Indians from the nearby Choctaw Academy, which was under the management of Col. Richard M. Johnson. One of these Indians, Sampson Birch, was ordained to the ministry by John Taylor, Silas M. Noel, and others, who called him "our dear Brother of the forest."

"Redstone Hall": There is some controversy as to whether this place or the Murphy house at the Forks of Elkhorn was the setting for Mary J. Holmes's *Marian Grey: The Heiress of Redstone Hall*. But when it is observed that in the early deeds, "in the forks of the Elkhorn" included not merely the immediate junction, but an area extending several miles up between the two branches, it will be seen that this location agrees in every particular with that described in the book.

The Harmony Presbyterian Church was organized in 1832 by the Rev. John Todd Edgar, of Frankfort. The lot was deeded by Joel Scott on September 22, 1832, to a committee composed of James F. Bell, of Scott; William Buford, of Woodford; and Joseph H. Davis and Andrew J. Alexander, of Franklin. The deed provided that there should be no burying ground on the land, and that if the premises should cease to be used as a place of worship, the title should revert to Joel Scott, his heirs, executors, or assigns.

There is a tradition that the congregation met for some time in the Baptist meetinghouse at Big Spring, their own house of worship being built by John Regis Alexander in 1840.

Some of the ruling elders were D. C. Humphreys, George Wythe Lewis, John Regis Alexander, and Thomas Martin, and in the congregation were the Alexander, Blackburn, Ferguson, Gratz, Lee, (R. S.) Todd, and Steele families, and many others.

The Rev. Robert G. Brank, of Muhlenberg, is said to have been one of the early pastors.

The congregation eventually became so small that about 1864 the organization was dissolved, whereupon many of the members united with the Midway Presbyterian Church. The Scott heirs exchanged this property for the old Forks of Elkhorn Church house and grounds.

The will of Francis Peart, in Woodford County, 1815, directed that much of his property should be given to the County of Woodford for a free school, to be maintained by the rent of the land. The school or college was to be called after his name, and to be built on land on South Elkhorn in Woodford and Scott where John Frauner was living at that time. What disposition was made of this bequest is not known.

Charles Alexander, a half brother of Robert Alexander, is said to have had an academy on the Leestown road, probably in the thirties. There is a tradition that the Big Spring meetinghouse was used for a school, but no dates are mentioned, though 1838 is given as a year in which Lyman W. Seely was conducting a school for girls in the vicinity of Spring Station.

"Woodburn," acquired by Robert Alexander, of Scotland, in 1790, has been continuously in the family ever since. It is famed alike for its scenic beauty, so often described by writers from the East, and for its blooded stock, the annual Thoroughbred sales in the past century being events of nation-wide interest. One enthusiast wrote that for lovers of fine stock to come to Lexington and not visit Woodburn would be equal to seeing Hamlet with Hamlet left out.

John Regis Alexander, also a half brother of Robert, came from Virginia and settled at what is now known as the Crosby place, "Roslins," on the old Lexington road. So many emigrants in covered wagons camped at his spring for the night that he used to call this road "The Old Missouri Trail," but because of his foresight in planting trees along both sides, "Shady Lane," a hundred years later, is advertised as one of Kentucky's scenic attractions.

"Nantura," the home of celebrated horses, was purchased in 1795 by the grandfather of the equally celebrated turfman, John Harper, who envisioned horses running "from eend to eend." On this farm may be seen the graves of Ten Broeck and Longfellow, marked by imposing marble monuments.

Wallace Station was named for Judge Caleb Wallace, ardent proponent of higher education, who was instrumental in the establishment of Washington and Lee, Hampden-Sidney, and Transylvania. He came in 1782 from Lunenburg County, Virginia, and settled in this vicinity, and his son, Samuel McDowell Wallace, built the brick residence which was in recent years the home of Senator Henry L. Martin.

Mrs. Carrie Moore Nation, the Kansas "saloon smasher," lived for five years at "Glenartney," near Midway. She was born in Garrard County, and came here with her parents about 1854, when she was nine years old.

The Woodford Presbyterian Church was described as "Shannon's Meeting House near Lewis's big sinking spring" when the Woodford County Court held its first session there in 1789. The deed was made in 1795 by Andrew Lewis, of Bath County, Virginia, for his brother John, the trustees being William Kinkead, James Dickey, and Thomas Bell.

The first pastor was the Rev. Samuel Shannon, who served until 1806, when he took charge of the churches on Upper and Lower Benson, in Franklin County. Judge Caleb Wallace, who had been a Presbyterian minister for ten years before studying law, was a presiding elder, and among the families of the congregation were the Alexanders, Colemans, Flemings, Gardners, Guyns, and Shipps.

This church merged with the Versailles Presbyterian Church in 1873. The building was eventually removed, and now only a few tombstones remain to mark the site.

The Dorsey Tavern was established about 1842 by Patrick Dorsey and his wife Sarah, and was afterward occupied by Wheeler Wiggs, and later by A. M. Perham. Its chief item of interest is the tradition that Mrs. Mary J. Holmes lived there while collecting material for *Tempest and Sunshine,* and other Kentucky stories.

On Glen's Creek was a schoolhouse built probably before 1827, when Pluright and Ruth Sisk deeded to Elijah Pepper, James Garnett, and Bernard Gaines a lot "for the use and benefit of a school whereon a stone Schoolhouse now stands known by the name of 'Glen's Creek English Institute.'" In 1830 it was advertised by J. H. W. Isett, Jr., in the *Frankfort Commentator* under the title, "Glenn's Creek Select School." He described it as being "handsomely built of stone, and situated in a respectable and healthy neighborhood," and stated that board could be furnished in the families of Charles Cotton and Bernard Gaines.

In that era of private schools it flourished for years, but was finally abandoned, and the building was recently demolished.

Cyrus McCracken built a mill on Glen's Creek in 1789. It was a sawmill, which would require more space for the transportation of its products than would any of the numerous gristmills in that section, and it was perhaps because of this that the McCracken's Mill Road was soon established, and in 1798 was extended to the mouth of Glen's Creek.

It was in this building that the Glen's Creek Baptist Church held its first meeting in 1801. After many years of service, the walls of the old mill are still standing, and now constitute the basement of a residence built on the site.

When Thomas Railey built his home on a high cliff overlooking the river, he named it "Clifton" for an old homestead in Virginia. The village which afterward grew at the foot of the hill was known by the same name, though futile attempts were made in later years to call it "Woodford City," and then "Cicero." Clifton was once a flourishing little milling and shipping point, but owing to the encroachment of the river and other factors, it is now best known as a summer camp site, and as the boyhood home of Clifford K. Berryman, the Washington cartoonist. C. K. Berryman and William E. Railey, the historian, were great-grandsons of Thomas Railey.

The Macedonia Presbyterian Church was organized in 1832 by the Rev. William Montgomery King. The Rev. John Newton Blackburn was one of the early ministers. In 1847 Richard S. Taylor and his wife Jemima deeded the lot to the elders, William W. Hawkins, John H. Berryman, Samuel S. Graham, and Isaac S. Whittington.

Many years later the congregation moved to Clifton, and in 1926 merged with Grier's Creek. The old Macedonia building was afterward used by a colored congregation.

In 1830 a lot on the hill between Millville and the river was deeded by Michael Mitchell to Bernard Gaines, Charles Ware, Thomas Winn, Elijah Pepper, William Hawkins, Michael Mitchell, and Randolph R. Darnell, trustees of the Glen's Creek Republican Meeting House, which was for the use of all denominations. Known as "The Old Stone Church," it was for three generations a tower of strength to that region. In 1845, under the sponsorship of William H. Whittington, a great revival was held there by John T. Johnson, R. C. Rice, and other noted pioneer preachers. In later years it was a popular gathering place on Sunday afternoons, when people for miles around would meet for Sunday school, after having attended services at their own churches in the morning.

After the Baptist and Christian churches were built at Millville in the nineties, the building was abandoned and eventually taken down. When Robert Watts bought the lot in 1938, the deed, in order to fulfill all legal requirements, had to be signed by a representative from each of the white Protestant churches in Woodford—twenty-five in all.

Millville was so called because of its various mills. In 1819 Isaac Miles and Roderick Perry each petitioned the court for permission to build "a water grist mill" on Glen's Creek, the Miles mill to have a dam extending three and a half feet above the surface of the water, and the dam at Perry's to be three feet.

Isaac Miles built his mill on the south side of the creek at Millville. After continuing there for many years, the business was moved by his grandson to Frankfort, where the same brand of flour, "J. E. M.", is still being sold, though it is now manufactured in Lexington.

Roderick Perry built his mill farther down the creek, on the west bank near the end of Blanton's lane. His heirs sold the plant in 1836 to Joseph Major, who operated a cotton factory there, and who was succeeded by Sidney and Peyton Johnson with a wool-carding mill.

Besides these there were Randolph R. Darnell's gristmill, Joseph Gorbut's woolen mill, several sawmills and a wagon factory.

The Shiloh Methodist Church, on Glen's Creek, was built in 1871 on land given by Eli and Susan Rosell. It was active for only about twenty-five years. It is recalled that in the congregation were the families of Stephen Tutt, Mrs. Georgianna Johnson, —— Latta, and Dr. J. M. Botts, who often conducted the services. One of the pastors was the Rev. Joseph Young, and another was the Rev. —— Ditsler, who is said to have preached on alternate Sundays at Cedar Chapel, across the river on the Lawrenceburg pike in Franklin County. Cedar Chapel was built sometime before 1860, and was attended by the Patties, Richardsons, Vaughans, and other families in the neighborhood, in addition to the students of the nearby Kentucky Military Institute, whose head, Col. R. T. P. Allen, was himself an ordained Methodist minister. Several members of the Kavanaugh family preached there.

Since many of the early boundaries were marked by trees, it is not surprising that, nearly a quarter of a century after the line was run between Woodford and Franklin, the Legislature should find it necessary to appoint a committee to again "run and distinctly mark the line between the said counties." This was done about 1822 by Willis Blanton, Richard Fox, and Daniel J. Williams, the trees on the line being marked with "5 Tomahawk chops on both sides."

FORKS OF ELKHORN CHURCH

"Put on plenty, Bob."

At this command the black giant knelt on the hearth with his armload, and with a practiced hand laid on the wood so expertly that the sparks flew upward in showers and moisture foamed at the ends of the sticks, while the smoke added its pungent quota to an atmosphere overcharged already with the human aura, and redolent of garments made of freshly cured skins.

The firelight flickered on a crowded room, for the Reverend William Hickman was conducting a service, the first to be held in the neighborhood, and the people had come gladly to hear him. There were mothers surrounded with wide-eyed small children—the older ones having slipped outside to play in the snow as a respite from the long sermon—fathers sitting or leaning against the wall, and in the farthest corner a group of colored servants, timid, but glowing with delight at the sound of words and phrases they had not heard since they left Virginia.

With the replenishment of the fire, the exhorter seemed to increase in fervor, for the winter day would soon be drawing to a close, and it was not safe to be in the woods at night. Some families had miles to travel, to the protecting vicinity of Haydon's Station on the west, Gore's toward the northwest, Innes's on the north, Blackburn's Fort on the east, and Anthony Thomson's stone castle toward the south. Those in the immediate neighborhood depended upon Major's Station at the home of John Major, where this first public service of worship was held in Franklin County.

It was in the year 1788, and the settlers in the Dry Run neighborhood, having attended to their immediate physical needs, were now beginning to be conscious of their craving for spiritual nourishment.

Life was not easy for those pioneer Baptist families. Back in Virginia before the Revolution they had been bitterly persecuted by the Church of England. But, as William Hickman wrote: "The Baptists in those days were much despised, which caused Christ's sheep to huddle closer together, and to love each other better than when there was no opposition."

The persecution finally became so grievous that the congregation of Upper Spotsylvania decided to come to Kentucky, which was described at that time as "a vortex of Baptist preachers." Accordingly one Sunday in September, 1781, after their morning worship these people with many of their relatives and friends took the Bible and the bell from the church they were leaving, and with all their worldly goods, started on what was truly a pilgrimage of faith.

Most of the men and some of the women were on foot, the others being on horseback, or, in case of illness, on litters. As the journey progressed, and traveling became more difficult, they were forced to abandon, piece by piece, many of their cherished household possessions, and those who had been taught to shun the "night air" were glad to find shelter for sleep under leafy boughs cut and leaned against a tree.

But worse was to come. Their store of bread became moldy, freezing weather set in, the sheltering leaves disappeared, and after an attack by the Indians, they were afraid to kindle fires. At one time the sleet and snow delayed them so that they traveled only thirty miles in three weeks. Throughout all these trials, however, they never lost hope, nor failed to set apart a time for worship.

It is a profitable experience to go out among the hills on a wintry day and try to picture our courageous kindred as they came over the sleet-covered mountains, gaunt and tattered, huddling under overhanging rocks for shelter from the driving rain, wading sometimes breast-deep through icy, treacherous streams, or pushing forward determinedly in the face of a blizzard—trembling with exhaustion, but with each labored step witnessing anew to the sacred principles of religious freedom.

In December, 1781, they finally reached their destination, and settled at Gilbert's Creek, in what is now Garrard County.

After two years this famous "Travelling Church" moved again, this time to South Elkhorn in Fayette County, and it was from that locality that William Hickman and several other families came to the Forks of Elkhorn.

This was one of the characteristic episodes of American history, and while not so spectacular as some others it was a positive influence in setting the standards of Christian living in the Bluegrass.

John Taylor wrote, "It was a gloomy thing at that time of day to come to Kentucky," but William Hickman said of his first view of it in 1776: "When we came to the beauty of the country, I thought of the Queen of Sheba, that came from the uttermost parts of the earth to hear the wisdom of Solomon, and she said the half was not told. So I thought of Kentucky; I thought if I never could get but ten acres of land, I determined to move to it."

Others had different impressions. One man found the cane in Woodford growing too luxuriantly to suit him, so he moved south of the river, where the land was thinner. Another found the gentle slopes in the eastern part of Woodford quite monotonous, and located on the hills of Anderson.

The streams were at that time the main highways. One man received a grant of a large tract south of the Kentucky River. As an inducement to get his relatives in Virginia to move here he offered them farms, but he was careful to give away the part farthest from the river, retaining for himself what was then considered the choicest portion. But in the course of time highways were built through the despised outlying farms, leaving to the descendants of the generous one only his hills and his river.

One writer calls attention to the fact that most of the early churches were named for streams or springs, and the reason for this is obvious.

John Filson wrote in 1784: "The Elkhorn lands are much esteemed, being situated in a bend of Kentucke River, of great extent, in which this little river, or rather large creek, rises. Here we find mostly first rate land, and near the Kentucke River second and third rate. This great tract is beautifully situated, and covered with cane, wild rye, and clover; and many of the streams afford fine mill sites."

As late as 1819, an act was approved by the Legislature to incorporate a company to improve the navigation of Elkhorn "commencing at the mouth thereof, on the Kentucky River. thence up Elkhorn to the forks thereof, thence up the nortl fork to the neighborhood of Georgetown and from the forks up the south fork to the neighborhood of Lexington." This was to be accomplished by a system of locks, with the builders being granted the right to pass through any mill dam. Subscription books were to be opened at Cole's Tavern, Georgetown, Lexington, and Versailles.

In the story of his life, written about 1827, William Hickman tells of his coming to this neighborhood:

"About that time the Forks of Elkhorn began to settle. Mr. Nathaniel Sanders, old brother John Major, brother Daniel James, old William Haydon, old Mr. Lindsay and a few others had moved down, and as there was a prospect of a large settlement Mr. Sanders named to his neighbor, Major, that it would be right to get a minister to come down and live among them, which pleased Major, he being an old Baptist. They consulted who they should get, and having a small acquaintance with me, Mr. Sanders named me; this was strange, as Mr. Sanders was a very thoughtless person about his soul. However, they agreed among themselves to make me a present of 100 acres of land; this was unbeknown to me till afterwards.

"On a very cold night Brother Major came to my cabin, about 20 miles from his residence. When he came in, upon being asked to sit down he said: 'No, like Abram's servant I will not sit down till I have told my errand.' He then told what had brought him to see me and gave me till the next morning to return him an answer.

"We passed a night of prayer—it was a night of deep thought with me, for I wished to do right. I was halting between two opinions, and when I reflected that the Forks of Elkhorn was exposed to the savages, and there was no settlement from there to the Indian town, I thought it would frighten my wife and children: however I consulted them about what I should do." They were willing to go however, but he still had to gain the consent of the congregation for which he was preaching.

Then: "Instead of writing, I first went to Bro. Major's, and from there to Mr. Sanders. I was astonished; his wife was an old professor of religion, and he walked with me to the very spring I now live at on his own land and showed me where I was to settle.

"I said to him, 'Sir, you don't care about religion, I want to know why you wish me to come.' His reply was, 'If it is never any advantage to me it may be to my family.' It started tears to my eyes, not knowing what Providence had in view, I however concluded to move as soon as possible, and my son William being married, he came down and built a cabin between Christmas and New Year's, 1787.

"On the night of the 17th we arrived at my son William's cabin. I had sent down an appointment to preach on Sunday at Brother Major's, where almost the whole inhabitants came, I suppose about thirty whites and a few blacks. I hope I was looking to the Lord. I took this subject, 'Let me die the death of the righteous, and let my last end be like his.'

"It was a blessed day; I think four or five experiences came from that day's labor, and, among the rest, Mr. Sanders.

"About this time there was a great fall of snow, and the balance of February and all March were very cold, but not enough to hinder the meetings * * * No weather scarcely stopped us, and we thought but little of the Indians. When April came it brought a fine spring, and we began to talk of becoming an organized church."

The first entry in the minute book is: "In answer to a call of the arm of the Church of South Elkhorn for helps to look into our Constitution, the helps came according to appointment the 7th of June, 1788. There was sent the following helps from our Mother Church (South Elkhorn), George S. Smith, Andrew Hampton, Alford Willi——, and John Price. Likewise from Clear Creek, John Taylor and Samuel Dedman. The following helps being present were called in to assist, viz., Robert Fryer, William Scholl, Peter Scholl, and John Glover, members from Marble Creek Church.

"After coming under examination, judged expedient and so pronounced us a Constitution on the principles of the Elkhorn Association. The members considered in the Constitution you find by name as follows:

William Hickman, Sr.	Nath'l Sanders
Mack McDaniel	Wm. Haydon
Thomas Hick——	Benj. Haydon

Thos. Essex	Lucy McDaniel
Will Bledso	Rebekah Hicklin
Jas. Ferguson	Mary Jam——
Wm. Hickman, Jr.	Ann Haydon
Thomas Hickman	Margaret Cook
Paschal Hickman	Betsy Major
Elizabeth Hickman	Susannah Major
Obedience Hickman	Mary Peak
Sally Hickman	and three colored members

"Opened door for the reception of Members and received

John Major, Sr.	Sarah Sanders
Elizabeth Major	Philemon Thomas
William Hall	Richard Thomas."

According to the custom of the time, they met on Saturday for the transaction of business, leaving Sunday free for worship.

In August the congregation met "at the Arbor" and selected Nathaniel Sanders and John Major as deacons. In the choice of a minister, however, they were divided in sentiment, and this feeling continued until October, when the "disaffected party gave up that Bro. Wm. Hickman, Sr., act as pastor of the church," and in November, with the aid of helps from Clear Creek and South Elkhorn, he was declared Minister of the Church. In his words, "They were pleased to call me to go in and out before them."

This seems rather discourteous, after inviting him to come down and live among them, but the Baptist Church could not have survived if it had not been made up of strong-minded individuals.

In May, 1789, certain members were appointed to seek out the most convenient place for a meetinghouse, and to fix what size would be most suitable. In July the committee reported their decision that 24 by 32 feet would be the most suitable size, but in September it was decided to defer the building that fall and winter.

The location of the building needed careful consideration, for these farsighted men realized that, for travel, roads were beginning to be used instead of waterways.

Since at that time only a few roads had been laid out, it was agreed that the meetinghouse would be most accessible if placed near the crossroads formed by the Steele's Ferry and the Lexington-Leestown roads. Accordingly, on June 1, 1795, John Brown, in consideration of the sum of one dollar, etc., sold to William Hickman, John Edrington, Edmund Ware, and Thomas Hicklin a parcel of land containing 13 poles "for the use of the Regular Baptist Church at the forks of Elkhorn forever * * * * and to no other use, intent, or purpose whatsoever."

In that same year the house was built by Nathaniel Sanders. It was, John Taylor wrote in 1824, "a framed meeting house not far from where the brick now stands, and was the first house of worship of any kind on the north side of the Kentucky River."

There was comparative safety in the Dry Run neighborhood, though farther toward the Ohio River the Indians were very dangerous. But William Hickman felt a great responsibility for the spiritual condition of the people living in that territory, and endured many hardships in carrying the Gospel to them.

Some time after he came to this community Mr. Hickman received an urgent invitation from the sons of Brackett Owen, who lived in that part of Jefferson County that is now Shelby, to come down and preach in their neighborhood. Since their mother was "an old professor," he accepted the invitation and made an appointment for a certain time. The Owens were formerly neighbors of the Major family, and William Major planned to go with Mr. Hickman. Benjamin Haydon was to be their guide, and a Mrs. Pulliam, of Frankfort, wished to go under their escort to visit relatives.

A few days before the appointed time the weather turned extremely cold, and Mr. Hickman, who dreaded cold more than Indians, decided that it would be unwise to attempt the journey. Since William Major insisted, however, they went to Haydon's Station about noon, where they found that Benjamin had gone across the river to hunt for his horses. As they could not go without a guide, Mr. Hickman was secretly relieved, especially since there was no way to cross the river but "in a little tottering canoe." They had to go on to Frankfort to tell Mrs. Pulliam, and Benjamin's mother thoughtfully sent along his good clothes, in case they should change their minds.

Mr. Hickman wrote of Frankfort, "At that time it was a perfect forest, there being only two little cabins in it." Dusk falls early in Frankfort, and when they reached Mrs. Pulliam's the shadows were lengthening, and the cold becoming more intense.

Stamping and tingling, they entered the room to be greeted by the blissful aroma of a fine turkey which Mrs. Pulliam was cooking before the fire.

Preachers in that time, even as now, were susceptible to a good dinner, and the mercury suddenly seemed to rise with Brother Hickman's spirits. "I told her to have it done, and I would go to the river bank and call Benjamin Haydon."

South Frankfort at that time was worse than a forest, for it was full of sinkholes and tangled with wild grapevines. After some time Benjamin answered and came on across. He had not found the horses, but a relative of Mrs. Pulliam's volunteered to lend one, so after a short time they were ready to start.

They had to cross the river one at a time, swimming their horses by the side of the canoe. When finally they were all over, and had their horses saddled, the moon was shining, though at times during the trip it would be snowing. They had to cross Benson nineteen times, sometimes on ice, and as he said "Some steps would bear us, the next break in." They passed a number of evacuated cabins whose owners had been killed or driven away. They reached their destination about two in the morning, and were put to bed where they stayed till about noon, while runners went out to different forts to call people to the meeting. Mr. Hickman's party was guarded to the river by twenty or thirty men, and the procession, he said, "looked more like going to war than to meeting to worship God."

On July 24, 1790, the Mount Gomer (Mt. Pleasant) Baptist Church was organized. The first meetinghouse, near the site of the present one, was built in 1791 on a high bluff overlooking Elkhorn Creek at Stedmantown. It was of logs, afterward covered with weatherboarding, and Ebenezer Stedman described it as he first saw it in 1833:"It looked at first sight like it had been built before the flood, and had floated and lodged on the hills like Noah's Ark. A look inside showed the seats made out of poplar slabs from the sawmill, with legs, and they came through the slabs, which made it quite unpleasant to sit down on."

A deed was not obtained until 1794, when Samuel Montgomery sold for five shillings to Moses Bledsoe, Benjamin Craig, Conrados Piles, Ernest Martena, John Edwards, Benjamin Perry, Francis Jackson, and Daniel James "a certain lot of land containing one acre, whereon the meeting house now stands, known by the name of Mongomer Meeting house." Some other families in the early congregation were those of Haydon, Head, Church, Long, Blanton, Oliver, and Poindexter.

It is said that this church was organized on the precept of Matthew 18:15, "If thy brother shall trespass against thee, etc.," and perhaps because of this it was not always in complete harmony with the other churches in the district.

Among the early pastors were F. H. Hodges, who served for thirty years, Isaac Crutcher, and William C. Blanton.

In 1801 the name was changed to "Mount Pleasant," and under this name it continued to bless the community until sometime within the present decade.

The summer and fall of 1791 William Hickman spent in Virginia, widening his horizon by preaching in many counties.

It seems unaccountable that keepers of the record should write pages on the small disagreements in the congregation, and let major tragedies go unmentioned.

In 1792 Hosea and Jesse Cook and their sisters, Margaret Mastin and Bathsheba Dunn, were living with their families at Quinn's Bottom (also called Innes's Bottom), a little settlement on Elkhorn about four miles from Frankfort. One day in April, as the Cooks were shearing sheep, the Indians made a sudden attack and killed them both. One fell on the doorstep of his cabin, and the two women, who were inside with three small children, pulled in his body and barred the door. They had a gun, but their only bullet was too large, so in terror and desperation Mrs. Elizabeth Bohannon Cook bit the bullet in two, loaded the gun, and fired through an opening between two logs, killing one of the Indians who were trying to beat down the door. Then the attackers mounted the roof and set fire to it, but one of the women climbed to the loft and put out the fire as often as it was started, using whatever the other woman handed up—water, eggs, and at last the blood-soaked jacket of the dead man.

The Indians finally left, but not until they had killed Lewis Mastin, the husband of Margaret, and two sons of Bathsheba and William Dunn.

A few days later Jared Demint, a nephew of Louis Easterday, was captured by the Indians on Eagle Creek, and twenty-five men from Scott County came down to search for him, stopping at the home of Louis Easterday, who had a still house. Here they imbibed too freely, and when they came to their senses, they found that the wily Indians had stolen their horses.

Young Demint was held captive in a cave on Glen's Creek, and he escaped within a few days, but his would-be rescuers had time for some serious thinking on the subject of intemperance before their horses were finally recovered.

In 1794 a day was set apart as a day of fasting and prayer, and in 1796 is an entry: "It is agreed that it is fault to omit washing one another's feet." How long this latter custom was continued we do not know, but William Graham made for the ceremony a copper basin which is now treasured as an heirloom by his descendants.

Viewed after a century, many of their decisions seem as unreasonable to us as our own will seem a hundred years hence. One entry states: "Agreed that it is wrong in the sight of God for church members to go to dances, horse races, cockfights, or barbecues, also wrong for church members to dress themselves or their children in a superfluous manner." William Hickman's son was excluded for joining the Free Masons, and another poor unfortunate "for his blasphemous expressions while in a state of insanity."

On the other hand, they were far in advance of their time in paying their pastor a stated salary—the general idea at that time being that virtue is its own reward.

They also imposed a strict rule: "It shall be the duty of all free male members missing two Church meetings to come forward the third meeting and give the Church their reasons for so doing." Since families were large and must be transported on horseback it is obvious why the ruling was restricted.

The Forks Church has always been noted for its thoughtful care of its unfortunate members. One item tells of employing a hand at the Church's expense to work for a brother in distress, and another speaks of levying on the Church for 200 pounds of pork and six barrels of corn for a poor widow, while in another, a committee sent to ascertain a good sister's needs reported that all she wanted was a wheel. (To those brought up in the gay nineties, this comes as quite a shock, until we realize that she meant a spinning wheel!)

About 1800 a great religious revival, embracing all denominations, swept the country. People would travel sometimes as much as a hundred miles to the famous camp meetings, at which the attendance in some cases is said to have been 20,000 persons. The services would continue without intermission throughout the day and night for a week at a time, with several exhorters discoursing simultaneously in different parts of the grove.

Though historians have given much publicity to the "jerks," shouting, and other extraordinary manifestations of religious fervor by those affected, the more thoughtful have seen in this movement "the first practical example of the possibility of the union of God's people in Christian worship." Ultimate results were the changing of many of the rough customs of the time, and the turning of men's thoughts to the evils of slavery. One leader said, "This revival cut the bonds of many poor slaves."

The Baptists nearly trebled their membership during this period, and William Hickman writes that he baptized more than 500 persons in two years.

The South Benson Church, in Franklin County, was constituted in February, 1801, by William Hickman, Sr., Warren Cash, and John Penny. The following members were dismissed from the Forks Church to join the congregation: William Hickman, Jr., and wife Obedience; Gilbert and Lucy Christian; John

Major; Nancy Berryman. Thomas Berryman was one of the first messengers to the Association.

The meetinghouse was located near Bridgeport, on the road leading to Farmdale. The first pastor was William Hickman, Jr., who preached there for many years, being followed by John S. Major. Others who served in the early days were A. R. Macey, William C. Blanton, and John Brown, who was a son-in-law of William Hickman, Jr.

Between 1824 and 1830 the church was divided over the doctrines taught by Campbell, and sixty-six members withdrew, creating soon afterward the Bridgeport Christian Church.

A clipping from an old scrapbook tells of the fame of the "June meetings" at South Benson, when on the first Sunday in June the entire countryside would dress in their best and turn out for the all-day meeting, which was known far and wide as the chief social and religious event of the year.

In 1883 the Evergreen Church was built, and in a few years more the South Benson Church ceased to function. The brick meetinghouse, which was built about 1843, is now used as a tobacco barn.

In April, 1801, the following members were dismissed to join a congregation up the North Fork of Elkhorn (the locality now known as Switzer): Thomas Bradley; Elijah, Charity, and Andrew Rogers; Elijah and Conny Anderson. One record states that this church was organized by William Hickman and George Eve, and that there were nineteen members in the original congregation. Among the earliest ministers to the congregation were William Hickman, George Eve, Jesse Vawter, John H. Ficklin, Mordecai Boulware.

In that same month, "at the request of an arm of the Church at the Mouth of Elkhorn and Cedar, by Bro. John Bartlett," the following members were dismissed to constitute a church in that place: William Gore; Sister Gore; William Rowlett, Sr.; Sister Rowlett; Daniel Rowlett; Nancy Rowlett; William Rowlett, Jr.; Elijah, Charity, and Kezia Calvert; Sister Stephens; John and Sally Bartlett; James Haydon. Some of the messengers sent to the Association were Berry Lamb, William Holloman, and W. Graves. The church was afterward called "Zion," and in 1802 there were forty-five members, but there is little more to be found concerning it.

The Forks of Elkhorn Church, however, continued to be the most prominent. In a Frankfort newspaper of 1802 appears a summons with the notice that by the direction of the court, "a copy of this order be published in the *Palladium* for two months successively, another copy set up at the door of Hickman's meeting house, on some Sunday immediately after divine service; and another copy set up at the door of the State House, in the town of Frankfort." A similar notice, shortly afterward, was ordered to be posted at "Croucher's meeting house, in Franklin County"—evidently Mount Pleasant, where Isaac Crutcher began his ministry.

Glen's Creek Church in Woodford was organized May 13, 1801, at Mrs. McCracken's sawmill, about three miles from Versailles.

Dr. W. J. McGlothlin, in his *History*, names the ten charter members as: James Ford, Seth Ramsey and wife, William Green and wife, Joseph Walden and wife, Samuel Berry and wife, Jane Samonis. James Ford and Lewis Garnett were the first deacons.

The first house was built about 1805, on land which is now a part of Hereford Farms, being known as the Hezekiah Winn place. On October 7, 1811, James Stapp sold to the congregation one acre for ten dollars.

The first pastor was William Buckley, who had charge of the congregation until about 1813. The next was John Edwards, from Shelby County, who continued until 1826, when he went to Missouri, and the third was Edmund Waller, who was in charge until his death in 1843.

In 1846 a committee was appointed "to get up a Sabbath-school and Bible class."

Since with the building of new roads another site seemed more desirable, in 1878 the present building was erected at the intersection of the Steele and McCracken's Mill pikes.

There were many tombstones in the old churchyard, but they have entirely disappeared, and the logs in the original building are said to have been used in constructing a barn on the old Mastin place.

Other members of the early congregation were: Joel Achly, Ann Angness (?), Lucy Atwood, William Bridgford and wife, Lucy Boulware, Jeremiah and Frances Buckley, Samuel Buckley and wife, Thomas Buckley, William Buckley, Joseph Bundrent (Bondurant?) and wife, William Burrus, wife, and daughter, Edmund Chapman, Whitfield and Sary Collins, Nancy Davenport, John Dawson and wife, Betsy Edwards, John and Narcissa Edwards, Lucy Edwards, Pheby Elnander (Alexander?), Betsy Fogg, Obed Fogg, Ann Gaince (Gaines?), James and Nancy Garnett, Louis Garnett, William and Lucy Garnett, Elizabeth Goode, John Green, Jane Green, Willis Hawkins, Ann Henry, Jane Hill, Sally Hunter, Richard Jesse, Andrew Jones, Thomas Jones, Mary (?) Long, Reuben Long and wife Jemima, Patsy Meridith, Sary Minter, John and Ann Mullican, Jane Mullican, Nelly Naul, Ann Negnan (?), Nancy Ramsey, Nancy Rarden, —— Rarden, William Rarden, John Read, Mary Read, Lucy Reaves, Benjamin Salley (Sallee?), John and Annie Sercy, Richard and Mary Searcy, John and Betsy Sheets, Mary Shepard, Richard D. Shipp, Richard and Elizabeth Shipp, Narcissa Shipp, Salley Shipp, Betsy Slaughter, Robert and Lucy Slaughter, Henry Stone, Reuben Sullenger, Gabriel Sullenger, Patsy Tuggle, Fanny Turpin, George Twyman, Mildred Twyman, John West and wife, Hannah Williams, Polly Willis.

In the records of the Forks of Elkhorn Church we find: August, 1805. "The Church Profess's to be grieved with Grassy Spring Church—Drew up their Complaints and Sent them by the following Brethren, James Haydon, Carter Blanton, Abraham Gregory, Daniel Peak, and Theodorick Boulware to Enquire and make report at our next meeting."

Grassy Spring Church (also called Hopewell) was organized some time before 1800, it is said, by Isaac Crutcher, who was the first pastor. It was located on the original road from Frankfort to Versailles, between the sites of the Forks of Elkhorn and the Glen's Creek Churches. A part of the lot was given by Richard Fox, and the remainder by Thomas Hinton, who, in his will (1829) specifies that it is to be for the use of any denomination of Christians.

Some doctrinal difference between it and the other Baptist Churches seems to have existed from the beginning. In 1824 there was a disagreement with the Association, and in 1830, we are told, the congregation voted unanimously to become a Christian (Disciples) Church, and as such it continues.

Though no record of its early history exists, the following families are known to have been in the congregation at that period: Bailey, Ballard, Blackwell, Blanton, Crutcher, Fogg, Gibbany, Graddy, Hall, Hawkins, Holloway, Parrish, Shipp, Stephens, Thompson, (George) Todd, Ware, Whittington. Of the few older tombstones remaining, one is of Isaac Crutcher (1767-1837), one of Reuben Daniel (1772-1857), and one, which is broken, of ——— Alexander, who died in 1830.

The settlers' first thoughts, after home and church, were for a school. Though their living conditions were primitive, they brought with them from Maryland and Virginia memories of classic training which challenged their ambition to produce equal educational advantages for their own children. With this in mind, we may be sure that the first institution of learning they set up was something more than a "blab school."

Whether this was the school on John Major's farm is not known, for information concerning it is singularly lacking. The only two persons who might be suggested as having taught there were the Rev. John Price, who taught a grammar school attended by Abraham Cook, and Philip S. Fall, who took charge of an academy in the district about the time he united with the Forks Church.

It was evidently started very early, for in November, 1805, there is a record: "Agreed by the Church that subscriptions be put into the hands of our Brethren William Samuel, Carter Blanton, and Thomas Settle to raise money to repair the schoolhouse which is in partnership between the Church and the subscribers to the schoolhouse."

September, 1807. "Bro. Wm. Hickman came forward and informed the Church that he was distressed on account of the practice of slavery as being tolerated by the members of the Baptist Society, therefore declared himself no more in union with us, or the Elkhorn Association. Therefore the Church considers him no more a member in fellowship.

"Pluright Sisk withdrew for the same reason."

For some time there had been in the churches a growing sentiment against slavery, some members even refusing to commune with slaveholders. On Craig's Creek in Woodford, Carter Tarrants and John Sutton had in 1806 organized "New Hope," a church for those who believed in emancipation, and it may be that William Hickman and Pluright Sisk were affiliated with it after they withdrew from the Forks Church.

But in the course of time people began to feel that slavery was a problem for the State, and not for the Church. So it is not surprising to read that in November, 1809, "Bro. William Hickman came forward and offered his membership, and after some conversation he was restored to membership and his former standing." The following year he again took charge of the Church as its pastor.

It may seem inconsistent that William Hickman and Pluright Sisk are each listed in the census of 1810 as owning one slave, but since the historians tell us that the situation of an emancipated slave in that period was far more unhappy than that of his brother in bondage, we may be sure that the servants in those two households benefited by their masters' principles.

The church at the Big Spring, at what is now Spring Station, in Woodford, was organized in October, 1812, and the congregation erected a large stone building for their house of worship.

From the Forks Church the following members were dismissed to join the constitution: Abraham and Mildred Gregory, Jesse and Nancy Cole, Prudence Blackburn, Catherine Smith, Walter and Agnes Ayres. George Blackburn was a charter member, and Judge Henry Davidge was also mentioned as a loyal supporter. William Hickman, Thomas Suter, and S. M. Noel were some of its ministers. John Taylor wrote of it: "After Mr. Noel and Mr. Creath served Big Spring for one year, for about two years past they have been served by the well known Mr. John Edwards. This church has only had a gradual growth from the beginning; they do not now perhaps exceed fifty in number—but they are a well-disposed, loving body of brethren."

It is thought that services were discontinued there about 1846, and in 1853 the property was sold to R. A. Alexander.

The stately old meetinghouse, which is still standing, is now used as a farm building.

The War of 1812 took its toll from the congregation. William Hickman wrote in after years: "My first wife died the 9th of June, 1813. Sorely distressed in mind about the massacre of her son, Pascal, at the river Raisin, she pined away and died." He married his second wife, Mrs. Elizabeth Abbett, the following year.

On the second Saturday in February, 1816, the following members were dismissed to join a constitution in Frankfort: Simon and Philadelphia Beckham, Mrs. Polly Hickman, Sally Cunningham, Patsy Ransdale, Betsy Loughborough, Sally Bacon, Benjamin and Letitia Edrington, Jane Daniel, Susanna Graham.

The church was organized on February 26, the first meeting being held at the home of Simon Beckham. There were thirteen charter members: Rev. John and Elizabeth Taylor, John Epperson, Elijah Stapp, Jeptha Dudley, and all those dismissed from the Forks Church, except Susanna Graham, Letitia Edrington, and Philadelphia Beckham, who joined later.

The first sermon was preached to the new congregation by Rev. Silas M. Noel. The first deacons elected were Joseph Edrington and John W. Wooldridge.

Meetings were conducted in the homes of the members, at the court house, and the State House until 1818, when they were held in the "House of Public Worship," a building on the southwest corner of the Old Capitol square, which had been erected with the proceeds of a lottery, and which was used also by the Presbyterians and the Methodists. This building burned in 1825, and the Baptists erected their first meetinghouse in 1827.

The earliest pastors, in order of service, were: Henry Toler; Jacob Creath and Philip Fall; Silas M. Noel; Porter Clay; George Blackburn.

In December, 1817, the Forks of Elkhorn Church had a membership consisting of twenty-five white males, fifty-four white females, and forty-seven slaves.

A constitution in the Forks of Elkhorn in Franklin County; otherwise known as Buck Run Church, was organized in January, 1818, at Isaac Wilson's. From the Forks Church were dismissed to join it: John and Susanna Price, Isaac and Lucy Wilson, William Forsee and wife, Frances Castleman, Nancy Triplett, Sarah Head, Lucy Nall, and Love Fuller. Other members named by John Taylor were: John, Elizabeth, and Benjamin Taylor; Presley and Fanny Neal; Julius and Elizabeth Blackburn; John and Catherine Graves; Elizabeth Gatewood; Lewis and Jane Nall.

The first building was located on the Wilson farm near what is now the intersection of the Spring Station and Georgetown pikes.

John Taylor preached there once a month for five years, and other ministers in that early period were William Hickman, Silas M. Noel, James Suggett, John H. Ficklin, Mordecai and Theodoric Boulware, Addison M. Lewis.

In 1824 John Taylor wrote of it, "Taking this little young church by and large, they are rather a happy people than otherwise—and though that warm glow of brotherly love is not often seen among them, they are peaceable among themselves * * * * We have very few black members among us, and another thing in our favor, we have very few rich men among us—for very often by rich men and negroes the cause of religion suffers much—for while one is above, the other is below its natural Godlike dignity."

In 1888 the building was taken down and removed to the Forks of Elkhorn, where services are usually conducted twice a month.

1819. "Whereas Samuel Gravit was excluded from this Church at their January meeting in the year 1802, and the charge standing on our record for pilfering a pair of gloves and for falsities, and some testimony coming before this Church, that proves his innocency, the Church has restored him in fellowship. Brother Samuel Gravit is granted a letter of dismission."

How did those men feel? Some may have quoted the Scripture about abstaining from all appearance of evil, but surely there must have been some who wrestled nightly in prayer for forgiveness for having deprived their fellow man of the benefits of church life through so many years.

And what of Samuel Gravit? Did he forgive them, or was he embittered for the rest of his life? It is actions such as these that make the study of history valuable to later generations.

April, 1819. "The Church hath agreed to give up the old schoolhouse, all except the stone chimney, for the benefit of Zachariah Pulliam and Ezra Richmond, on condition that the church shall have liberty to have their Church meeting in the new schoolhouse."

The oldest inhabitant remembers a pile of stones near the site of the old meetinghouse, which may have been the remains of "the new stone schoolhouse."

The lot containing the meetinghouse, schoolhouse, and graveyard had been increased to include 1¼ acres, and on July 8, 1809, Daniel E. Brown, a son of the original owner, granted to the trustees a title to it.

In 1812 there was started a movement to build a new meetinghouse. Various sites were inspected, and at one time they had agreed to buy 1½ acres from Giles Samuel; but in 1816 they concluded to build a new brick church 50 by 30 by 16 feet "on the lot where the old church stands." On the various committees appointed for these transactions were John Price, Silas Noel, Carter Blanton, William Samuel, Benjamin Edrington, William Ware, Theodoric Boulware, John Major, Joseph Edrington, and William Graham.

In April, 1817, they decided to build a new house whenever the sum of two thousand dollars was raised, but in June of that year they planned instead to repair the house and build a frame addition on the north side, about twenty-four feet square, sufficiently high for a gallery above.

July 1819. "This Church has agreed to give up the meeting house to Mr. Bennett Settles, the undertaker of the new meeting house."

No record of the long deferred date of building has been found, but in his autobiography William Hickman wrote: "Thanks be to God, the Lord has put it in the hearts of the people to build a good brick meeting house for the worship of God, and friends not in the society have been the greatest subscribers. We hope the hand of the Lord is in it." With a building program on hand, the Church may have considered the ninety-seven dollars raised for William Hickman for the year 1826 a very reasonable salary.

Brother Hickman was growing old. In 1823 John Taylor wrote of him: "Though now about 76 years old, he walks and stands as erect as a palm tree, being at least six feet high, rather of a lean texture, his whole deportment solemn and grave. His mode of speaking is so slow that the hearers at times get ahead of him in the subject before they get it from him."

It may be that William Hickman himself felt a lessening of his powers, for in 1827 he wrote: "We have now to lament the barrenness of the times: for a number of years we have had but small ingatherings, though we still wish to wait on the Lord, hoping to see better days. The old Mother Church at the Forks of Elkhorn is getting naked and bare, the Lord has taken a number of the leading members home to glory. * * * * For several years we have set apart every Sunday and Wednesday night for Prayer meeting, and have attended so far, and hope to keep on.

"Dear Brethren, don't neglect us. As poor as we are, who knows but the Lord will still remember in mercy, and we may yet enjoy better days?"

If he could have foreseen what an instrument of salvation the Forks Church was to be in the next hundred years, he might have said with the Psalmist:

"The Lord is good; his mercy is everlasting:
And his truth endureth to all generations."

The year 1830 was marked as the time of the great cataclysm in the Baptist Church, brought about by the teachings of Alexander Campbell. To the staunch Baptists it was unthinkable that any in their own congregation should forsake the teachings of their fathers, and they trembled for the souls of the errant ones. Some of these were their own brothers, who had learned to pray at the same knee, and huddled together in the same trundle bed.

In a moving appeal they set forth to the divergent members many considerations, beseeching them to think of the feelings of old Brother Hickman, and to regard "the peace, the happiness, and the welfare of Sion."

But it was in vain. The dissenters, equally as conscientious as their brothers, having heard a call, "went out, not knowing whither they went." Strained and sorrowing, they could only say to the anxious ones, "Brethren, pray for us."

It is a sad chapter, written in pain and grief, and it can scarcely be read without tears.

Finding their efforts fruitless, the Baptist leaders accepted the decision in a manner befitting the gentlemen that they were, and the two congregations lived together in an apparently amicable relationship. The Baptists retained the second Saturday and Sunday; while the new denomination chose the third, and under the leadership of C. H. Trabue, W. H. Whittington, and others, continued there for several years. They soon agreed to share the expenses for fuel and for a housekeeper, and often one congregation would "borrow" the house from the other for some special meeting.

About this time, too, the colored people were allowed to meet there separately, so there was the unusual situation of three congregations using one building. A few years before, John Taylor had written of them: "The poor blacks, whose voices generally exceed the whites, have learned many of those precious songs; they are now abundantly stirred up to a devotional spirit; they flock together and in the dead time of night you may hear them at a distance praying to, and praising God with charming sound. And as you travel the road in day time, at their business you hear them singing with such heavenly melody, that your heart melts into heavenly sweetness."

But now a change was in the air. Abolitionists were coming from the North and creating so much dissatisfaction that in 1831 it was recorded: "On motion the Church took into consideration the meeting of the Blacks at this place, and the Church thinks it proper to discontinue their meetings in the future at this place, either by day or night."

On January 24, 1834, William Hickman went to South Benson to preach, and as he was returning home after dinner he felt ill. Stopping in Frankfort at the home of one of his friends, he asked that a pallet be made on the floor. Here he lay throughout the afternoon, repeating passages of Scripture, and gradually growing weaker, until at last, with the firelight flickering as it did on that winter evening long ago when he first preached to his beloved people, he was granted the fulfillment of his prayer, "Let me die the death of the righteous, and let my last end be like his."

The *Frankfort Commonwealth* for January 28 had a brief notice: "Died—In this county on Friday last, the Rev. William Hickman, sen., at a very advanced age."

At the February meeting is recorded: "Resolved, that the members wear crape on the left arm for 30 days in memory of our aged and revered Brother William Hickman." Fifty dollars was appropriated for tombstones for him and his two wives' graves. (His remains, and those of his wife, were removed to the D. A. R. lot in Frankfort Cemetery in 1928.)

To him was given, also, the fulfillment of another desire. Several years before his death he had written of the Forks of Elkhorn Church: "This Church I hope to serve until I am laid in the dust, for they have ever manifested their love and esteem to me; they lie near my heart; I wish to live and die with them, and hope to spend a blessed eternity with them, when parting is no more."

At the April meeting in 1835 the leaders promoted a characteristic and thoughtful act which earned for them the gratitude of Kentuckians for the next hundred years: "On motion and second, Bro. John Stephens is appointed by the Church to have the old Church book bound together with the new one, in order to preserve the records for future generations."

Eben Stedman wrote in his journal: "For two years we heard most remarkable stories about Rail Roads. One said that he had seen carriages drawn on a Rail Road by steam; he was put down as a Munchausen. Another said he rode on a coach that went so fast that he had to breath through a brass tube made on purpose so that the speed would not take their breath away, and some told such stories that the people would not believe anything they would say."

A Louisville firm made a small locomotive and portable track, so arranged that one person could ride around the room. This was exhibited in Frankfort, Georgetown, and Lexington, "admittance one dollar to see the great wonder * * * * The excitement got up by this little model of a Rail Road in Lexington did not stop till a company was formed and a charter obtained for the Lexington and Louisville Rail Road. A flying machine in this day would not cause half the excitement that the little car and track is, in Lexington."

In January, 1835, a train was run from Lexington to Frankfort, over the first steam railroad built west of the Allegheny Mountains, and the second in the United States.

The cars were about twelve feet long, seating ten or twelve persons inside; and on the roof, which was reached by a stepladder, were also two long seats placed back to back. These cars were drawn by "locomotive steam engines of great power and speed," which were fired with wood stacked at intervals along the track.

Since the railroad was built almost within sight and hearing of the meetinghouse, no doubt many a staid old family mare forgot her dignity at the sight of the noisy monster tearing through the country at the amazing speed of fifteen miles an hour!

But to a Kentuckian, nothing will ever take the place of a horse. About this time the Frankfort-Versailles turnpike (Highway 60) was built, and several of the older roads were abandoned. With the advent of macadamized roads, vehicular travel became so popular that in 1838 the Elkhorn Association appealed to the Legislature to open the tollgates for free passage for persons attending church services.

The well-to-do could afford wheels, but there were some who must continue to go on horseback, and it was perhaps as a sop to their discontent that in 1837 it was decided to build a saddle house.

There is a story of one family who came out in a fine new carriage, but soon afterward their feelings were outraged at finding chalked across the shining surface

> "Who'd have thought it?
> Turnip greens bought it."

It would be interesting and romantic to learn the date of the first buggy-ride, for it was then that girls learned poise. In a buggy, one cannot work off a bad temper by scolding one's horse, or by dashing ahead and flirting mud on an unwelcome suitor.

The record states that there were eighty-one members of the Forks of Elkhorn Church in December, 1839. There is a list of members marked 1839, but it seems that only the first fifteen of the men and the first nineteen of the women were in it, the other names being added later. The list includes:

John Stephens, Sr.
William Graham
Reuben Crutcher, Sr.
Henry Crutcher, Sr.
William H. Martin
Ezra Richmond
Joel Scott
Thomas Foster
Gabriel Smith
Nathan Ayres
Isaac Crutcher
Levi Crutcher
Lewis Blackburn
Harrison Hancock
Enos Johnson
Francis Graham
John Foster
James Bridgford
W. N. Ayres
Thomas G. Guthrie
Edward M. Ayres
James Dark
Robert W. Scott
John R. Scott
——— Pilcher
John Crutcher
Isaac Wilson
John Wilson
Silas Macy

R. T. Macy
A. W. Macklin
John Macklin
C. F. Hendrix
James T. Dillon
Joseph Lambkin
Richard M. Jones
John Brydon
George M. Williams
Fielding Ramsey
William P. Robertson
Roberson Crutcher
Seth Ramsey
Timothy Hughes
Martha Crutcher
Susan Major
Rebecca Blanton
Susannah Crutcher
Margaret Graham
Sally Neal
Isabella Samuel
Frances Gibson
Lucy Foster
Eliza Richmond
Ann Schockley
Sarah Stephens
Artimesia Stephens
Mary R. Ayres
Letitia Hancock

Deborah Scott
Eliza Crutcher
Susan Crutcher
Hannah Stockdell
Susan E. Jones
Priscilla Graham
Catherine Graham
Nancy Hearn
Martha Ann Foster Ayres
Frances Elizabeth Foster Ayres
Margaret H. Jones Ayres
Agnes Smith
Sidney Jane Scott
Lucinda Dark
Durana Jane Pilcher Pratts
Eliza Ann Crutcher Hancock
Anna Pilcher
Elizabeth W. Scott
Sophia Hancock
Margaret Davis
Mary Hancock Crutcher
Polly Wilson Reed
Jane Wilson
Sarah Hendrix
Elizabeth Hendrix
Eunice T. Macklin

Ann Dillon
Elizabeth Lampkin
Mary Bryden Reed
Laura Taylor
Elizabeth Rodgers
Nancy Ramsey
Martha Williams
Cynthia Robertson
Mary Smith
Martha Wilson
Mary Hancock
Mahala Howe
—— Thompson
—— Tinder
Nancy Ramsey
Elizabeth Hancock
Scythy Ann Brightwell
Martha Brightwell
Huldah Carter
Gabriella Smith
Sarah Crutcher
Agnes Craig
Lucy D. Lewis
Mary Craig
Sarah Dixon
Susan R. Lewis
Mary Hendrix

The trustees in 1841 were R. W. Scott, John Scott, Levi T. Crutcher, Gabriel Smith, and Walter N. Ayres.

In the late thirties the abolitionists increased their activities, and many slaves were running away. Henry Clay says that up to this time there had been a "progressive melioration" in the treatment of slaves, but they were becoming so rebellious that their privileges had to be curtailed. One minister told of being constrained to use firearms to bring one to obedience, and in this he was upheld by all the congregation except Isaac Miles. In 1839 it was reported that the colored people had had such a disorderly meeting that the housekeeper was forbidden to give them the key to the building thereafter without a special order. A little later it was decided to "appoint four colored brethren to watch over the conduct of their other brethren."

Collins' *History of Kentucky*, in reviewing the events of 1848, gives this item under date of October 7: "About 40 negroes in Woodford County have been furnished with free passes by abolitionists, and are to steal horses and ride off to Ohio tonight, but the plot is discovered and defeated."

The records of 1850 indicate that during this period the colored people had their meetings at separate times from those of the white people, though under strict surveillance, and the pastor of the Forks Church was commissioned to preach to them in the afternoon of the fourth Sunday of each month.

About this time "Buena Vista" came into the possession of Mrs. Robert Todd, of Lexington, whose stepdaughter, Mary, was the wife of Abraham Lincoln. This was a very old homestead, originally owned by Mrs. Sarah Gibson. There are two stone houses about twenty feet apart, and between them until quite recently was a well—a wise provision in case of Indian attacks. The two buildings were afterward connected by a large frame addition which is thought to have been built by William Samuel, who owned it later.

The Todds used "Buena Vista" as a summer home, and Mrs. Lincoln and the children used to spend much time there.

Duckers was one of the earliest stations to be established on the railroad. and as it is only about a mile from "Buena Vista," it is said that Mr. Lincoln used to come by train for some of his visits, though there is no record of their producing any excitement such as would be caused a hundred years later.

There is a neighborhood tradition that when Mrs. Lincoln went to see the Lewises at "Llangollen" she would take the most direct route, crossing the creek at what is now known as the W. B. Allen place, which at that time was occupied by the family of Mr. Isaac Crutcher. Once when a sudden storm came up, she hurriedly took refuge with the Crutchers, declaring that, though she wasn't afraid of lightning, the thunder just terrified her!

March, 1845. "By request leave is granted to the Reform Church to occupy this house on the last Saturday and Sabbath." This is the last date on which the Christian Church is mentioned, showing that the separation took place between this time and April, 1852, when James Mitchum Stephens wrote in his will a bequest for "the Reformed or Christian Church, that is to say to the members of that Church who recently worshipped at the Forks of Elkhorn."

The withdrawal was no doubt a relief to both congregations, for although their relations were friendly, no house is large enough for two families, and certainly not for three.

The greater part of the departing congregation, however, eventually merged with that of Grassy Spring.

The Church at this time enjoyed an era of comparative quiet. It was requested that the members supply themselves with Buck's Hymns, and an October record says: "It is agreed that we keep up our prayer-meetings, and that we change them from 4 o'clock (on Sunday evenings) to candle light, and that they be changed from the meeting house to the houses of the members during the cold weather."

In November, 1846, it was agreed that "the Church observe the 26th of this month as a day of Thanksgiving, according to the request of the Governor."

A sketch of the life of Robert W. Scott says that he organized a Sunday school at the Forks of Elkhorn Church in 1850. The early Sunday schools were quite unlike those of today, consisting chiefly in having the children repeat verses from the Bible which they had memorized during the week. The children found this much more agreeable than listening to long sermons, and soon there was much rivalry among the pupils as to the greatest number that could be memorized. One contestant used to tell how he would take his Bible to the cornfield with him, and memorize as he plowed—a verse to a row.

1854. The colored brethren formerly belonging to Big Spring wished to be organized as a separate congregation, and asked the advice of the Forks Church. After serious discussion and consultation with the neighboring churches, they were advised to abandon the idea of a separate organization, and to have membership with some of the regular churches.

September, 1854, "Brother Freeman called the attention of the Church to the proposition of the Franklin Association that each church hold a meeting of fasting, humiliation, and prayer in view of the low state of Religion and of the great drought which afflicts the country, and it is agreed to hold said meeting on next Monday."

The year 1854 is noted in history as the time of the great drought. Old people used to tell that huge cracks appeared in the earth, and trees were cut down in order that cattle could feed on the leaves after the pasturage was gone. The *Frankfort Commonwealth* for that year states that many cornfields were literally scorched, as with fire, and the river fell ten feet below the navigable stage. The Ohio River could be forded in many places. On the fourth of September the thermometer registered 100 in the shade, after a period of three months in which there were only five days under 90, and very few under 95.

God has a direct way of talking with country people in which city dwellers cannot share—through the weather. To those in town, it is usually a matter of wraps or umbrellas, but to farmers the heavens literally declare the glory of God, for on a favorable season depends the conditions for months to come.

But on October 12 there was an all-night rain of "unprecedented copiousness," of which the writer said, "If the earth had not been so dry that it absorbed like a sponge, we should have had a sudden and very destructive flood." The river rose five feet the next day, mills began to run again, pastures freshened, and the people felt that their prayers had been answered.

The "low state of religion" may be evidenced by the following story:

"In January, 1857, the venerable Joel E. Scott, Sr., addressed the following letter to the church clerk:

"'Dear Bro.—I am informed that my sons, Robert W. and John R. Scott, my brothers in Christ, Alex Macklin and D. C. Freeman, have allowed dancing to be carried on in their houses during Christmas week just past. I make a charge against them.

"'Joel E. Scott.'

"The delinquents were cited to appear, promised not to offend again, and were excused."

It may also be noted that those of that generation handed down the tradition that the Forks Church was then the real style center of this section, and their description of the glamorous garments worn suggested the "superfluous manner" of dressing which was so strongly condemned some fifty years previously.

It is an adage that fine clothes call for fine surroundings. In 1858 it was decided that two stoves "adapted to burning coal" should be bought for the use of the Church. The next year the house was whitewashed and painted, and a dozen hymn books were ordered.

Did those who kept the record feel that it was inconsistent to have any suggestion of war on pages devoted to the service of the Prince of Peace? There is nothing to indicate that a war was in progress, though many of the church families had sons who wore the gray.

After the war, a spirit of progress was in the air. People realized that the meetinghouse was inconveniently located, because the branch on the east often rose above fording point, and the steep road up the hill became too heavy for vehicles.

There are two persons living in the community at this time (1938) who remember attending services in the old building. Mrs. Eugene Wolf, of Frankfort, tells of attending services at what she fondly calls "The Hickman Church," with her father, William O. Morris. J. B. Tharp was preaching, and he had just declared "He who eats till he is sick must fast till he is well," when her father told her she could go out and play. She recalls vividly the locust blooms, the blue jays, and the post and rail fence around the yard.

She tells also of an evening service, at which Isaac Crutcher stood before the congregation with a candle in one hand and a hymn book in the other, "lining out" the hymns, one of which she remembers:

> "Time is winging us away
> To our eternal home,
> Life is but a winter's day,
> A journey to the tomb."

Charley Hancock, an old colored man at "Hickman Hill," remembers going to the old church, and sitting in the gallery with his mother.

About this time the Presbyterian church known as "Harmony," which was located a mile or two farther east on the Leestown pike, dissolved its organization, and the property reverted to Robert W. and John R. Scott, who proposed to exchange it for that of the Forks Church.

In January, 1866, a meeting was held to discuss the proposal, and it is recorded, "with three or four exceptions many think the spiritual welfare of the church will be much enhanced by the change of location."

The exchange was made in that year, being transacted by Levi T. Crutcher, W. N. Ayres, G. W. Robb, and Timothy Hughes, trustees. Some time after the old brick building was abandoned, Robert W. Scott sold the part of his farm on which it stood to Hillery Bedford, who used the material in constructing the residence now owned by Sam A. Mason.

1866. "Moved and seconded that we invite our colored brethren and sisters to meet with us on the 4th Sabbath of this month, that we may advise with each other as to the relations we sustain to each other and to the Church." These items show the true quality of the leaders in the Forks Church, who were concerned not for the loss of their property, but for the future of those dependent on them.

Early in 1868 a new list of the colored members was made, and it was decided to drop from the list the names of all whose whereabouts were not known to the Church, as well as those who expressed indifference to remaining. In October of that same year the record states: "Whereas it has long been painfully apparent that the colored membership of this Church no longer feel Christian sympathy and interest with her, and have failed to participate in its ministrations, there fore, be it resolved: that said members be henceforward dropped from the roll of the Church as members, and debarred from the privileges of the Church, but the Church will be glad to retain in membership any who shall signify in two months a desire to walk with the Church in the future, and shall give evidence of Church fellowship."

This was no doubt a great relief to those in charge, who for years had borne the increasing weight of responsibility for the colored people.

As for the latter, though a few retained membership in the Forks Church, the majority grouped together in churches of their own, and, true to their early training, became excellent citizens.

At this period, and for some time thereafter, the neighborhood school was conducted in an old house that stood a short distance west of the present church building. The story is told of one of the teachers that he once went to spend the night with one of his patrons, and liked it so well that he stayed on for twenty years. It was too far to walk to school, and when the visit threatened to become indefinite his host very generously supplied him with a piece of land to raise corn for his horse.

And now appeared the triumph of mind over matter. As he went to school each morning, the teacher would ride slowly up one row of corn, hoeing as he went, and would repeat the process on another row as he returned in the afternoon. But the story ended before the size of the corn crop was disclosed.

The children of those days were an irrepressible lot, and one teacher would very obligingly stretch out on a bench with his old coonskin cap over his face, and sleep throughout the noon hour. Another, however, was more exacting, and the children would have to comb his hair and perform various other small services before he would consent to doze off and let their joy be unconfined.

During school hours, however, things were vastly different. They were practical-minded men who designed that building, and they had the conviction that the children should keep their eyes on the old blue-backed speller. Accordingly, they placed the windows so high that the only way the little prisoners could look out was by climbing on benches or leaving the door open.

But youth will be served. Since the outside was forbidden, they must make the best of things within, so it may not be surprising to learn that one of the pupils married her teacher!

Among the teachers recalled are: Rev. Nathan Ayres; Anthony Martin; Miss Hunter Poynter (the mother of Marvin H. McIntyre); Edward M. Ayres; Miss Mary Williams; Thomas Gibson; Miss Kate Thompson (sister of Dr. Wilson Thompson); Miss Sarah Poynter (Mrs. Griffin); Nathaniel Porter (the husband of "Sunshine"); Charles Parrent; "Yankee Weed" (his real name unknown, he was so called because he came from the North and wore blue clothes).

The records from this time on are not so heterogeneous as the previous ones, but they have a forward trend which strengthens the heart and augurs well for the future.

The people, having been disciplined by their long and patient oversight of the colored members, and having disposed of their charges in the best possible manner, were eager to go forward. Sermons could now take on a more intellectual tone, in conformity to the tastes of a well educated audience.

Best of all, the Church, now free from incumbrances within its own organization, could lift its eyes to wider fields, and begin to assume its share in fulfilling the Great Commission.

In 1867 it was planned to reopen their Sunday school, and soon afterward they were having two prayer meetings a week —the usual one on Wednesday, and one for the young men on Sunday evening. An offering was made for the German Baptists in Kentucky.

February, 1873. "Permission was granted to Mr. Howard Gratz to set a tablet in the wall of the church, commemorative of the virtues of our departed Brother Walter N. Ayres." The tablet is inscribed:

IN MEMORY OF

WALTER N. AYRES

BORN MAY 11, 1820;

DIED JAN. 14, 1872.

A MAN WITHOUT GUILE

In 1874 a committee was appointed to see H. Crutcher regarding exchange of land, and fencing. The next year the schoolhouse was removed from the church lot.

In December, 1875, is a note regarding lamps which had been bought by "Brother Seay." These were probably the first used by the congregation.

Rev. F. H. Kerfoot and T. W. Scott, in November, 1875, were appointed a committee to procure photographs of the former pastors of the Church to be placed in the Church Bible. Shortly afterward, Mr. Scott was also designated to make a list of all the members who had ever belonged to the Forks Church. This was quite in keeping with the practice of the congregation to preserve records, but if the collection was made it was evidently misplaced or scattered in later years.

In August, 1884, in planning for the meeting of the Association in Freeman's grove, "It was resolved that only a plain dinner would be furnished." As far back as 1846, when it was resolved that "It shall be the duty of R. W. Scott, W. N. Ayres, Robinson Crutcher, and Lewis Blackburn to use their best exertions to prevent the sale of any cakes or refreshments on the usual meeting days of this Church," and at intervals thereafter, these good resolutions had been made—but all in vain, for the basket dinners were an integral part of the history of the Forks Church, and have had their share in the making of Kentucky's reputation. Superfine cooking depends on love and pride and skill and background, and when good church women with all these qualities come in juxtaposition with the choicest products of carefully tended cows and pigs and chickens, the results are beyond any description, and are enjoyed in anticipation, realization, and retrospection.

For several years no records were kept, but the book shows that at the business meeting in September, 1885, G. W. Robb made a motion that attention be called from the pulpit next day to Spencer's *History of Kentucky Baptists,* and its purchase by the brethren be recommended. In that same year Mr. T. W. Scott, who knew the value of written records, arranged for the book an account of the important events between 1876 and 1885.

It was during this period that new seats and other improvements had been provided, but one thing which has been most beneficial to the Church was the organization in 1876 of the Women's Missionary Society. Emancipation brought freedom not only to the slaves, but also to their mistresses, for women, being obliged in many cases to do their own work, began also to do their own thinking, and from this time forth we find them sharing in every permissible phase of the Church's activity.

It was about this time that the organ was bought, and among those who played it are recalled Misses Mary Wasserboehr, Jennie Robb, Adelia Crutcher, Eva Cook, Martha Freeman, Jennie Crutcher, and Mrs. Susie Brown.

Having been called to the ministry, John R. Sampey, on his twenty-second birthday, September 27, 1885, was ordained in the Forks of Elkhorn Church by a presbytery consisting of Dr. William M. Pratt, of Lexington; Dr. James P. Boyce, first President of the Southern Baptist Theological Seminary; Dr. R. M. Dudley, of Georgetown College; Dr. George F. Bagby, pastor of the Frankfort Church; and Rev. Ben T. Quin, of Franklin County. It was a lengthy and trying experience, but, like another youth who sat in the temple in the midst of the doctors, he increased "in favour with God and man."

In formulating a set of Church laws in 1886, it was agreed that public dancing, habitual theater going, and card playing should be regarded as violations of the rules of the Church, but within the next year this was rescinded, with the understanding that such things be treated as the Scriptures direct.

The neighborhood was changing. Tobacco raising was beginning to be done on a large scale, and this was bringing into the community many families from other sections of the State. The young pastor felt that these newcomers should be attached to a Church home, and consequently, in August, 1886, he held a two weeks' revival of which it is recorded, "and from the beginning to the end of the meeting the presence of the Lord was felt among his people."

At this meeting, which Dr. Sampey considers one of the most enjoyable in his experience, the membership was increased from seventy-three to a hundred and fourteen, many of the additions being the children of the older families of the Church.

The protracted meeting was always the great event of summer, the calendar being consulted weeks ahead, and the date set for the time of the full moon, to make traveling easier.

The whole family went, and everyone prepared for it: the father stopping the work on the farm a little earlier; the mother hurrying about supper; the youths soaking their buggy wheels to eliminate the rattle; the girls fresh and vivacious after their naps on the cool parlor floor; and the "company," who had been invited to make their visits at this time, putting on stylish new clothes.

There is something irresistible about a protracted meeting. Young people of all denominations would come, sometimes for long distances; for youth happily has nothing to do with creeds, and the longer the drive, the better.

People would assemble in the early evening, in time for greetings and fellowship and important communications before the services began.

First in order would be the happy, vigorous singing, followed by earnest prayers and impassioned exhortation, leading up to the tense appeal of the invitation, and culminating often in a sweep of Pentecostal ecstasy so fresh from heaven that even the most casual attendant must be touched by the holy fire.

Then the crowning joy of the service—the confession. It never fails to move those who hear it, while its meaning to the man of God can be judged only by his face, which is as the face of a bridegroom.

There was yet more. After the benediction and goodbyes were said, there was still the long ride homeward through the perfumes of the summer night, past fields and trees all vibrant with the chant of lesser creatures making their own joyful noise unto the Lord. Rolling gently along in the moonlight, singing, discussing the meeting, or sitting silent, wrapped in the afterglow of the Presence or lost in the surge of new aspirations— these things, too, must be accounted to the glory of the meeting.

Baptism in the country, too, is impressive. "Here is water" is sufficient, whether it be in a paved baptistry or the wayside pool, but those who are baptized within four walls miss from their lives something of the physical fellowship with the scene on Jordan. The thin, faraway quality of the singing, the fresh smell of the water lapping at our feet, the coolness of the wind on our wet cheeks, and over all the blue heaven from which the dove descended—the association of all these things, together with the strong spiritual emotion, bring their share of enrichment to the newness of life in which we walk thereafter.

There is at the present time a tendency to make the religious experience a thing of reason rather than of emotion. But while it is essential that we should be ready to give "a reason of the hope" that is in us, yet an emotional emphasis is often more lasting than is a rational one, and no one of us having a store of memories such as these to feed upon can ever be entirely desolate.

A golden milestone in the life of the Church marked the one-hundredth anniversary of its organization. Two days were set apart for the celebration, and plans for the program included a speech by W. N. Pratt on "Revivals in Kentucky," reminiscences by Thomas J. Stevenson and F. H. Kerfoot, and a speech on "Daddy Hickman" by T. W. Scott. While few details are recalled by those who were present, it is certain that the occasion was observed in an appropriate manner.

The farsighted interest of this Church in its members is revealed in a resolution passed in 1890, by which the members residing in other communities were to be invited to attend a meeting on the second Saturday in June, and state whether they would be willing to take their letters and connect themselves with churches near their present homes. This is a perpetual problem of the churches. Long years before, John Taylor had written on the subject: "A man is always interested in the friendship and confidence of the people among whom he lives * * * * and if a man is so superior that others can do him no good, why should he be so churlish as not to be willing to do others good, and not wrap up his little musty letter, as the man did his talent, and not put it to usury in that heavenly commerce that the Lord has directed, between one Christian and another?"

Shortly after its organization, it is recorded that the Church gave permission to certain members to "exercise their gifts," and this policy of encouragement has advanced with the years. No talent within range of the Church's influence is allowed to lie unheeded. The organ was first played by Miss Mary Wasserboehr, who was an Episcopalian, and within the knowledge of the present generation persons of nearly every denomination have enjoyed a most harmonious relationship in the service of this Church. Miss Sue Poynter, a Methodist, was a favorite leader of the young people, and in 1894 she was appointed to assist Mrs. C. T. Freeman in soliciting weekly subscriptions.

The year 1904 marked the beginning of Dr. Sampey's second pastorate here, which was an important period in the life of the Church. After an unusually successful meeting, he pointed out to the congregation the fact that, since they all lived in comfortable homes in a prosperous community, it was scarcely fitting that they should worship the Lord in a leaky, decrepit old structure which had been built by slave labor at a cost of only five hundred dollars. Week after week he proclaimed his conviction, each time with a different text and sermon, but always to the same end—a new building which should cost about eight thousand dollars.

Finally the decision was made, and a campaign was started to secure the money. It was a popular enterprise, for everybody loved the Forks Church, and families outside the congregation were glad to be invited to have a share in the good work.

After the funds were assured, the next problem was the location—more important, after all, than the building itself.

About 1901 an interdenominational chapel had been built at Ducker on land given by D. C. and M. C. Darnell. It was easy of access, and for several years, under the leadership of Miss Dora Lucas and others, a Sunday school was conducted there on Sunday afternoons.

The traction line between Lexington and Frankfort was built in 1907, and soon the trend of building was toward the Frankfort-Versailles pike. Seeing this, the trustees of the Forks Church reasoned that since there would always be a village at Ducker, and a village needs a church, they would move theirs to the vicinity. Their decision has long since been justified, for in 1912 that section of the county was re-districted, and the chapel was converted into a public school, thus drawing more families into the neighborhood, while the building of new homes has slowly but surely increased.

Accordingly, on February 16, 1912, the trustees, H. P. Mason, Jr., L. C. Stafford, and S. J. Gibson, bought from J. F. and Myra B. Epperson a lot containing about one acre, lying immediately north of Ducker on the cross pike which leads from Ducker to the old Lexington-Leestown pike. On this they erected, at a cost of about nine thousand dollars, a modern brick building containing thirteen rooms, and with a seating capacity of three hundred.

The work was completed in the early fall, and the congregation moved at once to their new home.

It was a relief to those to whom the old building was hallowed by long association, that it was soon taken down, and was not allowed to disgrace the community through years of ignominious misuse.

The opening service in the new church was celebrated with an all-day meeting, at which the proud and happy members of the congregation were hosts to their admiring friends. It was not until sometime in the following spring that the building was dedicated, with Dr. E. Y. Mullins, of the Southern Baptist Theological Seminary, making the principal address.

Records covering the period between 1900 and 1920 have not been found. Other pastors came and went, but there were many achievements and events of that time which cannot be recalled.

The return of Dr. Sampey to the Forks Church in 1920 may have been the answer to William Hickman's prayers for his beloved people, for with the whole world demoralized and distracted by war, his steadying presence brought to the congregation a sense of reassurance and hope.

His thought during this period was for the spiritual life of the people, and to this end the congregation, which numbered two hundred and eighty, was divided into groups of ten, each group being in charge of a deacon or a deaconess. These deacons and deaconesses were pledged to care for the souls of those for whom they were responsible, to visit and interview them individually, and to pray for them by name. At the end of the year a spiritual inventory was taken, disclosing results which are apparent even to this day.

The record shows that in 1921 the following women were elected as deaconesses:

Mrs. W. C. Smith	Mrs. D. C. Darnell
Miss Georgia Crutcher	Mrs. S. J. Gibson
Mrs. Clarence Montague	Mrs. Carroll Tutt
Miss Lula Hearn	Miss Loulie Gibson
Mrs. Frank Watts	

Mrs. Henry Shumate and Mrs. J. F. Lippert were later added to the list.

Junior deaconesses chosen were:

Mrs. Walter Lewis	Mrs. Helm Lucas
Mrs. Harry Moore	Mrs. James Yeary
Mrs. Joe Jones	Miss Emma McChesney
Mrs. A. W. Lippert	Mrs. Spillman Campbell
Mrs. Curtis Lucas	Mrs. J. F. Lippert
Miss Georgianna Tutt	

Junior deacons chosen in 1923 and 1924 were:

Helm Lucas	Henry Shumate
Walter Lewis	J. B. Redmon
Nelson Webster	W. H. Montague
A. W. Lippert	W. C. Smith
Curtis Lucas	

In 1937 a wedding was solemnized at the church, calling attention to the fact that there have been eight that can be recalled:

Thomas L. Gibson and Lizzie T. Ayres—June, 1874
Duane Brown and Susie Ayres—September, 1877
Thomas Shaw and Lizzie Thompson—July, 1879
William B. Quinn and Mary Lizzie Hearn—October, 1880
S. J. Gibson and Cynthia Thompson—October, 1898
B. T. Bedford and Sidney Ayres—April, 1901
Wilburn Anderson and Georgia Shryock—November, 1923
Samuel Shryock and Caledonia Bidwell—1937

And so the valiant little Church goes on with its ministrations—a Christmas tree or a Daily Vacation Bible School for all the children in the community; a "shower" for a family whose home was burned; an entertainment to aid in buying an appliance for a crippled person; a chair for the office of a young doctor coming into the community; disused pews given to a colored church.

Nor are the members self-centered in their giving. They were outstanding in their contributions to the Seventy-five Million Dollar Campaign, and in addition to their offerings for foreign and home mission work, they send food to the orphans in Louisville, and many other gifts that are unrecorded. During the flood of 1937, arrangements were made to care for a number of refugees from Frankfort, but after the building was warmed and preparations well under way, the victims, who were enjoying their importance, refused to leave the scene of excitement.

One reason for the continued vitality of the Forks Church is that thoughtfulness and loyalty are promoted by the observance of special occasions. In early times, whole days were set apart for fasting and prayer, and now the people gather to celebrate the anniversary of a beloved pastor, to join in a memorial service for those departed, or, frequently, for a happy evening party in honor of new members.

In the phraseology of the Baptist Church is a beautiful and expressive word—watchcare. The lonely we have always with us, but in this day of small and widely separated families, when ties of blood mean so little, the comfort and value of having a Church home are brought to mind by reading in the record of some member of the congregation, and seeing the name of the participant prefixed by "our brother," or "our sister." The fact that in the early records individuals were designated merely as "Brother Smith," or "Sister Jones," without any sign of possession, gives evidence of an increasing sense of responsibility on the part of the present generation.

Rev. Leo Green, in August, 1934, received sixty-four additions in a protracted meeting which the record designates as "one of the greatest revivals ever held in this church." These substantial increases seem to have come in cycles: in 1840, in 1858, in 1885, in 1904, in 1921, and in 1934, though many outstanding members have been received at other times.

On June 12, 1938, the Church held its Sesquicentennial celebration. A large crowd was present, and in the assembly were descendants of many of the early church families, including those of Bartlett, Blackburn, Blanton, Crutcher, Gibson, Graham, Hancock, Haydon, Loughborough, Montgomery, Onion, Ramsey, Samuel, Thompson, and Ware.

It was a day of tender memories, of happy fellowship, and of earnest rededication. Dr. Sampey, who led the service, took his text from Hebrews 13, in which Paul, after having shown forth the mighty accomplishments brought about by the faith of those who had gone before, exhorts his hearers to follow the faith of their leaders. In like manner the speaker reviewed the history of the Forks of Elkhorn Church, beginning with the persecution in Virginia which led William Hickman to come to Kentucky. He told of the persistent faith of the leaders throughout the long period of physical and spiritual vicissitudes, and of the responsive attitude of the members, who gave their best. Because it uses the material it has, and because of its missionary spirit, he expressed great confidence for the future of the Church which he called "a monument of God's love and mercy." He spoke feelingly of his own long association with the Church and said that, like William Hickman, he felt toward it as to no other.

The pastor, Rev. H. T. Busey, and Rev. Leo Green added much to the program, and messages from former pastors were read.

In 1886, at the beginning of Dr. Sampey's pastorate, there were seventy-three members, but at the time of the Sesquicentennial there were 246.

The list of pastors, as arranged by Dr. Sampey, includes:

1. Wm. Hickman, a constituent member, June 7, 1788, but became pastor November, 1788. He died Friday, January 24, 1834. Was pastor for over 45 years, except for 26 months, 1807-1809
2. Addison M. Lewis, 1834-1838
3. B. F. Kenney, 1839
4. Josiah Leake, 1840-1842
5. Y. R. Pitts, 1843-1851, 1854-1860
6. Wm. F. Broaddus, 1852, January to May
7. A. Broaddus, June, 1852–December 1853
8. J. B. Tharp, 1861-1865, November, 1872-1874

9. Nathan Ayres, 1866
10. Thos. J. Stevenson, 1867-1870
11. C. W. Dicken, 1871—October, 1872
12. F. H. Kerfoot, 1875-1877
13. John A. Broadus, 1877-1880
14. Geo. W. Riggan, 1880-1885
15. John R. Sampey, 1885-1891, 1904-1915, 1920-1926 (23¼ years)
16. W. C. Tyree, October, 1891—May, 1892
17. D. G. Whittinghill, June, 1892—August, 1894
18. J. D. Robertson, December, 1894—June, 1897
19. R. W. Weaver, June, 1897—June, 1899
20. C. C. Coleman, October, 1899—April, 1901
21. L. B. Warren, April, 1901—April, 1902
22. J. W. Cammack, May, 1902—May, 1904
23. W. D. Byland ⎱ 1915-1919
24. Claude D. Boozer ⎰
25. W. A. Keel, 1926-1929
26. Otho A. Eure, 1929-1931
27. E. L. Hontz, 1931-1933
28. J. Leo Green, 1933-1935
29. H. T. Busey, 1936-1938

Associate pastors were J. W. Decker and L. F. Marsh.

Insofar as can be ascertained, the deacons, past and present, have been:

John Major, 1788	John Scott, 1841
Nathaniel Sanders, 1788	Isaac Wilson, 1845
Anthony Thomson, 1789	Robert W. Scott, 1847
John Edrington, 1789	George W. Robb, 1866
Edmond Ware, 1792	Lewis Crutcher, 1866
William Hicklin, 1794	Thomas W. Scott
Abraham Gregory, 1804	C. T. Freeman
Jesse Cole, 1804	Preston L. Gibson
Carter Blanton, 1810	Hillery M. Bedford
William Graham, 1814	W. B. Quin
Henry Crutcher, 1832	S. J. Gibson
Nathan Ayres, 1840	T. W. Freeman

Samuel A. Mason	Nelson Webster
Will Seay	Walter Lewis
D. Cotton Darnell	Calvin Long
H. P. Mason, Jr.	Frank Hill
Jeff King	Owen Crutcher
W. H. Montague	A. W. Lippert

There is a thriving Sunday school, graded for efficiency. Since its organization there have been twelve superintendents:

R. W. Scott	W. G. Crutcher
T. W. Scott	D. C. Darnell
G. W. Robb	S. J. Gibson
L. H. Crutcher	S. A. Mason
Will Seay	H. P. Mason, Jr.
Wilmott Freeman	Walter Lewis

An excellent preparation for the next century of service was instituted on April 10, 1938, when Harry E. Moore was ordained to the ministry. This young man is the fruition of seven generations of the Crutcher family who have been loyal workers in the Forks of Elkhorn Church. Representatives of four generations were present on this occasion—his grandmother's aunt, Miss Georgia Crutcher; his grandmother, Mrs. Mamie Burke Shryock; his mother, Mrs. Julia Shryock Moore; and himself.

After thoroughly questioning the candidate, and finding him satisfactory, Dr. Sampey, from the riches of his own observance of young men in the ministry, gave him three pieces of advice: First, to be scrupulously honest and careful in regard to financial transactions; second, to so conduct himself that no breath of social scandal can ever be raised against him; third, to avoid laziness in his preparation for service.

At the conclusion of the ceremony, the congregation followed the fine old custom of going forward in procession to give the right hand of fellowship to the young minister. This may not mean so much to those in the pews, but to the person so honored it is a lasting encouragement and a priceless memory.

Another important action of that year was the increasing of the pastor's salary so that he would be able to live in the community. It changes one's outlook on life to know that the pastor, instead of being seen only in a Sunday mood, may appear at any hour of the week, with encouragement and sympathy and help in all the affairs of life.

Aware of these things, we of the passing generation may well stand by, serenely confident, while youth, which so easily adapts itself to changing world conditions, carries our cherished ideals on into the unending future.

———

ADDENDA

On Sunday morning, October 17, 1943, before the congregation assembled, the Forks of Elkhorn Church building caught fire and was destroyed, with all its contents.

It was a tragic loss, but, as William Hickman so long ago observed, adversity makes Christ's sheep huddle closer together. The unconquerable people immediately began meeting at the Woodburn School, and continued there for more than two years. As soon as the war was over, and material once more available, they started rebuilding, and this Christmas season of 1945 finds in their carols a new note of joy for the coming restoration of the beloved sanctuary.

SUPPLEMENT

TO

FORKS OF ELKHORN CHURCH

"The beauty of the service, the sweet neighborhood quality of the congregation, the plain fact that everybody was kin to everybody else, and the knee-deep bluegrass, was all Kentucky and nothing but Kentucky."

—*Vachel Lindsay*

FOREWORD TO SUPPLEMENT

In writing both History and Supplement it has been a pleasure to find those whom I consulted so gracious and eager to assist, and to them all I am most grateful. Especial thanks are due to the officials of the Southern Baptist Theological Seminary and the State Historical Society for their continued assistance; to Miss Hattie Scott, who so freely and generously opened her files for my inspection; to Mrs. H. R. Crager, always alert for records that might help me; to Mr. George Crutcher Downing, whose encouragement and aid have so many times revived my flagging zeal; to Mr. William E. Railey for his kind permission to use whatever I needed from his *History of Woodford County;* and to my own family, who have "borne with me" for many long months.

No space is devoted to bibliography, for this book has been ripening through so many years that it would be impossible to recall every source of information. Much of it was absorbed in childhood, and if, according to a Bluegrass tradition, no horse will ever amount to much unless he has drunk of the waters of Elkhorn Creek, then surely it must add something to any chronicler to have sat at the feet of old men and women while they discussed Lafayette's visit and Campbell's preaching and the Beauchamp case from contemporary points of view.

In this Supplement I have endeavored to tell something of the families who worshiped at the Forks Church during the first half century of its existence, and to trace their lines "within holloing distance," as the pioneers themselves might say, of the present generation. There were some about whom no information is available except the year in which their names chanced to be mentioned in the minutes, but it is something to know that they were here.

Since in many cases the records of a family are gathered from widely separated sources, and are put together by piecemeal, it is impossible to know the succession in which the children were born, and no responsibility can be assumed for the order in which they are listed.

This is written for the younger generation only, for when people reach a certain age, no amount of court evidence and no number of family Bibles can make them believe that the comfortable old family records and traditions that they heard all their lives are not entirely accurate. (I have reached that age myself.) My information has come from many sources, and I have tried to keep separate the proven from the traditional. Appalling and inexcusable errors will be found, over which I shall be distressed, but they will be corrected by those who follow us. A considerate genealogist leaves some plums on the tree for his successor.

On reading a biographical sketch of any prominent man of the nineteenth century, one gathers that he was the center of his universe, and the women and children of his household were mere satellites tiptoeing past the room in which the Great One sat basking in his own effulgence and planning tomorrow's greatness. But now it is recognized that every member of the family has his value, even the frail little babies who remained here only a few weeks having added their sweetness to the life of the household. It may be thought that the unmarried ones are relatively unimportant, since they do not carry on the line, but they have a great part in shaping the life of their clan, and thus affecting the entire community by cherishing and perpetuating old traditions, fostering family pride, and exemplifying graces and embellishments of life which busy parents lack opportunity to teach.

Though some of those listed here deserved and won high honors, yet I have endeavored to keep these records as impersonal as possible, evaluating persons solely by their known service to the Kingdom. The titles, Doctor, Judge, and so forth, are used merely to distinguish one person from another bearing the same name.

Some persons are mentioned in the record in such a way that it is uncertain whether they themselves, or only their servants, were members of the Church, but as even in the latter case the masters would indirectly receive some benefit therefrom, their families are listed. Added to the list are several well known families who did not belong to the Forks Church, but were affiliated with it through marriage with some of its members.

Vague generalizations in historical writing passed out with feather beds, and to meet present-day demands for conciseness I have given the time and the place of each event whenever it was known. The letters and short words used in the records are not abbreviations (which would call for periods), but code words: F is Franklin County; W is Woodford County; s, son; dau, daughter; b, born; m, married; d, died; r, received; dis, dismissed by letter; ret, returned; c, consent. The mark ° after a surname indicates that more information may be found in the record of the family of that name. Those members having the numeral "1" following their names joined the Church before 1800; those designated by "2" joined afterward.

Names of the second generation are marked by numerals, and those of the third by letters. To trace the membership of a large family, it is more easily understood by making a chart of the names, placing the progenitor in the first column, the first generation in the next, with brackets after each generation for the children of the next. But when families repeatedly intermarry through one generation after another, who but an expert at hopscotch would venture to chart them?

To those who are interested in our upstanding relatives of long ago, these records are offered in the spirit of fellowship, while those who consider genealogy a waste of time are referred to their Bibles for precedent.

EARLY MEMBERS OF
FORKS OF ELKHORN CHURCH

ABBETT—Nancy, 1
Fanny, r 1824

Lewis Pines, Jr., a half brother (brother-in-law?) of William Hall, in his will, Spotsylvania County, Virginia, 1787, indicates that his sister Nancy m James Abbett. James was in F 1796, and the records imply that some of their children were: 1, James, Jr.; 2, Garnett; 3, Peggy Miles°; 4, Elizabeth Miles; 5, William, m Lorena Wade, F 1814. Jonathan Abbett m Nancy Oliver°, F 1809, and went to Henry. Fanny Abbett Neal° was a stepdaughter of William Hickman.

In Woodford, William Abbit m Margaret Campbell, 1798; Maria Abbett m John D. Mitchell°; and Nancy m Charles Robinson. Robert and Larkin were in Woodford.

ABBOTT—Charlotte, r 1831

William Abbott lived south of the river, F 1796, and in 1810 had a family of seven. William H. Abbott m Judith Shockley°, F 1841.

ADAIR—Benjamin, r and dis 1811
Betsy, dis 1811
Samuel, 1802

Benjamin Adair came from Flat Lick Church, in Bourbon. He m Elizabeth Mastin°, F 1801, and in 1801 had a family of seven. Samuel Adair m Nancy Cropper (c Bela), W 1803, and his will, W 1804, mentions a son, William.

ALLEN—Polly Read, dis 1802

James Allen m Mary Read°, W 1802, and they went to Nelson. There were many Allens in Woodford, where they were connected with the Berry, Buford, Coleman, Cox, Craig, Crittenden, Garrett, Hieatt, Mitchum, Quarles, Scott, and other families. Francis, Hugh, and four Johns were listed in the census of 1810. John Allen m Nancy Ford°, W 1817.

In F 1801 were William Allen and Charles, who lived on Salt River and was the father of Sarah Anderson°. Joseph W. Allen m Lucinda Anderson°, F 1826.

ANDERSON—Conny, dis to N. Fork Elkhorn 1801
Elijah and Wife, 1800   Sarah, dis 1818

In this vicinity were several members of the Anderson family, who were connected with the Stouts. Joseph Anderson, a preacher, was on the south fork of Griers Creek, W 1789.

One Joseph Anderson, of Woodford, bought from Achilles Stapp a farm on North Elkhorn, F 1792. His wife was Constance Peak°, and their children were: 1, Elijah, m Rachel Downing, F 1810; 2, Sally Smith°; 3, Betsy, m Bartes Boots, Jr., and went to Indiana; 4, Presley, m Sally Ross°, F 1818; 5, Rebecca West°; 6, Spencer P., m Catherine Hicks (dau William and Mary Harris Hicks), W 1825, and lived in Woodford; 7, Mildred Yancy°; 8, John; 9, Ellen Samuel°. Several of these children went to Marion County, Missouri.

Reuben Anderson (1765-1857) was on Elkhorn, F 1796. His wife was Sarah ———, from New Jersey, and they had: 1, Pamelia Bacon°; 2, Polly Wilson°; 3, Lucinda Allen°; 4, Penelope Hart Wingate°; 5, Harry I., m Adaline Hickman°, F 1825; 6, Charles S.

Amos Anderson owned property in Frankfort in 1800. In 1819 his heirs were listed as: Elizabeth, his widow, who m second William Smith, and: 1, Thomas; 2, Milly; 3, Henry; 4, George; 5, Sarah. One Amos m Sarah Rowland, W 1794.

Andrew Anderson, of Fayette, bought from David Stout a farm on South Elkhorn, W 1801. He had a family of twelve, among whom were: 1, Andrew, Jr., m Eliza (Woodruff?). One Andrew m Sarah Allen°, F 1810; 2, Nehemiah; 3, Reuben (m Elizabeth Bailey, dau John and Elizabeth, W 1815?); 4, O.H.P., m Catherine ———; 5, Penelope Stout°. One Reuben Anderson m Rebecca Kay (dau James), Fayette 1810.

Robert Anderson came from Pennsylvania. His father (John?) was born in Scotland. Robert m Amanda Edwards°, W (1859?) They lived at what is known as the Seay place, near Valley Farm, and were the parents of Mrs. Randolph Cotton, of Woodford.

James Anderson m Sally Kersey, W 1792. James m Eliza Wilson, F 1808, the bond signed by William H. Wilson; James m Nancy Butler (dau John), F 1810.

ANDREWS—Alexander, 2, withdrew 1802

Alexander Andrews, perhaps a connection of the Todd family, was on Elkhorn, F 1803, but in 1810 was in Woodford with a family of seven. His wife was Ann Livingston, and children mentioned were: 1, Alex G., who speaks in a deed of owing his mother a large money debt and "a larger debt of gratitude"; 2, Elizabeth Hackett Andrews; 3, Mary Todd Andrews; 4, Sarah L. Foster°; 5, Ann H. Foster°.

Their home was near the present home of J. H. Morrow, on the Frankfort-Versailles pike, but there is nothing but an old well remaining to mark the site. Alexander died about 1819, and there is a tradition that three women of his family who afterward lived in the house alone were murdered one night. A neighbor's slave was suspected, but his master sold him down the river before he could be apprehended.

Alexander G. Andrews sold land to Richard Crutcher, 1826.

APPLEGATE—Rachel, dis 1802

Richard Applegate, who probably came from New Jersey, mentions in his will, Scott 1800, his wife Rebecca and children: 1, Mary; 2, Rebecca; 3, Alletta, m Peter Lantamon in Maryland; 4, Cather Leman; 5, Elizabeth McCan; 6, Alse Walls; 7, Benjamin (m Lucy Hughes, Shelby 1790?); 8, Daniel, m Rachel Lindsay°, W 1790, and they went to Shelby. Their sons were: Lindsay, Jesse, Lisbon. They went to Missouri in 1843. 9, William.

John Applegate m Nancy Ford, Scott 1810.

AYRES—Walter, r 1811, dis to Big Spring 1812, ret 1837
Agnes, r 1811, dis to Big Spring 1812, ret 1837
Nathan, r 1834, dis 1841
Mary R., dis 1841   Edward M.

Walter Ayres (1779-1838) son of Nathan and Mary Leake Ayres, was born in Buckingham County, Virginia. He m his stepsister, Mary Agnes Maxey°, 1800, and the next year they came to Woodford and built what is known as the Owsley home, on the Lexington-Leestown pike. Their children were: 1, Edward M. (1804-1879), m Margaret H. Jones°, W 1840. They lived in Frankfort, and their children were: a, Agnes Jane, m William Y. Campbell, F 1860; b, Hugh Rodman, m his cousin, Effie L. Ayres (dau Thomas Burge and Deborah Jones Ayres,

of Ohio); 2, Judith Watts°; 3, Jane L., m Rev. Noah Flood, W
1838; 4, Nathan, m Mary Richmond°, F 1829. He went to
Missouri, but after several years he returned and spent his time
in preaching and teaching. 5, Elizabeth Gerard° (see Garrard),
lived in Missouri; 6, Mary Robinson°; 7, John, also of Missouri;
8, Walter N., m first Martha Ann Foster°, F 1841, and after her
death m her sister, Frances Elizabeth Foster, F 1843, and they
had: a, Thomas; b, Martha Scott°; c, Edward W., m Susan
Scott, and they built the brick house at the old Martin place,
now owned by John Lewis Thomas; d, Lucy, m George P. Mc-
Credie, and went to Missouri; e, Maxey Thompson°; f, Elizabeth
Gibson°; g, Susan Brown°; h, John W., who went to Missouri;
i, Mamie Runyan°; j, Nathan, who went to Texas; k, Roberta;
l, Margaret, m J. Terrill Stribling, and went to Norborne, Mo.

Thomas Ayres m Mary Sneed° (widow of Benjamin), and in
1801 they went to Gallatin, where he died in 1811, leaving his
wife and: 1, Daniel Coleman, m first, Susan Sale, Gallatin 1805,
and had Robert, Thomas, Sandford, James, William (second,
Malinda Hopper, Owen 1839?); 2, Lewis; 3, children of son
Thomas Cornelius. The family lived in Owen, 1823.

John Ayres was in Woodford, 1805, and James had a family
of three in 1810. Samuel m Elsey Malone, W 1821, and went
to Gallatin. Azariah and Joseph were in Mercer, 1795. Thomas
Ayres m Polly Stribling, Clark 1807; Edward S. m Lucy Ann
Goodrich, F 1827.

Maxey: Rev. Edward Maxey was one of the group of William
Hickman's friends in Virginia who, when they were persecuted,
would hold little meetings among themselves. He m Mary
Bondurant (who afterward m Nathan Ayres), and their children
were: 1, Ephraim; 2, Elizabeth, m Col. John Moseley; 3, Ann,
m Richard Lafon; 4, Philip, m his stepsister, Betsy Ayres; 5,
Agnes Ayres; 6, Nathaniel. One record says Edward's dau, Mary,
m Joseph Ford°. Several of these families came to Kentucky.

BACON—Betsy, r 1820, dis 1831
Nancy, r 1820, dis 1822
Sarah, to Frankfort 1816
Sister, other denomination, 1834

Lyddall Bacon, Sr. (s Langston and Sarah Miller Bacon) of
New Kent County, Virginia, m first Anne Apperson. Their chil-

dren were: 1, John (1767-1817), who settled on the Frankfort-Owenton road, m first, Anne Patterson°, and they had: a, Charles, m Caroline Castleman, 1821. John m second, Elizabeth Ware°, F 1799, and they had: b, Anne Apperson Fall°; c, Sarah Ware (1802——); d, Williamson, m Ann Maria Noel°, F 1824; e, James, m Alice Riggs, 1836; f, Richard, m Elizabeth E. Terrill; g, John Mosby, m Sarah Jane Haggin, 1835; h, Elizabeth P. Bryan°; i, Albert Gallatin.

2, Sarah (1769——); 3, Lyddall, Jr., m Martha Graham°, and they had: a, Edmund; b, John; c, William Robinson, m Judith Bacon, and their daughter Caroline m Joseph Cox and was the mother of Miss Jessie Cox, of Frankfort; 4, Langston (1777-1845), m Sarah Samuel°, and they had: a, Robert, m first —— Jeffries, of Owensboro, and second ——. His children were: Langston, Martha, Mary, William; b, Langston; c, Giles; d, Joyce; e, Sarah; f, Mary. Langston lived in Frankfort, in the house now occupied by Robert R. Gum, at 108 Clinton Street. The family afterward went to Missouri. 5, Edmund, m first Elizabeth Pemberton°, and second Pamela Anderson°. His daughter Elizabeth m Gideon Shryock, F 1829.

Also descended from Langston and Sarah Miller Bacon was Edmund, who m Mary —— and came to Frankfort. Their children were: 1, Edmund. One Edmund m Sarah O'Nan, F 1822; Edmund A. m Rebecca Hawkins°, F 1826; 2, Alexander (1806-1850), m first Rachel A. Graham°, F 1835, and second, Elizabeth C. Graham, F 1836, the bond signed by Francis Graham; 3, Eliza Roberts°; 4, Richardson; 5, Mary; 6, Susan H.; 7, Virginia P.; 8, Alice Martha Ann Cox°; 9, Sarah E. Several members of the family went to Jefferson County, Indiana.

BAINBRIDGE—Peter, 1801, dis 1819

Peter Bainbridge (1761-1826), son of John, was born in Maryland, and came to Kentucky in 1797. He was ordained to the ministry in 1790, but afterward practiced medicine, going to Glasgow, Ky., 1813, and to Mississippi in 1825. He m Eleanor J. McIntosh (dau Gen. Alexander McIntosh), and two of his children were: Eliza, m James Shackleford, Garrard 1805; Eleanor, m Judge George Robertson, Fayette 1809. Kezia Bainbridge m Isaac E. Gano°. Some of the family went to Owen. Absalom was in Shelby, 1800, and one Absalom in W 1801.

BAKER—John, 1801-1805
Joseph and Wife, 1801
Betsy

John Baker m Ann Jackson°, W 1791. He owned land on Glen's Creek, but had a family of five, F 1810. Nancy Baker (dau John) m John Roberts°.

Robert Baker m Clauda ——. They lived in the western part of Franklin, and his heirs, 1820, were: 1, Reuben, m Betsy Robinson, F 1795, and two of their children were Rosanna Pemberton° and Lucretia, m Turner Satterwhite, F 1822; 2, James, m Peggy Roberts°, F 1797; 3, Nancy, m Samuel Hutton; 4, Sally, m Peter Jordan, F 1804; 5, William, m Pitty Robinson, F 1801; 6, Betsy, m William S. Watkins, F 1796; 7, Jane Pemberton°; 8, Thomas. They owned land on Hammond's Creek. William Baker m Elizabeth Gravit°, F 1828.

Nicholas Baker m Lucy Lampkin°, Culpeper County, Virginia, 1791, and they came to Woodford, going later to Indiana. Their son Daniel m Elizabeth Lampkin, W 1816. William Baker m Patsy Woolfolk°, W 1798, and they had: a, Dr. William; b, Caleb W.; c, America, m Fleming Garnett°.

BALDWIN—Polly Peak, dis 1804

Polly Peak° m —— Baldwin. Daniel Baldwin was one of the original members of McConnell's Run Church. His will, Scott 1822, names his children: Daniel; Thomas; Jeremy; Moses, m Mary Lambert, 1794; Joseph; Deborah, m John Stewart, 1794; Mary Oxley; Elizabeth Roly (?).

John Baldwin m Elizabeth Rogers, W 1791. James had a family of seven, F 1810. John Page m Rachel Baldwin (dau Sarah), F 1821. Some of the family located in Owen.

BALLARD—William, 1800

Johnson Ballard and his two brothers came from Virginia to Woodford. Johnson m first Bettie Eastham, Culpeper 1791, and had a family of seven, W 1810. Their children were: 1, William, m Polly Taylor°, and they had a dau, Sarah Ann Elizabeth. William died F 1823. 2, Lucy Hughes°; 3, Elizabeth, m —— Burns, and they had: a, James; b, dau m —— Berry. 4, Benjamin, and other sons.

Johnson m second Isabella Sparks°, and in 1825 they sold their home on the Frankfort-Versailles road to John R. Morris and moved to the Swallowfield neighborhood. Their children were: 5, Mildred, m Moses Harrod, Owen 1835, and went to Missouri; 6, Fanny; 7, B.; 8, Johnson.

George Ballard was in Woodford 1796, and in 1801 William and George were in Scott. John Ballard m Susan Mitchum, 1823.

BARTLETT—Harry, 1, dis 1809	Henry
Sally, 1	James, 1
Elizabeth, 1	Frances, 1801
John, 2, dis to Mouth of Elkhorn 1801	
Sally, 2, dis to Mouth of Elkhorn 1801	

William Bartlett (1696-1775), of Spotsylvania County, Virginia, m Susannah Davis (dau John and Susannah Wyatt Davis). Their children were: 1, Major Harry, m Sarah Crane (dau Col. John). They were living on the river in Mallory's Survey, F 1795, and their children were: a, Henry, d 1794; b, (John C., of New Orleans, m Margaret Nicholas of Lexington, 1811?); c, Thomas. One Thomas and his wife Dicey were in Shelby, 1820; d, Elizabeth Gale°; e, Phoebe Sanders°; f, Polly Hickman°; g, Sally, m James Banks, F 1798, and they were the parents of Nancy Redding°; h, Frances, m first, Westley Hardin°, and second, Thomas Parrent, Jefferson 1828; i, Ann, m George Alsop, Jr., 1786, and they had: Sarah; Elizabeth Edrington°; Henry; Guilford D., m Caroline Jones, Jefferson 1826; Permelia Hawkins; George; Nancy; Louisiana, m F 1826 Samuel W. Mayhall, whose grandparents, William and Helen Murtaugh Mayhall, came from Ireland about 1771. Samuel and Louisiana Mayhall were ancestors of Mrs. Paul R. Davis, of New London, Mo.

2, Capt. Thomas, m Mary Foster (dau Anthony and Sarah). He came with his family and was living on Glen's Creek, W 1792, but they went to Henry about 1800. One record says he died in 1809, but the will of one Thomas, Henry 1817, names his children: a, Harry (m Margaret Goode°, Henry 1804?); b, Major Anthony, who lived in the vicinity of Spring Station while in Woodford, m Nancy Blackburn°. They went to Newcastle, Ky., where he died 1819. Their children were: George

B., m Mary M. Jackson°, W 1817; Prudence Moore; Thomas J., m his cousin, Mrs. Henrietta Blackburn Flournoy; William B.; Anthony W.; Edward B. (m Ann T. Sanders°, Grant 1834?); Mary; Eliza; c, Edmund. One Edmund m Sally Sneed°, F 1807; Edmund m Mrs. Jane Speer, Henry, 1815. His will, 1835, mentions his son Edmund; granddaughter Thomas Ella Bartlett (dau Thomas), evidently the one who m Dr. William T. Shortridge, of Fulton, Mo., Fayette 1849; dau Patsy Samuel°; Mary, wife of John Taylor; Philadelphia, m Henry Owen; d, James; e, Foster. One Foster m Jane Scott (dau Elijah), Henry 1804; one m Elizabeth Claggett, Henry 1837; f, Betsy Jackson°. One record adds: g, Polly, m Erasmus Simpson, W 1797.

3, William. One record says his wife was Mary Crane; another says Mary Davis. He died in 1777. 4, Susannah, m Thomas Collins; 5, Anne Montague°; 6, Isabella Graves°; 7, Sarah, m Thomas Perry.

John Bartlett, who m Sally Gore° and lived near the mouth of Elkhorn, might be classed with the family of Major Harry, were it not that a family record states that Major Harry's son John m Margaret Nicholas. John Bartlett's will, F 1834, mentions his wife Sally and children: George W.; James Scott; Jane; Willis (m Lucinda Hawkins, F 1816?); Anthony (m Sarah Ann Hall°, F 1830?); Elizabeth; Emily, m John S. Dorman, F 1835; Thomas, m Mary B. Haydon°, F 1821; John G. (m Sarah A. Ireland, Henry 1826?); Sally, m first Innes Haydon°, second ――― Cirlot; Susan (m Lewis Christopher, F 1825?); Maria, m first ――Tyler, second ――― Bostwich.

One Thomas Bartlett had a family of seven, F 1810. Lucinda (dau Thomas), m Joseph McKee, F 1832. William, m Dicey Goode°, Henry 1802. Thomas, m Sally Lindsay° in Virginia, and their sons were Robert and Thomas. Roswell Bartlett was in F 1797.

BASHAR—Mordecai, 1801

BEALL—Asa, 1801

Charles Beall, of Jefferson County, Virginia, owned land near the Forks of Elkhorn. His wife was Tabitha ――― (who afterward m Joseph Swearingen), and their children were: 1, Asa, who m Jane Edwards°, Bourbon 1799, was in this section for several years, but he sold his land to John D. Graves and others, and probably went to Bourbon about 1807; 2, Priscilla, m Edward O. Williams; 3, Susanna Edwards°; 4, Elizabeth, m Richard Turner, and had Tabitha and Ninian. She was living in Montgomery County, Maryland, 1826, when she sold land near Woodlake to John D. Graves.

Richard E. and Margaret Beale, of Fauquier County, Virginia, sold land in the vicinity of Beal's Run to George Blackburn, W 1794. Richard was in Woodford the following year.

BECKHAM—Simon, r 1812, to Frankfort 1816
Philadelphia, r 1812, to Frankfort 1816

Simon Beckham was in Scott, 1806. Simon and Philadelphia sold to George W. and James Gale a lot in Frankfort, 1818. He died F. 1830.

BERRY—Samuel, to Glen's Creek 1801
Mary, to Glen's Creek 1801

Samuel Berry was here in 1788. His farm was listed in 1800 as being on Glen's Creek, but his home in later years was in the Grier's Creek neighborhood. His wife, Mary, is thought to have been a daughter of Joseph Allen, of Spotsylvania County, Virginia, and their children were: 1, Allen, m Sally Blanton°, W 1803; 2, Samuel; 3, Elizabeth Hughes°; 4, Nancy Long°; 5, Susanna; 6, Rachel Smith°; 7, Mary Smith°; 8, James; 9, William. One Susan Berry (dau Samuel) m James H. Garnett°.

Evidently related to Samuel was Benjamin Berry (1757-1838), who m first Mary Allen, and second Nancy Blanton°. He lived near Clifton, and was the father of eighteen children, including Sally Ford° and John, m Rebecca Morrison°, W 1821. Benjamin was the grandfather of Permelia Berry Crutcher°.

Elijah Berry m Milly Stapp°, W 1803. Many of the Berry family lived in Mercer.

BERRYMAN—Nancy, 1800, dis to South Benson 1801

This may have been Nancy Emerson (dau Samuel), who m Thomas Berreman, Lincoln 1794. Thomas Berryman (Bereman) came from New Jersey to Kentucky in 1783, and was living south of the river, F 1796. In 1811 Thomas and Nancy sold land to the Greshams, and in 1817 to George Butler. They went to Mercer, where Thomas was living in 1832.

Thomas A. Berryman was in Owen, 1825.

No relationship is known between this family and the Berrymans of Clifton, who came from Virginia.

> BLACKBURN—Jonathan, r 1811
> Prudence, r 1811, dis to Big Spring 1812
> Julius, 1811
> Lewis, 1837, dis 1842

George and Julius Blackburn were in Kentucky in 1789, living at "Blackburn's Fort," which they built at what is now the farm of Mrs. James Withrow at Spring Station. There is some confusion about the relationship, for there is one tradition that George and Julius were brothers, and another that George and Gideon were brothers. Records from different sources state that George and Julius and Mildred were children of Edward and Anne, and grandchildren of William and Elizabeth; that Julius was the son of Henry; and that Gideon was the son of Robert and —— Ritchie, and grandson of Benjamin.

George Blackburn m Prudence Berry in Louisa County, Virginia, 1771, and they had: 1, Nancy Bartlett°; 2, Col. William B., m Martha Watkins (c Henry Watkins), W 1802, and they had: a, Henrietta, m first Dr. David Flournoy, second Thomas Bartlett°, third Frank P. Holloway; b, Henry C., m Susan Chiles, F 1837; c, Prudence; d, Jonathan. 3, Rev. Jonathan T. (1776-1834), who seems to have had no regular pastorate, but preached at various churches. It was said of him, "For his kindness and benevolence he elicited the veneration of all who knew him." He m his cousin, Prudence Buford°, 1796, and they had a son, Major William B., who m Mary A. Bohannan°, Fayette 1818, and went to St. Louis in 1845. 4, Elizabeth, m first Francis Peart, W 1801, and second Samuel Lewis°; 5, Mary, m Capt. George Holloway, and they had: a, Frank P., m first Mary Blanton°, and second his cousin, Mrs. Henrietta Bartlett; b, Mary Ann, m Dr. Leonard Hodges; c, George, m first Mary Hodges, F 1830, and second Mary Snodgrass; d, Mildred; e, Georgianna, m first William T. Willis, and second John W. Johnson°; f, Martha.

6, Rev. George, who was a charter member of Big Spring Church. He was ordained in 1825, and John Taylor wrote of him: "He is a pretty good preacher; his delivery is not quite so ready as that of some men, but his ideas are very good." Spencer's *History of the Kentucky Baptists* says: "He continued to develop his powers till he came to be regarded as a strong preacher, and was one of the leading ministers of his day, in Kentucky, in the benevolent enterprises of his denomination. He was chairman of the meeting that organized the Kentucky Baptist Convention in 1832, and was a member of its first executive board." He m first Julia Flournoy, and second Mrs. Anna E. Branham (see James), F 1832. His will, F 1837, names the children of his first wife: a, David; b, Elizabeth F. Branham°; c, Prudence, m Capt. William Hunt, F 1836, and they were grandparents of Mrs. Sam A. Mason, of Frankfort; d, Notley; e, Ann S.; f, Cassandra; g, George.

7, Edward M., m Lavinia S. Bell (dau Capt. John), Fayette 1801, and their children were: a, George E., m Isabella Buck°, F 1831, and they lived for a time at the homestead afterward owned by Dr. Sullenger, at Jett; b, Churchill, m Frances J. Hale°, W 1847, and they went to Arkansas; c, Edward, m —— Calhoun; d, Henry, m —— Bryan, in Fayette; e, Gov. Luke P. (1818-1887), physician and statesman. In 1835 he fought the cholera scourge in Versailles when all the other doctors were gone. Later, he successfully combated epidemics of yellow fever in the South and elsewhere, though his advanced ideas about quarantines aroused much opposition, and his scientific observation that yellow fever ended with the arrival of frost was considered farfetched. As Governor, he is remembered for his drastic prison reforms. He m first Ella G. Boswell, Fayette 1835, and second, Julia M. Churchill, 1857; f, William, m Henrietta Richardson Everett (dau Columbus P.); g, James, m Mrs. Henrietta E. Blackburn, his brother's widow, and they were the parents of Judge James W. Blackburn, of Frankfort; h, Senator Joseph Clay Stiles, m first Theresa Graham, and second Mrs. —— Blackburn; i, Mary, m Buckner Morris, of Chicago; j, Elizabeth, m Gen. Thompson B. Flournoy; 8, Margaret Trotter, m John Kinkead, W 1809; 9, Churchill, m first Eleanor Arnold, and second Lydia Paxton; 10, Mildred, m William White, and their dau, Prudence, m Abijah Withers, W 1830; 11, Luke; 12, Prudence. In her will, W 1836, Mrs. Prudence Berry Blackburn, the mother of this family, touchingly expressed a prayer that her dear children would love one another and live together in friendliness.

Since no written outline of the family in Scott has been found, the following records are incomplete: Julius Blackburn (———-1821), after leaving "Blackburn's Fort," settled in Scott near the Woodford line, and was a charter member of Buck Run Church. His wife was Betsy Scruggs, and some of their children were: 1, Julius, m Caty ———, and lived in Calloway County, Missouri; 2, Thomas (1788-———), m Wilanna Burbridge (dau George and Mary Hord Burbridge, who came in with the Travelling Church), and they had: a, Lycurgus; b, Sydney; c, Mary, m Dr. Henry Herndon, Scott 1838; d, Susan, m Judge Morrow; e, Martha; f, Wilanna, m Rev. Thomas McKee; g, Robert, m ——— Marsh, and went to Natchez, Miss.; h, Burbridge, m Emma Macklin°; i, John; j, Betty, m Dr. Charles Horace Benton, and they were the parents of Miss Lena Benton, of Frankfort; 3, William, m ——— Herndon, and went to Henry; 4, Dr. Churchill, who lived at his father's homestead, "Warwick," m first ——— Glass, second Elizabeth Elley, Scott 1840, third Mrs. Lizzie Blackburn Branham; 5, Martha, m ——— Forsee; 6, Nancy (?), m first ——— Branham, and second (Nimrod?) Martin, and went to Missouri; 7, Milly, m ——— Price, and went to Louisville, where their dau Lizzie m first ——— Weir, and second ——— Meriwether, and was the mother of Mrs. William E. Bradley, Sr., of Woodford County.

Another record says Julius Blackburn, of Franklin County, m Nancy Scruggs (dau Thomas), and they had: 1, Ely, m ——— Offutt; 2, Sally Ann, m ——— Glass; 3, Polly, m William Sinclair; 4, ———, m Asa Sinclair.

Churchill Blackburn, of Frankfort, m Virginia Norris (dau Nelson Norris, of Cincinnati), 1840 (or 1841).

The parents of Lewis Blackburn, a relative of the Blackburns at Spring Station, died when he was very young, and have not been identified. He lived at Fisher's Mill, between Georgetown and Midway. He m Sarah Ann Hancock°, F 1835, and their children, as remembered were: 1, Sophia, m Allen

Sutton, of Versailles; 2, Mary Crutcher°; 3, Jennie, m ——
Beard; 4, Phronie, m first —— Blackburn, and second Matt
Martin°, of Midway; 5, Bettie, m William Burke, of Versailles;
6, James Harvie, m Laura Neil, and they had: a, James Edward,
father Dr. W. P. Blackburn, Frankfort; b, Lewis; 7, William.

Rev. Gideon Blackburn (1772-1851), a Presbyterian minister,
m his cousin, Grizzella Blackburn (dau John and Jane Blackburn, of Jefferson County, Tennessee), and they came to Woodford, going later to Illinois. Their children were: 1, Rev. John
Newton, m first Isabella Berryhill, and second Catherine
Edwards; 2, Betsy Henderson; 3, James Harvie (1799-1818);
4, Samuel; 5, Jane, m W. M. King, Jefferson 1826; 6, Gloriana;
7, Grundy Henderson; 8, William; 9, Gideon; 10, Anderson.

Alex Blackburn was in Franklin County, 1801, and the heirs
of Samuel Blackburn were there in 1809.

Hale: Smith Hale (Heale), s George and Sarah Smith Heale
of Virginia, m Nancy Douglas, and they came to Woodford and
settled on what is now the Ben Hieatt farm near Duckers. He
died in 1817. His children were: 1, Lewis, m Letitia Flournoy
and lived at what is known as the Dr. Thompson place, at
Duckers. They had: a, Cassandra, m Walter Buck°; b, Fannie
Blackburn°; 2, Sarah, m first Hiram Moffett, and second William
H. Patterson, W 1818, and went to Missouri; 3, Margaret, m
Capt. —— Morey, and went to Missouri; 4, Maria, m Edward
Payne; 5, Jane; 6, Susanna Martin°; 7, Antionette, m Dr. Azra
Offutt, of Jessamine, 1828; 8, Catherine, m Nathan Payne; 9,
Eliza, m first William Hamilton, W 1810, and second Marquis
Calmes°, Jr. William Florence m Letty Hale, W 1808.

BLANTON—Carter, 1, dis 1831   Polly, r 1811
          Susanna, 1, dis 1831   William, r 1828

This compilation of Blanton records is from many sources,
and is subject to much correction.

Thomas Blanton, of Lancashire, England, was in Virginia,
1682. His will, probated in Essex County, 1699, mentions his
wife Jane, daus Elizabeth and Jane, and sons Thomas, John,
William, and Richard. The will of Richard (Spotsylvania, 1734)
mentions his wife Elizabeth, daus Priscilla, Elizabeth, and
Mary; sons Richard and Thomas who came to Kentucky.

Richard Blanton (son of the first named Richard) was the sheriff of Frederick County, Virginia, and his grandson, Harrison Blanton, said that he always told them that the first of his official acts was to apprehend and to confine in jail his friend, the Reverend Joseph Craig, for preaching the Baptist doctrine.

Richard lived to be over ninety, and probably did not come to Kentucky until long after the arrival of his brother Thomas. One record says that he died at the home of his daughter, Nancy Crutcher, and that he and his wife, who was Nancy Sneed, were buried in the Grassy Spring churchyard. Another record says they lived in a house on the hill back of his brother Thomas's home, and were buried there in the family graveyard.

Their children were: 1, John. One John Blanton m Margaret Green, W 1794. One John, said to have been born in Cumberland County, Virginia, 1752, was in Shelby, 1800 and for some time thereafter. Others in Shelby who may have been his children were: a, Jesse, m Sarah Cozine, 1800; b, Ann, m Joseph Oliver, 1800; c, Catherine, m John Martin, 1802; d, Patsy, m Thomas Fitzpatrick, 1805; e, Edmund, m Sarah ———, and died in Mississippi. 2, Charles, died in Virginia. It is said that he was the grandfather of Dr. Lindsey Hughes Blanton, who was pastor of the Versailles Presbyterian Church, 1857-1861.

3, Richard (———-1809?), m Sally Combs°, 1790, and they lived in Frederick County until 1799, when they came to Fayette County, Kentucky. Their children were: a, Harrison (1791-1879), m Betsy Dudley°, Fayette 1813. They settled at Leestown, and had: Sallie; Elizabeth; Mary, m Frank P. Holloway; Catherine Morris°; Alexander, m Emma Swigert; Sarah, m Thomas H. Taylor; Benjamin, m Alice Bacon, and they were the parents of Miss Elizabeth Blanton, of Frankfort; Lucy Virginia, m John McFarland; Thomas; b, Betsy Combs°; c, Sythy Vaughan° (1795-1837); d, Kitty Bedford°; e, Lucy Bedford°; f, Nancy, m John Clay (s Henry and Margaret Helm Clay, of Bourbon), Fayette 1823, and had: Harrison B., m Betty Gass; Sallie, m Henry Gaitskill; Margaret Elizabeth; Henrietta; Richard Henry; John Carter, m Laura Hume; Sythe; Thomas H., m first Hetty M. Talbott, second, Mrs. Mollie Collins; Mary C.; Martha N., m Emil F. Nelson; Susanna; Lucy Letitia.

4, Carter (1765-1835), m Susanna Snead°, Caroline County, Virginia, 1787. They came to Kentucky about 1790, and lived between Jett and Millville at the homestead lately occupied by Redd Crutcher, which they sold to Richard Crutcher in 1831, and went to Farmdale. Their children were: a, Margaret Vaughan Coleman° (1788-1860); b, Polly Snell°; c, Robert; d, Birdet A., m first Polly Daniel°, Christian 1818. They were living in Christian in 1830, but went later to Missouri. The will of Burdett C. Blanton (evidently their son) of Boone County, Missouri, 1869, mentions Susan S. Wigginton, Robert W. Blanton, Ann Eliza Forbis, and Thomas H. Blanton, of Missouri, and Burdette A. Blanton and Mary L. Blanton, of Carroll County, Kentucky. Birdet A. Blanton and his wife also had a daughter Betty, m —— Howard. Birdet m second Mrs. Marcia Scott°, Carroll 1853. e, Henry, m first his cousin, Susan Sneed Blanton, Gallatin 1820, and they had: Bettie; Susan; Dr. Carter, of Hickman, Ky., who gave his life for the yellow fever patients; Margaret, m Davis E. Beck, Owen 1850; Dr. William Henry. Henry m second Mrs. Sallie Green Craig, Owen 1840. f, Rev. William C. (1803-1845), was ordained at South Benson, 1833, and preached at Mt. Pleasant, North Fork, and neighboring churches. He m Mary R. Hawkins°, F 1827, and they had: Susan Sneed°; Caroline; Mary C.; Lavinia H. Sneed°; William C., m first Hannah Margaret Montgomery, Shelby 1852 and second Georgeanna ——; g, Eliza Daniel°.

5, William, m Elizabeth Ware°, F 1796, and they lived in Gallatin and later at New Liberty in Owen, selling Elizabeth's portion of "Wareland" to Lewis Crutcher in 1825. William died about 1831, and his heirs were: a, Edward B., m Lydia Ellis°, Gallatin 1827, and they had Elizabeth Sybile and William; b, Thomas Bullock; c, Susan Sneed, m Henry Blanton; d, Agnes Jeffries Green°; e, Sarah West°; f, William; g, Kitty; h, Jane. The will of William's wife, Elizabeth, Owen 1845, mentions an adopted daughter, Mary Ware.

6. James, m Jane Smith, Gallatin 1806. He owned property in both Frankfort and Gallatin. His will, Gallatin 1815, mentions his wife Jane and: a, Elizabeth, m Willis Tandy, Gallatin 1826, and had James W.; b, Nancy Owen°; c, another daughter (Mary D. Ellis?); d, Thompson. 7, Peggy Vaughan°, died in Virginia; 8, Mrs. —— Daniel°; 9, Nancy Crutcher°.

Thomas Blanton m Jane Moore, and was in Kentucky in 1788. He settled on a large tract of land near Grassy Spring Church, and built his home where the residence of W. E. Bradley now stands. The spring in front of the house was designated on an early map as "Blanton's Big Boiling Spring." His name does not appear in the Woodford tax list after 1803. His children were: 1, John, m Nancy Robinson. He died about 1808, and in 1822 she bought property in Mortonsville from George Robinson, of Fayette. Their children were: a, Sally Taylor°; b, Thompson, m Elizabeth Thomson°, W 1812, and went later to Lincoln County, Missouri; c, Willis (1787-1859), m Rebecca Ware°, 1812. They lived at "Mt. Vernon," known as the Levi Crutcher place, at Jett, and their children were: John William (m first Elizabeth Ann Samuel°, F 1835, and they had: Rebecca, Willis, Horace, Isabella, Churchill; he m second Lucy Buck°, and they had: Charles Buck, Keith, Willis); Sarah Ann Porter°; Horace F. (m first Martha Lamb, and had Martha; m second, 1848, Elizabeth Thompson, and had John William and Edward; m third, 1856, Mrs. John Kane, and had Elizabeth Ann; m fourth, 1864, Henrietta Stevens, and had Nettie, Horace, Mary); Maria Louise (m Nathaniel Currier); Elizabeth (m John Y. Mills); Agnes; Rebecca. One record states that Willis Blanton, of Frankfort, m Martha Daniel°.

d, Richard Strother, m Maria Sneed°, F 1819, and they had Richard Horace; e, Elizabeth Shipp° (1798-1866); f, Dr. James F., who, when he sold land to Willis Blanton, F 1822, was living in Lexington with his wife Catherine, but in 1828, when he sold his land on Glen's Creek to John M. Hopkins, was in Warsaw, Ky., with a wife Hester. In 1854 he was in Owen where his dau Nancy, m David L. Simpson, 1847. g, Horace; h, Nancy, m William Wood, W 1812; i, Dorothy, m John Hopkins, W 1820, and they went to Lincoln County, Missouri; j, Benjamin, who had a farm on Dry Run, F 1812, but may have been in Owen, 1829. He was in Lincoln County, Missouri, in 1832. His wife was —— Robertson, and their son John lived in Hannibal, Mo.; k, Thomas (1795-1826).

2, Mary Fox° (1772-1861); 3, James, m Nancy Warren, W ——. They had land on Craig's Creek, and in 1810 had a family of ten. He died about 1813, but his family remained in

Woodford for several years afterward. The records indicate that some of their children were: a, Elizabeth Rutherford°; b, Harriet, m Aaron Grider, W 1820; c, Parthena, m Ferguson Hudson, W 1821; d, Hardin. 4, Phoebe Rout°; 5, Elizabeth Bain°; 6, Lindsay. One Lindsay m Mary H. Taylor, Jefferson 1811; 7, Nancy Berry°; 8, Sally Berry°; 9, Thomas, m Ann Christopher, W 1801, and in 1810 they had a family of nine. In 1816 they sold their farm on Clear Creek to William Singleton, and are thought to have gone to Missouri.

John Blanton m Ann Hughes (dau Benjamin), Jefferson 1806. Nancy Blanton m Robert Sanders°. William C. Blanton, Jr., was associated with Orville Blanton and his wife Martha R., and Mrs. Harriet B. Blanton who m Samuel Theobald°, both in Frankfort and in Greenville, Miss., but the connection is not known. They may have been descendants of Edmund Blanton.

Combs: Conflicting records state that John Combs (1725-1785), son of Joseph Combs, of Stafford County, Virginia, m Sytha Bullitt (dau Benjamin and Elizabeth Harrison Bullitt), and their children were: 1, John, died in Virginia; 2, Cuthbert, died in Clark County, Kentucky; 3, 4, 5, Ennis, Joseph, and Fielding, came to Kentucky, but returned to Virginia; 6, Elizabeth, m Marquis Calmes°, of Frederick County, Virginia; 7, Sarah Blanton° (1774-1849); 8, Capt. Benjamin (1749-1838), who came to Clark County, Kentucky. He m Sarah Richardson°, and they had: a, William R., m Elizabeth Blanton°, Fayette 1811, and they were the parents of Lucy, Sarah, and other children (a record states that one dau m James M. Stephens°); b, Fielding A.; c, Marquis; d, Samuel R.; e, Elizabeth; f, Marian, m John R. Price, Clark 1805; g, Gen. Leslie (1793-1881), of Lexington, who worked so unsparingly during the cholera epidemic of 1833. He m first Margaret Trotter, and second Elizabeth Brownwell.

BLEDSOE—Joseph, 1	Judith, 1801
Abraham, 1, dis 1804	Milly, dis 1807
William, 1	
Elizabeth, 1, Mouth of Kentucky, 1800	

There is much disagreement concerning the parentage, the wife, and the sons of William Bledsoe, whose will was probated in Culpeper County, Virginia, 1770. Records agree that he came from England in 1725, and that he was the father of: George; Milly Weatherall; Mary Powell; John, who m Elizabeth White, and died in Clark County, Kentucky, 1799; William; Hannah Cave°; and Moses, but one record assigns to him Aaron and James, while another gives him Abraham and Joseph.

Some of the family came into Kentucky with the "Travelling Church." Rev. Joseph Bledsoe (b 1738) organized the congregation that remained at Gilbert's Creek as a Separate Baptist Church, and was in charge of it until his death. He m Elizabeth Miller, and some of their children were: 1, Rev. Moses, who m first Sally Tandy (dau William and Jane Tandy, of Fayette), and second, Lucy Jamison (dau Thomas and Lucy Ball Hackley Jamison), Clark 1797, and was the father of Dulcenia Harrison° and others. 2, Joseph, m Agnes Hickman, Bourbon 1797, and they went to Lexington, Mo. Their son, Rev. Hiram, m Susan Hughes, Bourbon 1819, and was the father of Robert D., who m Alice Green°. 3, Judge Jesse (1776-1836), m Sarah Gist (dau Col. Nathaniel), 1801, and spent his later years in Texas; 4, Elijah, m Judith Jamison (sister of Lucy). One record says Rev. Joseph m second Elizabeth Chapman, and they had a son John, b Creelsboro, Ky., 1801.

A group settling in this neighborhood included: 1, Joseph, perhaps the one who m Mary Saunders, Lincoln 1784, since he had a wife, Mary, F 1798. His will, Gallatin 1812, mentions a wife Nancy, but there is some disagreement about his children, John, Moses, and possibly Aaron, who m Eleanor Bond, Gallatin 1833. 2, Isaac, brother of Joseph, m Elizabeth Craig° (dau Benjamin), W 1793. His will, Gallatin 1825, mentions his heirs: Ezekiel, Watts, Job, Elizabeth Bledsoe. Lydia Easterday° is also mentioned as his daughter. 3, James Bledsoe m Judith ——, Culpeper, County, Virginia, 1785, and their dau, Sally, m John Tandy, Jr., F 1801. James died in 1799, and his widow m William Forsee°. 4, Abraham, here in 1791, also went to Gallatin. 5, William, m Winifred Reed°, of Culpeper, and they settled at Quinn's Bottom, on Elkhorn. He died in Gallatin, 1817. 6, Jacob was here in 1796, and Elizabeth was on Elkhorn, F 1801. In Woodford were Benjamin, m Isabella Thomas, 1790; William, Jr.; Elizabeth, m John Adams, 1797. Moses O. Bledsoe m Sophia Taylor (dau Samuel), F 1809.

Records show that one Isaac Bledsoe was killed in 1793, leaving a wife Catherine.

In Gallatin, Zachary Bledsoe m Ann Shelton, 1814; Jemima m Robert Johnson°; J. S. m Elizabeth Sanders°, 1815; George m Polly Wade, 1824; Anne m George Collins, 1825; Winna m Solomon Ellis, 1829.

Cave: Benjamin Cave came with the Bledsoes from England to Orange County, Virginia. He m Hannah Bledsoe (dau William), 1720, and among their children were: 1, John, m Mildred Bell, of Culpeper, and died in Scott County, Kentucky, 1810. Various records give his children as: a, Richard, m Sally Wood (dau Thomas), W 1792; b, Susan, m Thomas Wood; c, Henry (m Peggy Hawkins, W 1790?); d, Nancy, m William Kelly; e, William; f, Rebecca Haydon. His will mentions a granddaughter, Polly Burdett; 2, William, m Mary Mallory, and had Rev. William, who came to Kentucky with the "Travelling Church," and organized the Bullittsburg Church in Boone County. He m Margaret Threlkeld (dau John and Nancy Johnston Threlkeld), W 1784, and their son Daniel m Mary Holton (dau Lewis) of Gallatin (see Lindsay); 3, Rev. Richard, m Elizabeth Craig° and they had: a, John; b, Richard; c, Mary Rice; d, Hannah Graves°; e, Jeremiah, m Polly Graves°, 1808; 4, Anne, m first Philemon Kavanaugh°, and second William Strother; 5, Elizabeth Johnson°.

One Richard had a family of seven, W 1810; and Reuben had nine, including Mary, m John Cave, W 1816. One John Cave m Mary Harris, W 1816.

One record states that Matilda, eldest dau Capt. John Cave, of Woodford, m John Kirtley, and died in Boone County, Kentucky, about 1843.

BOHANNON—Larkin, 1802, dis 1803
        John, 1, restored to fellowship 1814
        Eleanor, 1

It is claimed that there are two distinct families in Kentucky: the Bohannons, descendants of Duncan or Dunkin and Sarah Bohannon, said to have come from England to Jamestown in 1690; and the Bohannans, whose ancestor, Ambrose Bohannan, is said to have come from Scotland to Gloucester County, Virginia, in 1700. But court records show that Dunkin Bohannon was living in Charles County, Maryland, in 1662, and in Gloucester County, Virginia, 1674.

Of the first family was Robert Bohannon (s Dunkin and Sarah), m Basheba ——, and their son, Elliott (1729-1781), who m Ann Walker and lived in Culpeper, had: 1, Richard (1748-1815), who was in Kentucky in 1789, and lived for several years in Woodford, but in 1798 went to Floyd's Fork in Jefferson. He m first Elizabeth Blackburn°; second, Catherine Herndon in 1789; third, Deborah Pearce (dau George), Shelby 1806. His children mentioned in his will were: a, Richard; b, Larkin, m Elizabeth Garnett°, W 1802; c, George m Franky Burton (dau John), W 1795; d, Julius, m Nancy Pearce (dau George), Jefferson 1801, and had Willett C. and Polly Branham°; e, Elizabeth, m John Burton, Jefferson 1809; f, Jane; g, Ambrose; h, Pearce; i, William; j, Henry. Ann Branham° may have been another daughter. One Richard Bohannon and his wife are said to have given the land on which the old Flat Rock Christian Church, near the Shelby line, was built about 1833.

2, Mildred, m Robert Gaines; 3, Ambrose, m —— Gibbs; 4, Elliott (1753-1824), settled on Elkhorn in Woodford. He m first in Virginia, and his second wife was Mary (Aylette?). His children were: a, Juretta, m Josiah Collins, W 1791; b, Rebecca, m first Elliott Kirtley, W 1798, and they were the parents of Laura Taylor°; she m second Bennett Osborne; c, Mary, m Jeremiah Burton, W 1798, and lived in Jefferson; d, Ann, m Elijah Kirtley, W 1798; e, Simeon, m Sally Calmes°, W 1803, and went to Jessamine; f, Eliza, m Benjamin Bondurant, W 1806; g, German, m Sallie Hamilton, 1808, and they had: Albert, m Henrietta Long, W 1836; Eveline Southworth; Susan Stout°; Isabella Gates; Mary Neet; h, Milly, m Isaac McCuddy, who had a family of five, W 1810; i, Olivia; j, Elliott (1791-1818). 6, John, m —— Lewis; 7, Mary, m —— Herndon.

Dr. Richard Banks Bohannon (s Richard B. Bohannon), came from Virginia to Woodford and lived first in Versailles and then on Grier's Creek. He m Fannie Menzies, W 1807, and they had: a, Francis, m —— Potts; b, Betty, m Capt. William W. George; c, Ophelia, m first, Virgil McCracken°, second,

Edward B. Wood, W 1836, third, Major Humphrey Jones; d, Henry Buford, m Mary Todd° and went to Missouri.

John Bohannon m Helen Cook° in Pittsylvania County, Virginia, 1774. They came to Mercer in 1779, and were on Glen's Creek, W 1789. He spent his last years in Shelby, where the settlement of his estate in 1837 indicates that his children were: 1, Elizabeth Montgomery°; 2, Rachel Montgomery; 3, Joanna Mitchell°; 4, Henry S., m Philadelphia Gale°, F 1820; 5, John (m Elizabeth Lane, Shelby 1810?). William Bohannon; Abraham Bohannon, who m Prudence Jones, W 1797, and went to Shelby; and Elizabeth Bohannon, who m first Jesse Cook° and second Joseph Edrington° were evidently closely related to John. There were many intermarriages among the Bohannon-Cook descendants in Shelby.

Austin Bohannon lived on Big Benson, and m Mrs. Elizabeth Jackson°, F 1799—perhaps his second marriage, since in 1810 he had a family of thirteen. Some of his children were: 1, Betsy, m John R. Crockett, F 1815; 2, Patsy Moss°; 3, Polly, m Abraham Louderback, F 1813; 4, Milly, m Robert Knox, F 1817, and went to Gallatin; 5, Sally, m Richard Berry, F 1825. Austin Bohannon was living in Kenton in 1845.

Ambrose Bohannon, of Gloucester County, Virginia, m first —— Lafon, and second, Elizabeth Gregory. His son, Col. Joseph (——-1811), of Essex County, m Elizabeth Lafon (dau Capt. Richard), and they are said to have been the parents of Capt. William Bohannan, who settled in Fayette near Fort Spring, but came to Versailles and lived for several years. His estate was settled in Fayette, 1820. Family records say that his wife was Frances Hipkins, but court records show that she was a daughter of Major Thomas Sthreshley, and that she m second Solomon Hoggins, F 1823. Capt. William's children were: 1, Richard A., m Josephine A. Gray (dau Joseph), F 1831; 2, Susan, m W. B. Ratliff, F 1823; 3, Adaliza, m James N. Clark, F 1829; 4, William T.; 5, Sophronia L. Gale°; 6, Martha Major°; 7, Mary Ann Blackburn°, who was mentioned in the will of John O'Bannon, W 1810, as his wife's niece. One William m Jane Wilcoxon, W 1808.

BOWLER (Boulware)—Ritchie, 1		Patsy
	Esther, 1	Emily, r 1828
	Theodorick, 1	Logan, r 1828
	Polly, 1	
	Caty, 1	
	Ramsey, 1801-1814	

One record says that the Boulwares are of Irish descent, and another says they are Huguenots. Ritchie or Richard Boulware came from Essex County, Virginia, to Garrard County, Kentucky, in 1780 or 1784, settling in Franklin about 1790. His wife was Esther Ramsey°, and their children were: 1, Rev. Mordecai, who was licensed to preach at the North Fork Church, 1813, and was ordained soon afterward. He succeeded John H. Ficklin at North Fork, and preached there from 1816 to 1825. He m Polly Wooldridge°, Clark 1797, and their dau Maria m James Quinn (s Benjamin and Sarah French Quinn), F 1813, whose descendants went to Missouri. 2, Ritchie, m first Susanna (dau John Major, Sr. and widow of Robert Wooldridge), F 1801, and had five children, including Emily (m Dr. Lyle, Mexico, Mo.), and Richard Logan, Hopkinsville, Ky.; he m second Mildred Waller (see Watts), F 1831, and they had a son, Richard Abraham. 3, Rev. Theodorick (1780- ——), attended a grammar school taught by Elder John Price. He m first Susan Kelly° in 1808, and they had Stephen, James, Theodorick, Daniel, Jane, Cordelia Rogers°, Susan, Jephtha, Isaac.

Theodorick preached at Stamping Ground and Georgetown, and received a call to preach in Cincinnati at what was then a large salary—nine hundred dollars a year—but he declined the offer because he did not wish to bring up his children in a city. He removed with his family to Missouri in 1827. He m second Mrs. Elizabeth H. Offutt in 1855.

John Taylor said of him: "He is much of a preacher, and considered very orthodox by all the high toned predestinarians— his preaching bears the semblance of a man snuffing a candle, as if he would take away from true religion all the superfluities that could possibly mingle themselves with it—some are of the opinion that at times he snuff's a little too deep; he has a greater aptitude to trim hypocrites than to invite poor sinners to come to Christ."

4, Ramsey, m Lucy Ford°, W 1805, and their dau Frances m
William Clore, Oldham 1839; 5, Catherine Pulliam°; 6, Patsy
Shely°. One Patsy Shely m Abner Wood, Gallatin (1837?).
After the death of Ritchie Boulware, Sr., in 1795, his widow
bought a farm between "Ingleside" and the home of Edmund
Vaughan, Sr.

Shely (Sheley, etc.): John Sheley came from Holland to
Jefferson County, (now West) Virginia, 1750. He m ——
Dunn, and they had: 1, David; 2, Maj. John (1757-1825), a
member of Washington's surveying party, m Anne Ridgeway,
1778, and they came to Kentucky in 1806, locating in Scott.
Their children were: John; Benjamin, m Patsy Boulware, F
1815; Harrow, m Sally Kelly°; Singleton; Van, m Martha Moore,
W 1825; George, m Sally Brooking, W 1834; Reason, m Nancy
White (dau William), F 1820. The family went to Missouri.
Michael Sheely m Agnes (Evans?), W 1798.

BRADLEY—Thomas, dis to North Fork Elkhorn, 1801

Thomas Bradley (1767-1820), son of Robert and Anna
Williams Bradley, came from Spotsylvania County, Virginia,
and was at Bryan's Station, where in 1788 he m Philadelphia
Ficklin°. Their children were: 1, Robert, m Nancy Pulliam; 2,
William, m first Sally Jenkins, 1818, and second Mahala Kirk-
patrick, 1826; 3, Henry, m Maria Jenkins, 1808; 4, James F., m
—— Keller, 1810; 5, Margaret, m William Huddleson; 6, John;
7, Mary; 8, Jeptha D., of Lexington, m Ann Eliza Suggett°,
Scott 1834; 9, Joseph Leeland. Thomas was living on Elkhorn,
F 1795.

Thomas Poe Bradley, born in Virginia in 1784, m Fanny
Bush, Scott 1804, and they went to Calloway County, Missouri,
1828. They had: F. B.; Lucy; Thomas; Milton.

Charles Bradley m Elizabeth Walton, Culpeper County, Virginia, 1799. They came to Woodford and located on Glen's
Creek. Among their children were: 1, Judith, m William A.
Pierce, 1820, and they were grandparents of Mrs. A. F. Peters,
of Frankfort; 2, Benjamin C., m Susan Mary Jones°, 1840; they
were parents of Miss Sue Bradley, Duckers; 3, Elizabeth Jones°.

Suggett: From various records is gathered the information
that Lieut. James Suggett came from Wales to Baltimore and

married (Elizabeth Smith?). His wife died after the birth of a daughter, and he m second Jemima Spence (dau Patrick and Jemima Pope Spence). They lived in Orange County, Virginia, but his will is in Fayette County, Kentucky, 1786. In addition to daus Jemima Johnson° and Catherine Merry, they had: John (1751 -——) m Mildred Davis, 1772 (one record says Milly Piersall). They came to Scott with their family: 1, Rev. James (——-1851) was ordained at Stamping Ground 1810, and preached at Clear Creek and other places until he went to Calloway County, Missouri, about 1822. There he was known as an organizer of churches and an able, zealous preacher. He is said to have been a fluent and witty speaker, and John Taylor is quoted as saying, "When I see Suggett in the pulpit, I think he ought never to come out of it, and when I see him out of it I think he ought never to go into it."

He m first Sarah Redding°, and they had Thomas, James, John, Edgecombe, Joseph, Henry, Benjamin, William, Malinda, Nancy, Catherine, Susan. He m second Mrs. Jane Jacoby, 1843.

2, William, m Betsy Castleman°, W 1797. They had: a, Ann Eliza Bradley; b, David C., m Mary Samuel°, and their children were: Judith Ann, m John Wickliffe Bradley; Sophronia, m Alfred D. Offutt; Almyra, m Anderson Chenault Brown, and they were the parents of Miss Mary S. Brown, of Georgetown; Samuel, who went to Texas; Benjamin; Lucy. 3, Elizabeth Thompson°; 4, John, m Milly (or Winifred) Craig, and went to Missouri; 5, Sallie (1790-1857), m Jack Wickliffe Bradley, and they were ancestors of Victor Bradley, of Georgetown; 6, Catherine, m John I. Johnson; 7, Edgecombe Polk, m first —— Nash, and had Letitia Peak°; he m second Polly Swetnam°, and their dau Cynthia m John Duncan and was the mother of Mrs. Harvey Shropshire, of Georgetown; 8, Polly Viley°; 9, Milton, m Annora Craig.

BRANHAM—Jane, dis 1833, Other denomination 1834

There were many Branhams in this section, but because of the destruction of records in Scott, the families cannot be classified.

Albert G. Branham m Jane Elizabeth Major°, F 1833. They lived in Missouri, and their children were John T., Ellen, Sallie, Laura, Mary, Olivia, Albert, Alvin.

Tavner Branham (s Spencer and Sarah Bourne Branham, of Virginia) settled in Franklin on Cedar Creek, though after his death in 1818 some of his children were in Scott and some in Owen. His wife was Elizabeth Burbridge (dau Thomas), and their children were: 1, Thomas, m Elizabeth ——, and was on North Elkhorn with a family of ten, F 1810; 2, John, m Fanny Vawter°, F 1801; 3, George; 4, Mildred, m Valentine Swisher, F 1801. (Valentine Switzer came from Switzerland about 1750-1770 with his brothers John and Nicholas, and settled in Hampshire County, Virginia. In early records this name was Switcher, then Swisher, and when the railroad was built in the vicinity about 1885, the station was named in honor of the family, "Switzer."); 5, Sally; 6, Nelly, m John G. Jenkins; 7, Linsfield, m Polly Vawter°, F 1807, and they were ancestors of Miss Helen M. Crane, of Detroit; 8, Daniel, m Theodosia Hampton, F 1812; 9, Francis. Thomas Gaines and Jacob Swan, mentioned in a settlement of 1818, may have been sons-in-law.

John Branham, a brother of Tavner, evidently went from Woodford to Scott. He m Letitia ——, and died in 1824, leaving: 1, Henry, m Mary ——; 2, Tavner (1786-1831), m Ann Hicks, W 1814, and they had: Elizabeth, Amanda Dunlap, Martha Starks, Sarah Jane Gay, Susan Davis Parrish; 3, Robert, m Nancy Stapp°; 4, Susan Stapp°; 5, William, m Mary Stapp°; 6, Sanford, m Matilda Brooking°, 1817; 7, Elizabeth Stapp°; 8, Beverly, m Martha T. Brooking°, W 1818.

Daniel Branham m Ann Bohannon°, W 1790. His will, Jefferson 1812, mentions his wife and children: Patsy; Julius; Richard; Elijah; and George Bohannon, uncle of his son Richard. Richard Branham, Jr., m Polly Bohannon, Jefferson 1819.

Richard Branham m Polly Bohannon, F 1797. The will of one Richard, Scott 1814, names his wife, Hannah, and sons William; Harbin, m Eleanor Scott°; Tavner; James; George.

Robert Branham (also written Brenham) m Mary Fox°, W 1807. He sold land to Lewis R. Major, F 1833. His children were: 1, Dr. Richard F.; 2, Charles; 3, Robert; 4, Louisa, m first, Rowland M. Thomas, Shelby 1827, second, —— Applegate, third, Gen. Thomas N. Lindsey, F 1853.

Benjamin, William, Gaydon, and James were in Scott before 1800. Benjamin m Nelly Miller, W 1792, and one Benjamin m Sally Stanford, W 1824. William Elzey Branham m Elizabeth

F. Blackburn°, W 1833. In Franklin, Benjamin m Mary James°, 1809; John H. m Anne James (see Blackburn), 1818. Harriet (dau Sally) m Gervas E. Russell, 1816; Sarah (dau Sally) m John L. Moore, 1823.

Fox: Arthur and Richard Fox, twin sons of William and Mary Kendrick Fox, of Mecklenburg County, Virginia, came to Kentucky about 1784. Arthur m Mary Young (dau Richard and Mary Moore Young), 1786, and went later to Mason. Richard taught for a while in the fort at Lexington, but came later to what is now Woodford, and was one of the founders of Versailles. He m Mary Blanton°, and they lived in a stone house which stood until recent years on an elevation opposite the McKee home on the Frankfort-Versailles pike. His grave, near by, is within a small enclosure. He gave a part of the land on which Grassy Spring Church was built.

Their children were: 1, Lucy, m first Obadiah Sullivan, W 1803, and they had: a, Richard; b, Daniel; c, Polly, m Bacon Bush, of Anderson, and they were the parents of Mrs. William Saffell, of Frankfort. Lucy m second, Capt. Archibald Morrison, 1815, and they had: d, Robert; e, Sidney Louise, m 1842 Col. E. G. Sebree, of Trenton, Ky., and they were grandparents of Miss Marguerite Banks, of Washington, D. C.; f, Sarah, m Garland H. Withers, of Danville, W 1834; g, Lucy (m Joseph Roberts, W 1841?). Capt. Morrison had by a former marriage: Elizabeth New°; Martha Ann, m William L. McQuire, W 1819; Rebecca Berry°; Jane; Mary; Archibald (m Elizabeth Tyre, W 1857?). 2, Newton, located near Hopkinsville; 3, Mary Branham; 4, Elizabeth; 5, Sidney Louise, m first William Allen Pruett, W 1822, and they had: a, Martha, m —— Redd. Sidney Louise m second John L. Herndon, of Georgetown, W 1833, and they had: b, Julia, m Jefferson Polk, of Des Moines, Iowa; c, Lucy R., m —— Thompkins, of Des Moines; 6, Martha, m her cousin, D. C. Freeman°; 7, Richard L., m his cousin, Sarah Ann Williams (dau Thomas and Mary Fox Williams); 8, William K.; 9, Eliza Jane, m William McBride, W 1828; 10, Julia Ann, m Milton Withers, W 1835, and went to Missouri.

BRIDGEFORD—James, 1843

William Bridgeford was living in Scott in 1805, but on Buck Run, W 1807. His will, W 1810, mentions his wife Lucy and children: James; Thomas; Johnson; Lucy; Mary; Judy; Richard, m Nancy Guthrie°, W 1808, and in 1810 they were in Woodford with a family of four.

William T. Bridgeford m Lucinda Moss°, F 1837.

BRIGHTWELL—Martha, 1847
Scythy Ann, 1847

Martha Brightwell (1772-1856) was the widow of William Brightwell, of Spotsylvania County, Virginia. In 1848 she bought land from the Hall family, and her home, "Mt. Lebanon," was on the site of the house until recently occupied by Mrs. John Shryock. Her children were: 1, Scytha Ann (1815-1852); 2, Thomas J., died 1860; 3, Nancy, m —— Wright and went to Montgomery County, Missouri; 4, William J., m Ann E. Penn, Scott 1840, and lived in Gallatin; 5, Wesley; 6, Huldah. Thomas J. and William J., after the death of their mother, sold the farm in 1860 to Levi Crutcher.

Also in the neighborhood were William Brightwell, m Mary Johnson°; and Thomas, m first Ellen Johnson, F 1837, and second, Mary Tyre, W 1852. Waller L. Brightwell m Parmelia Mitchell°, W 1821 and went to Platte County, Missouri; Margaret Brightwell m Valora Sample, W 1842.

BRISTOW—Rebecca, r 1828, dis 1830

James Bristow m Rebecca Jackson°, W 1801. Samuel Bristow m Ann Long°, F 1820; William m Sarah Lewis°, F 1821.

In 1801 Livin Bristoe was in Woodford, and Henry was in Shelby.

BROWN—George, Sr., 1801   William, Jr., 1801
John, 1790   Polly, 1801-1803
Jesse   Betsy, 1801-1803
Daniel, 1801   Sally, 1801-1803
William, 1, dis 1803   Sally, 1812, dis 1817
Elizabeth, 1, dis 1803
George, Jr., Jefferson Co., 1807
John, Jr., 1801, withdrew 1802—no more of us

The Browns came to Kentucky with William Hickman, who speaks of "Father Brown and his lady" as being very old, and says that their daughter Obedience married his son, William Hickman, Jr.

Though the court records of this family are very confusing, they make it appear that one George, who owned land on South Elkhorn, had: 1, John (——- 1806), from whom the original church lot was obtained, m Nancy (Elam?) and they had: a, William; b, Daniel E., m Elizabeth Finnie°, W 1805, and had a family of seven, F 1810. He is thought to have been the father of James D. Brown, who m first, Sophia F. Cox°, F 1830, and second, Virginia Ann Lewis, F 1838, the mother of Albert Duane Brown, m Susan Ayres°. Other children of Daniel E. may have been Emsey, m Francis M. Taylor, F 1831; (a dau m Reuben Gale°?); and Judith Sheets°. He sold his farm in 1819 to William Samuel. c, Polly, m George Brown, Sr.; d, Obedience, m Gilbert Pew, F 1805, and they had John Pew. 2, Jesse, who in 1807 sold land to James Davis. He m Eliza Scrogin, W 1792, and they had: George, Preston, James, Robert, Leven, Joseph, Sally, John, Jesse, William. 3, Daniel, had a family of four, F 1810; 4, Obedience Smith°; 5, Patsy Church°.

William Brown, Sr., and several members of his family took their letters in 1803, and probably went to South Benson. His will, F 1816, names his wife, Elizabeth, and: 1, George, Sr., m Polly Brown, F 1801; 2, John. One John m Nancy Hickman°, F 1810, and went in 1817 to South Benson, where he was ordained in 1820. In 1830 he left the Baptist Church to follow the teachings of Alexander Campbell. 3, William; 4, Daniel; 5, Stephen, m Sally Bailey°, F 1816; 6, Jesse, m Phoebe Bailey°, F 1816; 7, Benjamin; 8, Polly; 9, Betsy; 10, Sally Bailey°; 11, Nancy Bailey°.

John Brown, Jr., m Sally Settle°, F 1806; Polly m Thomas Settle°; Sally m Charles Stephens°; Mrs. Eliza m Martin Sheets°; Daniel m Polly Johnson (dau William), F 1807; Robert m Mrs. Permelia Prewitt (dau William White), F 1822; Peter m Betsy Cunningham°, F 1811.

In Woodford, Daniel Brown m Betsy Hart, 1805; Jesse m Lydia Bevis (dau William), 1812.

Another family was that of Berryman Brown, who m Mary Noel° in Essex County, Virginia. They went to Caroline, where he died, and in 1782 she came with her family, first to what is now Mercer, and later to Franklin. The children were: 1,

Charles, m Mollie Sneed°. They lived on Salt River, and had, besides other children, John, m Sallie Sneed°. 2, Scott, m Lucy Munday, Mercer 1797, and they had: a, Patsy, m first, Samuel Arnold, and second, Nicholas Green°; b, Affiah Daniel°; c, Lavinia, m Newton K. Henry; d, Meredith, who was killed by oxen running; e, Capt. Harrison, m Martha Jane Henry, 1840, and lived on the McCracken pike in Woodford; f, Belinda, m Albert Dillon, F 1828; g, Ruth, m James McFerran, F 1836; h, Ann, m John Mayhall, F 1855; i, Gen. Scott; j, Judge Reuben, m Edna Mayhall, F 1873, and they were the parents of Scott, Ray, and Harry Brown, of Frankfort.

The old home of Scott Brown on the Nineveh pike is still standing, and in good condition.

3, William, m Sally Payne, F 1801, and their children were: a, Berryman, m Kitty Marshall; b, Samuel, m Elizabeth Samuel; c, Scott, m Salinda Henry, 1828; d, Madison; e, Lucinda; f, Maria. 4, Margaret Daniel°; 5, Sarah Graves°.

Rev. John Brown, a Presbyterian minister of Rockbridge County, Virginia, came first to Woodford, and in 1796 to "Liberty Hall," in Frankfort. His wife was Margaret Preston, and their children were: 1, Senator John, m Margaretta Mason (dau Rev. John, of New York), 1799, and it was she who, in the garden of "Liberty Hall," established in 1810 the first Sunday school west of the Alleghenies; 2, William; 3, Mary, m Dr. Alexander Humphreys, and they were the parents of D. C. Humphreys and Eliza Todd°; 4, James; 5, Dr. Samuel, of the Transylvania Medical School, who obtained from Jenner some of the newly discovered cow-pox virus, and brought it to this country imbedded in balls of beeswax in his pockets. In 1802, while other doctors hesitated to use it, he vaccinated about five hundred persons in Lexington, the first town in America in which smallpox vaccination was successfully performed. 6, Dr. Preston, of "Sumner's Forest," in Woodford, m Elizabeth Watts°, and they were the parents of Mrs. Orlando Brown, of Frankfort, and Mrs. Robert W. Scott.

One John Brown settled on Glen's Creek in Woodford, where he died in 1822, leaving his wife Nancy and a large family, among whom were: 1, Susan, m first Roderick Perry, W 1801, and their dau Mahala m Samuel Pepper and was the grandmother of Miss Laura Pepper, of Frankfort; Susan m second, James Edwards°. 2, Polly Garnett°.

Oliver Brown m Nancy Garnett°, W 1801; John m Nancy Glenn, W 1806; George T. m Sally Perry, W 1808; John m Nancy Perry, W 1811.

Bailey: The Baileys came to Kentucky with the Hickmans and Browns, and apparently settled near Bridgeport. The will of Abraham Bailey, F 1835, mentions his children: 1, Benjamin; 2, Jeremiah; 3, George; 4, Mary Brown°; 5, Sally Brown°; 6, Archibald, m Sally Brown, F 1808; 7, Jesse, m Nancy Brown, F 1815; 8, Phoebe Brown°; 9, Susan; 10, Obedience. Other children of Abraham were: 11, Shelah, m Mary Church°, F 1815, and they built and operated "Bailey's Tavern" at Bridgeport, which is now the home of Warwick Emmitt. They were the parents of Churchill Bailey and others. 12, William; 13, Abraham, Jr., m Eliza Hickman°, F 1819, and they had: America, George, James, Francis, Martha, Lilas, Mary, Obedience, Lydia. 14, —— m —— Palmer.

In Woodford, William Bailey m Polly Crutcher°, 1815, and they had: 1, Delia, who married very young, and started with her husband to California in a covered wagon. They were never heard of again, and are supposed to have been killed by the Indians; 2, Albert, m Laura ——; 3, William, who lived on an old road leading from Duckers to Grassy Spring Church, m first Delia Simmons (dau S. and N. Simmons, of Bullitt). He m second Mary Ann Stephens°, F 1860; 4, Elizabeth Johnson°; 5, Sarah O.

Benjamin Bailey m Susan A. Craig, W 1791; one Benjamin Bailey m Frances Nall°, W 1810.

Church: Robert Church, of Culpeper County, Virginia, m Margaret Campbell in 1773. They came to Kentucky with their family in 1785, and settled on Main Elkhorn, where many of their descendants now live. They were the parents of: 1, Henderson, m Charlotte White, and their son, James B., m Dorothy Brydon°, F 1821; 2, Thomas, employed by the Government as an Indian scout, m Mary White (dau Ambrose), 1793, and they were ancestors of Miss Drue Church; 3, Robert, m Patsy Brown°, W 1794. Their children were: a, James, m Polly Moss°, F 1818. They lived in the neighborhood of Peak's Mill, and were grandparents of Mrs. C. M. Jackson, Mrs. Virgil Gaines, Mrs. George Hannen, Sr., Mrs. Milton Arnold, Sr., Zach and John Church, of Frankfort, and great-grandparents of Judge Church Ford, of Georgetown; b, Polly Bailey°; c, Nancy Lewis°; d, Sally, m —— Satterwhite; e, William, m his cousin, Catherine Church; f, Bidsey, m Jeptha D. Boots, 1833.

4, Richard, m Anne Lewis°, and they were the parents of Susan Oliver°; 5, William, m Kitty Oliver°, 1807; 6, Mary, m —— White; 7, Ida.

> BRYANT (Bryan)—Morgan H., 1801, dis 1810
> Betsy, 1811
> Peggy, 1811, dis 1824
> "Sister", 1819
> Nancy, dis 1827

The will of Morgan Bryant, Fayette 1804, mentions children Rebecca and Morgan, and grandchildren Joseph and Mary Bryant. One Morgan Bryan was in Shelby, 1795. The estate of Morgan Bryan was settled in Henry, 1815. Martha Bryan, who m Daniel Gano°, had a brother Morgan, b 1773. One Morgan H. Bryan m Sally Hunt (dau John), Fayette 1805. He was on Elkhorn, F 1801-1807.

Morgan H. Bryan, of Jefferson County, Kentucky, bought a lot in Frankfort from Benjamin Hickman, 1823. In 1845 the children and heirs at law of Morgan H. Bryan, deceased, of Boone County, Missouri, who sold the lot to Ellen Fox, were listed as: 1, Sally McClelland; 2, Milton Bryan and wife Zerelda; 3, John H. and wife Ann Eliza; 4, David M. Hickman and wife Cornelia; 5, William W. Bryan; 6, James H. and wife Mary A.; 7, Thomas W. and wife Jane N.

Thomas Bryan m Nancy Haydon°, F 1802, and they lived between Daniel Peak's and "Melrose," at the former home of the Rev. John Gano. Their children were: 1, Rozette D., m William A. Chinn, F 1820; 2, Sarah Ann, m William D. Coryell, of Mason County, F 1832; 3, Harriet; 4, Emeline; 5, Eliza, m Brinkley Morris, F 1825, and they had Eugene and Henry; 6, Martha Gayle°; 7, Mary F., m William A. Goreham, F 1827, and they had a dau, Mary C.

Thomas Bryan's widow and children sold property in 1837 to Peter Dudley, and to Dr. Francis Lloyd in 1840.

Betsy Bryant m first Thomas H. Gouldman°, and second Archibald L. Bryant, F 1826; James Bryant m Sally Gray (dau

James), F 1805; the records state that Thomas L. Bryan m Jane
Martin°, January, 1812, and Esther Forsee° in July, 1812, both
in Franklin County. James M. Byran m Sarah S. Macey°, F
1827; T. C. Bryan m Elizabeth P. Bacon°, F 1839. Stephen Bryant m Sally ———. They lived at Camp Pleasant, on Main
Elkhorn, and were the parents of Virginia Ann Hawkins°.

Presley Bryant m Nancy Miskil, W 1792, and they were
living on the river, F 1801. His will, F 1815, names his wife
Nancy and: 1, Rawley; 2, Sarah, m Jesse Moore; 3, Nancy.

BRYDEN (Brydon)—John, 1847

Robert and Barsheba Brydon were in Lincoln, 1789. Robert
m Polly Edwards°, W 1794. He lived on Elkhorn, and in 1810
had a family of ten. His will, F 1827, mentions his wife Mary;
a granddaughter, Katherine (see Robinson), and children: 1,
Dorothea Church°; 2, Margaret; 3, John, m Mary Shackelford°,
F 1831; 4, James (1816-1856); 5, William, m Nancy Head°; 6,
Barbara; 7, Robert, m Nancy Brydon, F 1836; 8, Stevenson (1812-
1866), m Hester L. Clark (dau Harriet), in 1843, and their children were: a, Frances M., m Thomas Reuben Long° (s Benjamin
and Julia Jackson Long), 1862; b, Hally A., m C. S. Hampton,
1871; c, Ellen H., m Robert Long (brother of Thomas R. Long),
1871, and they were the parents of Mrs. James Arnold, whose
home is at the site of Gore's Station on the Frankfort-Owenton
road.

Barbara Brydon bought land from Uriah Edwards, F 1796,
and sold to John Major in 1800.

BUCK—Charles, r 1813, dis 1817
Polly, r 1813, dis 1817

Three sons of Charles Buck, of Virginia, m three daus of
William and Isabella Calmes Richardson°. Charles Buck, who
is said to have gone from Westmoreland to Frederick County,
Virginia, m first ——— Earle, and had: 1, Col. John, m Miriam
Richardson°. They came to Woodford, where he died 1816.
Their children as recorded were: a, Charles, m Polly Price°. In
F 1833 their home near the Forks of Elkhorn was sold to the
French family by his heirs: Elizabeth, Ann, Isabel Blackburn°,
Samuel C., Mary Charles, Lucy P. Blanton°, Waller, Charles.
b, Peter Chew, m Mariam Price°, Fayette 1811, and they lived

on Craig's Creek. There is much confusion over the names of the two Price sisters who m Charles and Peter C. Buck, and conflicting statements have been published. c, John, m Anice Buck (dau Rev. Thomas); d, William, m Maria Flowers, 1822; e, Sarah R., m Charles Cotton (s William and Frances Taylor Cotton), 1819; f, Elizabeth, m Thomas Helm, 1797; g, Ann, m Meredith Helm; h, Isabella, m Willis Field, 1805; i, Amelia, m John N. Buck. One John Buck lived on Grier's Creek.

Charles Buck m second Mrs. Letitia (Sorrel) Wilcocks (see Ewing), an aunt of his first wife, and they had: 2, Capt. Thomas (1756——), m Ann Richardson°, and they had: a, William R. (1776-1823), m Lucy Blakemore (dau George and Elizabeth Mauzy Blakemore, of Warren County, Virginia), 1802; b, Marquis C., m Elizabeth Drake; c, Dr. Isaac Newton, m first Susan Taylor, and second Janet N. Buck; d, Henrietta Calmes°; e, Isabella R., m Hezekiah Conn; f, Mary Ann, m George Bayley; g, Rebecca, m William R. Ashby; h, Elizabeth, m George Neville Blakemore, 1814; i, Letitia, m John Mauzy Blakemore, 1820. 3, Charles, m Mary Richardson°, and their children were: a, John, m Sarah Catlett; b, Rev. William Calmes (1790-1872), m first Maria LeWright, and second Miriam Field. He is said to have been the one to whom the Baptists owe their deliverance from prejudice against missions. He went to Union County in 1820, and in 1836 to Louisville, where he labored for the cause of missions. In 1841 he took editorial charge of *The Baptist Banner and Western Pioneer,* which he conducted for nine years. In 1850 he went to Alabama, where he continued his religious writing. He spent his last years in Waco, Texas. c, Charles L., m Lucy Bayliss, and they had Col. John W., who m Mary Belle Sutton°. They lived between Midway and Georgetown, and were the grandparents of the author, Charles Neville Buck, of Louisville; d, Letitia, m George Catlett (s Robert and Mary Floyd Catlett), and they had a large family. They removed to Morganfield, Ky., 1816. e, Samuel, m Mary Bayley; f, Mary, m Dr. William Bayley; g, Rev. Thomas, m Amelia Dawson.

Calmes: Gen. Marquis Calmes (born 1755?), of Huguenot ancestry, was the son of William Waller and Lucy Neville Calmes, of Frederick County, Virginia. He came first to what is now Clark County, Kentucky, and later to Woodford. He helped to lay off the town of Versailles, and it was he who named it.

"Caneland," the home of General Calmes, which was recently destroyed by fire, was located on the Big Sink road on land now belonging to the Dunlap heirs.

He m Priscilla Hale° (dau George and Sarah Smith Hale), Fauquier County, Virginia, 1782. In his will, W 1834, he mentions these children: 1, Nancy, m Dr. William R. Jennings, of Tennessee, W 1825; 2, Priscilla, m Joel Kirtley, W 1821; 3, Miriam (1797-1881), m Thomas Eastin, of Clark, W 1823; 4, Sally Bohannon°; 5, William; 6, Marquis, who went to Missouri, m his cousin, Mrs. Eliza Hale° Hamilton, W 1836; 7, George (m Elizabeth Downy, Clark 1819?); 8, Spencer, m Henrietta Buck°. (One Spencer Calmes m Sally Edwards, dau William, Clark 1817). Spencer was the father of Marquis and Waller. 9, Fielding.

> BUCKLEY—Jeremiah, r 1804, to Glen's Creek 1811
> Frances, r 1804, to Glen's Creek 1811
> Elizabeth, r 1805, dis 1813
> Samuel, r 1805, to Glen's Creek 1812
> Thomas, r 1807, to Glen's Creek 1812

Jeremiah Buckley and his wife Frances lived at Clifton, and had a family of twelve, W 1810. Jeremiah was on the tax list, F 1813. Three daughters were: Cynthia, m Henry Stone, W 1811; Nancy Stout°; Mary, m Samuel McGuire, F 1824. Elizabeth Hinton° was probably another daughter. Rev. William Buckley was ordained at Glen's Creek, 1807, and was preaching in Trimble County, Kentucky, in 1816. William Buckley m Polly Webb (c Aaron), W 1800; Nancy Buckley m Reace Williamson, W 1818.

Hinton (Henton): Thomas Henton was the son of William and —— Henton, of Rockingham County, Virginia. He m Christine Brennen, and they settled in Woodford near the site of Grassy Spring Church, for which he gave a part of the lot. Their children were: 1, Cassius Casper, m Hannah Sisk°, W 1809; 2, Guy; 3, George H., m Elizabeth Buckley°, W 1812; 4, John B., m Polly Martin°, W 1815; 5, Chris; 6, Catherine, m Reuben Cluff, W 1811; 7, Elizabeth; 8, Persis, m James Gibbany,

W 1818; 9, Thomas (1797-1869), m first Mildred and then Nancy
Darnaby (daus Edward and Mildred Ellis Darnaby), and was
the father of Mildred Thompson° and of the Hentons now living
in Woodford.

BUFORD—Mrs. Elizabeth, r 1812, dis 1815

Thomas Buford, Jr., of Middlesex County, Virginia, m Elizabeth ——, and they were the parents of Agatha Twyman°;
Elizabeth, who m Jeremiah Early, 1728 (see Scott); and John,
m Judith Early, and lived in Culpeper. John and Judith had,
among other children: 1, Henry, m Mildred Blackburn°, Bedford
County, Virginia, 1771, and they were the parents of Prudence
Blackburn°. 2, Capt. Simeon, m Margaret Kirtley, 1777, and
they came to Barren County, Kentucky. Three of their sons
came to Woodford: a, John, m first Nancy Hickman°, and
second Mrs. Ann Howe° Watson, and had a family of five, W
1810; b, Col. William, m Frances Walker Kirtley, Barren 1801.
They lived at "Free Hill," now the Alexander home, near Spring
Station, and had several children, including Margaret Twyman°
and Gen. Abraham, of "Bosque Bonita"; c, Simeon (1787-1859),
m Elizabeth Twyman°, 1806, and in 1834 they went to Missouri,
settling near Glasgow. Their children were: Manville, m Elizabeth Shelby; Legrand, m 1838 Eusebia Mallory; Adeline, m
John S. Nowland; Almira, m 1831 Capt. John V. Webb; Elizabeth G., m 1835 Judge John S. Ryland. 3, Abraham, who settled
in the part of Woodford that is now Scott. He m Martha
McDowell, and their son, William McDowell, m Margaret Elizabeth Robertson°, 1828, and lived at "Elkwood," the Cannon
home near Midway.

Charles Buford m Henrietta P. Adair (dau John), F 1821;
Legrand Buford m Jane E. French (dau William and Polly
Taylor° French), F 1828.

BULLARD—William, 1   Sister, 1798
                Catherine, 1

The Bullards were connected with the Woolfolks. Reuben
Bullard, of Caroline County, Virginia, m Catherine ——. He
died about 1781, and she came first to Woodford and later to
Shelby with her children: 1, Reuben, m Betsy Gill, Shelby 1803,

and they had: a, Elizabeth; b, Lucinda; c, Richard; d, Nancy Jane; e, William. One William m Lydia Foree, Henry 1831, and died in Shelby, 1846, leaving his wife and sons, Reuben, William, and James; f, Reuben; g, ———. Some of this family went to Illinois. 2, Elizabeth Sanders°; 3, William, m Agatha Branham (dau William Samuel°, Sr., of Henry?), F 1799, the bond being signed by ——— Hickman and Ambrose Jeffries; 4, Caty, m George Gill, Shelby 1800; 5, Nancy, m James Morton, Shelby 1810; 6, Fanny. One Fanny (dau Reuben) m Nathaniel Richardson°.

Richard Bullard m Catherine Benson (dau Charles), of Culpeper County, Virginia.

CALLENDER–Philip, r 1810, dis 1815

Philip Callender m Belinda (or Malinda) Yancey°, Culpeper County, Virginia, 1805. He witnessed the will of Robert Fenwick, F 1807, but he died in Owen, 1829, leaving his wife and: 1, Emily, m Austin Shelton, Owen 1826; 2, Richard, m Matilda Martin, Owen 1831; 3, Polly, m Nelson Parish, Owen 1831; 4, Lucinda Garnett°; 5, America, m Joseph Poland, Owen 1840; 6, John, m Sarah A. Baldwin°, Owen 1837; 7, Morten.

David Corbey (?) m Patsy Callender, W 1809.

CALVERT–Elijah, 1, dis to Mouth of Elkhorn 1801
Charity, 1, dis to Mouth of Elkhorn 1801
Keziah, 2, dis to Mouth of Elkhorn 1801
Elizabeth

Elijah Calvert had a family of four, F 1810. His home on Cedar Creek was evidently in that part of Franklin which was given to Owen, since he was listed in Owen after 1819. His dau, Nancy, m first Paul Grugin, F 1799, and they had: 1, Charity, m Barnett Harrod, Henry 1824; 2, Elizabeth, m Benjamin Harrod, Henry 1824; 3, William K., m Mary Rogers, Owen 1830; 4, Keziah; 5, Thomas. Nancy m second Presley Neale°.

Peyton and Thomas Calvert had families of eight each, F 1810. Keziah (dau William) m William Curry, F 1801; Martin m Elizabeth Cox°, F 1813; Celius m Lucy Hardin°, F 1814, and was in Owen, 1826; Elizabeth Ann m Humphrey Sparks°; Isaac, on Steele's Branch, F 1820, was the father of Mary Sparks°; one Isaac m Dorcas Hampton, F 1836.

Presley Calvert m Isapena Johnston, W 1797. In Scott were Christian and Presley, 1801, and John and Presley, 1805. Obed Calvert m Elizabeth Lindsay°, Scott 1825.

Judge A. D. Calvert, of Swallowfield, represents the family in Franklin County.

CAMPBELL—Peggy, 1802, dis 1820

Mrs. Peggy Campbell m William R. Wilson, F 1826, the bond being signed by Garland Lillard. Thomas W. Twyman° m Margaret Campbell, W 1843, with the bond signed by John W. Redd. Rachel Robinson° m —— Campbell, and had Martha and Isabel.

CARTER—Huldah, r 1847, d 1849

Margaret and Thomas Carter sold land in Franklin and Scott to Philip Hudson, F 1823. John Carter sold land to Isaac Wingate, F 1865.

CASH—Brother, 1800

Warren Cash (1760-1850) m Susannah Baskett (dau Elder William and Mary Pace Baskett), of Goochland County, Virginia, 1783. They came to what is now Woodford, where in 1785 they were baptized in Clear Creek by John Taylor, who considered them "the first fruits of God in the wilderness of Kentucky." They went to Shelby, and were among the founders of Beech Creek Church, of which Warren was ordained pastor in 1799. He was "a plain, sound, practical preacher." They went later to Nelson, and then to Hardin, where their son, Rev. Jeremiah Cash, m Sarah Jewell, 1809. Archibald Cash m Betsy Enlow, Hardin 1813; Warren T. Cash m Kitty Duvall, Hardin 1822. William M. Truman m Emily S. Cash, Hardin 1843, Warren T. Cash, Jr., stating the bride was of age.

CASTLEMAN—Fanny, 1811, to Forks of Elkhorn 1818

Lewis Castleman m Jemima Pearsall in Virginia, and they came to Woodford and settled on Clear Creek. Their children were: 1, Jemima, m Silas Douthitt, W 1790, and went to Henry; 2, Elizabeth Suggett°; 3, John, m Fanny Gatewood°, and they have descendants in Gallatin. They were the parents of Jemima

Fuller°, and were the grandparents of David E. Castleman, of Covington, who m Lee Hawkins° (granddaughter of William S. and Katherine K. Hawkins); 4, Lewis, m Ann Dudley°; 5, Jacob, m Sarah White, and their dau, Mary H., m Daniel Weisiger, Jr., 1819; 6, Sarah Hawkins°; 7, Kesiah, m Gabriel Tandy, of Carroll; 8, David, who lived on North Elkhorn, m first Mary Breckinridge (dau John), and second Virginia Harrison (dau Robert C., Sr.), and was the father of Gen. John B. Castleman, of Louisville.

Gatewood: The will of Augustine Gatewood, Jessamine 1802, names his wife Betty; daus Fanny Castleman°, Elizabeth, Mary; and son Richard.

CHRISTIAN—Gilbert, dis to South Benson 1801
Lucy, dis to South Benson 1801

One Gilbert Christian went from Scotland to Ireland in 1702. He m Margaret Richardson, and they came in 1726 to Pennsylvania, and in 1732 to Augusta County, Virginia. Their children were: 1, John, m Margaret ——; 2, Robert; 3, Mary, m first John Moffett, and second James Trimble; 4, Major William (—— -1776), m Mary ——, and their two sons were: a, Patrick, father of Martha Richards°; b, Gilbert, m Lucy Richards°. He owned a farm on Dry Run, F 1796, and in 1806 sold land on South Benson to George Brown. Elizabeth Lewis Thomas, who m Eleazer Haydon°, and Mary Oldham Thomas, who m John Montgomery°, are listed as (adopted?) daughters of Gilbert Christian.

His will, Hopkins 1812, mentions his wife Lucy; sons Gilbert and Benjamin; daus Lucy, Pamelia, Sally, (Neelly?), and Patsy Guiler or Guyler. Another record adds sons Philemon and Richard.

John Christian, of Hanover County, Virginia, m Judith Pate (dau Jeremiah), and they came to Lexington, Ky., where he died in 1792. Among their children were: 1, Paul, b 1772, m Mary King Sutton°, 1799, and they went about 1830 to Huntsville, Mo. He was the father of: a, Virginia Yates°; b, Napoleon B., m Patsy Swetnam°, and they went to Randolph County, Missouri, where he died 1869; c, Caroline Swetnam°, and others. 2, Betsy Bacon°; 3, Jane Oliver°.

One Christian family in Fayette descends from William Christian, who m Anna, a sister of Patrick Henry, in Virginia, and came to Kentucky very early.

CLEMENS (Clements)—Bernard (or Barnett), dis to Mouth of Elkhorn 1801

Bernard Clements (1757- ——) m Sally Gore° in Charlotte County, Virginia, about 1784, and they were on Elkhorn, F 1796. Their children were: 1, Allen, m Polly Triplett°, F 1808; 2, Catherine Stephens°; 3, William, who went first to Owen and then to Henry; 4, Jane; 5, Sally, m Presley Arnold, F 1817; 6, Osten; 7, Nancy.

Gustave was in Henry, 1822, and Abraham was in Owen, 1825. Joseph m Eliza Rowlett°, Owen 1831.

Hannah Clemens m William R. Hawkins°.

CLIFT—Horatio, 2, 1802

Horatio Clift m Nancy Edrington°, F 1799. He was living in Woodford in 1805, and in Bracken in 1810.

COLE—Jesse, 2, dis to Big Spring 1812
Nancy, 2, dis to Big Spring 1812

Various origins have been assigned to the Coles, but Judge Redmond S. Cole, of Tulsa, Okla., who has made a nation-wide study of the family, states that those from Pennsylvania, who originally spelled the name *Kohl*, went to the vicinity of Roanoke, Va., and later to Missouri and other places in the West, were an entirely different family from those who came to Woodford. He could trace no relationship between the two families. Mrs. Ann Lindsay Grigson says in her book that the family is of English descent, and that Richard Cole came from Virginia to Kentucky and settled in Woodford. He came from Culpeper County, and is thought to have been a son of John Cole, whose will was probated there in 1757. One record indicates that Richard lived for several years in King George County, Virginia.

He came to what is now Franklin County, where in the summer of 1785 he assisted Humphrey Marshall in surveying the site of Frankfort. He afterward went to Woodford and settled at what is known as the Waits place on the Lexington-

Leestown road, which was known for many years thereafter as "Cole's Road." Here he conducted a famous inn, "The Black Horse Tavern."

His first wife was Ann Hubbard, and he m second Emsey James, W 1795. The children of Richard (1729-1814) and Ann were: 1, John, m Nancy Hines, and lived in Barren; 2, Richard, Jr. (1763-1839), m Sallie Yates°, and continued to operate the tavern after his father's death. His children were: a, Polly Finnie°; b, Elizabeth Martin°; c, Sallie Lewis°; d, James, who m his cousin, Sallie Lindsay°, and they had Zerelda and Jesse Richard; e, William Y.; f, Jesse. One Jesse F. Cole m Fanny Rice (b William), F 1815; g, Amos (1798-1827), m —— and had a dau, Sarah Ann. 3, Jesse, m first Nancy Sparks°. He owned several tracts of land on Elkhorn near the Scott County line, but went later to Ripley County, Indiana. His second wife was Mrs. Elizabeth (Roberts) Hyatt. He died 1857, leaving: a, Charles; b, Jeremiah, m Rebecca Young; c, Elizabeth, m Noah Ransdall; d, John (1801-1875), m Sarah H. Collier; e, Mary, m —— Young; f, Jesse; g, Milly, m —— Salyers; h, Nancy, m Hezekiah Evans; i, Elizabeth, m —— Jones; j, Willia Washington; k, Henry Clay.

4, Rachel, m Willa Jett (s Peter and Rebecca Bowen Jett), of Stafford County, Virginia, and she came to Kentucky after his death. Their children were: a, Richard Cole, who came to Kentucky and m first Lucy McCoy (dau William), W 1811. He m second Susan T. Miller about 1823, and went to Daviess, where many of his descendants are now living. b, Thomas (1787-1858), m Elizabeth Swetnam°, Scott 1815, and they had: George Hiram, m Lettie Finch; Elvira; Mary; Elizabeth Edwards°; Thomas J., m Virginia Darnell°; Louisa, m George Diuguid; William Willa, m first Fannie Gaines°, and second Sarah Ellen Coleman°; Sydney, m A. W. Cromwell; Virginia, m Edward Cromwell. Thomas Jett came to Kentucky about 1812, and conducted a school in Georgetown. He settled in 1822 at what is now Jett, where he lived first at "Luckenough," and then at "Arrowhead Farm."

5, Betsy, m —— Snape, and went to North Carolina or Tennessee; 6, Sallie Graves°; 7, Alice Lindsay°; 8, Lucy, m Jonathan Cropper, W 1794. The Coles are long-lived people, but Lucy died early, leaving a daughter who was reared by her sister, Alice Lindsay. Jonathan Cropper m Polly Foster, Scott 1796.

The graves of Richard and Ann Cole and some of their descendants are in the burying ground at "Cole's Tavern."

Jesse Cole m Sally Chinn (dau Ann), Green 1806; William Cole m Martha Bass (dau Joseph), Green 1806.

Swetnam: George Call Swetnam m Mary Sutton°, Albemarle County, Virginia, 1794. They came to Scott, and their children were: 1, Elizabeth Call Jett°; 2, William, m Nancy Pitts°; 3, John, m first Sarah Goff (dau Thomas) Clark 1818, and second Mary Belmear. He went to Howard County, Missouri, 1827, and was the father of twenty-two children. 4, Sidney, m Susan Hardin; 5, George, m Caroline Christian°; 6, Henry Harrison, m Rachel Wilhoit, and lived in Owen; 7, Temperance, m Robert Grimes; 8, Malvina Pitts°; 9, Fannie Pitts°; 10, Patsy Christian°; 11, Cynthia Pitts°; 12, Polly Ann Suggett°; 13, Harriet Shipp°. Many of these families went to Missouri.

COLEMAN—Mrs. Peggy, r 1812

Capt. James Coleman (1750-1825) s Robert Edward and Sally Lightfoot Coleman, m Sarah Taylor° in Orange County, Virginia, 1780, and they came later to Woodford, where they lived at "Stonewall," on the Versailles-Midway road. Their children were: 1, Edward Spillsbee (1786-1860), m Margaret Vaughan Blanton°, and settled at Coleman's Spring in South Frankfort in 1806. They had: a, James Carter, m Ann Eliza Mills (dau Charles and Tabitha Buckner Daniel Mills) Todd 1832, and their dau Sarah Ellen m William Willa Jett°, F 1874, and had: Carter Coleman; Elizabeth; Charles Mills; Ermina (who m W 1910 Dr. Matthew Cotton Darnell, and has Helen; Rev. Jacob; Dr. Matthew; Mills; John Dunlap; and Susan); and Dr. Richard Lawrence. b, Susan, m Thomas Torian, F 1833, and went to Texas; c, Lucretia; d, Richard, m Catherine Samuel°; e, William Burdette, m Jane Gayle° and lived at Minorsville. They were ancestors of Mrs. Alvin Stilz, of Lexington; f, Margaret, m Grandison Owen, and they were the parents of Lee A. Owen, of Jett; g, Sarah Sneed°; h, Edward Chapman, who went to Missouri. One Chapman Coleman m Mary Ann Carter, Lincoln 1838.

2, James, m sisters, Sarah Taylor°, W 1828, and Mary Taylor°, and had: a, Sarah, m William R. Giltner, W 1853; b, Mary (1832?-1892.), m first John I. Finch, W 1852, second Thomas Allen°, third Warren Viley°. James Coleman m third Mrs. Martha (Lawless) Harris, 1836, and their children, who lived near Louisville, were: c, Martha; d, James; e, John, m Amanda Herndon, and was the father of Chapman, of O'Bannon; f, Charles, m Jennie Copp; g, Lucinda, m James C. Herndon, and they were the parents of Miss Henrietta Herndon, of Pleasureville.

3, Ann-Mary Sutton°; 4, Lucinda, m Jeffrey Bondurant, of Oldham, W 1828, and they had: a, Dr. Coleman, m Mary Woolfolk°, b, Joseph. 5, Sarah, m Dr. John James Thomasson (s Poindexter and Sarah Dupuy Thomasson); 6, Chapman, m Ann Mary Crittenden (dau Gov. John J. and Sarah Lee Crittenden), and their children were: a, Florence, m Patrick Joyes; b, Cornelia, m —— Marriott; c, Eugenia; d, Judith, m Charles Adams, and went to California; e, Sallie; f, Gazaway; g, John; h, Chapman, m Jane Hendrick (dau Rev. John R.) of Frankfort. 7, Catherine, m William Woods, W 1815, and they had: Sarah Ann, James Henry, and William Coleman, who went to Missouri.

Thomas Coleman, of Caroline County, Virginia, m Millicent Winn, and they had Mary Sutton°, Caroline Sutton°, Nancy Yates°, and others.

John Winston Coleman (s John and Lucy Chiles Coleman), m Louisa Sutton°, Fayette 1822, and they were the parents of David S., who m Judith A. Chiles (dau John and Mary Brooking Chiles), and had John W., who m Mary Payne and was the father of John Winston Coleman, Jr., of Lexington.

Thomas Coleman, of Orange County, Virginia, m Mrs. Susanna Strother Hawkins°. They came to Woodford and settled near Mortonsville. Their children were: Nancy George; Strother; Susanna Sublette°; John.

Sutton: John Sutton, of Albemarle County, Virginia, who was of Welsh descent, m Temperance Lane, and they came to Scott County, Kentucky, where he died in 1810. Their children were: 1, John (1759-1826), m Mary Coleman°, and they had: a, Col. John, Jr., (1780-1830), who went to Jefferson County, m first Mary Coleman°, W 1807, and they had three children:

Alfred Orville, m Eleanor Root (dau Charles), Jefferson 1836; Ann Mary, m Samuel S. Givens, and went to Union; Sarah Taylor Woolfolk°. Col. John m second Emily Smith (dau William), 1821. b, Millicent, m Joel Crenshaw, Scott 1801, and they had ten children; c, Temperance, m Richard Lightbourne, 1802, and they had a large family, including Richard P., who m his cousin, Sarah Sutton, and was the father of Sarah, m George McCready these being the parents of Dean Richard L. McCready, of Louisville; d, Mary King, m George Jones, Scott 1809, and they had eight children; e, Thomas; f, Dr. William Loftus (1797-1862). Known as the father of the Kentucky State Medical Society, he was its first president, and it was due to his efforts that the law was passed requiring registration of vital statistics. He practiced in Morganfield until 1833, and then in Georgetown. He m first Mary Buck° Catlett (dau George and Letitia Buck Catlett), Union 1820, and they had: Dr. George, m Mary F. Wallace, 1846; Mary Belle Buck° (1823-1907); Dr. John, of Midway, m Mrs. Ellen Lamb Richmond; Thomas. Dr. W. L. Sutton m second Nancy Cooper, 1837, and their children were: Daniel; Dr. William H., who went to Dallas, Texas. Dr. W. L. Sutton m third Mrs. Ann Tibbs Webb, 1843, and they had: Annie, who m Joel C. Tarlton, and was the mother of Mrs. B. M. Goldsborough, of Georgetown; Caroline; Henry Craig, of Webb City, Mo., who m Katherine Brown.

2, Robert (1761?-1828), m Caroline Coleman°, and their children were: a, Mary King Christian°; b, Milly, m first Philip Bradley° (s Robert and Hannah Johnson Bradley), and second Samuel C. Scroggin.

3, Capt. William, m Sarah Pendleton Buckner (dau William and Sallie Thomas Buckner), and they settled near Georgetown. After his death in 1820 she went to Shelbyville. Their children were: a, Demetrius, m Caroline Grant; b, Parmelia; c, Paulina, m first William McMillan, 1817, and second George William Hardin, Scott 1819; d, Pendleton Lane; e, Cordelia, m Benjamin Buckner, 1823; f, Ellen, m her cousin, Alvin Lightbourne, 1846; g, James Monroe, m first Margaret Patterson, 1829, second Mrs. Miller, third Mrs. Holland, fourth Mrs. Marks; h, Sarah, m Richard P. Lightbourne; i, Temperance Reubena, m Thomas B. Caldwell (see Macklin), 1828; j, Williametta, m Henry H. Ready,

Scott 1830; k, Juliet, m Dr. William Morton; l, Unetta, m Walter Carr Chiles, and they were the parents of Mrs. Louisa Thomas, of Frankfort.

4, David (1776-1839), m Juliet May (dau John), Fayette 1803, and they lived in Lexington. They had: a, George Washington (1804-1870), m Laura Grosvenor, from Connecticut, Fayette 1828. They lived between Lexington and Georgetown, and their dau Louisa m the Rev. John N. Norton, who was rector of The Church of the Ascension in Frankfort, 1846-1870, and for whom the Norton Infirmary in Louisville was named. b, Louisa Coleman°. 5, Mary Swetnam°.

Yates (Yeates): Dr. Michael Yates, of Caroline County, Virginia, m Martha Marshall, and many of their descendants came to Kentucky. It is said that there were seven children, but records differ as to their names. A deed, W 1800, mentions as legatees of Michael Yates: 1, William and Sarah Yates. One William (possibly Michael's grandson) was in Scott, 1796-1812; 2, John, m Ann Coleman°, 1785. They remained in Virginia, and some of their children were: a, Michael Warfield; b, Millicent, m Henry Yates; c, John Marshall, m Virginia Christian°, 1818, and went to Randolph County, Missouri. 3, Michael; 4, Patsy, m Richard Johnson, and they were living in Spotsylvania in 1803.

Another son was: 5, Abner, m Ann Hawes (dau Thomas and Elizabeth Fisher Hawes). They came in 1788 to Fayette, where he died in 1791, leaving his wife and: a, Henry, went to Virginia and married his cousin, Millicent Yates, in 1809. They settled in Gallatin County, Kentucky, and among their children was Governor Richard Yates, of Illinois. Henry m second Mary Ann Shroff, 1834 and third, Elizabeth McMillan, 1836. b, Martha Ellis°. 6, Marshall Yates was evidently another son.

Joseph Yates m Mary Thomas, Orange County, Virginia. They went to Maryland, and then to Kentucky, where he died in Scott, 1814. They had eleven children, including: Judge Hiram, who m Margaret Porter, of Woodford, and went to Lewis County, Missouri; John T.; Ann Bond; Sarah; Joseph; Samuel; Franklin.

Sallie Yates m Richard Cole°, Jr.; Dorcas Yates m Garnet Lambert, W 1794; Mary Yates m Joseph Covenhoven, W 1794.

Colquit—Sarah, r 1791

Mrs. Sarah Colquit was the mother of Mrs. Sarah Gibson°. Her first husband was evidently a Samuel, as her will, F 1796, speaks of her son, William Samuel°; her deceased daughter Ann Garnett; her son-in-law John Garnett°; her grandson Waller Garnett; her dau Sally Gibson.

Jonathan Colquit, of Halifax County, Virginia, died 1801, leaving a son Ransom, who m Susanna Baker, 1785. Ransom E. Colquit m Nancy Boggess (dau Joseph), F 1805; Ransom Howly Colquit was on the tax list, F 1805. One Ransom was in Henry 1818, and in Owen 1819.

Cook—Margaret, charter member	Seth, 1
Jesse, 1789	Nicy, 1
Hosea, 1789	Nancy, Sr., 1
Abraham, 1, dis 1798	Nancy, Jr., 1
William, 1	Vine, 1796

Mrs. Margaret Cook came in 1780 with her husband and family from Franklin County, Virginia, to Kentucky, and settled on South Elkhorn on a farm north of Henry Crutcher's and east of Thomas Hicklin's. The father died a few months after their arrival. In one year William Hickman baptized nine of the children.

After the death of Margaret Cook in 1798, many of the family went to Shelby. Her children were: 1, Jesse, m Elizabeth Bohannon°, and they had William and Seth (see Edrington); 2, Hosea, m Elizabeth Edrington°, W 1791, and they had a son, Hosea; 3, Rachel Murphy°; 4, Bathsheba Dunn°; 5, Helin Bohannon°; 6, Rhoda, m —— Jameson; 7, William, m Keturah Crutcher°, F 1798, and they went to Shelby, where he died in 1816; 8, Seth, m Frances Wilkerson, W 1797. His will, Shelby 1840, names his wife and: a, Sarah, m Abram Kesler, Shelby 1815; b, John; c, William. William W. Cooke, of Nashville, m Phoebe Gerrard°, Shelby 1807; William B. Cook m Betsy Sacre (dau Elizabeth), Shelby 1811; William m Hannah Miles° (dau John, Sr.), Shelby 1825. d, Nancy Casler; e, Polly Montfort; f, Malinda Brumley; g, Ann Guthrie°; h, Seth; i, Frances; j, Jesse; k, Jane; l, Daniel; m, Martha.

9, Margaret, m first Lewis Mastin°, and second James Hacket, F 1797; 10, Eunice Miles°; 11, Rev. Abraham (1774-1854), m

Sarah Jones, F 1795, and their dau Elizabeth m John Johnson, F 1824. They went to Shelby, where he was ordained in 1809. After his ordination, he preached at Christianburg and Indian Fork, but would accept no pay for his services. In 1851 he went with his family to Missouri. John Taylor said of him: "This precious servant of the Lord preached with great effect among the people—some souls will remember what he said in this, and the world to come."

William Cook m Polly Cannon, W 1802; Hosea Cook m Elizabeth Livingston°, W 1815. In Shelby, Nise Cook m Hosea Dunn, 1814; Mrs. Betsy Cook m Israel Christie, 1815; Hercules Agee m Rhoda Bohannon, 1821; Hosea Cook m Rhoda Agee (widow Hercules), 1823.

Cosby—William, r 1828

William H. Cosby m Sarah Minter (dau Rev. Joseph and Jane Trabue Minter), W 1810. Their children were: 1, Eliza Jane; 2, Lucy Trabue° (1813-1892); 3, Joseph; 4, Mary; 5, Elizabeth, m Alford Fox Hough; 6, William Henry, m Eliza F. Porter, and lived in Missouri; 7, Sarah Ann.

Elizabeth Cosby m Joseph Minter, W 1811.

Coster—Nicholas, 1802

Cox—Elizabeth, dis 1827   Alfred, 1858

There were several lines of the Cox family in this community. Three families which appear to have been related were those of Capt. John, Benjamin S., and Thomas.

The record of Capt. John Cox (1750-1828), of Brownsville, Pa., states that he m Elizabeth Marlow, of Maryland, 1775. They came to Kentucky and settled on Elkhorn, F 1802. Their children were: 1, Judge William M., who went to Missouri; 2, Benjamin, m Betsy Tate°, F 1805, and their dau Polly m Henry Hockensmith and was the grandmother of Mrs. C. W. Martin, of Franklin County; 3, Thomas; 4, Nancy; 5, Polly; 6, Priscilla, m John Wallace; 7, Letitia, m Aaron Townsend; 8, Elizabeth; 9, Samuel; 10, Rev. Jacob M., who went to Indiana about 1820, m first Araminta Julian Tate°, F 1817, and they had six children. He m second Martha Christian Hudson, of Georgia.

Benjamin Sedwick Cox was born in Maryland, 1748. He m
Gressel Lindsay°. He was in Fayette, 1788, and in 1797 bought
from Joseph and Chloe Fenwick a farm on Main Elkhorn. Their
children were: 1, Benjamin S., m Elizabeth Ann Moss°. They
were in Woodford, 1834, and in 1846 went to Missouri. Their
children were: a, Curran M.; b, George W. L., m Martha Bacon°;
c, Jacob B.; d, Sydney A.; e, John Rowan; f, Margaret, m ——
Grable; g, Mary, m —— Means; h, Elizabeth, m John W.
Moutray, and they were the grandparents of Miss Myrtle
Tennant, of Wellington, Kans. 2, William L., m his cousin,
Mary Jane Lindsay°, F 1807, and they had Trouisant, who went
to Oklahoma; 3, Jacob, m Maria Fenwick (dau Cornelius and
Annie Fenwick), F 1812, and they had: a, Annie Maria; b,
Annie Maria; c, Louis L.; d, Isabella C., m Gen. Sidney Sherman,
F 1835; e, Caroline McLean, m Kosciusko Morgan, 1843, and
they went to Morgan's Point, Texas. They were the parents of
Mrs. H. H. Craig and Mrs. Fanny Allen, of Frankfort. f,
Cornelius, m first, Sallie George, and second, Nellie Stedman; g,
Leonard J., m Sophia Cox Stedman (dau Eben and Mary Ann
Steffee Stedman), and they were the parents of Jacob L. Cox,
of Frankfort; 4, Catherine Craig°; 5, Gressel, m —— Manning,
in Piqua, Ohio. Nancy Cox (dau Benjamin S.), of Fayette,
died 1803, aged twenty years.

Thomas Cox also lived on Elkhorn. He evidently married
first a daughter of Thomas Lloyd°, and had a dau, Martha Lloyd
Cox, who m Robert Bratton, F 1817. Thomas Cox m Ann Janey
Smith (niece of Thomas Lloyd°), W 1793. His heirs, F 1828,
were: 1, Francis; 2, Jacob; 3, Jane; 4, Catherine, m Jesse Hockensmith, F 1831; 5, Emily; 6, Elizabeth, m John Thomas Bratton;
7, Priscilla, m Charles O'Hara (s Kean), F 1814; 8, Etheldra, m
first, William Taylor, F 1817, and second, John Page, F 1822; 9,
Thomas Lee Cox.

Samuel Cox came with his family to Kentucky, and died
before 1795, when his widow, Agnes, and children signed a deed
of emancipation. His heirs, mentioned in a deed, F 1803, in
which they sold their farm to John Major, were: 1, Agnes
Moxley°; 2, Hannah, m James Hampton; 3, Samuel, m Nancy
Woolfolk°, W 1795, and lived in Pendleton County, Kentucky,
for a while, going later to Sangamon County, Illinois; 4, Ann

Cox. Whether this family is identical with a Franklin County family with similar names which is mentioned in the D. A. R. Lineage Book is not known.

Jesse Cox m Jane Roach (dau Simeon and Jane Roach, who went from Culpeper County, Virginia, to South Carolina), and they had: 1, Sophia F. Brown°; 2, Alfred W., m Henrietta C. Scott, W 1852, whose descendants live in Lexington. Mrs. Jane Roach Cox m second Charles C. Black°.

On Cedar Creek was Asa Cox, who had a family of eleven, including Elizabeth Calvert°.

About 1808 Russell and Benjamin Cox and their families located in the part of Franklin that is now Anderson. One record states that they came from Rowan County, North Carolina, and another says they came from Virginia. Also in Franklin were: Ancil, m Polly Buckhannon, W 1816; Tunstall; Nathaniel; Ambrose; Er; and Bradley. In Woodford were: William; John; Thomas; Tench; Peter; Daniel; James.

Another Benjamin Cox, brother of Col. Isaac Cox, of Cox's Station in Nelson, was born in Maryland, 1767. He came to Kentucky and m Sarah Piety (dau Austin and Sarah Polk Piety), and they lived in Shelby. Two of their sons were: 1, John Crittenden, m Eliza Garrett (dau Willis), Shelby 1830, and they were grandparents of Miss Sarah Wallace Smith, of Frankfort; 2, Austin P., who lived in Frankfort, m Rebecca Phillips (see Graham). They were grandparents of Miss Helen Austin Cox, of Wellington, Kans. Col. Isaac Cox was the ancestor of Mrs. Osso W. Stanley, of Frankfort.

Among the many Cox records in Franklin are: Elizabeth (dau Elizabeth), m Graves Hancock°, the bond being signed by Benjamin Cox and Sarah Tate; Elizabeth, m Daniel Oliver°; James, m Sally Esom (dau James), F 1799; Ann, m William Haydon°; Kitty, m Solomon Haydon°; William, m Phoebe Haydon° (dau Webb), F 1808; Jacob, m Sally Thompson, F 1822; Jacob, m Cassandra Talbott, F 1834, the bond signed by James Bratton; Anthony, m Nellie Murphy, F 1818; Francis, m Julian Cox (dau Benjamin), 1827; Francis, m Rebecca Hockensmith (dau Jacob), 1832; Araminta, m Anthony Smither°; Eliza M. (dau Benjamin), m Samuel Luckett, 1827; Mary W. (dau Thomas), m James Bratton, 1829, the bond signed by Jacob Cox;

Priscilla R. (dau Benjamin), m William McKim, F 1831; Samuel, m Margaret Gaines, 1825; Sowell, m Louisa Moxley°, 1817.

In Woodford, James Cox, m Nancy Martin, 1814; James, m Jane Stevenson, 1819; James, m Polly Stevenson, 1825; Timothy, m Elizabeth Owen°, 1824; Thomas, m Matilda Peters (dau James), 1825. Elizabeth Cox was the mother of Harriet H. Davis°.

Black: Charles C. Black went from Madison County, Kentucky, to South Carolina, where he married Mrs. Jane Roach Cox°. They returned to Kentucky about 1821 and settled on North Elkhorn, near Switzer. Their children were: 1, Elizabeth Macklin°; 2, Sarah, m Charles C. LeCompte, F 1853; 3, Stephen, m Lydia Macklin°, F 1864. In 1869 they bought from the Freeman heirs "Silver Lake Farm," which is now the home of their grandson, Charles W. Black.

> CRAIG—Benjamin, r 1789, gone from us 1793
> Nancy, 1789, gone from us
> George, dis 1800
> Agnes, 1848   Mary, 1848

Rev. Toliver Craig (1705-1796), posthumous son of John and Jane Taliaferro Craig, was born in Spotsylvania County, Virginia. He m Mary Hawkins (dau John and Mary Hawkins) and they and several members of their family came to Kentucky with the "Travelling Church" and were in the siege of Bryan's Station. Toliver and his wife came to "Craig's Fort," near Versailles, in 1783. Their children were: 1, Captain John (1730-1815), m Sallie Page. They came also to Woodford, but in 1793 went to that part of Campbell that is now Boone. They had: a, Elijah; b, Benjamin; c, Frank; d, Philip; e, Betsy Johnson°; f, Polly Cave°; g, Sally, m John Bush, W 1792; h, dau m Thomas M. Prentiss; i, John H.; j, Lewis, m Kitty Cox°, and their son, Henry Harrison, was the father-in-law of Mrs. H. H. Craig of Frankfort. 2, Toliver, m Elizabeth Johnson. They were in Woodford in 1790, but went later to Great Crossings in Scott. Their children were: a, Johnson; b, William; c, Toliver, m Patsy Wright; d, Elijah; e, Nathaniel; f, John, m Alice Todd°, Botetourt County, Virginia, 1792; g, Polly, m —— Gholson; h, Nancy, m —— Bell.

3, Rev. Lewis (1737-1825) was twice imprisoned in Virginia for preaching doctrines not in agreement with the Church of England. He was the pastor of the "Travelling Church," and continued the work at South Elkhorn until 1792, when he went to Maysville. In that vicinity he organized other churches, and, "became, in a manner, the father of Bracken Association." John Taylor described him as "a great peace-maker among contending parties, better acquainted with men than books; never dwelt much on doctrine, but mostly on experimental and practical Godliness." His wife was Elizabeth Sanders°, and their children were: a, Frances Childs; b, Polly Thomas; c, Sally Davis; d, Eliza; e, John; f, Whitfield; g, Lewis; h, Elizabeth Bledsoe°; i, Catherine Hawkins King.

4, Elijah, m Frances Smith. He came in 1782 to what is now Woodford, and built a fort five miles from Versailles. He is said to have preached in Frankfort about 1785. He afterward went to Lebanon (now Georgetown) and had charge of an academy. Their children were: a, Lydia, m —— Grant; b, John; c, Simeon; d, Joel; e, Lucy Pitts°; f, Polly. 5, Joyce, m John Faulkner. They were in Fayette in 1788, and were the parents of Martha Stephens°; 6, Jane Sanders°.

7, Elizabeth Cave°. 8, Rev. Joseph (1741-1819) also was imprisoned in Virginia for preaching the Baptist doctrine, but his preaching through the bars of the jail gave him so much publicity that his persecutors thought it best to release him. He m Sallie Wisdom, and they lived in Woodford. Their children were: a, Reuben, m Fanny Twyman° (dau Dudley); b, Jane, m Robin Asher; c, Sally, m —— Allen; d, James, m Sally Mitchum (dau Dudley and Susan Allen Mitchum), W 1798; e, Thomas, m Polly Wisdom; f, Samuel, m Patsy Singleton°; g, Joseph, m Polly Parker; h, Phoebe; i, Elijah W., m Almira Grosvenor, 1821; j, Lucy Dupuy°; k, Elizabeth; l, Polly, m James Mitchum (brother of Sally), Fayette 1808.

9, Benjamin (1751-1822), m Nancy Sturman. As he was one of the men to whom the Mount Pleasant Church lot was deeded, it is possible that he and his wife were members of that congregation after leaving the Forks Church. About 1799 they went to Gallatin, where he laid out the town of Port William (Carrollton). Their children were: a, Joseph; b, Nancy, m John B.

Bernard; c, Elizabeth Bledsoe°; d, Silas, m Paulina Peak°; e, George (m Elizabeth Morton, Clark 1805?); f, Sally Price°; g, Thomas (was he Stuman Craig, who is recorded as marrying Elizabeth Easterday°, Gallatin 1809 or 1819, and Phoebe Easterday, Gallatin 1822?); h, Benjamin, m Elizabeth Morris; i, Levi, m Catherine Craig; j, Polly O'Neal°; k, Lewis, m Milly Smith.

10, Jeremiah, m Lucy Hawkins°, and they probably lived in Woodford. Their children were: a, Elijah; b, Hawkins, m his cousin, Patsy Craig; c, Cerena; d, Lewis.

Ezekiel Craig m Fannie Guthrie°, W 1827.

CRUTCHER–Brother	Eliza, r 1830
Patsy, 1801	Levi, r 1832
Henry, r 1819	John, dis 1842
Susan	Mary Hancock
Reuben	Roberson
Elizabeth, r 1829	Sarah, 1848
Isaac, Jr.	

The name Crutcher (also written Croucher, Croutcher, Critcher) is said to be English, meaning, "Those who live at the Crossroads."

Henry Crutcher (————-1807) of Caroline County, Virginia, bought from Lewis Craig in 1796 a farm south of the Lexington-Leestown road, some of which is still in the possession of his descendants. He m first Susannah ————, and they had: 1, Joanna (1762- ————), m first ———— Sale, and second James Sacra, F 1801. One James Sacra had a family of eleven, F 1810, but Joanna and her husband perhaps went later to Shelby, where there were many intermarriages among the Sacra and Cook families in the next generation. 2, Rev. Isaac (1767-1837), m first Nancy Blanton°, Caroline County, Virginia, 1790, and they had: a, Richard, m first Pamelia Berry°, W 1823, and had: Susan Ann, m James M. Starks; America, m B. F. Starks; Dr. James, m Fannie Foree and went to Henry; Mary; Nancy, m ———— Withers; Martha; Jefferson, m Alpha Herndon; Lewis; Washington, m first Virginia Redd, and they were the parents of Mrs. Thomas Dunlap, of Versailles, and Redd Crutcher, of Lexington; he m second Mary Cardwell; Lafayette, m Anna Graves, and they were the

parents of Mrs. W. G. Simpson, of Frankfort, and Arthur Crutcher, of Woodford.

Richard Crutcher m second Mrs. Elizabeth McKnight, W
1842, and their dau Florence m George T. Cotton. He m third
Mrs. Fannie Mudd. In 1831 he bought from Carter Blanton
the farm on the Jett-Millville road which is now known as the
Redd Crutcher place.

b, Lewis, m Narcissa Deering°; c, Mary Bailey°. Rev. Isaac
m second Fanny Hutchinson, W 1804. He m third Nancy Graddy
(dau Jesse and Viola Dale Graddy), by whom he had: d, Thomas,
m first (Martha Edwards°, W 1834?), and second —— Holt,
and they were the parents of Dallas C. Crutcher, of Frankfort; e, William, m Susan Scearce (dau Henry and America Berry
Scearce), W 1841, and was the father of Dr. W. L. Crutcher, of
Frankfort; f, Jesse Graddy, m Martha Pittman (dau Asa and
Nancy Trabue° Pittman), 1845, and they were the parents of
Richard L. Crutcher, of Frankfort, who m Emma Stephens°,
and was the father of Mrs. Charles Morris, Mrs. Frank Heaton,
and Mrs. George Stone, of Frankfort; g, Sally, m John Weathers,
W 1823; h, Nancy Blackwell°.

Isaac Crutcher lived on a farm adjoining that of Carter Blanton. He was licensed to preach at Mount Gomer (now Mount
Pleasant) in 1796. With Joseph Craig and Robert Asher he constituted Grier's Creek Church some time after 1798, and there
is a tradition that he organized Grassy Spring Church and was
its first pastor. Joseph Craig said of him, "He left behind a
good name."

3, Elizabeth Pemberton°; 4, Keturah (Catherine) Cook°.

Henry Crutcher m second Martha Beasley (dau William and
Ann Jennings? Beasley), of Caroline. Their children were: 5,
Henry, Jr. (1780-1852), m first Susanna Hancock°, W 1802, and
they had: a, Eliza Hancock°; b, Laetitia Hancock°; c, Levi Todd,
m Rebecca Dixon°, and they lived at "Mt. Vernon," which he
bought from Willis Blanton, F 1832. Their children were: John;
Llewellyn; Newland Maffitt, m Mary Ellen Giltner, and they
were the parents of B. Todd Crutcher, of Frankfort; William
Price; Washington T.; Martha; Susan, m William Shryock, and
they were ancestors of Rev. Harry E. Moore, Jr.; d, John, m
Mary French (dau Hiram and Margaret Hardin French), and
they had: Kate, m J. C. Risque and was the mother of Dr.

Clarence Risque, of Shelbyville; Elizabeth; Callie, m George Lockett; e, Thomas m Nancy Wakefield, and went to Shelby; f, Bartlett, m Mary Hancock°, and their children were: Cordie; Younger, m Emma Burke; Garrett, m Mary Blackburn°; Adelia, m —— Cook; Mary Ellen, m Curtis Burke, and went to Mo.; Frank, m —— Bright, went to Shelby; Georgia; g, Harry.

Henry Crutcher, Jr., m second Susan Shipp°, W 1851. They lived near Duckers at the Poynter place, now owned by Quarles Thompson.

6, Reuben (1782-1863) lived in the house now occupied by the Wardle family, just east of Henry Crutcher's old home. He m first Elizabeth Onion°, 1802, and their children were: a, Isaac, m Elizabeth Ramsey°, and they had: Lewis, m Effie Britton, and they were the parents of Mrs. George Glass, of Wilmore; Elizabeth Seay°; b, Eli; c, William; d, James, m Martha Major Thomson°; e, Reuben, m Sallie Craig°, and they went to Warsaw, Ky.; f, Lewis, m —— Craig°; g, Thomas J., m first Mary ,Louise Thomson°, W 1834, and second Zoraida E. Thomson°, W 1838. Their children were: John; George; Mary Louisa; Ann, m Jerry V. Downing, and was the mother of George Crutcher Downing, of Washington, D. C.; Elvira; Thomas; h, Austin Robert, m Susan Hancock, and they lived in the house now occupied by Mrs. John Hogan. Their children were: Reuben; Sally, m Joseph Towles; Sophia, m William Miles; Elizabeth, m —— Goucher; Mary Williams°; Matilda Blackburn°; Laetitia.

Reuben Crutcher m second Sarah Scandland°.

Seay: John Peter Balee, the son of a French nobleman, came to Philadelphia, where in 1772 he m Elizabeth Baker. They came later to what is now Shelby County, Kentucky, and had nine children, including: 1, Elizabeth, who m Leroy Edwards°, and had, besides other children: a, Effie, m William Mount, and they were the foster parents of Elizabeth Redding, who m Dallas Crutcher°; b, Mary, m Fields Britton, Shelby 1834, and they were the parents of Effie Mount Crutcher°; 2, Susan, m Samuel Seay, and they had: a, Joel; b, Benjamin; c, Adam; d, Elizabeth; e, Mary; f, Martha, m Cyrus Pendleton; g, Samuel, m Elizabeth Crutcher°, F 1856, and they were the parents of William Seay, one of the present deacons in the Forks of Elkhorn Church; h, Robert, m Mary Gregg; i, William, m Martha Williams°, F 1854.

CULLENS—Charles, r 1814, dis 1817

One Charles Cullen, who had fifteen children, came from Caroline County, Virginia, to Georgetown. Charles and Eleanor (Peak°?) Cullen, of Scott, sold land to Isaac Wilson, F 1822. James Cullen m Fanny Webster°, W 1812.

CUNNINGHAM—Sally, to Frankfort 1816

John Cunningham m Sally Hickman°, F 1799. In 1800 he bought from Elisha Lindsay the farm at Jett which until recently was owned by the Cromwells. He sold this land to Edmund Vaughan in 1802, and went to Frankfort, where in 1810 he had a family of five.

James Cunningham m Jane Gibson°, F 1799; John Cunningham m Elizabeth Gibson°; Betsy Cunningham m Peter Brown°; Fountain Cunningham m Sally Taylor, F 1824. Rev. R. M. Cunningham, was the father of Arianna Hickman°.

The will of Hugh Cunningham, W 1820, mentions his wife Elizabeth, and sons James, Thomas, and John. Elizabeth Cunningham m Moses Boone°.

CURLEY—Letia Ann, dis 1829

William Curley m Letitia Ann Hathaway°, W 1829.

DANIEL—Mrs., r 1812   Eliza, r 1829, dis 1829
          Jane, to Frankfort 1816
          Permealey, r 1820, dis 1826

John Daniel came from Virginia, and was in what is now Shelby, 1789. His children were: 1, Thomas, m first Mary Sneed°, and they had: a, Pamela Pace° (1799-1878); b, Nicholas M.; c, Polly S. Pace°; d, Rev. Littleton, m Sarah Wilkerson, 1832, and they were ancestors of Mrs. V. E. Richardson, of Mt. Vernon, Ill.; e, Eliza M., m Rev. George Allen, 1834. These families all settled in Illinois. Mary Sneed Daniel died about 1812, and Thomas Daniel m second Nancy Maddox°, 1815, and they had Rev. Thomas M., m Ollie Bondurant.

2, Walker, who laid out the town of Danville; 3, Robert, who m Mary Trigg (widow of Stephen), Lincoln (1783?), and whose will was probated Shelby, 1797; 4, Martin, m Patsy Meriwether (dau Nicholas and Elizabeth Meriwether), Jefferson 1788, and they had: a, Walker, who is thought to have been the one who m Elizabeth Blanton°, F 1827, and they were the parents of Walker, of Shelbyville, who m Mattie Boone Wilson and was the father of William, Carter, Walker, and Mattie Van Dyke; b, Eliza M.; c, Polly; d, Frances; e, Patsy; f, Martin.

5, Samuel Coleman, m Nancy Brackett (dau John and Mary), Jefferson 1798, and their children are listed as: a, John; b, William; c, Walker, m Mary Ann Smith, Ohio County, Kentucky, 1825; d, Elizabeth, m Thomas Lynch (Shelby 1823?); e, Polly; f, George; g, Coleman; h, Brackett; i, Martha, m Nathaniel Thomas, 1833; j, Robert; k, Matilda, m William C. Maddox°, 1835; 1, Ann, m Thomas Smith (1831?); 6, Betsy, m Nicholas Meriwether, Jefferson 1786, and their descendants went to Louisiana and Mississippi; 7, Sukey, m John Morris, Jefferson 1790; 8, Mrs. —— Clark.

William G. Daniel was in Frankfort, 1810, with a family of two. He died in 1813, and his widow, Jane, m James Shannon, F 1817. They owned land on Benson, F 1836.

James Daniel, of Christian, was the father of Polly Blanton°.

Benjamin Daniel (1770-1844) m Margaret Brown°, Caroline County, Virginia, 1790, and they came to Mercer. Their children were: 1, Coleman (1791-1863), who went to Louisville, m Elizabeth Kaye (dau Frederic), Jefferson 1817; 2, Phenton, m Henry Smart, Mercer 1810, and they had: a, James; b, Jane Pattie°; c, Benjamin; d, Bell; e, Martha; 3, Mary Graves°; 4, Owsy or Osway, m Eliza Vaughan°, F 1830, and their children were: a, Mary Phenton, m —— Green°; b, John William, m Mrs. Ann Foree Satterwhite; c, Eunice, m John Butler, of Bridgeport; 5, Mercer, m Affiah M. Brown°, F 1829; 6, William, m Eliza ——, and they went to southwestern Kentucky, where they had three children. One William Daniel m Eliza Sutton, F 1825; 7, Martha Blanton°; 8, Eliza Graves°; 9, John (m Mary Wickersham, Mercer 1834?).

Reuben Daniel (1773-1857), s Jacob and Mary Daniel, was born in Caroline County, Virginia, and was buried in the Grassy Spring churchyard. One Reuben m Ebby Kirkpatrick, Jefferson 1801. Sally Daniel m Joseph Pitts°.

Pace: John Pace had a family of five, W 1810, and Joel Pace had ten. Joel moved to Jefferson County, Illinois, some time before 1819. His son, Joel, Jr., m Pamela Daniel°, 1822, and they also went to Illinois. Their children were: a, Mary Eliza, m Warren McCreery; b, Charles, m Susan A. Taylor; c, Letitia, m J. P. Haynes; d, Williamson; e, Edward, m Mary Woodin; f, Newton Carter, m Anna Bogan; g, Isabella F., m Charles W. Povey; h, Addison. Joseph Pace (twin of Joel, Jr.) m Mary Daniel°, 1827, and their children were: a, Susan, m George Dillingham; b, Pamelia, m James Dillingham; c, Elizabeth, m J. B. Allen; d, Thompson, m Mrs. Herons; e, Dr. Thomas; f, Mary Ann.

James Atwood m Polly Pace, W 1809; Nathaniel Goodrich m Martha Pace, W 1816; William Jackson° m Letitia Pace.

DARE—O., dis 1801

DARK—James, dis 1842
        Wife, dis 1842   Lucinda, dis 1842
The record states that James Dark died 1871.

Jane Dark was in Fayette, 1790. William Dark m Susan Trumbo (dau Caty), Bourbon 1832.

DART (or Hart)—James, 1

DAVENPORT—William, r 1819

Jonas Davenport (———-1802), of Jessamine, m Alice Redd (dau Mordecai and Agatha Minor Redd), W 1791. They had these children: 1, Samuel; 2, Polly; 3, Nancy; 4, Elizabeth; 5, Lucy Major°; 6, Rev. William (1801-1852), m Eliza A. Major°, Christian 1819, and their children were: William, Chastain, Benjamin, Jackson. As Rev. William's parents died when he was very young, he made his home with his aunt, Mrs. Williams, of Scott County. After his marriage he lived in Fayette until 1825, and then removed to Christian, and while there was converted to the teaching of Campbell, and became a minister in the Christian Church. In 1835 he and his family, in company with his wife's relatives, removed to Woodford County, Illinois, where they established Walnut Grove Academy, reorganizing it in 1855 as Eureka College. He died in Nebraska City, Nebr.

Fortunatus Davenport m Mary (Nancy?) Williams°, W 1811; Charles M. Davenport m Mary Harrison, Jessamine 1821. Powhatan Davenport was in Woodford, 1822.

Davis—James, 1, r 1799, dis 1802   Wood
    Frances, 1, dis 1802   Margaret, dis 1840

James Davis is said to have lived at "Valley Farm," which he bought from Jesse Brown in 1803. He was in F, 1796, and in 1801 owned land in both Scott and Shelby. In 1810 he had five in his family, but the only known descendants were Lutie Davis, who m Samuel Parrish, and their dau Anna May. One Lee Davis is said to have had a health resort at "Valley Farm." James Davis's estate was settled by Thomas Davis, F 1820. Joseph H. Davis and his wife, Harriet R., sold land to Joel Scott in 1831 and 1837, and they, with Thomas and Elizabeth Davis, of Virginia, sold to Nancy Bryan, F 1835. Joseph H. Davis m Harriet Cox°, W 1821.

Capt. Samuel Davis (1758-1806), who was in F 1796, bought from John and Chinoe Smith, W 1802, a farm on the Leestown road which probably was what is now known as the old Freeman place. He was buried in the old Forks churchyard. Nothing is known of his family except that it evidently was his widow or his daughter, Sarah, who m James H. Martain, Sr.°, and inherited this farm. She afterward married John P. Porter°.

John Wood Davis was on Elkhorn in Scott, 1795-1801, and John W. Davis was in Woodford, 1802. Also in Woodford were Richard, Henry, and Patrick, on Elkhorn 1799; Thomas on Clear Creek; John on Dry Run; William on Elkhorn; Solomon and Elijah on Glen's Creek, 1800.

Eli (Elijah?) Davis m Tabitha Elizabeth Jones°, W 1795; Handy T. Davis m Ann Whittington°, W 1827, and they went to Indiana. William Davis m Henrietta Nall°, W 1822.

Thomas W. Davis lived on Cole's Road at "Pine Grove," now known as the Slack place, which had rooms for slaves in the basement. He m first Jane Kinkead (dau John and Margaret Kinkead), W 1795, and they were the parents of: 1, Preston, m Amanda Caroline ————, and they went to Davidson County, Tennessee. He m second Sarah Lee (dau Henry and Frances Lee, of the vicinity of Leesburg, and granddaughter of Hancock and Mary Willis Lee, of Virginia), W 1803. Their children were: 2, Hancock W., m Margaret Kinkead, W 1832; 3, Sanford (I. or J.), m Lucy ———— (see Elliott), and went to Fayette; 4, John H.; 5, Jeptha D., m Margaret ———— (whose mother probably was Mrs. Martha Elliott° Moore Guthrie), and they lived in Scott.

Thomas W. Davis died W 1830, and his heirs sold the property to D. C. Humphreys in 1851-1859.

DEERING—Simeon, r 1814, dis 1817
Barbara, r 1814, dis 1817

Robert Deering m Agatha Twyman°, and they came from Albemarle County, Virginia, to Franklin County, Kentucky. They settled on Benson, but the family went later to Barren. One Robert Deering was killed by falling from a horse, F 1822. The records indicate that some of their children were: 1, Walker (———-1844), m Sallie A. McClelland (dau Henry and Betsy Mc-Clelland), F 1801, and for several years they lived on Elkhorn, and later in Frankfort, where he made plows. He finally settled on the Frankfort-Versailles road in Woodford, where he built the brick house that was for many years the home of the Morris family, but is now owned by the Kings. The census lists him as living in Frankfort in 1810 with a family of ten, of whom some were: a, Narcissa Crutcher°; b, John Granville, m Susan Brassfield, W 1836, and they went to Missouri; c, Emily, m Henry Hardie, W 1830; d, Isyphena Morris°.

2, Simeon m Barbara Caplinger (dau Jacob), W 1798. They lived south of the river in Franklin County for some time, but were in Scott, 1820. They were the parents of Elizabeth Edrington°; 3, Nancy, m George Eaton, F 1803; 4, Mary, m John Younger, 1796; 5, Susanna, m first ——— Foster, and second Waffer Payne, 1796; 6, Betsy, m Jacob Caplinger, F 1809.

Betsy Deering m John Hendricks°; Barnaby Worland m Catherine Deering, W 1828; Catherine Samuel° m ——— Deering; Twyman Deering m Milly Crenshaw, Barren 1808; John W. Deering m Ann Dimick, Scott 1835.

Morris: John Risk Morris (1798-1876) m Isyphena Deering, 1823. They lived at the Deering homestead in Woodford, and three of their sons were: John, m Cordelia Sargent°; James, m Mary L. Deering; and Edwin, m Edmonia Stephens°, and they were the parents of Judge Leslie W. Morris, of Frankfort.

William Morris (———-1829) and his wife Sally lived in Woodford near Fort Spring, having in 1810 a family of eleven. Some of their children were: 1, William Mason (1799-1883), who lived near Mortonsville, m first Pamela Walker (dau William and

Rosanna Darnell Walker), W 1820, and they had: a, Mariam Jane, m William G. Collins. William Mason m second Priscilla Collins Lancaster, and they had: b, Lewis William; c, Samuel; d, John; e, James; f, Mary Hester; g, Antoinette, m G. W. Dixon, and their daughter Daisy m —— Middleton; h, Fanny, m I. Newton Gray, and their daughter Fanny m A. M. Sublette; i, Bettie, m Price Hawkins, W 1853; j, Julia. 2, James, who lived near Stamping Ground, m Winneford Harbour, and their son William Overton m Mary Catherine Hendricks°, and was the father of Mrs. Eugene Wolfe, of Frankfort; 3, Thornton, who lived first in Frankfort and then in Henry; 4, Elizabeth, m Elijah Eaton, W 1822, and they were the parents of Mason and Betty. Several members of this family went to Henry.

Another John Morris (s William Morris of Virginia) m Ann Innes (dau Harry and Elizabeth Calloway Innes), F 1802, and they had eleven children, of whom one was Charles, m Kitty Blanton°, and they were the parents of Miss Virginia McF. Morris, of Frankfort.

DENNEY—Jane, dis 1817

Fielding Denney m Jane Hicklin°, F 1816.

Aaron Denney was in Woodford in 1790; Simon was in Scott, 1795-1797, and Lewis and Fielding in Scott, 1800.

DENT—Peter, 1, dis 1791   Mary, 1, dis 1791

Some of the Dent family came from Maryland. John Dent m Ann Lynn, who after his death m James Finnie, of Spotsylvania County, Virginia.

Rhoda Dent m first Eli Chinn, and second Capt. John Metcalfe, of Fauquier County, Virginia, and was the mother of Governor Thomas Metcalfe.

DILLON—James T., r 1841   Ann

James Dillon, of Irish descent, m Ann Bibb Thomson°, and they lived at the place adjoining the old Harmony Church which is now owned by Newton Williams. A family record says they had six daughters: 1, Elvira; 2, Eveline; 3, Ann; 4, Melita, m John Hardwick and had two sons; 5, Elizabeth, m Marion Jackson and had a dau Melcina who m —— Christopher; 6, Cordelia, m Major Bluett and had Edward, Charles, Melita, Mary,

and Ann. After his wife's death James Dillon and his daughters
went to Missouri.

Harriet Dillon (dau James) m William C. Johnson, F 1818.
Franklin Dillon, s James and Phoebe Dillon, was born in Virginia and died F 1860, aged fifty-two.

DIXON—Sarah, 1848

John Dixon m Sarah McCracken°, 1790, and they lived near
Switzer. Their children were: 1, Matilda; 2, Sophia Hancock°;
3, Sarah Yancey°; 4, Cyrus, m Mary Hair (dau Nathan), Owen
1827, and they lived at "Mt. Lebanon," the Brightwell place,
and had a son, William, and two daughters; 5, Ann; 6, Rebecca
Crutcher°; 7, Merit, m Lovey Williams°, W 1829; 8. Elizabeth
Williams°; 9, Mary, m Martin Bates; 10, Willis, m Sallie
Williams°. James Dixon m Nancy Morton, W 1814.

McCracken: One record says that Ovid, Seneca, Isaac, William, Cyrus, and Elizabeth McCracken were born in Ireland and
came to America before the Revolution. Other records say that
Ovid went to Indiana, Isaac and William were killed at Blue
Licks, and that Seneca lived in Maryland, and that his son Cyrus
came with his family to Kentucky, but was killed by the Piqua
Indians in 1782, while serving under George Rogers Clark.

The children of Cyrus McCracken were: 1, Capt. Virgil, of
Woodford, who died 1813, leaving his wife Martha and: a, Sally;
b, Polly; c, Martha (Williams°?); d, Cyrus, d W 1829; e, George,
d W 1830; f, Virgil. 2, Ovid, at Glen's Creek Church, 1805. One
Ovid, who may have died in Meade before 1832, m Susan Garnett°, W 1818; 3, Seneca (1757-1829), who is said to have explored Kentucky in 1775, but returned to Maryland for the Revolution. One record says he brought his family to Kentucky in
1783, and another says 1793. He settled on what is now known
as the Baker farm, at the Forks of Elkhorn. He m first Margaret
Williams°, probably in Virginia, and they had: a, William; b,
Sarah Shipp° (1780-1854), who was born in Virginia. Seneca
m second Rebecca Reynolds, and their children were: c, Otho
(1790-1878) m first Jane Bell, F 1832, and second Sallie Wilson,
in Missouri, 1843; d, Osborne, m first Monomia Carter, F 1819,
and second Sally Porter°, W 1829. They went to Missouri, and
their children were Jane, William, Laura, and Samuel Porter;

e, Mary, m first Charles Stewart° (s John Stewart, who came from Virginia to Henry), F 1821, and second Greenberry Simpson, Henry 1843; f, Elizabeth, m Capt. John Hamilton, F 1816, and they went to Missouri. They were ancestors of Mrs. W. W. Hunter, of Coshocton, Ohio; g, Margaret, m Asa Scott, F 1827. The family burying ground at the Forks of Elkhorn contains the graves of Seneca and his second wife, and also those of Nancy and Merit McCracken, who probably were Seneca's children.

4, Cyrus, who had a sawmill on Glen's Creek. His will, W 1795, mentions his wife Elizabeth and: a, Ovid; b, Virgil; c, Cyrus; d, Ruth, m Owen Powell, W 1800; e, Sally West°; f, adopted John Shepherd°; 5, Sarah Dixon° (1774—).

Virgil McCracken m Sallie Caldwell (dau Henry), W 1800; Virgil m Martha Irwin, Fayette 1811; one Virgil m Ophelia Bohannon°; William m Jiney Ellis°, W 1800; Cyrus m Catherine Allen, Fayette 1815.

Dowden—Susannah, 1

The Dowden family came from Maryland. Sarah Dowden was in Bourbon, 1787.

Susanna Dowden m John C. Lindsay°. Rebecca Dowden (dau Nathaniel and Susanna) m John Quisenberry°. One Nathaniel Dowden was in Woodford, 1791.

Thomas Dowden m Elizabeth Darnell°, W 1819. They lived near Mt. Vernon Church in Woodford, and were the parents of: 1, Elizabeth, m Madison Vaughn, and their son, Darnall Dowden, of Bagdad, Ky., m Ambie Grey, and the father of Mrs. Everett Caldwell, of Catlettsburg, Ky., and Erle C. Vaughn, of Lexington; 2, Jane, m —— Watts; 3, Columbia, m Silas Mahuron; 4, Rev. Darnell, m —— Snider, and they were the parents of six children. He was licensed to preach in 1841. He went to Leitchfield, and later to Breckinridge and Meade counties. Spencer says: "He was a preacher of excellent acquirements and a high order of talent, and a writer of considerable ability." 5, Clementius; 6, Edmonia, m —— Shelburn.

Michael Dowden m Catherine Stucker (dau Margaret Miles), W 1789; Catherine Dowden m George Groves, W 1791; Willis Dowden m Paulina Mitchell, W 1835.

One Nathaniel Dowden was in Mercer, 1794-1799. The will of Nathaniel Dowden, Shelby 1846, names his wife Agnes and children: James, John, Nathaniel, George, Ashford, Joshua, Willis, Elizabeth, Nancy Knight, Susan Ransdal, Mary Freeman, Mahala Underwood.

Darnell (Darnall, Darneal, Darneille): Joseph and Dr. Aaron Darnell, who were second or third cousins, came from Fauquier County, Virginia, to Woodford.

Joseph (s Jeremiah and Katherine Holtzclaw Darnell) m Jane Ashby (dau Capt. Jack and Jane Combs Ashby), and they lived at "Bosque Bonita" on the Versailles-Midway road. Their children were: 1, Jacob, m Pattie Shrewsbury, 1814, and it was some of their children who began using the form "Darneal" as their surname. They were the parents of: a, Martha, m William Shrewsbury, W 1832; b, Mary Jane, m Joseph A. Peters, W 1836; c, John S.; d, Julia, m Marshall Hurst; e, Elizabeth; f, Josephine; g, Jonathan Swift, m Catherine Hunter°; h, William Pitt, m Ann Richards; i, DeWitt Clinton; j, Edward, went to California; k, Joseph Morgan, went to California; l, Samuel S.

2, Edward, m Phoebe Dale, W 1817; 3, Lewis, m Elizabeth ——; 4, Jeremiah; 5, Betsy Dowden°; 6, Lucy, m Shelby Prewitt, W 1823; 7, Catherine, m Joseph Cross, W 1805; 8, Dolly Owen°; 9, Rosannah, m William Walker (see Morris), W 1803; 10, John.

Dr. Aaron Darnell (1761-1816) was in Lincoln, 1789, and in Woodford, 1791. He m Jane Railey (dau John and Elizabeth Randolph Railey), W 1797, the bond being signed by her brothers, Thomas and Randolph Railey. They lived first on Griers Creek and then on Glen's Creek. Their children were: 1, Elizabeth Pope, m Aaron Mershon, W 1820; 2, Randolph Railey, m Attalanta Whittington°, W 1827, and they had: a, Aaron, m first Catherine Hawkins°, 1828, and second Sarah E. Pepper (dau Samuel and Mahala Perry Pepper); b, William, m first Sarah Taylor°, and they were the parents of James S. Darnell, of Frankfort; he m second Mrs. Eleanor Taylor° (dau Burket and Ellen Nall Yancey, and widow of Frank Taylor); m third Bettie Swindler; c, John Railey Long, m Susan Frances Cotton (see Sublette), W 1858, and they had a large family, including D. Cotton Darnell, of Duckers, and Dr. M. C. Darnell, of Frankfort; d, Southy, m Sarah Webb, and they were parents of Miss Vassie Darnell, of Chicago; e, Virginia Jett°; f, Attalanta Edwards°; g, Charles Randolph, m first Bertha Railey (dau Richard H. and Katherine Hawkins Railey); he m second Margaret Holloway; m third Sallie Huckaby.

3, Virginia, m John A. Markley, W 1831, and they were grandparents of Mrs. Ferdie B. Ireland, of Madison, Ind.

DUCKER—William, r 1828, dis 1833
Mary, dis 1833

William Ducker was in Frankfort, 1810, with two in his family. He m Mary Johnston, F 1815. They bought land from Capt. James Porter in 1820, and probably built the old log house which until recent years stood east of the depot at Duckers. In 1832 they sold their property to the Lexington and Ohio Railroad Company. They were mentioned as heirs of Henry Johnson, of Scott, in 1834.

Enoch Ducker (1789-1871) was born in Pendleton. He came to Versailles and m first Nancy Clayton, W 1819, and second Mrs. Mary Craig (wid William M.), W 1846 or 1848. Nathaniel Ducker, who also came from Pendleton, was in Shelby, 1811. Nancy Ducker (dau Nathaniel) m Abraham Ducker, F 1815. Ephraim was in Franklin, 1801; James in Shelby, 1803; John in Campbell, 1832.

DUN (Dunn)—Barsheba (Bathsheba), 1, dis 1802
Lewis, r 1820   Wife, r 1820

William Dunn was in Woodford, 1791. His wife was Bathsheba Cook, and their dau Molly m John Roberts°. The family probably went to Shelby, where Hosea Dunn m Nise (Eunice) Cook, 1814.

EASTERDAY (Yesterday)—Susanna, 1, dis 1809
Louis and Wife, r 1820

The name *Easterday* was usually pronounced *Yesterday*.

Christian Yesterday, Sr., Christian, Jr., and Martin were in Frederick County, Maryland, 1778.

Lewis (Ludwig) and Daniel Easterday were on the tax list, W 1794. Lewis m Susanna Martin°, W 1791, the marriage being witnessed by Rich Booler (Boulware?). They began their married life on the farm southeast of the station at Jett, originally known as "Luckenough," but now marked "Winding Way." They went to Gallatin in 1809, but returned in 1820, and sold "Luckenough" in 1822 to Thomas Jett.

The records indicate that they had these children: 1, Elizabeth Craig°; 2, Thomas, m Paulina Baker, Gallatin 1816, and they had: Telitha, Sophia, Lewis, James C., Theodosia, Abraham; 3, Lewis, m Lydia Bledsoe°, Gallatin 1816, and they had; Florence, Thomas, Susan; 4, Jane, m first William E. Davies, Gallatin 1820, and second ——— Searcy; 5, Susanna Montgomery°. Others who may have been their children were Phoebe Craig° and Francis Easterday, m Sarah Davis, Carroll 1842, and they had James, Sarah, and perhaps others.

Thomas Easterday m Susanna Farris (dau Isaac), Carroll 1849. One Thomas was a doctor.

EDDINS—Joseph, r 1812, dis 1818
Nancy, r 1812, dis 1818

Joseph, Nancy, and Milly Eddins were charter members of Mt. Vernon Baptist Church, in Woodford, which was organized about 1820. Three daughters of Joseph Eddins were: 1, Peggy Triplett°; 2, Kitty Williams°; 3, Sally, m Christopher Stratton, W 1818. Emily Eddins, who may have been a daughter, m Alexander Hufman, W 1824.

Charles Eddins, who came from Virginia to Woodford, was the grandfather of William Eddins of Frankfort. One Charles Eddins m Mary Hunter, Owen 1848. William Ethington m Sarah Ann Eddins (dau Benjamin), W 1834.

EDRINGTON—John, 1789   Joseph, 1801, dis 1817
Margaret, 1   Elizabeth, 1801, dis 1817
Benjamin, r 1801, to Frankfort 1816
Lettice, r 1801, to Frankfort 1816
Polly, 1801   Lucretia, 1829

John Edrington came with his family from Virginia, and in 1791 bought land on Dry Run from John H. Craig. His farm adjoined those of Carter Blanton and Benjamin Garnett. He died F 1808, and the records indicate that he and his wife Margaret were the parents of: 1, Jane; 2, Polly; 3, John, m Loveday Jackson°, W ——, and they went to Henry; 4, Joseph, m Mrs. Elizabeth Bohannon Cook°, W 1793, and had a family of eleven, W 1810. Some of their children were: a, John Price, m Sarah Beeler; b, Joseph C.; c, Elbridge G.; d, Capt. H. S.; e, Benjamin F., m Ann Milburn; f, Rebecca Taylor°. They lived at the "Mack Shaw place" between Jett and Millville, but in 1820 they sold it to Isaac Crutcher and went to Hickman, Ky.

5, Benjamin, m first Lettice Hickman°, W 1792, and they had a family of seven, F 1810, including John, m Sarah Thornton Yancey°, W 1812, and Sarah Sheets°. Benjamin m second Mrs. Mary Hall Jackson°, F 1817, and third Elizabeth C. Alsop (see Bartlett), F 1830; 6, Rebecca Settle°; 7, Nancy Clift°; 8, Elizabeth Cook°.

Thomas Edrington m Elizabeth Deering°, F 1814; Fidelia Edrington m James Ellis°. In Woodford, Fielding m Elizabeth Williams, 1810; Price m Ellen Livingston°, 1815; John M. m Lucy B. Johnson, 1829. Benjamin and William were in Mercer, 1796.

EDSON—see Eidson

EDWARDS—Haden, 1800   John, 2
                Susannah, 2, dis 1818

Haden Edwards, grandson of Haden and Penelope Sanford Edwards, of Bourbon, and son of John and Susanna Wroe Edwards, m Susanna Beall°. He bought from Benjamin Craig in 1796 land on the north fork of Elkhorn a mile above the Forks, and in 1800 he sold to William Hubbell a tract "beginning at the butment of Haden Edwards' mill dam, northwest to Nathaniel Sanders." He went to South Carolina before 1809, when he sold to Ezra Richmond a tract beginning at the mouth of Dry Run and continuing up South Elkhorn. In 1810 he was in Georgia, and several years later was in Frederick County, Virginia.

John and Susan Edwards, of Bourbon, sold land near James Haydon to Asa Beall, F 1801. This family came from Stafford County, Virginia.

Uriah Edwards, of Spotsylvania County, Virginia, m Mildred Head (dau Henry and Frances). He died in 1781, and in 1789 his widow was in Kentucky with her children: 1, John (m first Dorothy Gatewood, dau Henry and Mary?) was living on Elkhorn, F 1795, but settled later near McCracken's mill in Woodford. A family record says this John was the son of John Edwards who came from Wales to Virginia, but Uriah Edwards had a son John, and he came to Kentucky with the family.

John's will, W 1814, mentions his wife Nancy and: a, Rev. John, m Narcissa Shipp°, 1802. He went to Christianburg, Ky., in 1803, but in 1809 returned to Woodford and preached at Hillsboro and Glen's Creek and Big Spring until 1826, when he went to Missouri. In 1810 he had a family of six, including a son Wiley; b, Fielding, m Jane Wright, W 1822, and they were the parents of Davis, who m first Amanda Latta, F 1854, and second Ann Mary Mastin (dau John Gilbert and Jane Miller Mastin°), 1863. William H. Edwards and others, of Woodford, are children of the last marriage; c, Benjamin, who died W 1814, leaving his wife Lucy, and: Benjamin, John, Nancy; d, Uriah, died before 1814, leaving sons Fielding and Benjamin. e, Wiley (1787-1847), m Nancy Sullenger°, W 1811, and they had: Affiah; John; Frances (m first Hiram F. Beasley, W 1833. They went to Newcastle and their dau Affiah, m Judge Pryor. Frances m second Caleb Matthews); Thomas S., m first Susan Hawkins° (dau William S. and Katherine Keith Hawkins), W 1840, and second Eliza Hawkins (dau William, Jr., and Elizabeth Sublett Hawkins); George (m Elizabeth Jett°, 1843, and they lived for many years at the Thomas Blanton place near Grassy Spring now owned by W. E. Bradley. They had a large family, including Miss Mary Edwards, of Versailles, and Thomas W., m Attalanta Darnell°, and went to Texas); Ann (m a relative, Thos. Jefferson Ford of Newcastle, W 1845); Henrietta (m John Connell, and they were the parents of Edgar, m Nannie Ferguson); Amanda Anderson°; Waller; William (m Mary Ferguson°, and they were the parents of Van H. and others). f, Lewis; g, Moses; h, Mildred; i, Polly Brydon°; j, Elizabeth (m Leonard Brasfield, W 1823?); k, Nancy.

2, Uriah, who in 1795 bought from Lewis Craig a farm on Elkhorn a mile above the Forks. Uriah and wife Elizabeth sold to William Gaines, F 1799, land that formerly belonged to John Edwards. He had a family of seven, F 1810, but evidently went with his family to Henry about 1815. The records indicate that he was the father of: a, John (m Polly Martin, dau Elizabeth, F 1798?); b, Uriah. One Uriah m Sally Underwood, F 1807, and Uriah m Mrs. Nancy Church, F 1808; c, Bennett (1783-1852), m his cousin, Margaret N. Edwards (dau Benjamin), F 1812, and they had Elizabeth Moss° and Ninian, m Ellen Edwards, F 1838. One Bennett Edwards m Mrs. Eliza Owen° Adams, F 1827; d, Elizabeth, m first Wm. Marshall°, and she m second George Ward; e, Fielding; f, William, m Elizabeth Marshall°, Henry 1818; g, Moses.

3, Rebecca, m Reuben Hawkins°; 4, Elizabeth, m Elisha Hawkins°; 5, Benjamin, m Elizabeth Pemberton° and settled on Benson. He died F 1846, leaving his wife and: a, Charlotte; b, Mary Heaton; c, John; d, Rebecca; e, Elizabeth Hickman°; f, Bennett; g, Janette, m Morgan Jenkins, F 1834; h, Margaret's heirs. 6, Moses, m Lucinda Berry (dau Henry), W 1798. They appear to have lived in Franklin, then in Woodford, where in 1810 he had a family of eight, then back to South Benson in Franklin. Their dau Lucinda, m Beckwith Baker, F 1818. 7, Milley; 8, Mary.

Simeon Edwards, said to have come from North Carolina, m Mary Edwards, W 1792, and in 1806 was living near what was later known as the John Morris farm on the Frankfort-Versailles road. Joseph Edwards had a large family on Clear Creek.

Listed as infants of William Edwards, W 1793, were Cornelius (m Polly Williams°, W 1803?), and James (m Nancy Searcy, W 1801?). The will of one James, W 1839, mentions his family: 1, Nancy, m Oscar Pepper, W 1845; 2, Cornelius; 3, James, m Mrs. Susan Perry (see Brown), W 1829; 4, Thomas, m Nancy Hiter, W 1834; 5, Mary Whittington°; 6, Martha Crutcher°; 7, Lucy, m David Paxton, W 1818; 8, Marilla Hale; 9, Martin, m Mary Y. Hiter, W 1839.

Robert Stubs m Sarah Edwards, W 1791; Presley N. Edwards m Naomi Darneal, W 1842. James S. Edwards (s Isaac) m Mrs. Hannah Stout°, F 1809.

EIDSON (Eadson, Edson)—John, 1803
Betsy, dis 1818

George Eidson was in Clark, 1796. John was in Franklin, 1810, with a family of eight. The will of James Eadson, F 1807, mentions his sister Nancy and his niece, Lucy Kelly. It is witnessed by Sucky Hambelton, Mary Martain, and Landon Sneed. The settlement of the estate of Edward Edson, F 1807, indicates that his children were: Sarah, Nancy, John, James, Blanton.

Nancy Eidson m Dr. Landon Sneed°; John m Betsy Haydon°, F 1805, and went to Henry.

ELAM—Elizabeth, 1789

Mrs. Elizabeth Elam m Francis Hall, Shelby 1797.

Richard Elam (orphan of William) was bound to Daniel James, W 1790. The will of John Elam, W 1794, names his sister, Anne Brown, and his nephews, William and Daniel Brown. Benjamin Elam had a family of eleven, W 1810. One Benjamin was in Franklin, 1817. Thomas Elam m Mary Ann Furr (dau Arlimacia), W 1826.

One John was in F, 1795-1808. John F. m Harriet S. Farmer°, F 1830.

ELLIS—Delila, r 1828

The Ellis family came to Kentucky with the Travelling Church. Capt. William Ellis, Jr., whose ancestors came from England to Spotsylvania, was the military leader of the caravan. He m Elizabeth Shipp° in 1786, and died in 1800. Hezekiah Ellis, who was also of this family, was imprisoned in the Fredericksburg jail in 1775 for publicly denouncing British tyranny.

William and Eleazer Ellis were in F, 1795. One William m Nancy Foster°, the bond signed by Thomas Foster, Bourbon 1816. They came to Franklin, and are said to have lived on the old Frankfort-Versailles road at what is known as the Harry Shaw place, now owned by Green Lyon. In his will, F 1850, he mentions his wife Nancy, a brother James, and a nephew Benjamin Ellis. One James m Fidelia Edrington°, F 1822. Elizabeth Ellis, in her will, F 1833, mentions her son Benjamin and other children.

Eleazer, father of Nancy Rowlett°, had a family of nine, F 1810, and Jacob had three. One Eleazer m Isabella Hale, Owen 1822. Jesse, who m Diana Sheets°, F 1796, had a family of seven, but went later to Owen. Israel m Nancy Hall°, F 1807, and in 1810 was in Frankfort with a family of three. One

Israel m Polly Hardin, Owen 1826. William m Elizabeth Taylor, F 18 ?.

In W 1810 were Jesse, Sr., on Glen's Creek with four, Leonard with ten, and Jesse, Jr., with three. In 1792 Hetty (dau Jesse, Sr.,) m Hugh Ferguson°, and Sally m Joseph Hunter. In 1796 Jonathan m Betsy Shepherd, and Nancy m William Shepherd. William, Sr., on Glen's Creek, was the father of Jiney McCracken°. Jesse m Esther Alexander, 1804; Hezekiah m Sarah Hurst, 1812.

Henry Ellis m Martha Yates°, Gallatin 1809, and they went to Sangamon County, Illinois.

ESSEX—Thomas, 1788, long absent in 1792

One Thomas Essex m Anne Essex (dau Dr. Essex, of Tennessee), Fayette 1817. Thomas m Carsiah Edelin, Hardin 1818 or 1819.

EWELL—Betsey, 1812, dis 1819-(r 1825?)
Priscilla, 1812, dis 1819

Elizabeth Hale (dau George and Sarah Smith Hale°) m —— Ewell. Solomon Ewell (s Elizabeth) was bound to Allen McCurdy, F 1813, and in the same year his brother Charles was bound to Edmund Bacon. Jesse Ewell m Elizabeth Ewell (dau Elizabeth), W 1819. The will of Elizabeth Ewell, Shelby 1859, names her dau Ophelia, wife of William F. Caplinger.

Sally Ewell m John Bartlett°, the bond being signed by Marquis Calmes. William Ewell m Sytha C. Baker, Clark 1818, the bond signed by George Calmes (see Hathaway).

EWING—Baker, 1804   Lettice, 1801

Two brothers, Charles and Robert Ewing, came from Londonderry, Ireland, to Bedford County, Virginia, about 1745, and married daughters of Rev. Caleb Baker.

Charles m Martha Baker, and several of their children came to Kentucky. They had: 1, William; 2, Robert; 3, Samuel, whose will, Scott 1808, names his wife Ellinor and children: a, Martha Murray; b, John; c, Joseph, died Scott 1840, leaving wife Polly and children, Martha Moody, Rebecca Ewing, Hetty Johnson, Darkus Rush, Priscilla Offutt, Nancy Ward, Joseph M., and

Alexander; d, William; e, Robert; f, James; g, Samuel; 4, George; 5, David; 6, Caleb; 7, Charles, whose son, Mitchell, m ——— Davis, and was the father of Elizabeth Gano°; 8, Mary; 9, Martha (m Charles Crawford, 1783?).

Robert m Mary Baker, and their children were: 1, Col. Baker (1750-1808), m Letitia Warren (dau William and Ann Wilcox Warren, and granddaughter of John and Lettice Sorrell Wilcox— see Buck), Lincoln 1784. About 1795 they came to Frankfort, where they lived for several years, but in 1805 he was living in Gallatin. One account says he died at his home in Franklin County, but another states that he started for New Orleans on a raft of lumber, and was never heard of again. His estate was settled, F 1818.

Baker and Letitia had: a, Ann Wilcox, m William Fauntleroy, F 1800, and they went to Gallatin; b, Dr. Robert M., who lived in Georgetown and was one of the founders of Georgetown College, m Margaret Gano°, 1816; c, Elizabeth K., m George Briscoe, Lincoln 1814, and went later to Illinois; d, Polly; e, William W., m ——— Combs; f, John L., m Betsy May, Mercer 1817, and they went to Illinois; g, Fouche T.; h, Letitia, m Jacob Spears, and they also went to Illinois; i, Baker Finis, m Sarah Moss Durham, Mercer 1823, and they were great-grandparents of Miss Hatabel Hyer, of Orlando, Fla.

2, Gen. Robert; 3, Young; 4, Judge Reuben; 5, Jane Kelly; 6, Polly or Patty; 7, Urban; 8, July or Martha Mills; 9, Sydney Ann Linn; 10, Chatham; 11, John; 12, Rev. Finis, m Margaret Davidson, Davidson County, Tennessee, 1793. He was one of the founders of the Cumberland Presbyterian Church.

Many of the children of Robert and Mary Baker Ewing located in Logan County, Kentucky, and several died in Missouri.

Richard Berry m Polly Ewing, Mercer 1794, and went to Missouri in 1820; Samuel Ewing m Jane Jackson, Lincoln 1795. George W. Ewing m Judith Trabue° (dau Jane), Bourbon 1829.

FALL—Philip S., r 1819, dis 1820

Philip Slater Fall (1798-1890) came in 1817 with his parents, James and Catherine Barrat Fall, from Brighton, England, to Logan County, Kentucky. In 1819 he came to Woodford to visit his cousins, the Trabues, and in that same year was licensed to preach at the Forks of Elkhorn Church, being ordained in 1820. In 1821 he m Ann Apperson Bacon°, and their children were: 1, James Slater, m Martha King, 1847; 2, John; 3, Elizabeth Sarah Taylor°; 4, Catherine Marianna, m Col. John B. Temple, 1853; 5, Caroline; 6, William Robinson, m Edmonia L. Taylor, 1860; 7, Philip Slater; 8, Albert Boult; 9, Alexander; 10, Henry Ewing.

Philip Fall shared with Jacob Creath, Sr., the pastorate of the Frankfort Baptist Church in 1821. A few years later he was converted to the beliefs of Alexander Campbell, and organized the First Christian Church in Louisville, the Vine Street Christian Church in Nashville; and in 1832, assisted by John T. Johnson, the First Christian Church in Frankfort.

In 1831 he bought "Poplar Hill," the Daniel Weisiger home on the Owenton road, and here for many years he conducted "The Female Eclectic Institute," a school for girls which he continued later in Frankfort.

FARMER—Mrs. Susanna, r 1812, dis 1815

Benjamin Farmer (1783-1837) was the son of Hezekiah and Elizabeth Cheatham Farmer, of Chesterfield County, Virginia. In 1807 he m Susanna Goode°, and they came to Franklin County and settled at Farmdale. Their children were: 1, John G., m Katherine Hawkins°, F 1835; 2, Silas Cheatham, m Huldah Crook, F 1831, and they had: a, Elizabeth, m John Aubrey, F 1853, and was the grandmother of Mrs. Russ Hughes, of Frankfort; b, George M., m Emma Payne, and they were the parents of Miss Huldah Farmer, of Frankfort; c, Ann Sargent°; 3, Thomas, m first Elizabeth Thomas, Anderson 1837, and second Fannie Garnett, of Owen; 4, Sally, m Jonathan Crook; 5, Tapley Joseph, m Mary Watts (dau Thurman), Anderson 1837; 6, Elizabeth; 7, Benedict (1821-1899), m Lucy Thomas, Anderson 1843, and they were the parents of Ben T. and William S. Farmer, of Frankfort.

Joel, John, and Elisha Farmer were in Franklin, 1795. Elias Farmer m Sally Roberson (dau Mills), F 1795; Harriet S. Farmer m John F. Elam°.

FENDER (?)—Brother, dis 1800
Wife, dis 1800

FENNELL—Abner, r 1814
Lucy, r 1814

They probably came from Scott, where others of the name lived. They were the parents of Polly Triplett°.

FERGUSON—Larkin, 1, dis 1798
Nancy, 1, dis 1798   Thomas, 1
James, 1   John, dis 1798
Lydia, 1   Lucy, dis 1798

Larkin Ferguson was in Fayette, 1787, and Larkin, James, and Thomas were in Woodford, 1791. Larkin died in Scott, 1821, leaving a son John and perhaps other children. James (1769-1822) m Lydia ——. They built their home in Scott, between Switzer and Stamping Ground, where their tombstones are yet standing. The records indicate that they were parents of Eunice; Thomas (1806-1871); and John Redd, who m Maria Macklin°, F 1825, and had: Alex M., James H., and Mallie Kelly°.

Thomas m Hannah Murphy°, F 1796. Thomas A. m Jemima Peak (dau Elizabeth), Washington 1825. Hugh m Hetty Ellis°, W 1792, and their dau Elizabeth m Francis Slaughter, F 1814.

One family of Fergusons was related to the Atwells and Hursts, and perhaps to the Lees. Henry Ferguson m Margaret Hurst (dau Peter and Ann Rust Hurst), 1829, and they lived on a farm formerly owned by Gersham Lee, on Cole's Road near the old Harmony Church. Their children were: Mary Edwards°, Lewis, James, Peter, Kate, Mildred.

FICKLIN—John H.

William and Sarah Ficklin came from England to King George County, Virginia, about 1710. Their son William m Molly Marye, and they had: 1, Thomas (1738-1812), m Mary Herndon (dau John and Mary Lewis Herndon), 1766. They were at Bryan's Station in 1781, and Thomas was a charter member of the Great Crossings Church, Scott 1785. Their children were: a, Philadelphia Bradley°; b, Rev. John Herndon (1770-1826), m his cousin, Anna Herndon, 1790, and they settled near Stamping Ground. It was in his barn, in 1791, that the McConnell's Run (now Stamping Ground) Church was organized under the preaching of William Hickman, and he was an early convert. He was licensed to preach in 1805, and in 1807 was ordained at North Fork by William Hickman and William Buckley, both ardent believers in emancipation. He preached at North Fork for several years, and was considered a good preacher, of strong intellect and sincere piety, though his views on emancipation were unpopular. He is thought to have spent his last years in Illinois, though his two sons, Asa and Benjamin, went to Missouri. c, Joseph, m Polly Campbell; d, Margaret, m Asa Piper, and went to Illinois; e, William, m Elizabeth K. Williams. 2, John, m Mary Price, of Jessamine; 3, James; 4, Charles; 5, a daughter.

One Thomas Ficklin, of Scott, died 1823, aged 81.

FINNEL—Lucy, r 1818

Edwin C. Finnell m Elizabeth C. Suter°, F 1827.

FINNIE—James, 1, dis 1811
        Benjamin, 1
        Elizabeth, 1

Capt. James Finnie (—— 1819), whose father came from England to Virginia, was in Fayette, 1788, and he and his brother John were in Woodford, 1791. They removed to Union County, Kentucky, about 1811.

James and his first wife (who may have been Ann, dau Dr. William Lynn, and widow of John Dent, of Frederick County, Virginia) had: 1, Nancy Williams°; 2, Elijah, m Polly Cole°, and they were grandparents of Mrs. Mary Finnie Shipp, of Midway; 3, John; 4, Elizabeth Brown°; 5, James; 6, Judith, m Thomas James, Union 1817. Capt. James Finnie m second Mary James, and their children were: 7, Alexander; 8, William James; 9, Melissa; 10, Thomas Lightfoot, m Malinda Ellen Threlkeld, Union 1831; 11, George Henry; 12, Silas Slaughter, m Elizabeth Buckham, 1845.

Col. John Finnie's wife was Rachel Taylor, of Clark, and they had a family of eleven, W 1810, including Mary B. T. Graham° and Susan Gibson, who m Nicholas Casey, Union 1815.

Jeremiah Luckett m Elizabeth Finnie, F 1818. John Finney m Elizabeth Edzard (dau William), F 1809; Robert Finney m Fanny Lucas, F 1811; William W. Finney m Polly Edzard, F 1813; Jane Finney m Andrew Williams°.

In Union County, Eleanor Finnie m Samuel Casey, 1814; Eliza m Peter Casey, Jr., 1818; John G. m Fanny S. Casey, 1824. In Barren, Henry Finney m Elizabeth F. G. Hayden, 1820.

FITZGERALD—Elizabeth, r 1811, dis 1815
    Betsy, r 1811, dis 1815
    Peggy, r 1811, dis 1815
    Nancy, 1800   Sister, dis 1806

James Fitzgerald was living north of the river, F 1801, and was the father of Nancy Lowry°. Betsy and Peggy were daughters of Elizabeth. Maryan had a family of seven, F 1810. In W 1810, Ellis had five, and Daniel, on Glen's Creek, had nine, but he was on Big Benson, F 1815.

FORBUSH (Forbis)—Sally, dis 1803

Isaac Forbis m Sarah Haydon°, F 1802. Some of the Forbis family went to Boone County, Missouri.

FORD—James, 1, to Glen's Creek 1801
   Lucy, 1, to Glen's Creek 1801
   Reuben, 1812-1818

James and Lucy Shipp° Ford came from Caroline County, Virginia, and settled near McKee's Crossroads. They had: 1, John, m Sally Berry°, W 1810, and went to Shelby, where he died in 1856; 2, Lemuel, m Hannah McDowell (c Margaret), W 1809; 3, Lucy Boulware°; 4, Thomas, m Alcy Graddy (dau Jesse), W 1819; 5, Susan Montague; 6, Nancy Allen°; 7, Lewis; 8, James, Jr. The will of one James Ford (possibly a grandson of James and Lucy), W 1879, speaks of his farm on South Elkhorn in Scott and Woodford, and mentions his niece Laura Sea; sisters Rebecca Montague, Lucy Turk, and Susan, wife of Nelson Alley; brother, Thomas J. Ford, who m Ann Maria Edwards°, W 1845.

Reuben Ford m Nancy Louderback (dau Abraham), W 1813; one Reuben m Rebecca Sheets°, F 1819. Reuben Ford, Sr. (s David Ford, of Richmond, Va.) died F 1856, aged seventy-two. The will of Bartlett Ford, F 1820, mentions his wife Nancy, sons George and Andrew Jackson, dau Nancy Robertson, and others.

One John Ford was on South Elkhorn, W 1791 and later. The Ford and Edwards families were related, and this John may have been the one who m Aphia Pattie° in Culpeper County, Virginia, and spent his last years in Henry.

Absalom Ford had a family of twelve, W 1810. It was his son, James P. Ford, who in 1867 introduced the famous bill by which Mortonsville came within one vote of becoming the State Capital.

Joseph Ford, of Buckingham County, Virginia, m Mary Maxey°, 1788.

Montague: The Montague family came from Normandy. The name was originally spelled *Montagu*, and authorities say that it should be pronounced with three syllables, as it has no connection with the two-syllable *Mon-tague*, which is a corruption of the Irish name *Mac Teague*.

Peter Montague came from England to Virginia in 1621. He m Cicely Jordan, and their son Peter II was the father of Catherine Twyman° and of Peter III, who had: 1, Thomas, m Grace ———, and was the father of Clement (1723-1791), m Anne Bartlett°. Clement's son Thomas came from Spotsylvania County, Virginia, to Frankfort. He m Agnes Ellis, and among their children were Mary Todd°, and Thomas, who m Susanna Ford°, W 1810, and had James T., William, Lucy, Lewis F., Lemuel, Henrietta, Susan, Martha, Elizabeth, Albert.

2, Peter IV, of Middlesex County, Virginia, was the father of Peter V (1732-1820), m Elizabeth Henderson, and had Andrew, whose son Thomas came from Orange County, Virginia, to Fayette, about 1809. His son, William Andrew, m Mary Ann Nutter, and they were grandparents of William H. and Clarence Montague, of the Forks Church.

Peter and Cicely Montague were also ancestors of the Deering family.

FORSEE—William, r 1810, to Forks of Elkhorn 1818
Wife, r 1810, to Forks of Elkhorn 1818

The Forsees (spelled also Farcy, Farsi, Forssee) were Huguenots. William m Mary Ann Smith°, 1783. They came to Kentucky in 1807 and settled on Elkhorn. Their children were: 1, George S., m Matilda Samuel°, F 1816, and they went to Owen. Their children were: a, George William, m Mary E. Rees, 1842; b, Churchill P., m first Ruth Chambers (dau Teletha), 1850, m second Nannie Craig, 1858, m third Miranda Duvall; c, James S., m first Louisa Beadles, m second Vincincia Threlkeld (dau Elijah), 1850. His children were: Emma Ruth Beck, E. T., G. W., Matilda Lee; d, Samuel Nicholas, m Anna Maria Hodges (dau Rev. Frank), and they were the parents of Miss Nannie Forsee and Mrs. T. E. Martin, of Stedmantown; e, Nancy, m Rev. Benjamin O. Branham, 1851; f, John Jamison, m Henrietta Threlkeld.

2, James; 3, Stephen; 4, Esther Bryan°; 5, William B., who lived in Gallatin, m Letitia Smith (dau John), Fayette 1822, and they had: Ann Martin, John, Samuel, Isabella, George, Mary, Martha. 6, Polly (mentioned in her father's will, F 1835, as Polly Macy, but a Polly Forsee m Bennett Moxley°); 7, Anthony R., m Eliza Ann Tandy (dau John), Gallatin 1825; 8, Peter N., m first Elizabeth T. Gray (dau Mrs. Nancy Tate°), F 1832, and second her sister, Sally Ann Gray, F 1835. He was in Clark County, Missouri, 1840, and was the father of J. W. Forsee. 9, Jane, m Rev. Farmer Rees, F 1822. Farmer Rees (1801-1854), of Henry, preached to the poor and practiced medicine for a living. He was ordained about 1849, and went later to Louisville as a city missionary. One Farmer Rees m Ann M. Buck, F 1839.

William Forsee m second Judy Bledsoe°, F 1808, and died in 1839.

FOSTER—Thomas, r 1828   Martha Ann
        Lucy, r 1828   Frances Elizabeth

The Fosters came from Spotsylvania County, Virginia. In Bourbon, Thomas Foster m Rhoda Howard, 1800; Thomas Foster (s John) m Frances Wilson, 1815, the bond being signed by Thomas Foster, Sr.; Jesse m Patsy Jones, 1822; Nancy m William Ellis°. Arthur and Thomas Foster were in Scott, 1801.

Thomas Foster (1777?-1842) came to Franklin County about 1828 and had a log tavern opposite the present home of E. D. Shryock at the intersection of the Lexington-Frankfort and Leestown-Lexington roads. His wife was Lucy Marshall°, and his children were: 1, Eliza W. Mitchell; 2, John Thomas, m Mary ———, and went to Missouri in 1850; 3, Martha Ann Ayres° (———-1841); 4, Frances Elizabeth Ayres°; 5, William Henry (m Ann Beavis, F 1830?); 6, Susan; 7, Judith Ann Jones°. Mrs. Lucy Foster m William Marshall°.

John Foster m Anna Graham, F 1804; Hezekiah Foster m
Ann H. Andrews°, W 1819; Thomas Foster m Sarah L. An-
drews°, 1819.

FULLER—Love, to Forks of Elkhorn 1818
William L. Fuller m Jemima Castleman°, F 1818. Gilbert
Fuller sold land to Benjamin Taylor.

GAINES—Jinney, 1
The will of Lewis Pines, Jr., Spotsylvania 1787, mentions his
sister, Jiney Gaines (see Abbett).
William Gaines was living on Dry Run, F 1795, but in 1801
and thereafter was on Glen's Creek in Woodford. His will,
W 1819, names his wife Jane and: 1, William. One William
and his wife Sarah sold land on Elkhorn to John Baker, F 1813;
2, Richard; 3, Thomas. One Thomas had a family of three, F
1810; 4, Franklin, on Stucker's Branch, W 1826; 5, Barnett, m
Patsy Poindexter°, F 1817, and they were the parents of Ander-
son, m Mary J. Gaines and had: John W., m Elizabeth Ann
Noel°, F 1868; James Barnett, m Lucy Spicer (dau William and
Susan Jane Gaines Spicer), 1862, and they were the parents of
Bowman Gaines and Mrs. T. J. Lewis, of Frankfort; William, m
Alice Jones; Quincy, m Margaret Nolan; Charles, m Ellen Noel°;
Lucy Ann, m F. M. Shelton. 6, James, whose will, F 1859, men-
tions his wife Lucy and children: a, Thomas H., who went to
Newcastle, Ky.; b, Juliet, m —— Hockensmith; c, Susan Jane,
m William Spicer, 1841; d, Henry E.; e, William P., m Alice
Sullivan; f, Westley, m Susan M. Spicer, F 1856; g, George
Washington, of Anderson. 7, George.
Connected with this family was James Henry Gaines, of
Woodford, who m Juretta Gaines, and they were the parents of
Rev. Virgil M. Gaines, for many years an elder in Grassy Spring
Church.
Robert Gaines m Ann Jenkins, Spotsylvania County, Vir-
ginia, 1783. They came in 1809, and his will, W 1833, names
his wife and children: 1, Richard; 2, William; 3, James; 4, John
Robertson; 5, Lucy, m James Gaines; 6, Thomas.
George Gaines m Milly White, W 1812; James m Rebecca
Adams, W 1814; William m Juliet Hamilton, F 1817; Thomas m

Nancy Switzer, F 1826; John B. m Ruth Ann Hawkins°, F 1838, and they had: 1, Epaphroditus; 2, Mary Elizabeth Whittington°.

Another family was that of Robert Gaines (s William Henry and Isabella Pendleton Gaines), who came from Culpeper to what is now Anderson County, Kentucky. He m Elizabeth Long, and their children were: 1, Thomas (1771-1853), m Milly Row (dau Thomas and Rachel Keeling Row?), Orange County, Virginia, 1800, and they had: a, Harriet, m John Haley, of Mercer, F 1820; b, Edmund Pendleton, m first Nancy M. Foree, 1832, and had Jugurtha, m Lizzie Miller, 1857; he m second America B. Garnett°, W 1837; c, Thomas Row; d, Jinsey, m John T. Jordan, 1831; e, Rev. Keeling Carlton, who lived at Bridgeport, m Mariam Pulliam°, F 1834, and they were the parents of Prof. J. T. Gaines, long associated with the Louisville public schools, and were grandparents of Thomas Keeling Jett, of Jett, and great-grandparents of Mrs. Chester Harrold, of Gainesville, Fla.; f, Absalom; g, Rachel, m Abram B. Tinsley, Anderson 1836; h, Elizabeth, m Robert A. Armstrong, Anderson 1843. 2, John Long; 3, Richard, m Malinda Sanders, and their son Gabriel Hansford, m Ann McCormick and was the father of J. W. Gaines, of Lawrenceburg; 4, Elizabeth, m David Williams°, and they were the parents of Dr. U. V. Williams, of Frankfort; 5, Lucy (m Judge William Tipton?); 6, Amelia, m William Rice; 7, Robert; 8, Reuben.

James M. Tipton m Elizabeth Gaines, Anderson 1837; William Gaines m Catherine Pendleton, F 1852; William A. Gaines m Margaret Wood, 1854.

Of another family was Capt. Bernard Gaines (1767-1839, s Col. Daniel and —— Gaines, of Amherst County, Virginia), who m Catherine Fouace Cooke (dau John and Catherine Burton Cooke), W 1812. They lived on the Frankfort-Versailles road at what is known as the John Mastin farm, now owned by the King family. Their children were: 1, Elizabeth, m first Charles F. Nourse, and second Sylvanus W. Johnson; 2, Catherine Mary, m Oscar Pepper; 3, Gustavus Cooke, m first Ann Gibson°, 1843, and they were grandparents of Miss Annie Belle Fogg, of Frankfort. He m second Catherine Mary Cromwell, 1856, and they were the parents of Misses Nannie and Rachel Gaines, who, as Methodist missionaries, devoted their lives to service in Japan.

GALE (Gayle)–Rachel, 1
    Elizabeth, 1801, dis 1812
    Lucy, r 1820, dis 1829

With family names constantly repeated, and many records burned, this outline is far from satisfactory.

The will of Matthew Gale, Spotsylvania County, Virginia, 1779, mentions his wife, Judith (Purvis?), and children: Matthew and wife Mary; Joseph, wife Rachel, son John Edwards; Sarah Deatherage; John; Elizabeth Poole; Joyce Dudley°; Judith Barnaby.

Matthew (son of the first Matthew) m Mary ——, and he and his son Josiah were at Bryan's Station. He settled in the part of Woodford that was afterward Scott, and probably died before 1800. Their children are listed as: 1, Josiah. One Josiah m Elizabeth Bartlett° and lived on Elkhorn and Sulphur Lick. He had a family of four, F 1810. Josiah, Jr., m Susan White (dau William and Nancy Gale White). Two Josiahs were in Scott, one in Gallatin and one in Lexington, though their relationship is not known. 2, Robert D., Sr. (1777-1815), who came from Scott to South Benson in Franklin about 1810, when he had a family of six. His children have not been identified, though John E. Gale was administrator of his estate.

3, Matthew, Jr., m Sarah Penn (dau Thomas), probably in King and Queen County, Virginia. It was evidently after his wife's death that he came to Scott, where a burned fragment of his will (1798-1812) says: "mother, Mary ° ° ° ° Judith." His children are thought to have been: a, Elizabeth, who mothered the orphaned children of her brother John and her sister Mary, m first Paul Williams and second —— Smith, and went to Hannibal, Mo.; b, John (m —— Minor?), had: Elizabeth; Matthew, who is thought to have gone to Mississippi; and John Minor, who came to Frankfort and m his cousin, Elizabeth Stewart, F 1823. They built the house now occupied by the Rebecca-Ruth candy shop, and were the grandparents of Clarence Gayle, John W. Gayle, George L. Payne, and Dr. Flora Mastin, of Frankfort. Several of their children went to Henderson and Columbus, Ky.; c, Mary E., m Benjamin Stewart, of King and Queen. They died in Virginia, and Brooking Taylor was guardian of their children: Elizabeth Holmes, m John M.

Gale; and Sarah Ann, m William Holeman, F 1820; d, Nancy
Taylor°; e, George, m Sophronia Bohannan°, W 1813, and they
lived first on South Benson and then in South Frankfort, on
Third Street opposite the site of the present hospital. Their
children were: Mary Ann, m Robert Hogg Alves, and they were
ancestors of Mrs. Clarence Van Liew, of Frankfort; John; William, who went to Ohio. Sophronia died in 1822, and George
went to Henderson, where he m Jean Holloway, 1827, and had
other children. f, Josiah, who chose Robert D. Gale for his
guardian, F 1813; g, William Edwards, born in Prince William
County, Virginia, 1795, who chose Robert Gale as his guardian,
W 1812. He m Elizabeth Davies Walden, 1815, and they lived
for some time in Caroline County, Virginia, though he died in
Cincinnati and she in Fleming County, Kentucky.

4, John E. One John E. m Sarah Tull, W 1815. They lived
on Glen's Creek, but were in Jefferson County, Indiana, when
they sold their farm to R. R. Darnell, W 1833. 5, Judith.

Joseph Gale, son of the first Matthew, was in Fayette 1788,
but evidently died before 1792, when Rachel was listed in Woodford. They had: 1, John Edwards, and the records indicate
that they had also: 2, Nancy, m William White, F 1795, and
had: a, Permelia, m first James W. Prewitt, F 1815, and second
Robert Brown°; b, Nancy Shely°; c, Susan, m Josiah Gale; d,
Judith E., m George W. Gale, F 1811. 3, Capt. James, m Lucy
Sanders°, F 1800, and lived on the Frankfort-Versailles road in
the vicinity of "Melrose." Though listed with a family of eight,
only two are known: a, Joseph C., m Martha Bryan°, F 1828, and
they had James and Thomas B.; b, Reuben S., who died in 1828
and was buried in the Brown graveyard. His wife may have
been a daughter of Daniel E. Brown°; 4, Elizabeth Weston°.
One Reuben m Polly Pemberton°, Henry 1817.

A group living on Glen's Creek in Woodford included: 1,
Robert F., recorded as having been born in Caroline County,
Virginia, 1769. He m Elizabeth Wood, and they came to Scott
and afterward to Woodford, where he had a mill near the mouth
of Glen's Creek. He had a family of ten, including: a, Philadelphia Bohannon°; b, Mary, m Orman Brown, F 1823; c, Elizabeth, m Lloyd Hackett, Shelby 1827; d, Letha, m Richard Rad-
ford, of Shelby, W 1828. The family went to Shelby, and finally

to Missouri. 2, John E., who was living with Robert F. in 1824; 3, Judith, evidently a widow, was the mother of Louisa Samuel° and Elizabeth F. Johnson°, and perhaps of Valora Gale. 4, Thomas, born 1779, who owned land on Glen's Creek, 1812. He went to Scott, and then to Lewis County, Kentucky, where he died 1816. He m Nancy Miller, 1799 (who m Isaac Skinner 1820), and their children were: a, Margaret, m Joseph Rosson, F 1821; b, Walker (1813-1818); c, Mary Vaughan°; d, Catherine, m Preston Alexander, 1831; e, Robert D., d 1814.

George W. Gale m Judith E. White, F 1811, and they lived on Elkhorn. Mrs. Judith E. Gale m Joseph Trotter, F 1827.

William Gayle, said to have come from King and Queen County, Virginia, m Margaret Pitts°. His will, Scott 1817, mentions his wife and: 1, Caty; 2, Betsy; 3, Susan; 4, Julia, m David Elliott; 5, Dr. William (1790-1859), m Catherine Bentley Ballou°, 1818. They lived at Switzer, and were grandparents of Dr. J. W. Gayle, of Frankfort, and Miss Cordie Coleman, of Georgetown, and great-grandparents of Mrs. J. W. Lancaster, of Georgetown; 6, Josiah; 7, Temple; 8, Robert M.; 9, Nancy; 10, Younger. One record adds Henry, who is said to have gone to Owen.

Christopher, John, and Samuel Gale were also in Scott. The will of John Gayle, Owen 1849, mentions his wife Malinda; sons John, Robert, James, Thomas, and dau Joanna Leonard.

Dudley: Robert Dudley (1726-1766), son of Edward Dudley of Fredericksburg, Va., m Joyce Gale, 1746. Their children were: Robert; Capt. Ambrose; Joyce Quisenberry°; Peter; James; William.

Capt. Ambrose Dudley (1750-1825) m Ann Parker, 1773. He was originally a member of the Episcopal Church, but after hearing the imprisoned Baptists singing hymns in the jail in Fredericksburg he was converted to their faith and resigned from the army to become a preacher. He came with his family in 1786 to Fayette, and was engaged to preach at the newly organized church at Bryan's Station. He and his wife had: 1, Robert, m first Sarah W. Rodes (second, Ann Parrish before 1813?) and went to Christian in 1818; 2, William E., m Polly Smith, 1798, and they were the parents of Col. Ambrose W., who m Eliza G. Talbott, 1824, and lived at "Melrose," near Frankfort. 3, Gen. James, m first Polly Ferguson (dau Abraham), and second Mrs. Mourning (Goodloe) Royster, Madison 1824; 4, Jeptha, who came to Frankfort, m first Betsy Lewis (dau Thomas), Fayette 1805, and second Rebecca Trotter, Fayette 1817. One record says he m also Mrs. Sally Clay, sister of his first wife and widow of Gen. Green Clay, Madison 1813, and the Fayette records show that one Jeptha Dudley m Juliet Smith (dau Jane), Fayette 1824.

5, John, m Patsy Parrish (dau Timothy), Clark 1813, and went to Missouri; 6, Polly, m Maj. Benjamin Graves; 7, Dr. Benjamin W., the noted surgeon of Lexington, whose advanced ideas and skilled treatment proved so efficacious in the great cholera epidemic of 1832. He m Anna Maria Short (dau Maj. Peyton), Fayette 1821; 8, Gen. Peter, m Maria Garrard° Bourbon, 1815, and they lived on the Frankfort-Versailles road at what is known as the McMillan place, now owned by W. S. Morris; 9, Col. Ambrose, of Mississippi, m first ——— Ludlow, and second Mrs. Clarissa Cluny, in Cincinnati, 1837; 10, Elizabeth Blanton°; 11, Rev. Thomas (1792-1886), who was also a Baptist preacher, m first Elizabeth Buckner, and second Mrs. Caroline Russell Harrison (widow of Carter H. Harrison), Fayette 1848; 12, Parker, m Ann H. Taylor (dau Reuben), Fayette 1821, and went to Missouri; 13, Nancy Castleman°; 14, Simeon, m ——— Woodford and went to Missouri.

Ambrose Dudley and his son Thomas occupied the pulpit for a total of one hundred years.

GANO—John　　　　　Patsy, 2
　　　　Keziah, 1　　　Jemima, dis 1812

Rev. John Gano (1727-1805) was the son of Daniel and Sarah Britton Gano, of Hopewell, N. J., and was the great-grandson of Francis Gano, a Huguenot who settled in Maryland. The name was originally Gerneaux, but the Huguenots, when they left France, often made slight changes in their names, to avoid being followed.

John Gano was educated at Princeton, and was ordained at White Plains, N. J., in 1754. There is a tradition that it was he who immersed George Washington, and one account says that at the first inauguration President Washington called on John

Gano for a prayer, "so that his was probably the first public prayer calling for God's blessing on the new-born nation."

His first wife was Sarah Stites (dau John, of New Jersey), and their children were: 1, John S. (1756-1765); 2, Capt. Daniel, who came with Wilkinson, and helped to lay off the town of Frankfort. In 1809 he went to Scott, where he spent the remainder of his life. He m first Martha Bryan, 1795, and they had: a, Ezekiel Hopkins; b, William; c, Mary Forbis; d, Susanna Harriet. He m second Jemima Robinson°, 1808, and they had: e, John Price; f, Isaac E.; g, Daniel S. 3, Margaret Hubbell°; 4, Rev. Stephen (1762-1828) was a physician at Tappan, N. Y., but was ordained to the ministry in 1786. After preaching for some time in the vicinity of New York, he accepted a call to the First Baptist Church in Providence, R. I., the oldest Baptist church in the United States, where he continued preaching for the rest of his life. The Draper Mss. indicate that it was he who preached the first sermon in Frankfort. The family record states that he m Martha (Phoebe?) Bryan, of Rowan County, North Carolina.

5, Gen. John S., m Mary Goforth, and they lived in Cincinnati. Their children were: a, Daniel; b, Dr. John A., m Catherine Maria Hubbell (niece of Capt. William Hubbell), Scott 1821 or 1822, and they had: Mary, m Joseph Wright; John; Eliza; Aaron; Catherine Maria; William; Charles; Elinora, m William L. Hunt. 6, Susanna, died young; 7, Dr. Isaac Eaton, m Keziah Bainbridge°, Bourbon 1789, and they had Sarah F., m Andrew P. Hay, F 1815, and perhaps others. He practiced in Frankfort, and was postmaster there about 1800. 8, Sarah, m Dr. S. Thane, and they had: a, Sally; b, Mary Hubbell.

9, Gen. Richard Montgomery (1775-1815) m first Elizabeth Ewing°, F 1797, and went to Georgetown. They had: a, Mary, m Capt. John C. Buckner; b, Margaret Ewing°; c, Cornelia, m Capt. William Henry (s Gen. William, of Christian); d, Elizabeth, m Daniel Henry; e, Rev. John Allen, m Catherine Conn (dau Capt. William), Bourbon 1827, and they had: William; Rev. Richard M., who went to Dallas, Tex.; Fanny, m Noah Spears, Jr.; Robert; Stephen; Franklin, went to Texas; Eliza; John A., also went to Texas; Mary E., m John W. Buckner, of Bourbon. One record says he had a dau, Charity, who m Rev. William Price and went to Texas.

John Allen Gano was a friend of Alexander Campbell, and became an outstanding minister of the Christian Church. A great peacemaker, he was so influential that, of nearly ten thousand persons baptized by him, comparatively few ever returned to their worldly ways. f, Stephen F.; g, Richard. Gen. R. M. Gano m second Mrs. Deborah Winter Goforth (dau Daniel Winter and widow of Aaron Goforth), F 1814 (see Scott). 10, Susanna Price°; 11, William (1781-1798), of Cincinnati.

Rev. John Gano preached in North Carolina, New Jersey, Philadelphia, and New York before coming to Kentucky in the summer of 1787. He stayed in Lexington a year, and then came to Frankfort, where his son Daniel had already located. He says in his biography that he built a log house here in 1798, but he was living on his farm adjoining Daniel Peak's when his will was written. He soon had a large following, and in addition to his ministrations throughout the surrounding country he was engaged to preach twice a month at the State House.

His wife died in 1792, soon after coming to Frankfort, and about 1793 he m Mrs. Sarah Hunt Bryan° in North Carolina.

In his old age he was stricken with paralysis, but even after that he did not feel that his responsibility was diminished, and he would insist on riding horseback to his place of appointment, where he would be supported by a friend on either side, and would sit in a chair to preach. It was at this time that he wrote: "I sometimes wonder, why God ever conducted me to Kentucky, when so little fruit or good effect of my poor labours have appeared, at least to myself! why, in this half dead condition, I am yet continued in life! Yet, I have more cause to wonder, that ever God made me instrumental of good, at any time of my life, or any where in the world; and that I should be laid by, as an instrument out of use."

GARNETT—James, 1   Benjamin, 1801, dis 1803
         Ann, 1   Polly, 1801, dis 1803

The Garnetts came from Essex and Culpeper, Virginia. James and Ann Shipp° Garnett lived in the Glen's Creek neighborhood, and their names are on that church roll. The will of James, W 1808, mentions his wife and: 1, Lewis (m Eliza Hitt,

W 1824?); 2, grandson Thomas, son of deceased son Thomas; 3, James; 4, Anderson, m first Fanny Brooking°, and second Mary W. Ballard°, W 1824; 5, Anthony, who went to Christian, m Lucinda ——; 6, Fanny, m David Guernsey, W 1811; son-in-law William Garnett; son-in-law Elijah Burbridge (m Betty Garnett, W 1796).

Benjamin Garnett, who was highly praised by John Taylor in his "Ten Churches," m Polly Woolfolk°, W 1789. They lived in the old house now remodeled and owned by J. S. Simcox, on the Jett-Millville pike opposite the Redd Crutcher place. This place was sold in 1806 to Carter Blanton, and the Garnetts went to Shelby, where he became a successful minister of the Gospel. Records indicate that they were the parents of: 1, Sowell W.; 2, Richard, whose will, W 1833, mentions his wife Elizabeth and: a, America, m first Edmond P. Gaines°, and second Nicholas P. Green°; b, Mary; c, Martha; d, Elizabeth; e, Catherine McDaniel°; f, Moses; g, Harris. Mrs. Elizabeth Garnett sold her home on the McCracken road to William McDaniel in 1839.

Thomas Garnett was in W 1788, and probably went to Clark. His wife was Susanna (Pulliam?), and their children were: 1, Philip R. (m Elizabeth Dudley, Spotsylvania 1799?). He went to Jefferson, but was in W 1803; 2, Elizabeth R. Bohannon°; 3, William, who evidently was the son-in-law of James Garnett. He lived on Glen's Creek, but may have removed to Gallatin about 1820. Another William was on Clear Creek, W 1800, and Hugh and James were there in 1816. One William had a family of ten, W 1810. Susan (dau William) m Ovid McCracken°.

John Garnett (1750-1837) was living in the neighborhood of the Forks Church in 1794, and went afterward to the section of Gallatin that is now Owen. He m first Ann, dau Mrs. Colquit°, and had: 1, Waller, m Clara —— and lived in Owen. He m second Susanna Maddox, Gallatin 1809, and they had: 2, John M., m Elmira C. Pryor, Owen 1848; Jameson, m Lucinda Callender°, Owen 1835; 4, Milly Ann; 5, Phoebe, m Martin Jones, Gallatin 1808; 6, Nancy Adkins; 7, Sally Neal; 8, Susanna Ayres.

In Woodford, Nancy Garnett m Oliver Brown°; Charles m Polly Brown, 1807; James m Polly Garnett (dau James), 1810; Polly m Elijah Utterback, 1811; Reuben m Phoebe Claxton,

1815; Jane m John F. Kennedy, 1827; Nancy m Ezekiel True, 1838.

Woolfolk: Many of the Woolfolk family were in Caroline County, Virginia. Sowyel or Sowyell Woolfolk (1744-1830) was the son of Richard Woolfolk, who came from Albemarle County, Virginia and settled in Jessamine. Sowyel m Polly (Mary Netherland) Harris, and they lived at Elm Corner, in Woodford. Their children were: 1, John H., died 1813; 2, Col. Joseph H., m Martha Mitchum (dau Dudley), 1816; 3, Polly Garnett°; 4, Nancy Cox °; 5, Patsy Givens, m William Baker°; 6, Sowyel D., m Sallie Bowman, of Fayette; 7, Thomas H.

John Woolfolk, Jr., m Elizabeth Lewis in Virginia, and they were parents of Lucy Samuel°.

Richard A. Woolfolk (s Richard) m Sarah Taylor Sutton°, Jefferson 1828, and they went to Lincoln County, Missouri. They had a large family, including: 1, Mary, m Dr. Coleman Bondurant; 2, Sarah, m James Reed Major, and they were parents of Gov. Elliott W. Major, of Missouri.

Elijah Woolfolk, of Scott, m Phoebe Pitts°, and their children were: 1, Eleanor Hughes°; 2, Cordelia, m George E. Trimble, Scott 1855 or 1856; 3, Manie; 4, Elisa; 5, Adaline; 6, Nannetta Cullins°; 7, Dr. Josiah (1811- ——); 8, Jordan; 9, James.

GARRARD—George, moved away 1808

The tax list, F 1803, shows that George Garrard had land in Muhlenberg County, Kentucky.

Governor James Garrard (1749-1822) m Elizabeth Mountjoy in Stafford County, Virginia, 1769. He was active in the Virginia Legislature in procuring the passage of the famous bill securing religious liberty to the people. He came to Bourbon County, Kentucky, in 1783, after which he entered the Baptist ministry, preaching until after he was elected Governor in 1796.

Some of their children were: 1, Mary Edwards°; 2, John, m Sarah Shipp°, Bourbon 1805; 3, Daniel, m Lucinda Toulmin in Mobile, Ala., 1808, and they were grandparents of Mrs. Guy Barrett, Sr., of Frankfort; 4, Elizabeth, m James A. Brooks, 1810, and their dau Eliza m John Regis Alexander, 1849, and was the grandmother of Mrs. Polk South, Jr., of Frankfort; 5, Margaret, m Isham Talbott, F 1804. They lived at "Melrose," and were the parents of: a, Eliza Dudley°; b, Juliet Samuel°; c, William G., m Cordelia Wood, and they were grandparents of the Misses Lindsey, of Frankfort; 6, Maria Dudley°.

One record says that John Gerard, a first cousin of Governor James Garrard, though he spelled his name differently, came to Kentucky about 1795 and settled in Shelby. His children were: 1, Nancy, m John Newland, Shelby 1812, and they went to Ralls County, Missouri; 2, Phoebe Cook°; 3, William. One William Gerard was in Jefferson 1797 and for several years afterward, and William Garrard was there in 1808. William Gerrard published *The Argus* in Frankfort, 1806. He bought land from the Settle heirs, F 1818, and sold to Ezra Richmond in 1823. His wife was Nancy ———, and their children were: a, William, m Elizabeth Ayres°, W 1825; b, Edward; c, Mary Jane Martin°; d, Anne, m ——— Lyle. The family went to Ralls County, Missouri, 1828.

Isaac Garrard was in Shelby, 1794 through 1812, and Margaret Garrat was there in 1800. Uriah Garrard was in Woodford, 1791; John Garrard m Eliza Allen, W 1818. Presley and James Garrott were in Franklin, 1797.

GAYLE—see Gale

GIBBS—Thomas, r 1828, gone from us, 1831

In William Hickman's manuscript, written about 1828, he says, "Brother Gibbs, of Frankfort, meets with us."

Julius Gibbs (1753-1834), of Culpeper County, Virginia, m Agnes ———, and they had: 1, Betsy Guthrie°; 2, Milly Sisk°. He m second Catherine ———, in 1785, and their children were: 3, James, m Elizabeth Guthrie°, F 1811. His will, F 1873, names his wife Elizabeth and children: a, Elizabeth Ann (widow of John W. Bennett); b, James L.; c, William G.; d, Jacob C.; e, Julius C.; f, Thomas J., m Permelia Johnson, F 1833; g, Milly, widow of Jordan Gibbs. 4, John; 5, Polly; 6, Robert. One Robert m Fanny Pemberton°, and their son, John P., born near Versailles in 1825, went to Missouri. 7, Churchill; 8, Samuel C.; 9, Judith Roberts.

In 1794 Julius Gibbs and his family were in Scott, where he spent the rest of his life.

In the tax list of Jefferson, 1799, one Julius Gibbs is listed as owning land in Lincoln. C. J. Gibbs m Charlotte Potter, W 1836.

GIBSON—Sarah, 1   Elizabeth, 1800
        Phoebe, 1   Nancy, 1801

Two Gibson families came to what is now Franklin County. Mrs. Sarah Gibson (dau Mrs. Sarah Colquit) in 1790 bought from Benjamin and Nancy Craig the place on the Leestown road that is now known as "Buena Vista." She died in 1807, leaving: 1, Phoebe Martin°; 2, Betsy Sneed°; 3, Sally Robinson°; 4, James; 5, William, m Frances Samuel°, 1813, and their children were: a, John, died young; b, Lucy Woolfolk, m James E. Goodwin, W 1839, and was the mother of Frances Thompson°; c, Ann, m Gustavus Gaines°, and they were the parents of Fannie Fogg°; d, Spilsby Samuel (1821-1851); e, William (1822-——) m Isabella Loughborough, 1844, and they had: Thomas, m Lizzie Ayres and went to Texas; Preston Loughborough, m Mary M. Wilson°; Stonewall Jackson ("Josh"), m Cynthia Thomson°; Lucy Anna.

William Gibson, Sr., in 1817 bought John Samuel's farm at Duckers from the other heirs, and it remained in the Gibson family for more than a hundred years.

Henry Gibson died F 1801, leaving his wife Sarah and children: 1, Polly; 2, Elizabeth Cunningham°; 3, Jean Cunningham°; 4, James; 5, John, m Ann McCoun (dau Nancy), F 1796, and they were the parents of Elizabeth Mitchell°.

One James Gibson had land south of the river, F 1801. John Gibson was on Clear Creek, W 1807.

Samuel Gibson, who lived near Defoe in Henry, m Nancy Gill, 1828, and they were the parents of Mary Jane Hall° (1831-1854).

GOLDMAN—see Gouldman

GOODE—Robert, Jr., 1810-1811

The Goodes came to Kentucky with the Hickmans, with whom they were connected. Rev. John Goode, of Chesterfield County, Virginia, who m Sally Brown° in 1760, preached in the old Skinquarter Church in Virginia. One of their children was

Susanna Farmer°. John, Robert, and Fleming Goode were in Adair, 1810.

The will of Samuel Goode, Warren 1820, mentions his brothers, Robert and John C., and is witnessed by Sally C. Goode and John Quisenberry.

William Goode, of Essex County, Virginia, m Elizabeth Abbott, of Middlesex. His will, W 1821, names his wife Elizabeth and: William; Bivian; Walter, m Amanda Rankin, of Clark; George, m Eliza Stone, W 1826; Cordelia Tutt°.

Charles Goode was in Henry, 1811. Richard and Rebecca Goode, of Henry, had: 1, Joel; 2, Lemuel, m Martha Hancock°, Henry 1821; 3, Richard, m Polly Hancock°, Henry 1814; 4, Rebecca Bartlett°; 5, Margaret Bartlett°.

GOOLMAN—see Gouldman

GORE—Isaac, mouth of Elkhorn, 1801
Sally, mouth of Elkhorn, 1801
Nancy, mouth of Elkhorn, 1801
William, 1801, down on Elkhorn
Polly

When the country was being settled, Joseph Gore built "Gore's Station," a fortification near the present home of Guy Arnold, at the junction of the Owenton and Peaks Mill roads.

Isaac and Sarah Gore, of Charlotte, Va., were on Elkhorn, F 1796; they were parents of Frances Jackson° (1782-1856).

William Gore, on Elkhorn 1796, was the father of Susan Haydon° and Sally Bartlett°. William and Polly sold land to Stephen Bryant, F 1815.

One William Gore m Patsy Jackson°, F 1799; Patsy Gore m William Walker, F 1804; Patsy Gore m William C. Lee, F 1812; Joseph Gore m Polly Moxley°, F 1811.

William Gore had a family of six, F 1810, and Henry, who lived in Frankfort, had five. One Isaac Gore m Rachel Goodman (dau Avery), Garrard 1802.

GOULDMAN—Goldman, Elizabeth, dis 1809
Goolman, Betsy, dis 1824

Robert Goldman, who was in Woodford 1795, m Elizabeth Martin°, F 1804, the bond signed by Louis Easterday. The

estate of one Robert Gouldman was settled in Shelby, 1808, by
Elizabeth Gouldman, the other heirs being: 1, Sarah; 2,
Susannah; 3, Edward. One Edward and his wife were in
Natchez, Miss., in 1826. 4, Lucy Boone°.

Thomas Gouldman m Betsy Bryant°, F 1814. They may
have been related to the Grahams, as the date of his death,
1824, is recorded in William Graham's Bible. Mrs. Eliza B.
Goldman m Arch L. Bryant°. She bought land on Main Elkhorn, F 1825, from Enoch M. and Lucy Boone, Henry B. Truman
and wife Susan, of Meade County, Kentucky, and James B.
Trueman and wife Elizabeth, of Harrison County, Indiana.

> GRAHAM—William, r 1811
> Peggy, r 1811
> Susanna, r 1812, to Frankfort 1816
> Polly, r 1818   Catherine
> Priscilla   Francis, r 1840

Capt. Francis Graham (s William) came from Augusta
County, Virginia, and had a farm on Elkhorn, F 1796. He m
first Elizabeth Robinson, of Botetourt County, Virginia, 1768,
and their children were: 1, John H.; 2, David, on Benson 1811,
m Sarah Bacon°, F 1812, and they lived in South Frankfort.
3, George W., m first Susan Runyan°, F 1804, and they also
lived in South Frankfort. He m second Marilda (Tuper?), F
1854. He was the ancestor of Prof. Wayland Graham, Lyman
Graham, Mrs. John Rogers, and Miss Nonie Goodwin, of Frankfort, and of Senator G. G. Vest, of Missouri, author of the famous
tribute to the dog.

4, William (1768-1845), m Peggy Montgomery°, F 1798.
About 1823 he built and operated the Graham Tavern, which
stands by the side of the old Lexington road, north of the railroad at Jett. His children were: a, James, m first Polly Keller,
1824, second Nancy Sanders°, 1825, third Elizabeth Trotter,
F 1838; b, Ephraim; c, Nancy Hearn°; d, Polly Hancock; e,
Priscilla; f, William, m Mary Robinson°; g, Martha Elizabeth, m
Henry Vandegrift, F 1840; h, Catherine; i, Rebecca Mont-
gomery°.

5, Martha Bacon°; 6, Elizabeth Runyan°; 7, Robinson, on
Little Benson, 1813; 8, Francis, m Mary B. T. Finnie°, F 1808;

9, Priscilla Montgomery°; 10, Peggy, m William J. Phillips, F 1803, and they were the parents of Rebecca Cox°; 11, Catherine Samuel°, (1785- ———).

Capt. Graham m second Nancy Partlow°, F 1805. He died about 1809.

Rachel A. Graham and Elizabeth C. Graham were the first and second wives of Alex B. Bacon°. Jane Graham (dau Elizabeth) m John P. Shaw°.

Runyan: The Runyans are said to have descended from Vincent Rongnion (Roignon, Roygnon), a Huguenot who came to New Jersey in 1676.

Reuben Runyan was in Frankfort with a family of four, 1810. Some of his children were: 1, Mary Porter°; 2, Spencer, m Elizabeth Graham°, F 1804, and in 1810 they had a family of five; 3, Susan G. Graham° (1786-1849), joined the church at Clear Creek, 1800, and was baptized by "Old Father Cave"; 4, Naomi, m Ebenezer Huntington, F 1817. Reuben Runyan m Anna Watson, W 1801; Robinson G. Runyan m Elizabeth Smith, F 1831; Benjamin Runyan m Lucy Long°, W 1817, the bond being signed by Willis Long. Reuben, William, and Benjamin Runyan were in Owen, 1822.

One Reuben Runyan m Mary Trayne Greenwood, of New Hampshire, and it was she who in 1844 established in Frankfort the famous school for girls, "Greenwood Seminary." They were the parents of William Runyan, who m Mamie Ayres° and went to Missouri.

Reuben Runyan owned land on Cedar Cove Branch, F 1811.

GRAVAT—Samuel, 1801, dis 1819
Thomas, dis 1806

Samuel Gravat m Sally Page, a niece of John Mastin, F 1804. Thomas Gravat m Elizabeth Triplett°. Thomas and George S. were on Elkhorn, F 1809, and in 1810 Thomas had a family of five, and George had three, including Elizabeth Baker°.

Thomas P. Gravit m Jane Cox°, F 1830, the bond signed by G. Gravit; George S., Jr., m Ellen McDaniel°, F 1829; Jefferson m Elizabeth McDaniel, F 1832.

Hugh Gravatt was the father of Isabella Smithey°.

GRAVES—John, 1812

John Graves (probably John D.) was mentioned in connection with Jesse Cole, but it is not certain that he was a member of the Forks Church.

John D. Graves (1776-1848) walked from Maryland to Kentucky and settled in Scott. He came to Franklin about 1805, buying land in the vicinity of Woodlake and Spring Station from Asa Beall and Isaac Wilson. He m first Nancy Nall°, and they had: 1, Mildred; 2, Sarah Jones°. He m second Catherine Thomasson (dau Richard), and they had: 3, Susanna, m Joseph Falkner; 4, Martha; 5, John T., who had land in Lewis County, Missouri; 6, William L. (b 1814), who also went to Missouri, m Eliza Dunlap; 7, Elias; 8, Eliza, m William E. Featherston, F 1846. John D. m third Winnefred Nall°, F 1828, and fourth Nancy Poindexter°, F 1830, by whom he had: 9, Joseph S.; 10, George P.; 11, Lewis L. He also had a dau, 12, Fanny Smith°, but the records do not tell which of his wives was her mother.

Benjamin Graves m Sallie Cole°, and they lived between Lee's Branch and Beal's Run. The records indicate that some of their children were: 1, Nelson, who sold land on Elkhorn to Thomas H. Gouldman, F 1817. His will, W 1853, liberates his slaves and gives money to the Kentucky State Colonization Society. 2, Richard C., m Nancy Martin°, W 1818, and went to Cass County, Illinois; 3, William W.; 4, John C., m Susan McCoy (dau William, of Indiana), W 1821; 5, Thomas G.; 6, Nancy Johnson°.

Many of the lines of the Graves family throughout the Bluegrass descend from Captain Thomas Graves, who came to Jamestown, Va., in 1608.

Thomas Graves (1730-1801), son of Thomas and Ann Graves, of Spotsylvania County, Virginia, m Isabella Bartlett°, and they came with their family to Fayette as early as 1787. Their children were: 1, William, who remained in Virginia; 2, Bartlett, m first Frances Lane, Louisa County, Virginia, 1787; he m second Kitty Patterson, and third Elizabeth Leathers. 3, John, who came to Fayette, m Margaret Clore; 4, Susanna, m James Randolph; 5, Isabella, m John Hall; 6, Sally, m Samuel Graves, Louisa County, Virginia, 1783, and they came to Kentucky; 7, Mary, m Samuel Beeler; 8, Lydia, m John Graves, Louisa County, Virginia, 1784, and they came also; 9, Ann Hancock° (1756-1846).

Thomas Graves (1763-1845), son of Rice and nephew of the above Thomas, probably came to Fayette with this family, but he went later to Creelsboro, Ky.

Joseph and Mary Goodwin Graves, of Louisa County, Virginia, came to Fayette, and their son Joseph m Margaret Hayes (dau William and Lucy Gatewood Hayes), Fayette 1830, and was the father of Mrs. Lafayette Crutcher, Sr., of Woodford.

John Graves (1769?-1824) was one of the twelve children of John and Ann Rice Graves, of Culpeper County, Virginia. He came to Kentucky and m first Hannah Cave°, W 1790. Their children were: 1, Absalom, m Elizabeth Graves (dau Rev. Absalom and Felicia White Graves), 1816; 2, William Hawkins; 3, Mary, m Sydnor D. Hanks, W 1816; 4, Reuben, m Elizabeth Cox°, W 1822; 5, Judge Richard Cave, m first Lucy Mitchum (dau James and Polly Craig Mitchum), 1824, and second Mrs. Helen M. Scott, 1851; 6, Benjamin Taylor, m Lucinda Scearce (dau Laban and Jane Ashurst Scearce); 7, Joseph Craig, m Ann Kirtley, 1828. John Graves m second Mrs. Elizabeth Eve Graves, widow of his brother Stephen, in 1820.

Leonard Graves m Marah Gordon, Lincoln 1786. Leonard m Sally Brown°, F 1796, and his will, Mercer 1811, names his wife Sally and children: 1, Sally; 2, Tally; 3, James; 4, John; 5, Rice; 6, Levy; 7, Greenvil or Greenwell; 8, Scott, m first Mary Daniel°, and second Mrs. Betsy Prather; 9, Polly, m first —— Coghill, and second Alexander Newton; 10, Patsy, m Robert Alexander; 11, Levin or Living.

William Graves m Polly Graham, Mercer 1812. His will, F 1837, mentions his wife, Mary, and is witnessed by Scott Brown and John Arnold.

GREEN—John, 2, dis 1819
      William, to Glen's Creek 1801
      Nancy, to Glen's Creek 1801

Rev. John Green (s Nicholas and Elizabeth Price Green, of Culpeper County, Virginia), m Jane Hawkins. They were in Woodford, 1808, and lived for several years in Versailles, where Green Street was named for him. About 1820 he conducted a ferry across the river at the mouth of Glen's Creek, which he sold to Joshua McQueen in 1832. In 1831 they were in Owen, where he died in 1849. Their children were: 1, Samuel A., m America Roberts°, Owen 1837, and they had: a, Joseph; b, Mary, m —— Suter; c, George. 2, John; 3, Willis, m Artemesia Lillard; 4, Letitia Roberts°; 5, Elizabeth, m William G. Bower, Owen 1830; 6, Nicholas P., who lived near Farmdale, m first Mrs. Patsy Brown° Arnold, F 1829, and they had: a, Martha Thomas°; b, Scott, m Helen Henry; c, Ruth, m George Green; d, Dee, m Colon Jones. Nicholas P. m second Mrs. America P. Gaines°, W 1856. 7, Hawkins, m Jane Bulkley (?); 8, A. Morton (?), m Eliza Spencer; 9, Benjamin, m Becky Walker.

William Green (s Robert and Patty Ball Green), a cousin of Rev. John, m Nancy (?) Blackwell, and they also came to Woodford, where in 1810 he is listed with a family of three.

One John Green m Mildred Todd°, W 1809, and they had: 1, Maryan, m —— Boyd; 2, Elizabeth; 3, Martha, m William Louderback, Owen 1835. Martha Louderback m William Hodson°. John died 1813, and Mildred m second John Louderback, F 1818.

In Woodford were also James; Sarah; Henry; William, on Buck Run; Paul and Eli on Clear Creek; Edward and Jehu on Craig's Creek.

In Franklin, Eliza Green m Moses Long°; and Josiah Green m Rebecca Long°, 1814. Jeremiah and Josiah Green were on Elkhorn, F 1819.

Pascal Green m Agnes Blanton°, Owen 1826. His will, Owen 1852, names his wife and: 1, Elizabeth Ann; 2, Susan B. Roberts°; 3, Henry; 4, Edmund; 5, Alice R., m first C. B. McAfee, of Mercer, and second Robert D. Bledsoe°, and went to Missouri; 6, Robert S.; 7, Martha, m —— Owen, and they lived in Shelbyville; 8, Mary C. Gale°; 9, Sally C. Gale°; 10, John J.

William Green m Ann Marshall°, Lincoln 1790; William Green, of Henry, was the father of Lucy and Elizabeth Boone°; William Green m Lucy Boone°, Fayette 1810; Elizabeth Green m Benjamin Todd°; William Green m Elizabeth Sanford, W 1824.

GREGORY—Abraham, 1, joined Big Spring 1812
Millender, joined Big Spring 1812
Caty, 1

Abraham Gregory (1746-1815) bought from Robert Alexander, W 1797, the tract of land on which Spring Station is now located. His will mentions his wife Mildred, and leaves property to William, John, and William Moore Gregory, though their relationship is not stated. He emancipates slaves, gives money to Big Spring Church, and confirms the gift of the lot on which it is built. He leaves a horse and a hundred dollars to Elder William Hickman, and makes bequests to Abraham Smith, Abraham Watts, Abraham Sparks, and Gregory Young. His tombstone stood until recently in the family burying ground near Spring Station.

John Gregory was the son of William. After William's death, John and William Moore Gregory sold land to Thomas Bullock and Peter Watts, W 1826.

The will of Mildred Gregory, W 1820, mentions Mildred Waller, Mildred Guinn, Mildred Fisher, Mildred Yancey, Ann Maud Noel, Nelly Rodgers, Peter Watts, and Winny Nall, and was witnessed by Horace Waring, with Theodoric and Silas Noel as executors.

John M. Gregory (1758-1844) of Culpeper County, Virginia, m Barbara Hooper, 1787. They came to Woodford and lived on the Spring Station—Midway pike. Their children were: 1, Ann, m Merryman Stevens, and went to Boone County, Missouri; 2, Frances, m John C. Ruth, W 1821; 3, Mildred, m Frederick Junod, W 1822; 4, Sally; 5, Emaline or Evaline, m Joshua Lloyd, W (1850?); 6, Susan, m John Nicholson, W 1820; 7, Mary; 8, Elizabeth. John M. Gregory's will also mentions Manuel Gregory. His heirs sold the property to R. S. C. A. Alexander about 1851.

Jonathan and Stephen Gregory were in Woodford about 1800. Peter Gregory m Martha Minter (dau Rev. Joseph and Jane Trabue° Minter), W 1811.

Watts: Various branches of the Watts family in this vicinity have been traced to Edward Watts, of Spotsylvania County, Virginia, who died about 1750.

Among his children were: 1, William, whose son William (1724-1797) m Elizabeth ——. They came to Mercer, where they evidently spent their last years, but their tombstones may yet be seen on the Woodburn estate near Spring Station. Some of their children were: Mildred Gregory°; Eleanor Rodgers°; Richard, who came to Mercer; Peter (1756-1833), who came from Mercer to Woodford, but died in Shelby. He m Margaret Fisher, Lincoln 1785, and they had: William, m Sarah Smith, Garrard 1809; Ann, m Ezekiel Fisher, W 1815; Mary m John Gill, Mercer 1814; Mildred, m first Thomas P. Waller°, the records indicate that she m second William Waller°, W 1825, and third Richie Boulware°, Jr.; Abraham Gregory, m first Judith Ayres°, W 1823, and second Lucinda Robinson, Mercer 1825; Simeon R., m Sarah Pemberton°, W 1829, and went to Shelby; George W., went to Missouri.

2, Edward, whose family included two sons: Arthur, the ancestor of Mrs. Robert W. Scott°, and Edward, the father of Mrs. John Snell°.

One record says that John Watts (1730-1796), who came to Madison County, Kentucky, was the son of Thomas and Esther, and the grandson of Edward Watts, but another record states that he was the son of Thomas and the grandson of Francis and Ann Watts. He m Sarah Barnett, and some of their children were: Elizabeth Vawter°; Julius, who m Mary Eve, Orange County, Virginia, 1785; Judge John, m first Fanny Sebree, Culpeper County, Virginia, 1788, and second Mary Greenberry. He lived in Boone County, Kentucky, for several years, and went about 1810 to Dearborn County, Indiana, where he was known as both a judge and a minister of the Gospel. He died in Clark County, Kentucky, leaving a large family, among whom were Sarah and Frances Vawter°.

One John Watts lived for many years on Big Benson, having a family of three, F 1810. Some of his children were: 1, Edmund, m Apphia Lane°, F 1803; 2, Jeremiah, m Lucinda Lane°, W 1796, and they were ancestors of Mrs. Johnson Hearn, of Jett; 3, Bledsoe, m first Sally Searcy (dau Nancy Reardon), W 1807, and second Elizabeth Truman, W 1824.

William Watts m Nancy Vinzant, W 1791; Elizabeth Watts m George Mitchell°. Col. James Watts, of Virginia, m Margaret Patteson°, F 1817 or 1821.

GRUBBS—Polly, 1811, dis 1817

The Grubbs family is said to have descended from Peter Grubbs (Van Krupps), who came from Holland to Virginia in 1646. John Grubbs m Polly Gooch, Shelby 1811. John Grubbs was in Franklin, 1809-1816, and John A. Grubbs in 1815. One John Grubbs, born Hanover County, Virginia, 1751, died in Barren County, Kentucky, 1819.

GULLION—Jer'h, 1788

Jeremiah and Jack Gullion are said to have been the earliest settlers of Frankfort. Jeremiah, a noted Indian spy, built the first house where the Methodist Church now stands. He went to Gallatin, where his will, 1816, mentions his wife Belle and Jerry and John Gullion and others. Robert Gullion, a brother of Jeremiah, and Henry Gullion were also in Frankfort. The estate of Nathaniel Gullion, Sr., was settled F 1812, with Nathaniel, Jr., named in the settlement.

James Gullion m Sarah Demaree, Henry 1805; Anna m John Kelly, Gallatin 1809; Joseph m Margaret Wyant, Gallatin 1812; Jeremiah m Rebecca McGrew° (dau Alice), Henry 1813; Joseph m Sally Wood, Gallatin 1826; William m Elizabeth Wiley, Gallatin 1826; George m Susan Sale, Gallatin 1828; Henry m Sarah C. Jacobs, Carroll 1847.

From this family descends General Allen Gullion, of Carrollton and Washington.

GUNNELL—Betsy, dis 1821

Elizabeth Redd Major° m John T. Gunnell, of Christian County, Kentucky. She died soon after the birth of her son, Thomas Allen Gunnell, who was reared by his grandparents, Thomas and Susanna Major. He m Marian Wallace Thomson°, 1847, and lived in Saline County, Missouri.

Richard Gunnell was in Scott, 1799.

GUTHRIE—John, from Great Crossings 1804
          Margaret, r 1818, joined Unitarians 1826
          Polly, r 1818, joined Unitarians 1826
          Thomas G., dis 1840

Some historians claim that the Guthries are Scotch, while others say that the early forms of the name—Guttery, de la Gootrie—indicate Huguenot lineage.

One record says that Thomas and Mildred Howell Guthrie came from Fauquier County, Virginia, to Woodford in 1793, settling on the Lexington-Leestown road in the vicinity of Beal's Run. Their children were: 1, Mary, m John Frauner (see Smith); 2, Thomas, Jr., m Lucy (Woods?), and they had a family of seven, W 1810, including Fannie Craig°. They sold land to E. M. Blackburn, W 1826. 3, John, who presumably m first Mollie Bridgeford°, W 1802, and had a family of five, W 1810. He m second Margaret Tiller°, F 1814. He sold his farm on the north side of the Lexington-Leestown road to William Risk, W 1829. One John bought from Adam and Mildred Montgomery in 1828 an acre of land near what was later the site of the Harmony Church, and probably built a shop there. John Guthrie was south of the river, F 1805. 4, James, m Elizabeth Gibbs°, W 1802. He was in W 1801 and afterward, except through 1809-1813, when he was in Franklin at the site of what was later the Foster tavern. James and Elizabeth sold their farm in 1826 to George E. Gallaspie, and went to Shelby, where his will, 1840, mentions his wife and children: a, Jeptha D.; b, Thomas C.; c, Isaac N.; d, Julius G.; e, Elizabeth G.; f, Gabriel Smith; g, Granville C.; h, James G. Another record adds Agnes; Nathan; Mildred; William J.

5, William, m —— Yates°, and had a family of four, W 1810. William is listed in Mercer 1789-1800, in Woodford 1805-1814, in Mercer 1815-1817. One William m Catherine Reese, and one William was in Henry. 6, Nancy Bridgeford°; 7, Elizabeth Gibbs°; 8, Mildred Montgomery°; 9, Robert, m Sarah Long°, W 1815. They went to Henry, where their son John m Frances Owen° in 1840. 10, (Elder) Caleb, m Elizabeth Smith°, W 1817, and they went to Henry, where he died in 1878.

Others who were evidently grandchildren of Thomas and Mildred Guthrie were: James Guthrie, m Frances Smith°, W 1828; Nancy Sargent°; —— Guthrie, m Mrs. Martha Elliott° Moore; John Guthrie, m Eliza Wheat, W 1826; Willis and Sandy Guthrie.

Benjamin Guthrie came to Kentucky in 1783 with Richard Cave and Richard Johnson, and helped to build the Big Crossing Station in Scott for Robert Johnson. He m Frances ——, and they were on Glen's Creek, W 1810, with a family of seven, including: 1, Sally, m Edward Carter, W 1804; 2, Dahuldy, m William Gardner, W 1811; 3, Benjamin, m Catherine Ramsey°, W 1812; 4, Minerva Davis°. Norman or Norbourne Guthrie may also have been his son.

Alexander Guthrie, Jr. (s Alexander, Sr., of Cumberland County, Virginia) was in Woodford 1800-1806, but in 1808 was on Cedar Creek in Franklin, possibly in the section that was cut off in 1819 to form a part of Owen. He had a family of seven, F 1810, one of his children being Elizabeth Hardin°.

Sargent: The Sargents came from Person County, North Carolina, and were listed at various times in Franklin, Woodford, and Mason, before finally settling in Woodford, where William, William, Jr., Robert, and Drury were living in 1826, and perhaps later.

Capt. William Sargent was in Mason in 1803, in F 1805, and with a family of ten, W 1810. His wife was Mary Moore, and some of their children were: 1, John, in Mason 1797, in F 1804. He m —— (Pulliam?), and their children were: a, James Pulliam, (1806-1837), m Nancy J. Guthrie°, W 1827, the bond signed by Abraham G. Watts. They had: John Drury; Barbara Ann Stephens°; William Guthrie, who m Margaret Hawkins°, and was the grandfather of Mrs. W. O. Snyder, of Frankfort; James P. (Birdmore), who m Ann Farmer and was the grandfather of Mrs. James Dawson, of Frankfort. b, Mary Ann. Robert Sargent was the guardian of John's children, W 1824. 2, William, m Jane Davis Kyle, 1820. One William m Christina Rodgers°, W 1822. 3, Robert, who in 1821 bought from John Bell a farm "on the road leading from Blackburn's Tavern to Fox's cabins on the Frankfort road from Versailles." He m Mildred W. Gwyn, W 1828, and they had several children, including Mrs. John R. Morris°, of Woodford. 4, Lucy Tutt°; 5, Mary, m John W. Kyle, Mercer 1818. Capt. William may also have been the father of: Elizabeth Rodgers°; Benjamin Sargent, m Perlina Rodgers°, W 1825; Drury M. Sargent, m Permelia

Andrews Rodgers°, W 1825, and they had Churchill B. and John
W., who sold land to C. J. Blackburn, W 1849. Drury Sargent
m Rebecca Sanders°, W 1835.

Jeremiah Sergeant was in Woodford, 1791. James Sargent
was in Mason, 1797, and Joshua in 1803.

HALL—William, 1, dis 1803
       Sarah (wife of William), 2, dis 1803

The only available record of the Halls who settled here
states that William m N—— in Virginia. Whether it was he
who was the husband of Sarah is not known.

He was in Fayette in 1788, and in 1797 he owned the farm
on the Hanly road which now belongs to the Hancocks. He died
in 1817, leaving: 1, Jeremiah (—— 1825), m Mary Woold-
ridge°, F 1804, and they had: a, Emily Noland°; b, Thomas J.;
c, Sarah Ann (Bartlett°?); d, Mary Porter, m Lewis F. Vanden-
burg; e, Lucinda, m John Meredith; f, William C.; g, John W.,
m Mary Jane Gibson°, 1847, and they were grandparents of
Dr. G. C. Hall and Dr. L. T. Minish, of Frankfort. Jeremiah
lived on a part of his father's land.

2, Thomas (—— 1858), m first Mary B. Stephens°, F 1817.
Their children were: a, Susan, m Robert Bailey; b, Sarah Haw-
kins°. Thomas m second Mary Maupin (Gilbert) (Wright), and
they had: d, Harriet Jane, m Joseph Bailey; e, Anna Maria,
m Oscar Blakemore; f, Emma. Thomas lived at his father's
home place.

3, William (1783-1865), who lived near Bridgeport, m first
Mary Pattie°, F 1812, and second, Elizabeth Eloise Freeman°,
Anderson 1837, and they had: a, William; b, Eloise; c, Anna;
d, George Whitfield, m Ruth Flannagan; 4, Nancy Ellis°; 5,
Mary (1776-1830) m first John Jackson°, and second Benjamin
Edrington°; 6, Sally Hughes°; 7, Elizabeth, m first Paschal Hick-
man°, and second, William Littell, F 1823.

HANCOCK—Jemima, 2, dis 1803   Mary, dis 1837
           Susanna, 2   Eliza Ann Crutcher
           Harrison, dis 1840   Sophia
           Letitia, dis 1840   Elizabeth
           William, r 1834, dis 1837

The Hancocks in this community descend from John Hancock, of Virginia, who m Ann Graves°. They came to Woodford about 1800, then settled on Sulphur Lick, in Franklin County, about 1805, but went later to Ohio. Records from different sources assign to them these children: 1, Susan Crutcher°; 2, Bartlett, m Sophia Dixon°, F 1812, and they had these children, and perhaps others: a, George Washington, m first Eliza Crutcher°, 1844; he m second Mary Eliza Frazier, 1868, and they were the parents of George W. Hancock, of Jett; he m third Louisa Duffy, 1886. b, Mary, m Bartlett Crutcher°; c, Sarah Ann Blackburn°; d, Harry, m first Letitia Crutcher, and they went to Shelby; he m second Maria Davidson, from Madison, Ind. Some of his children were Nathan, George, and Bartlett; e, Susan, m Robert Austin Crutcher°; f, dau m —— Clark, near Switzer, and they had Robert, Washington, and others; g, Nancy, m Wesley Barger, of Shelby, and their dau m —— Henry; h, Letitia, m —— Kizer, of Bourbon, and they had a son Washington; i, Betty, m Robert Estes, of Scott, and they had James F.

3, Joel (1788-1863), had a son, Levi Bartlett, and twelve other children; 4, John, who is said to have gone to Hamilton, Ohio. One John, who lived at Graefenburg, west of Bridgeport, m Frances —— and had: a, Stephen, m Martha Lacy (dau Elijah), F 1822; b, Lewis; c, Elizabeth, m Edgar Jett°; d, Virginia, m John Walker Jett°; e, Thomas (1814 ——), m Nancy Gilpin, and went to Spencer, Ind.; f, Pamela, m Nathan Railsback, F 1822; g, George. 5, James; 6, William; 7, Henry Graves (1797-1876), m 1822 Sarah Watson, of Millville, and they went to Oxford, Ohio.

8, Isabella, m Henry Clem; 9, Graves, m Elizabeth Cox°, F 1810; 10, Thomas G., m Jemima Haydon°, F 1801. They lived on Elkhorn, and the records indicate that they had: a, James; b, Maria; c, John Bartlett; d, Jane Yancey°. 11, Nancy Jones°.

Other Hancocks were: Simon, in W 1791, owning land on Dry Run, F 1796, in Henry 1811, where he died about 1832. One Samuel m Martha Bartlett°, W 1796; Elizabeth (dau Samuel) m John Samuel°. Samuel Hancock was in W 1791, in F 1797. William, on Glen's Creek, was the father of Martha Stout°. William, Sr., on Griers Creek, m —— Wooldridge.

He died W 1826, leaving: 1, Obed, m Dicy Perry (dau Lewis), W 1790, and had a family of twelve, W 1810; 2, Hannah, m Robert Mosby, W 1792; 3, Edna Dehoney; 4, Teney; 5, William, Jr., m Mary Ann Wiles, 1815.

Sally Hancock m Joseph Layton, F 1823. Benjamin Hancock m Johanna Clarke. William Toreman m Ann Hancock (bond signed by Simon), W 1798.

HARDIN—Frances Bartlett, dis 1808, r 1813

The Hardins, who came from Virginia, were of Huguenot descent, the name being originally Hardouin.

Wesley Hardin, the founder of Hardinsville (now Graefenburg), m Frances Bartlett°, F 1808. They were living on Big Benson in 1819, but he died about 1822, and Frances m second Thomas Parrent, Jefferson 1828.

Col. John Hardin (s Martin, Sr.) came from Fauquier County, Virginia, to what is now Washington County, Kentucky, 1781. For his heroism in fighting the Indians the county of Hardin was named for him. His son, Senator Martin D. Hardin (1780-1823), m Elizabeth Logan, F 1809, and they lived with their children at "Scotland," which they bought in 1818 from the Samuels and Wares.

Elizabeth Logan Hardin m second the Rev. Porter Clay (brother of Henry Clay), at one time pastor of the Baptist Church in Frankfort. They went to Jacksonville, Ill., where he became an evangelist to the border settlements of Illinois and Missouri, preaching to white, black, and red men. He is said to have been the first to preach in the English language west of the Mississippi.

Mark Hardin (brother of Martin, Sr.) m Elizabeth Ashby, (dau Capt. Thomas, Frederick County, Virginia) and three of their sons were: 1, Benjamin, m Nancy Routt, Fauquier County, Virginia, 1785. They went to Kentucky and were ancestors of Bayless Hardin, of Frankfort; 2, Evangelist, with a family of twelve, F 1810, including Sarah Lindsay° and Elizabeth Kelly°; 3, Enos (also written Ennis), m Elizabeth Guthrie°. They came from Clark and, with others of the family, settled in Henry and in the part of Franklin that is now Owen.

Richard Hardin had a family of six, F 1810; James had nine; and Mark, in Frankfort, had six. Lewis m Elizabeth

Sheets°, F 1818; Nathaniel (s Benjamin) m Sarah A. Sanford°, F 1830; Haydon (s Martin) m Betsy Sisk°, W 1818.

HARRISON—Jemima, 1811, away in 1817

Joseph Harrison, of Louisa County, Virginia, m Margaret Richardson. He is listed among the defenders of Bryant's Station, though one record says his widow came to Fayette with her children after his death in 1788. They had: 1, Clara Morton; 2, Judah Graves; 3, Hiram, went to Jessamine; 4, Hezekiah, whose will, Fayette 1806, speaks of his wife Jane and six children; 5, Jemima; 6, Richardson; 7, Mildred, m Rev. William Payne (s Edward and Ann Conyers Payne); 8, Dulcena, m Jillson Payne, brother of Rev. William. She died in 1821, and he m second Mrs. Ann Stites, F 1822, the bond signed by Jacob Holeman; 9, Hosea; 10, Micajah, m Polly Payne, and their son, Micajah V., m Dulcenia B. Bledsoe°, Montgomery 1827, and went to Missouri.

In Woodford, Henry Harrison m Betsy Dale (c George), 1799, and they lived on Sinking Creek (Big Sink). He signed the marriage bond of Mourning Harrison Nall°, 1803. William C. Harrison m Levisa Hinton°, W 1829; Thomas M. Harrison m Elizabeth McGraw°, W 1829, the bond signed by Samuel Buckley.

Jeremiah Harrison came from England to Rockingham County, Virginia. He m Sarah Shipman, of Welsh ancestry, and they were in Woodford, 1790, settling on Sinking Creek. Their children are listed as: 1, Luke, m Edna Young (dau Nimrod), F 1811, and they lived on Glen's Creek; 2, Robert, m Rachel Williams°, W 1795; 3, Davis, who went from Woodford to Franklin about 1803; 4, Jane Hearn°. Some of this family went to Owen.

HART (Heart)—James
Lucy, r 1818
Eliza, r 1819, dis 1826

This name was sometimes spelled *Heart*, and pronounced *Hurt*°.

James Hart m Polly Telford, Scott 1801; Hugh Hart m Eliza Telford, Scott 1801; Betsy Hart m Daniel Brown°; John Hart m Susan Smith, F 1837.

John, David, and Charles Hart were in Mercer, 1789, and Nathaniel was in Franklin, 1803.

"Spring Hill," near Versailles, now known as "Hartland," was settled by Nathaniel Hart, Jr., and his wife, who was Susanna Preston. For over a century it was the home of this family, being owned until recently by their descendants, the Camdens. Nathaniel Hart, Jr., was a brother of Chinoe Smith°.

HATHAWAY—William, r 1825
Priscilla, r 1825

James Hathaway, of Fauquier County, Virginia, m Joanna Neville (dau George and Mary Gibbs Neville), and they were probably the ancestors of William, whose wife may have been Priscilla Ewell°. Letitia Ann Hathaway m William Curley°.

David and Jonathan Hathaway were in Clark, 1793. One Jonathan m Tompson Ann Henry (dau Joel), W 1825. He died the following year, and his widow m Benjamin P. Gray, W 1828.

HAYDON—James, 1	Nancy, 1
Betsy, 1, dis 1804	Benjamin, 1
Sally, 2	James, Jr., 1801, Mouth
Betsy, 2	of Elkhorn
William, 1	Abner, 1

The Haydons are said to have come from Hagadown, Denmark.

Thomas Haydon, who died in Spotsylvania County, Virginia, 1782, left several children, including: James; Ezekiel, who may have been the one of that name whose will was in Jessamine, 1818, and who was the ancestor of the Haydons on Clear Creek; Jarvis, the father of Abner; William.

James, m Elizabeth ———, and they lived for some time at Haydon's Station before going to Henry, where he died in 1815. Their children were: 1, John; 2, James; 3, Carey Allen; 4, Elizabeth Eidson°; 5, Martha Slaughter Roberts°; 6, Jemima Hancock°; 7, Nancy Bryant°; 8, Sarah Forbes°.

William Haydon built a cabin and raised a crop of corn a mile above Frankfort in 1776. His station was on the river at the mouth of Yeatman's Branch, which was known in early times as Haydon's Mill Creek. He went to Gallatin and spent his last years at Port William (now Carrollton). His wife was Ann Ballard, and some of their children were: 1, Benjamin (1760- ———), who went to Henry; 2, Sally, m Gersham Lee, Sr., and they went to Gallatin; 3, James (1766-1840), m Susanna Gore°, W 1792, and lived at Peak's Mill. Their children were: a, William G., m Elizabeth Long°, F 1813, and went to Illinois; b, Thomas, m first Sarah Hawkins°, F 1814, and second Dollie Ann Wallace°, and he was the father of Moses, who m Mary Webster° and had: William, m Teresa Shaw; Thomas, m Elizabeth Hunley; Mrs. George Gardner, and others, of Woodford; c, Benjamin, m Rhoda Hancock°, F 1816, and they had a son John; d, James, went to Owen; e, Mary Bartlett°; f, John G., m America (Vineyard?), Owen 1829, and had James and Thomas; g, Goar; h, Nancy, m Rowland Kendall; i, Elizabeth, m John M. Ireland, F 1838; j, Sarah, m Benjamin Harrod, F 1833; k, Fountain T., m Elizabeth Duvall (dau Rev. James), F 1841, and they were grandparents of Mrs. Emma Munday, Mrs. Kate Harrod, and Mrs. B. W. Wright, of Frankfort; l, Susan Ann Smither°; m, Bland, went to Owen; n, Innes, m Sallie F. Bartlett°, and had John, William, and Martha.

Also connected with this family was John Haydon, of Owen. His son Ennis m Matilda Thacker, and they were grandparents of Daniel Ennis Clark and Douglas Vest, of Franklin County.

Webb Haydon and his wife Elizabeth were on Elkhorn, F 1810, with a family of seven. The records indicate that some of their children were: 1, Francis S., m Milly Owen°, F 1804; 2, William, m Ann Cox°, F 1804; 3, Phoebe Cox°; 4, Solomon, m Kitty Cox°, F 1809; 5, Ruthy Sullenger°.

Joshua Jones m Mary Haydon (dau J. William), F 1796. Eleazer Haydon m Elizabeth Lewis Thomas (see Christian), F 1796.

HEAD—Benjamin   John Alfred, 1801
       Sarah, 1801, to Forks of Elkhorn 1818

John Alfred Head, of Culpeper County, Virginia, appointed his brother Hadley Head, of Woodford, to transact some business in 1794. One John A. Head came to Kentucky, and his will, Scott 1804, mentions his wife Elizabeth and: 1, William. One William m Sally Oliver, Culpeper 1792, and it may have been he who had a family of nine, F 1810; 2, Benjamin J. (1784-1862), m Martha ——. In 1840 he bought from Ezra Richmond what is known as the Colby Taylor farm on the Leestown-Lexington road, now owned by Quarles Thompson. In the graveyard are many tombstones, including those of John A. Head (1807-1840), and Harvey W. Head (1825-1845). Benjamin and Martha were the parents of Thomas Jefferson Head (1815- ——). He m Harriet A. Duvall, 1835, and some of their children were: a, Joel S., m —— Talbott, of Danville; b, Martha, m Dr. Green Pryor; c, Sallie, m —— Talbott; d, Mary Elizabeth, m Theodore Hockensmith, and they were grandparents of Hickman Darnell and Mrs. Ira Gray, of Cynthiana; e, J. A., m Alice Hardin; f, Benjamin, of Switzer. Jane Head m Alfred S. Ireland, F 1843.

3, Alfred. This was evidently John A. Head who m Polly Head (dau Benjamin), F 1805. His will, F 1847, mentions his wife Polly and: a, Joseph; b, Benjamin T.; c, William; d, Henry H. (m Elizabeth Long°, F 1840?); e, Alfred; f, Permelia Triplett°; g, Nancy, m Charles Story, F 1840; h, Sarah, m James Wright, F 1830; i, Francis. Several members of this family went to Daviess.

4, Anna, m —— Ransdale; 5, Sarah; 6, Fanny; 7, Elizabeth, m (Elijah?) Kendall.

To that part of Woodford that was afterward Franklin came Mrs. Grace Head, widow of Benjamin Head, of Culpeper, with her children: 1, Benjamin, m Milly Long, Culpeper 1785. They settled on Elkhorn, and he died in 1808, leaving his wife and: a, Moses, died 1816; b, Sally Smither°; c, Polly, m John A. Head (above); d, Grace, m first Joseph Moxley°, and second Benjamin Head; e, Benjamin T. (m Margaret?); f, Francis R.; g, Thomas Jefferson, m Rachel Boots, F 1827; h, John M. 2, Francis, m (Elizabeth?), and the records indicate that they had: a, Benjamin; b, John L., who went to Montgomery; c, Sally Long°; d, Polly, m Willis Johnson, F 1810, and went to Bracken. The widow of Francis m second Benjamin McAndre, W 1795, and they went later to Henry. 3, Mary, m Benjamin Perry, and they also went to Henry

Polly Head m Reuben Burton, W 1792. In Franklin, Benjamin T. Head m Nancy Sheridan, 1813; Benjamin T. m Eliz-

abeth Bohon, 1827; Milly m Joseph Bert, 1814; James m Fanny
Wetherspoon, 1828; John M. m Martha Luckett, 1829; John
m Lucy Payne (dau Lucy), 1830; Nancy m William Brydon°;
James m Martha Ann Sebree, 1838.

HEARN—Nancy, dis 1841

The Hearn (Heroun, Heiron, Heron) family came from
Normandy with William the Conqueror.

Jacob Hearn (1740-1808), who was a son of Edward and
Deborah Hearn and a grandson of Derby and Sarah Hearn,
of Maryland, m Janet Gilderoy and came with his family to
Versailles. Their children were: 1, Isaac, m Ann Hinton (dau
Alys Samples), W 1795, the bond being signed by Thomas
Hinton. They lived on Little Benson and had a family of nine,
F 1810, but went to Owen about 1817. Some who may have
been their children were: a, Thomas, m Polly Russell, Owen
1821; b, Isaac, m Susanna Harrison°, Owen 1824; c, Mary H.,
m James Harrison, Owen 1822; d, James, m Polly Baker, Owen
1823; e, Jacob, m Sarah Todd°, Jefferson 1829; f, Peter, m
Susan Taylor, Owen 1837; g, Sallie, m —— Baldwin; h, Joseph,
m Nancy ——. 2, Jacob (1770-1851), m first Jane Harrison°,
W 1796, and they went to Owen and afterward to Christian.
Their children were: a, Sarah, m Jeremiah Harrison°, Gallatin
1818; b, Louisa Smith°; c, Harrison, m Polly Smith°, and had
Thomas, Ethelinda, William, Clarinda, James; d, Warren, m
first Elizabeth Whittington°, W 1829, and they had Matilda,
m W. S. Wilson. He m second Jane Alexander, W 1834;
e, Elizabeth Thomas; f, Melvina Still; g, Luke. Jacob m second
Mrs. Mary Coleman, and they had Jacob MaGlothlin, born
1837.

3, Edward, m Vincincia Smith, W 1800. They also went
to Owen, and were the parents of: a, Margaret, m Elijah Threlkeld, Owen 1826, and lived in Henry; b, Elizabeth, m William
M. Smith, Owen 1833. 4, Elizabeth Johnson°; 5, Sarah Whit-
tington°; 6, Deborah Smith°.

7, Andrew (1766-1849), m Sarah Harbison (dau Catherine),
W 1804. They settled near what is now the south end of the
Hanly road, and built the house that is still occupied by their
descendants. Their children were: a, Charles Grandison, m
Evelyn Rollins, and they were grandparents of Mrs. B. F.

Fannin, of Frankfort; b, James, m Sarah Jane Threlkeld, Owen 1842; c, William H.; d, David, m Nancy Graham°, F 1829, and they had: James G., who lived at the old Graham Tavern, m Melcina Jane Johnson°, 1850, and they were grandparents of Miss Lula O. Hearn, of Jett, and Mrs. Edgar Riley, of Midway; Margaret, m Alexander Quin, and was the mother of W. B. Quin, of Jett.

HEART—see Hart

HENDRICKS—Bird, 2, dis 1802   Wife, dis 1802

Bird Hendricks died in Warren County, Kentucky, 1822, leaving property to his wife Catherine. The will of one Katherine Hendricks, W 1837, names her children: 1, Sally Hall; 2, Polly Cox; 3, Joseph; 4, Katherine Wilson; 5, John (m Betsy Deering°, W 1822?); 6, Henry; 7, Cornelius; 8, Ezekiel; 9, Lucy Strange; 10, Elizabeth. It is possible that this was Catherine Deringer, who m Henry Hendricks, W 1789.

Coonrod Hendricks m Judith Rice, W 1793. George Hendricks m Catherine Robertson (dau J. Suter°), F 1826.

HICKLIN—William, deacon 1794, died 1801
       Thomas, 1   F———
       Rebecca, 1   James, 1801
       Ginny, 2   John, 1801
       Robert, 1801-1804
       Betsy, 1801, withdrew 1802, restored 1814, dis
         1819
       Peggy, r 1818, dis 1819
       Rebecca, r 1818, dis 1819

Capt. Thomas Hicklin and his wife Elizabeth came from Augusta County, Virginia, and were living on Elkhorn, probably in the vicinity of Faywood, W 1790. The records indicate that their children were: 1, Hugh, who is said by one historian to have come to Kentucky about 1797, but one Hugh was in Shelby, 1792-1801, and perhaps later. The will of Hugh Hicklin, Harrison 1811, names his wife Elizabeth, sons John and Hugh, and several daughters. 2, William, m Margaret Thorn (dau James), W 1792. He was living north of the Lexington-Leestown road in F 1797. 3, Jonathan, m Jean Lockridge (dau Robert), W 1794, and had a family of eight, W 1810; 4, Thomas, Jr., m Rebecca ——. They lived in a log house at "Hicklin Hill" (now called "Hickman Hill"), south of Cole's Road as it crosses "Hicklin Branch" (now known as "Locust Creek" or "Hickman Branch"). Thomas died about 1804, and Rebecca, who had a family of seven, F 1810, died 1814. Some who may have been their children were: a, Jane Denney°; b, Moses; c, John. One John m Nancy Hicklin (dau William), Scott 1820. d, William. One William m Elizabeth R. Thomson°, and went to Greenup County, Kentucky. e, Thomas; f, Elizabeth. They sold their farm to Ezra Richmond about 1819.

5, Rachel, m James Lockridge, W 1801; 6, James, m Catherine Scearce (dau David and Cassandra Scearce), W 1810, and was deeded land on South Elkhorn by his father, W 1825. Some of the family were in Bath County, Kentucky, and some went to Lafayette County, Missouri.

HICKMAN—William, Sr., 1
        William, Jr., 1, dis to South Benson 1801
        Obedience, 1, dis to South Benson 1801
        Thomas, 1796
        Polly, 1, dis to Frankfort 1816

Paschal, 1790	John, 1801-1805
Betsy, 1801	Patsy, 1801
Sally, 1	Polly, 2
Benjamin, 1801	Betsy, r 1815

Reverend William Hickman, Sr. (1747-1834) was the son of Thomas and Sarah Sanderson Hickman, of King and Queen County, Virginia. His parents died when he was very young, and he and his sister lived with their grandmother until he was fourteen years old, when he was put out to learn a trade. In his new situation he fell into evil habits, and so continued until after he married. In 1770 he and his wife went to Buckingham County, where they became interested in the preaching of John Waller and James Chiles.

The next year they moved to Cumberland County, and there they saw their neighbors, the Bondurants, Maxeys, and Eppersons, being converted. After a while William's wife began to accept the Baptist doctrines, but of himself he wrote: "When I heard the truth preached it all condemned me. I often wished that I had never been born, or that I had been a brute that had no soul to stand before the holy God. For months I tried to pray, but thought I grew worse and worse, till all hopes of happiness were almost gone. My heart appeared to be as hard as a rock." He told of spending one night in utter misery, after which, "About the setting of daylight I got up and walked out. All at once the heavy burden seemed to fall off; I felt the love of God flow into my poor soul. I had sweet supping at the throne of grace—my sins pardoned through the atoning blood of the blessed Savior." On returning to the house, he continued, "I made no ado for fear of losing the sweet exercise. That was one of the happiest nights I ever experienced in all my life. The next morning when I arose and looked out, I thought everything praised God, even the trees, grass and brutes praised God." In the course of time he was baptized by Reuben Ford.

In the spring of 1776 William Hickman and several others started on a visit to Kentucky. They came to Harrodsburg, which, from his description, was an uncouth place, with smoky cabins and unwashed citizens. Thomas Tinsley was preaching there, and one day he said he would not preach unless William Hickman preached first. It was William's first effort, and he preached for fifteen or twenty minutes, "a good deal scared, but thinking that if I left any gaps down, he would put them up."

He returned to Virginia, continuing to preach, and in 1784 brought his family and settled in Fayette County.

In addition to his pastoral work in the Forks of Elkhorn Church, he was instrumental in organizing congregations at Glen's Creek, South Benson, North Fork, Mouth of Elkhorn, Stamping Ground, and other places, and attended to them in in their earlier years.

He has been described as a tall, erect man with a grave manner. John Taylor says of him: "His preaching is in a plain and solemn style, and the sound of it is like thunder at a distance—but when in his best gears, his sound is like thunder at home, and operates with prodigious force on the consciences of his hearers."

Family records state that his first wife was Mary Goode, a sister of Rev. John Goode, though he says in his manuscript: "My first wife was the daughter of John Shackleford, of King and Queen, as has been previously stated, by her we had thirteen children, seven daughters and six sons." A complete list of the names of their children has not been obtained, but some were: 1, Rev. William, Jr. (1767-1843), came to Franklin with his father and settled near him on Elkhorn. In 1801 he went with others to organize the South Benson Church, in which he was ordained in 1802. He preached there, and at times in the neighboring churches, throughout the remainder of his life.

He m first Obedience Brown°, whose family came to Kentucky with the Hickmans, and their children, as mentioned in his will, were: a, George, who was in Shelby, 1814. One George m Mary Grant, Shelby 1812, and Patsy (dau George), m James White, F 1831. b, Nancy Brown°; c, Lydia, m Capt. Francis Lockett, F 1831; d, Martha, m John P. Thatcher, F 1829; e, Eliza Bailey°. William, Jr., m second Eliza Edwards°, F 1835, and they had: f, Benjamin W.; g, John E.; h, Elizabeth P.

2, Lettice Edrington°; 3, Thomas, m Polly Bartlett°, W 1792. In 1810 he was in Frankfort with a family of seven. In 1829 his heirs, who sold land on Elkhorn to J. D. Brown, were: a, Thomas. One Thomas Hickman m Harriet Brooking°, W 1822; Thomas E. Hickman m Virginia Elliott°, W 1827; b, William (S.?); c, Joseph; d, Frances B., m first Tipton Lewis°, and second Lewis F. Stephens°. Mrs. Polly Hickman m Gen. Squire Grant, of Campbell, F 1828.

4, Capt. Paschal, for whom the county of Hickman was named in commemoration of his heroism at the River Raisin. He m Betsy Hall°, F 1797, and they lived in Frankfort. Their children were: a, Sally, m Gen. George W. Chambers, of Louisville, 1820 or 1821; b, Patsy, m first John Sproule, F 1818, and second Col. Benjamin Estill, of Abingdon, Va., F 1825; c, Susan, m William K. Trigg, and went to Missouri. Mrs. Paschal Hickman m second William Littell.

5, Benjamin, m Frances S. Littlepage, and they lived in Frankfort, on the triangular lot bounded by Main, Broadway, and High, "commonly called the Cocked hat Lott." Their children: a, Benjamin F., m Arianna Cunningham°; b, Emily Littlepage, m R. K. Woodson, F 1832, and they were grandparents of Woodson Coleman, of Frankfort; c, Louisa Frances, m Edward H. Watson, F 1835. 6, Sally Cunningham°; 7, Betsy Todd°; 8, Patsy Ransdall°; 9, Polly Hunter°.

10, (James?). Since William Hickman and his sons Thomas and Paschal owned land in Shelby, it is reasonable to believe that James, who settled in Shelby, was another son. The will of James Hickman, Shelby 1843, names his children: a, William; b, Thomas J.; c, John; d, Euclid; e, Benjamin H. (m Mary Jane Owen°, F 1833?); f, Caroline M.; g, Joseph and his dau Caroline; h, Ralph; i, Laurance; j, James, m Juliana Brooking°, Shelby 1825.

11, (John?). Nothing is known of him except that his name was on the tax list, F 1801-1802.

William Hickman's first wife died in 1813, and on December 25, 1814, he took for his second wife Mrs. Elizabeth Abbett, a daughter of Benjamin Dicken, of Scott. She had a son and two daughters by her first husband, and by William Hickman she had five more sons, of whom four were: 12, Edwin A.; 13, Ezra; 14, James H.; 15, John Gano, died in infancy. Mrs. Abbett's daughters were: ——, m Thomas K. Horn, and Fanny Abbett Neal°.

William Hickman's sister Elizabeth m first —— Mitchell, and had four children; she m second Edward Broaddus, of southern Kentucky, and had two more.

Moses Hickman (Hicklin?) witnessed the will of John Brown, F 1805. James L. Hickman, of Frankfort, m Maria Shackleford, Fleming 1818; Nancy Hickman m Joseph A. Hulette, F 1835.

David Hickman (s James and Hannah Lewis Hickman) was in Bourbon, 1795, and John was there in 1800. David m Clara McClanahan, and they were the parents of Nancy Buford° and Agnes Bledsoe°. Richard Shelby m Lydia E. Hickman (dau John L.), Bourbon 1833.

HILL—Hannah, r 1801, dis 1801

William Hill m Sarah Smith°, F 1798, the bond being signed by George Smith. One William Hill, F 1804, listed land in Shelby. Gamaliel Hill m Permelia Lewis°, F 1814; Zachariah Hill m Tabatha Walston, F 1838.

Robert Hill was in Mercer, 1795. George Hill m Jane Lee, W 1816. George P. Hill m Rhoda Sparks°, Owen 1821.

HITER—Elizabeth, r 1803, dis 1807

James Hiter m Betsy McGee°, F 1796. Charles Hiter m Betsy Oliver°, W 1794. Benjamin Hiter, a cousin of Charles, m Elizabeth Combs, and they lived in Woodford near Troy. After the death of Benjamin Hiter, Elizabeth Combs Hiter m Meredith Furr, and they were grandparents of W. D. Furr, of Frankfort.

HODSON—Joshua, r 1828
Polly, r 1828
Nancy, r 1828

John Hodson was in Scott 1806, and in Woodford 1815. John B. Hodson bought land on Elkhorn from James Rentfro, F 1809, and had a family of five, F 1810.

Andrew J. Hodson m Elvira Lewis (dau Fielding), Owen 1836; William Hodson m Martha Louderback (see Green), Owen 1838.

HOUGH—Joseph, 1801-1806

John and Aaron Hough were in Franklin, 1797, and John and Moses were on Elkhorn, F 1801. John Hough m F 1819 Mrs. Sally Witherspoon, who was the mother of: 1, Fanny Witherspoon, m James Harrod, F 1828; 2, Nancy Witherspoon, m Christopher Lee, F 1835; 3, Susan Freeman°.

HOWE—Mahala, r 1845

Edward Howe was living above the mouth of Cedar Creek, F 1800, and John Howe had a family of nine, F 1810.

John Howe m Sally Harris or Farris, F 1795; James m Margaret Grimes, F 1819; John m Sarah Parks or Parker, F 1820; Edmund m Nancy Buffin (dau Nancy Baker°), F 1817; Polly m Peter Keger (?), F 1837.

George Howe m Lydia Happy, Fayette 1825. Amanda Elizabeth Howe (dau —— and Virginia Happy Howe), of Stamping Ground, m Morton Brinker Hundley or Hundleigh, whose father came from England to Culpeper County, Virginia. The records indicate that they were the parents of Will T.

Hundleigh, the Kentucky landscape painter, and they were grandparents of Mrs. Nora Haydon° Maxwell, of Lexington.

Capt. Edward Howe m Nancy Lyne. He died at the age of eighty, W ⸱824, and was buried in the Pisgah churchyard. His dau Anne (1785-1835) m first Dr. John Watson, and they lived at the Crittenden home (now the Methodist orphanage), near Versailles. They had several children, including Dr. Edward H., who m Sallie Lee (Maria) Crittenden (dau Gov. John J. and Sarah Lee Crittenden), and was the father of Rear Admiral John C. Watson, and the grandfather of Miss Sarah Crittenden Taylor, of Frankfort.

Mrs. Anne Watson m second John Buford°.

HUBBELL—William, 2, dis 1811   Margaret, 1, dis 1811

Capt. William Hubbell (1757-1831) was the son of Hezekiah Hubbell, of Stratford, Conn. He m Margaret Gano° in Orange County, New York, 1779. They came to Kentucky and lived for some time between the Forks of Elkhorn and Woodlake, removing later to Scott. They had a family of six, F 1810, including: 1, William D., m Elizabeth Price°, F 1822; 2, Margaret. Catherine Hubbell Gano° was the niece of Capt. Hubbell.

HUGHES—Polly, r 1820

Abijah Hughes, of Welsh descent, whose family came from Maryland to Virginia, m Susanna Pace, and they came to Kentucky. They settled near Farmdale in Franklin County, and their children were: 1, Mary Ann, m Bartlett Lancaster, F 1822, and went to Iowa; 2, William, went to Shelby; 3, Quentin Durward, went to Indiana; 4, Martha, m —— Wallace; 5, Betsy, went to Indiana; 6, Louisa, m first —— Reading, and second Porter Coleman Reading, of Swallowfield; 7, Samuel, m Lucy Ballard°, Owen 1826, and their son Benjamin Samuel m Annie Winter° (dau John L. and Jane White Winter, of Fayette), and was the father of Mrs. Frank Hewitt and Mrs. E. H. Elliott, of Frankfort. Abijah Hughes was on the tax list, W 1810.

John Hughes (s Joseph and Sarah Swan Hughes), a relative of Abijah, m Elizabeth Berry°, W 1801.

Thomas Hughes m Sally Hall°, F 1802. He is said to have built the house on Todd Street in Frankfort which was afterward occupied by John W. Rodman, and in 1810 had a family of six, including Mary Vaughan°. John W. Hughes m Mary Rodgers° (dau Daniel), F 1829. James Hughes was in Franklin County, 1796, and John in 1810, with a family of nine.

Timothy Hughes, who joined the Forks Church in 1862, m Elenora Woolfolk°. They came with their family from Scott, and lived near Midway at "Pine Grove," which they bought from D. C. Humphrey in 1862 and sold in 1883 to John Slack, of Louisville. They were grandparents of Miss Mattie Hughes, of Midway.

John Hughes m Polly Holeman (dau Daniel), W 1805.

HUNTER—Polly, dis 1824

Capt. James Hunter m Polly Hickman°, F 1818. They went to Shelbyville, where he died in 1837 at the age of seventy-four.

William Hunter, in Frankfort 1810, had a family of seven. One William and his wife Ann went from Frankfort to Washington, D. C.

One James Hunter, of Philadelphia, had by his first wife, whose name is unknown: 1, James G. One Judge James G. was in Frankfort before 1800; 2, Robert. He m second Mary Stewart°, and they had: 3, Charles S., m Fanny ——, and their children were: Sarah, Margaret, Charles, James, and perhaps others. They were in Woodford 1810, but afterward lived in Franklin near the mouth of Glen's Creek.

4, William Stewart, m Catherine Canfield, W 1816, and they lived on the McCracken's Mill road. Their children were: a, Mary, m Randolph Railey, Jr.; b, William S., m Mary Brown; c, Elizabeth, m John Brown; d, James m Harriet Peters; e, Catherine, m Swift Darneal (see Darnell); f, Absalom C., m Edith Sanders°; g, Belle. 5, Sarah Long°. It is not known whether James Hunter, Sr., died in Pennsylvania or in Kentucky, but in 1806 his widow and children, who were then living in Woodford, arranged to settle his estate.

Another James Hunter m Jane Davis°, W 1812. He died W 1824, leaving his wife and: 1, John; 2, Sally; 3, Marian.

Joseph Hunter m Sally Ellis°, W 1792; Absalom Hunter m Nancy Sheets°, W 1808, and in 1810 was living in Versailles with a family of three; while Samuel Hunter had a family of four.

Stewart: Charles Stewart, of Bucks County, Pennsylvania, had four children who came to Kentucky: 1, William, who was killed at Blue Licks; 2, Robert, who was on the tax list W 1800 and a few years thereafter, but was living in New York City in 1807; 3, Hannah, m John Harris. Her will, F 1804, names children: a, John; b, Ann, m first Dr. Hugh Shiell, of Philadelphia, and second Judge Harry Innes, Lincoln 1792; c, Elizabeth Todd°; d, Sarah Smith; e, Mary Hanna; f, Rachel Harris; g, Hannah Harris. 4, Mary Hunter°. The wife of Achilles Sneed° is said to have been a niece of William Stewart.

Charles Stewart m Mary McCracken°, F 1821, and they lived in Eminence.

HURT—Hannah, r 1828

Richard and Hannah Hurt (written also Hart) were relatives of the Majors who went with them to Missouri.

Mourning Hurt m Mourning Oliver°, F 1817.

JACKSON—Cyrus, 1801   Mrs. Josiah, withdrew 1807
Madra, 1801

Francis Jackson came from Amelia County, Virginia, in 1787, and in 1792 was living in Woodford on Dry Run. He was a member of Mount Gomer Church. The settlement of his estate, W 1836, shows that he had eight heirs, of whom some were: 1, Madra, m Keziah Metcalfe, and went to Jefferson, where his dau Sabina m David S. Cox, 1840; 2, Rebecca Bristow°; 3, Eliza, m Abel Cook°, and went to Hickman, Ky.; 4, Nancy B. Long°; 5, John A., who probably went to Shelby; 6, Micajah.

Another family from Amelia was that of William Jackson, who sold land near Millville to Isaac Miles. His will, W 1795, names his wife Ann and: 1, Matthew; 2, William, Sr. (m Betsy Bartlett°, W 1792?); 3, Samuel; 4, Eady Rowlett°; 5, Anney Moore; 6, Martha Cousins; 7, Elizabeth; 8, Judith; 9, Sarah Ann Brown°; 10, John C. (Chandler?), evidently the one who settled near the mouth of Elkhorn and had, besides other children: a, Nancy Stephens°; b, Patsy Gore°; c, Sarah, m Zachary Duvall, F 1797; 11, Nelly, m Conrados Piles, and went to Henry; 12, Loveday Edrington°; 13, William, Jr.; 14, Ann Baker°; 15, Prudence, m Anthony Malloy, W 1793; 16, a grandson, Jesse

Montgomery Jackson. The will was witnessed by Isaac Miles and Anthony Bartlett.

John Jackson, said to be of the same family as Stonewall Jackson, m Mary Hall°, W 1793. He lived in Franklin, and in 1808 bought from Samuel Montgomery the farm now owned by Clarence Montague, at Jett. He died in 1815, leaving his widow and: 1, William, m first Letitia S. Pace°, W 1816, second, Mary Ann Mayhall, and third Sarah Mayhall (dau Timothy), F 1828. He lived near Bridgeport, and had: a, Joel, who went to Hawesville, Ky.; b, John, whose daughters m Taylor and William Parrent, of Frankfort; 2, Sally Vaughan°; 3, Elizabeth, m John Asberry, F 1814; 4, Nancy (m Seth Cook°, F 1815?).

John Jackson, who came from Scotland, m Alice Young (dau Col. Richard and Mary Moore Young), W 1792, and they lived in Versailles, where in 1810 they were listed as having a family of fourteen. Some of their children were: 1, Maria, m William Douglas Young, W 1811; 2, Alice, m Judge William E. Ashmore; 3, Richard G., m Mary Virginia Lafon°, W 1825, and they were the parents of Miss Sally Jackson, of Frankfort; 4, John C., m Lucy S. Lafon, W 1826. One John Jackson m Mary O'Bannon, W 1813.

Elizabeth Jackson m Austin Bohannon°; Reuben Jackson m Franky Gore°, F 1804, and they were the parents of Catherine Vaughan° and Julia Long°. Letitia Jackson m Robert Church°, F 1827; Elizabeth m James Kelly°; Margaret m James Rentfro°; Martha m Stephen Livingston°; Mary M. m George B. Bartlett°. Joshua Jackson m Margaret Underwood, W 1795; John A. Jackson m Susan Long° (dau Mary), W 1804.

JAMES—Mary, 1   Nancy, 1
       Sister James (Nancy Smither), dis 1815

Daniel James (1750-1824?), a cabinetmaker, came from Virginia, and was one of the early settlers of the community. He lived at Haydon's Station on a farm, which he sold to Benjamin Branham in 1824. He and his wife were members of the Mount Pleasant Church, transferring their membership to Frankfort about 1819.

His wife was Sarah Richards°, and they had a family of six, F 1810. Some of their children were: 1, Mary Branham°; 2,

Anne, m first John H. Branham°, and second Rev. George Blackburn°; 3, Susan, m Caleb Spencer, Henry 1814. Hugh James m Charlotte M. Irwin (dau Samuel), F 1800; William L. James m Matilda Pemberton°, F 1805; Sally James m William Napp, F 1798. Daniel settled the estate of Elzey L. James, F 1810. Daniel and Thomas were in Henry, 1811. Daniel died in Newcastle.

Rev. Daniel Field James "an eminently godly man," was the son of John and Clara Nall° James, who came from Culpeper County, Virginia, to Kentucky in 1785. He m Eleanor Evans, Pulaski 1816. They lived in Pulaski, and were grandparents of Dr. Samuel E. James, of Frankfort.

William James was in Scott, 1801; Joseph in 1811, and a few years later James, Benjamin, Wiley, and John, who m Mary Poor (dau Drury and Elizabeth Mims Poor), were also there. Some members of this family went to Covington, Ind., and some to Adairville, Ky.

Richards: The will of Philemon Richards, W 1794, names his children: William; Anne Chapman; Sarah James°; Lucy Christian°; Lewis; Benjamin; Philemon, Jr., whose estate was inventoried, Hopkins 1818.

JEFFREYS—Ambrose, 1801, dis 1810
            Agnes, dis 1810

Ambrose Jeffreys was living in Frankfort, 1797. He m Agnes Ware°, F 1805, and in 1810 had a family of three. He sold land to William Samuel in 1815.

Matthew Jeffreys (s John Jeffreys, of Mercer?) m Elizabeth Wooldridge°, F 1816.

JETER—Elisha, dis 1803

Elisha Jeter m Mary Mathews (dau James), W 1810. Fielding Jeter had a family of seven, W 1810. William Jeter m Susan Payne (dau Charles), W 1814; Hiram Jeter m Mahala Carson (dau Isabella), W 1825.

JOHNSON—Enos, dis 1841

Enos Johnson, who went to Missouri, has not been identified, though there were several Johnson families in the vicinity.

Col. Cave Johnson (1760-1850) was the son of Col. William and Elizabeth Cave Johnson, of Orange County, Virginia, and was an uncle of Elder John T. Johnson and Col. Richard M. Johnson, of Scott. He came to Kentucky in 1779, and was at Bryan's Station and later in Woodford. The records state that he m first Sally Keene, 1781; second Ann Keene, 1782; third Elizabeth Craig°, 1784. Children of the last marriage were: John, Sally, Benjamin, Younger, Nancy, Cave, Elizabeth, Catherine, Julia, Lucinda, Harriet, Jane, Polly. He was one of the surveyors who laid out the town of Versailles, but he removed to Boone County about 1796.

One Cave Johnson m Mrs. Margaret Keene, F 1836, the bond signed by Thomas Theobald. A letter from one Cave Johnson says his father m Mary Noel at Craig's Station, W 1790 or 1791.

David Johnson (s Isaac and Elizabeth Holeman Johnson, of Jessamine) m Polly Burch, Lincoln 1792, and went to what is now Anderson. Their children were: 1, Cave, m Marian Sublett°, W 1823, and they lived near Mortonsville for several years, but afterward returned to Anderson. They had: a, Sarah, m Jesse Mosby; b, Susan Martin°; c, Frances V., m James W. Howard (s Isaac and Lucy Willis Howard), 1848, and they were grandparents of Marion C. Howard, of Versailles; d, John, who went to Lebanon, Ky.; e (David?), the father of Holeman Johnson, of Salvisa, Ky. 2, Mary (1795-1825), m John Bond; 3, David; 4, Jack.

An old Bible record says: "Nellie Conway married James A. Madison, Sr.—12 children. Jane Madison married Fauntley Johnson, Dec. 9, 1812." In that same year Fauntley (Fauntleroy) and Jane Madison Johnson came from Virginia to Woodford and settled near Mortonsville. Their children were: 1, Madison, m —— Smither°. Madison C. Johnson died F 1890, leaving his wife Harriet. Madison L. Johnson m Virginia Wilkins (dau George and Frances Wilkins), W 1848. 2, Thomas D., m Mary Smith; 3, Eliza; 4, Permelia Smither°; 5, Nicey; 6, Minerva; 7, Sweden, m —— and went to Shelby; 8, William.

Jane Madison Johnson died in 1830, and Fauntley Johnson m Mrs. Marian Sublett Johnson (widow of Cave), W 1832. Their children were: 9, Benjamin C.; 10, Mary V.; 11, Fauntley (known as "Little Fauntley"); 12, Zachariah; 13, Nancy, m (W.

Holeman?) Martin°, and their son Woodford m Willie Collier; 14, Lewis, m Josie Manuel; 15, Andrew Broaddus, m first Nannie Ford, and second Emma ——. Fauntley Johnson m third his cousin, Sarah H. Johnson, W 1846.

Richard Johnson (1768-1854), a relative of Fauntley Johnson, was the son of Alexander and Mary (Lewis?) Johnson, of Virginia. He m Elizabeth ——, and they lived in the Millville neighborhood. Their children were: 1, Richard Fauntley ("Big Fauntley"), m Mary Adkins; 2, Yancey; 3, John; 4, Sarah, m Fauntley Johnson; 5, Nancy; 6, Ellen Brightwell°; 7, Mary Brightwell°; 8, Jane Alepha, m Benjamin Williams°, W 1839; 9, Elizabeth.

Isaac Johnson was living on the Steele's Ferry road, W 1794, and in 1810 one Isaac had a family of four, and another Isaac had ten. One Isaac Johnson lived in the vicinity of Millville, and his will, W 1826, is witnessed by Isaac Whittington and Andrew Hearn. His wife was Elizabeth Hearn°, and some of his children were: 1, Susan, m William Samples, W 1803; 2, Andrew, m Nancy Mitchell°, and their son, John William, was the father of Mrs. John Quinley, of Frankfort; 3, Isaac, m Mrs. Martha Davis, W 1827; 4, Arthur, m Elizabeth Gayle°, W 1830, and they went to Owen; 5, Jacob (1804-1854) m Elizabeth J. Mitchell°, F 1835, and one of their sons, James Clelland, m Mary Willis (dau William and Georgianna Holloway Willis), and was the father of Mrs. Frank Watts, of Versailles. Jane Johnson (dau Isaac) m John Warren, F 1809, and Jane Johnson (1797-1860), dau of another Isaac, m John Walker, W 1819, and died in Franklin County. David Johnson (s Isaac) m Sally Thurman, W 1794.

Edmund Johnson (s William and Sarah Johnson) m Betsy Peyton (dau William [or George] and Susan Cogell [or Cozell] Peyton, who m in Culpeper County, Virginia, 1792), W 1811. They lived at some period in Mercer, though their children were later in Woodford. They had: 1, Sidney; 2, Thomas, m Rebecca ——; 3, Peyton, m Elizabeth Bailey°, W 1848; 4, Henry W. (m Sally Graddy, W 1850?); 5, Paulina, m John Sullivan; 6, Melcina Jane Hearn°. One Peyton Johnson m Pamelia M. Johnson, F 1839. One record states that they married at Saundersville, which is said to have been located on Flat Creek.

Thomas Johnson appears to have lived on Clear Creek. His will, W 1792, names his wife Elizabeth and: David; Silas, m Nancy Poor, W 1814; Mary; Anna; Betsy; Sally.

Simeon Hifner, who came from Culpeper County, Virginia, m Louisa Johnson (dau Elizabeth), W 1827, and they were grandparents of Melvin B. Hifner, for many years superintendent of Woodford County schools.

Nancy Graves° m —— Johnson, and they were the parents of Benjamin and Nelson Johnson.

James Johnson (Johnston), a shipbuilder who was born near Richmond, Va., m Mary Jane Richardson°, F 1799, and they had: 1, William James; 2, Thomas; 3, Jane; 4, Nancy; 5, Martha; 6, Sarah; 7, Elizabeth. James Johnston sold land on the north bank of the river to John Richardson, F 1804.

Jones—Thomas, 1   Richard M., r 1841, d 1847
       John, 1791   Margaret H. (Ayres)
       Susan E., r 1840, d 1872

Thomas Jones was among the early members of Glen's Creek, and was listed, W 1800, as owning property in Shelby.

Thomas W. Jones, a relative of John Paul Jones, came from Pennsylvania and had property in Frankfort and on the river near Big Eddy. He m Susan E. Winter°, F 1814, and they were living in Lexington in 1823, though their children were here at a later period. They were the parents of: 1, Sidney Scott°; 2, Richard M., m Elizabeth Bradley°, 1843, and the records indicate that their dau Rebecca m first —— Leffler, and second George W. Gayle°; 3, Margaret H. Ayres°; 4, Deborah S. Ayres°; 5, Susan Mary Bradley°.

John Jones, who apparently lived in Woodford, was the father of Prudence Bohannon°, and John and Mary Jones were the parents of Tabitha Davis°.

One John Jones, who m Ann Marshall, bought land from S. M. Noel, F 1813. His will, F 1829, mentions his wife and children: 1, John J., m Judith Ann Foster°, and their children were: a, John Thomas; b, Lucy Marshall; c, Ann Cruse. 2, Mary C. McIlvain; 3, Ann, m George M. Parker; 4, Richard C. (on South Benson, F 1811?); 5, Elizabeth, m John M. Parker, F 1829; 6, Hamilton G.; 7, George W.; 8, Frances B., m George Mason;

9, Francis; 10, Susan R. In 1833 these heirs bought from L. R. Major a tract on which they built the brick tavern which they afterward sold to William W. Stephens.

Joshua Jones m Mary Haydon°, 1790; Abraham Cook° m Sarah Jones, F 1795; Lewis Jones m Sally Graves°, F 1818. Erasmus Jones had a family of four, F 1810; Richard C. had five; Robert had eight; William had four. Many of the Jones family lived in Scott.

Winter: The Winters were of Welsh descent. Daniel Winter came from Maryland, and was living in Frankfort, 1810. His children were: 1, Susan E. Jones°; 2, Deborah, m first Aaron Goforth, F 1805, second Richard M. Gano°, third Joel Scott°; 3, Jane, m F 1825 John Goodman, who made the first musical instruments in Frankfort, and whose descendants live in Louisville.

John L. Winter was the father of Annie Hughes.°

KELLY—Winney, r 1805, dis 1812

In the will of James Eadson, F 1807, he mentions his niece, Lucy Kelly, and the will is witnessed by Winiford Kelly.

James Y. Kelly (1765-——), s James and Susan Wilson Kelly, m Lucy (or Nancy?) Neale°, and they came from Fauquier County, Virginia, to Scott, about 1800. Their children were: 1, Susan Boulware°; 2, Sally Shely°; 3, James; 4, Nancy, m her cousin, George P. Kelly; 5, Elizabeth Rogers°; 6, Penelope, m her cousin, Thomas C. Kelly; 7, Spicer; 8, John.

The will of William Kelly, Scott 1835, names his wife Nancy, and children: Edward; Elizabeth Graves°; Milly Sutton°; James; grandchildren Louisa Swoop and William C. Boston. James B. Kelly m Mallie Ferguson°.

In Franklin, Andrew Kelly m Rebecca Onion, 1801; William L. Kelly m Elizabeth Rowan, 1803; Daniel m Sally Burchfield, 1810; Jacob m Elizabeth Hardin°, 1814; Amos m Elizabeth Jackson°, 1817; Thomas m Sarah Douthitt, 1822.

James Kelly m Hannah Smith, W 1804. William and James were in Woodford, 1790; and the will of Samuel, about 1810, mentions his brother John, of Indiana.

Jacob Kelly m Peggy Gore°, Culpeper County, Virginia, 1790.

KNAP—Susanna, 1801, dis 1803

Joshua Knap m Mrs. Susanna McDaniel°, F 1800, the bond being signed by Robert Finnie. They were living north of the river, F 1801.

LAMPKIN—Joseph, r 1841, dis 1843
Elizabeth, r 1841, dis 1844

Records show that some of the Lampkin family came from Culpeper County, Virginia, and settled in that part of Fayette which is now Jessamine, and some in Woodford near Millville.

Daniel C. Lampkin was in Woodford, 1791, and one Daniel was on Clear Creek, W 1800. The will of James Lampkin, W 1811, names his wife Sarah and children: Charles Harrison; William Muse; Presley Thornton; Lewis Washington; Peter; Charlotte Craig; Sally Parker; Betsy Pepper; Fanny Hayes; George Chatin; James Lewis; John B., who in 1810 had a family of four.

John R. Lampkin m Lucy Poor (dau Capt. Thomas and Susan Poor), W 1807; Daniel Baker° m Elizabeth Lampkin, W 1816.

In Culpeper were Sally and Anne Lampkin Jackson°.

LANE—Eliza, r 1828   Mary, r 1828

Edward Lane came from Orange County, Virginia, and settled in that part of Franklin that was afterwards Anderson. He probably was the owner of Lane's Mill, on Little Benson. He died Anderson 1831. His wife was Rhoda and their children were: 1, John; 2, Richard, died F 1812; 3, Garland, m Elizabeth McBrayer (dau James and Naomi McBrayer), F 1816; 4, Felix, m Harriet Poindexter°, F 1811; 5, Hasting, m Elizabeth Jewell (dau Basil), F 1810; 6, Nancy, m Benjamin Stanisberry, W 1800; 7, Alpha or Apphia Watts°; 8, Lucinda Watts°.

Peter Lane m Polly Cox°, F 1811, the bond signed by John Montgomery; Frances Lane (dau Mary) m Richard W. Herndon, W 1827; Daniel S. Lane m Nelly Florence (dau William), W 1817.

Poindexter: Thomas Poindexter (s John and Lucy Christian Poindexter, of Virginia) m Lucy Jones. He died in Franklin

County, Kentucky, about 1797. Their children are listed as: 1, Rev. John, m Elizabeth Thornton; 2, Gabriel (1758- ——) m ——, and had a family of ten, F 1810. He was the father of Harriet, and of Lucy, who m William P. Underwood, F 1802. Gabriel went to Clark County, Indiana. 3, Thomas, m Sally Ragland; 4, Robert, who had a family of eight, F 1810; 5, James; 6, Richard; 7, George; 8, Milly or Molly, m Garland Cosby, and had: Stith, Nicholas, Francis, Betsy, Garland. 9, Elizabeth Jones m Christopher Cammack, and lived in Frankfort; 10, Lucy.

William Poindexter in F 1810 had a family of ten, including: a, Martha C., m Bernard Gaines°, F 1817; b, Sarah, m James P. Hampton; c, Margaret, m John Hockensmith, F 1823. The Poindexters lived on Elkhorn.

Lewis—Joseph, 1, dis 1798	Lucy D., r 1848
Sarah, 1, dis 1798	Susan R., r 1849

Joseph Lewis witnessed the will of Mrs. Margaret Cook, and he and his wife Sarah went with the Cooks to Shelby, where his will, 1817, mentions: wife, Sally and: 1, Jesse; 2, Joseph, m Nancy Bell, Shelby 1804 or 1805; 3, Abraham, m first Christina Christy, Shelby 1805, and second Lucy Wilcoxon, Shelby 1821; 4, Rebecca (m Henry Lawson, Shelby 1821?); 5, Esther, m Samuel Prather, Shelby 1812; 6, Ann Miles°; 7, Susan, m Roger Ellis°, Shelby 1805; 8, Rachel; 9, Polly; 10, Isaac (m Margaret Bristow, Shelby 1810?); 11, Sally; 12, Martha; 13, Jemima; 14, Sarry; 15, Elizabeth; 16, Jonathan; 17, James.

Hon. John Lewis (1784-1858), s Zachary and Ann Terrell Lewis, of Virginia, m Jean Wood Daniel (dau Travers), in 1808. They came to Woodlake, and for many years had a famous school at "Llangollen." Their children were: 1, Frances Ann Mitchell°; 2, Rev. Cadwallader, m Elizabeth Henry Patteson°, 1839. They lived at "Belair," now owned by Mrs. Pollock Paynter, and were the parents of: a, William Jarratt, who m Louise T. Wallace°, and was the father of Misses Frances and Elizabeth Lewis, of Frankfort; b, John Alexander, m Margaret Jane Scott°, and was the father of Misses Sidney and Jane Lewis, of Georgetown. Rev. Cadwallader Lewis was ordained to the ministry in 1846, and preached at Frankfort, Versailles, Glen's Creek, and other churches in the surrounding territory. He was instrumental in organizing Providence Baptist Church, of which he was pastor from 1858 until his death in 1882.

3, Elizabeth Travers; 4, George Wythe, m Mary Jane Todd°, and they were the parents of George A. Lewis, of Frankfort; 5, Mary Overton; 6, John M.; 7, Jean Wood Patteson°; 8, Addison, m Mary G. Mitchell°; 9, Lucy Daniel (1826- ——), m James M. Hollady, of Spotsylvania County, Virginia, and they had: a, Louise Richmond; b, John Waller; c, James Minor; 10, Susan Raleigh Price°; 11, Waller; 12, James M., m Euphemia M. Todd°.

Rev. Addison Lewis, a brother of John, m Sarah Billingsly, and they were the parents of Virginia Ann Brown°. Rev. Addison preached at Buck Run, Great Crossings, and other churches in the vicinity, and went to Missouri in 1838.

One John Lewis, who had a mill near the Woodford Church in 1789, was the father of Samuel Lewis, who m first Esther (Whitley?), and had a family of five, F 1810. They evidently lived in the vicinity of Spring Station, owning land in both Franklin and Woodford. Samuel m second Elizabeth Blackburn° Peart, W 1817, and they had a dau, Prudence B.

Henry Lewis and his wife Scytha came from Bracken, and settled on Big Benson about 1808. His will, F 1831, mentions his wife and: 1, Charles B., m Paulina Routt°, W 1826. They went to Woodford, and later to Scott. Two of their children were: a, Catherine, m Leonard Fleming, of Midway; b, Eliza, died 1846; 2, Henry B., m Sally Cole°, W 1828, and they had: a, Sarah Vaughan°; b, Alice; c, Joseph; d, Perline Thomas°; 3, Nancy, m William White, F 1809; 4, Permelia, m first Gamaliel M. Hill°, and second William M. Stout°; 5, Sally, m Nimrod Mason, F 1813; 6, Polly; 7, heirs of Zachary Lewis. Zachary B. Lewis m Jane Mason, F 1813. One Zachary m Ruthy Roberts°, F 1815; Zachary m Nancy Church°, F 1826.

Charles and Henry B. sold the farm on Benson to James Roberts in 1836, and in 1860 they sold Cole's Tavern to Edward Waits, of Harrison.

John Lewis m Verinette Stephens°, F 1824; Tipton Lewis m Frances Hickman°, F 1811. Eliza Lewis (dau Henry) m John R. Nowland°.

LINDSAY—Vachel, r 1802, dis 1811
Ann, r 1802, dis 1811
Nicholas, 1
Mary, 1, to Mouth of Kentucky 1800
Rachel, 1

Anthony Lindsay (1736-1808) came with his family to Kentucky in 1784, and settled in the vicinity of Haydon's Station. In 1799 he sold to his son Elisha the farm which was owned in recent years by Marcus H. Cromwell. Some records say that he came from Maryland, and others, from Virginia, but the marriages of two of his daughters indicate that he may have lived for a time in each place.

In 1758 he m Rachel (Nellie) Dorsey (dau Nicholas and Sarah Griffith Dorsey), and their children were: 1, Kate, m her cousin, John Lindsay, in Maryland; 2, John C., m Susanna Dowden°, and went to Henry. (One John was in Frankfort, 1810, with a family of five.) Their children were: Kate; Betsy; James; Anthony; John; Orlando (m Sarah Hardin, dau Evangelist, F 1814?); Joshua, m Caty Mattox°, Henry 1818; Nathaniel; Hazel; and Cyrus; 3, Sally Bartlett°; 4, Nicholas, m (Mary?) Quisenberry° and they had four children. Their sons were Ross, who died in a blockhouse in 1812, and Vincent (m Patsy Warren, F 1814?), who went to Illinois.

5, Anthony, Jr. (1761-1831), m Alice Cole°, W 1788. In 1790 they went to Scott and built a fort called "Lindsay's Station." which was the nucleus of Stamping Ground. Many of their descendants live in Carroll County, Kentucky, and in Missouri and Illinois. Their children were: a, Gen. Jesse, m first Priscilla Ficklin°, and second, Mrs. Delia Scruggs; b, William, m Permelia Scruggs; c, Lucy, m Thomas Buford Scruggs; d, Richard Cole, m Julia Bond; e, Greenberry; f, Ann, m Abner Sanders°; g, Sallie, m her cousin, James Cole°; h, Elizabeth, m Obed Calvert°; i, John Cole, m Miriam Sneed Scott°, and they had: Judge Benjamin, m Helen Lindsay; Dr. William, m Nannie Brown; Carter Blanton, m Florence Cox; John Scott, m Juliette Lindsay°; Kate, m Dr. N. C. Brown; Mary; James Bond. j, James; k, Polly (1813- ——).

6, Vachel, who shared with Zachary Ross a farm on the east bank of the Kentucky River. He m Annie Quisenberry, Bourbon

1792. They moved to Dearborn County, Indiana, coming later to Gallatin County, Kentucky. Their children were: a, Thomas; b, Sallie; c, George; d, Vachel; e, Nicholas, m Martha Cave°, Gallatin 1842, and was the father of Mrs. Eudora Lindsay South, who about 1880 established at Jett a famous private school, "Excelsior Institute," which for more than thirty years was the standard of quality in education for this and the neighboring counties. Nicholas and Martha Lindsay were also the grandparents of Vachel Lindsay, the poet. f, Elijah; g, Charles, m Polly Lindsay, dau Anthony, Jr.; h, Polly; i, John; j, William.

7, Elizabeth, m Elisha Whitaker, of Shelbyville, W 1793; 8, Lydia, m first Jesse Whitaker (s John), W 1793, and second —— McCrockland; 9, Rachel Applegate°; 10, Charles; 11, Elisha, m Sarah Holmes (dau James), Shelby 1797. He died in Florida. 12, Lucy, m John Meek, Shelby 1813, and went to Indiana.

William Lindsay, of Maryland, died 1795, and his widow, Jane, came with her family to Kentucky in 1805. In 1808 she came to Frankfort, where she died in 1829. She had, besides several children who died in infancy; 1, John, who died about 1816; 2, Andrew Ross; 3, Elizabeth, m —— Swann; 4, Ann; 5, Grizzel, m —— Haws (one record says she m —— Cane); 6, Mary Jane Cox°.

Mary Lindsay m William Williams°.

Quisenberry (Cushinberry, Cresenberry, Coosenberry): Humphrey Quisenberry, of old Rappahannock County, Virginia, was the father of Thomas, whose son Aaron, born about 1725, m Joyce Dudley° and went to Orange County, Virginia. Their children were: 1, Aaron, m Sally Ellis°; 2, Moses, m Mary Gatewood (dau Henry), and came to Bourbon, where he died in 1792. They were the parents of: a, George, who went to Christian; b, John, who also went to Christian; c, Edward Sanford, who went to Logan County, Illinois; d, Ann Lindsay°. 3, William, m first Agnes Morton, of Orange County, Virginia, and second Mrs. Swann; 4, John, m Rachel ——, and came to what is now Clark County, Kentucky, but went later to Warren. Some of their children were: a, Nicholas, m Lucy Stephens, Clark 1805; b, Rebecca Ewing°. 5, George, m first Jane Daniel°, and second Peggy Reynolds; 6, Rev. James (1759-1830), m first Jane

Burris (dau Thomas and Frances Tandy Burris), 1776, and they were ancestors of Bayless Hardin, of Frankfort. He m second Chloe Shipp°, 1811. He settled at Howard's Creek, near Boonsborough, about 1885, and was the father of fifteen children. 7, Winifred; 8, Mary, m William Cooper; 9, Elizabeth, m Capt. David J. Pendleton.

John Quisenberry m Rebecca Dowden°, Bourbon 1791. Elizabeth Quisenberry m Zachary Ross°.

LIVINGSTON—Patsy, r 1820

Mrs. Sarah Livingston had a family of four, W 1810, but was in Frankfort in 1823. Her tombstone stood until recent years in the burying ground on the old Walcutt farm, formerly Haydon's Station.

The records indicate that some of her children were: 1, Elizabeth Cook°; 2, Ellen Edrington°; 3, Stephen, m Martha Jackson°, W 1812, and they evidently lived at one time in the vicinity of Gore's Station. In F 1836, Austin P. Cox was appointed guardian of the orphans of Stephen Livingston: a, Rebecca; b, William J.; c, John Henry; d, Martha Ann, e, Stephen, Jr.

LONG—Molly, 1811, dis 1824

The Longs in this section appear to have come from Orange and Culpeper Counties, Virginia.

The will of John Long, W 1797, mentions his wife Molly and: 1, Sukey. One record says that she married John A. Jackson°, while another indicates that she m Henry Reardon, and that her sister, 2, Jane, m John A. Jackson; 3, William (m Susan Holeman, W 1816?), lived on Griers Creek; 4, Thomas (m Nancy B. Jackson°, W 1810?); 5, Willis, m ——, and they were evidently the parents of Lucy Runyan°; 6, Sally, m Ransford Peyton. One Sally Long m Robert Guthrie°. Richard Long was named executor of this will.

The will of Reuben Long (s Richard), Culpeper County, Virginia, 1762, names his wife Elizabeth and sons: Gabriel, James, William, Anderson, Reuben, John. Reuben, John, and James were on the pension list, W 1810. Reuben was the father of Milly Mitchell°.

John Long (1749-1832) m Mary Haynes (dau William), Bedford County, Virginia, 1772. They came to Kentucky and were in the siege of Bryan's Station, locating in Woodford in 1789. In 1811 they were on Rough's Run, presumably at "Welcome Hall," the Henry Graddy place. Their children were: 1, Garrard (1773- ——) who about 1816 moved to Henry, where he had a mill. No wife's name is attached to any of his deeds in Woodford, but one Garrard Long, of Missouri, m Frances Elizabeth Peyton (dau V. Peyton), Bourbon 1835; 2, Lucy Whittington°; 3, James C., m Nancy Berry, 1802, and they had: a, John W., m first Jane Stevenson, 1824, and second Winifred Davidson, 1841; b, Eliza, m A. C. Scott°, W 1825, and they were ancestors of Miss Sarah Coleman Scott, of Frankfort; c, Kitty, m Augustus Bower, 1832; d, James L., m Louisa Jesse, W 1834; e, Sydney, m Fielding Evans, 1836; f, Henrietta Bohannon°; g, Mary Haynes, m John Hall°, W 1843, and they were grandparents of Mrs. E. B. Smith, of Shelbyville; h, William B., m Lucy Barkley, 1857; i, Ambrose D., m Mildred Bullock; j, Thomas Parker (m Nancy Jackson°?); k, Ryland D., m Mary Portwood, 1857.

4, John, m Polly Stevenson (dau Benjamin), W 1805. They appear to have lived on Glen's Creek until 1826, when they went to Versailles, and later to Clay County, Missouri; 5, Reuben, m first Sally Macey°, F 1802, and they had Leander M. (1804-1831); he m second Jemima Read°, W 1807. 6, Frances Marshall°; 7, William B., m Sarah S. Hunter°, W 1810. He died about 1825, leaving his wife and: a, Charles S.; b, James H. L. 8, Betsy McDaniel°; 9, Mary Brooking°; 10, Sally, m Robert Clark, W 1811; 11, Willis, who went to Henry in 1816, m first Harriet Thomas°, Henry 1817, and second Elizabeth Agun (dau William Agun, W), Henry 1829; 12, Anderson (1795-1810).

James Long evidently moved to Franklin County, where he died about 1812. Garrard Long was appointed as guardian of his infant heirs. James m Betsy ——, and their children were: 1, Zachariah, who located on Clear Creek; 2, Gabriel; 3, Virginia; 4, Elinor Scandland°; 5, Richard, m Sydney Harrod (dau Elizabeth Gordon Harrod), F 1819, and lived on the river in Franklin; 6, Armstead, m Pauline Peters (dau Lewis and Frances Waller Peters), W 1822, and they lived near Mortonsville. One Gabriel Long m Elizabeth Bowlin, Fayette 1816.

One John Long (———-1819) m Azubah Hawkins° in Culpeper County, Virginia, 1793. They came to Franklin and settled on Elkhorn. They were the parents of: 1, Ann (m Samuel Bristow°?); 2, Polly, m Benjamin Long, F 1811; 3, Elizabeth, m William G. Haydon°; 4, Rebecca, m Josiah Green°; 5, Moses, m Eliza Green°, F 1821, and their dau, Mary, m Lawson F. Noel°; 6, William, m Levina Green° (dau Jeremiah), F 1821. Azubah Long m John Knight, F 1833.

Gabriel Long (1791-———), son of Nicholas, m Katherine Macey°, F 1820. His nephew and adopted son, Robert A. Long, m Sallie Peak°, 1851. One Robert was on Elkhorn, W 1811, and for many years thereafter.

The Franklin census, 1810, lists Benjamin Long with a family of six, John with ten, Lawrence with three. Thomas P. with four, William with four, while in Frankfort was Thomas with four. Benjamin Long m Sally Head°, F 1807; Thomas P. m Charlotte Shoole, F 1807, the bond being signed by Robert Brydon. It was evidently their son, Benjamin, who m Julia Jackson°, F 1831, and was the father of Thomas Reuben, who m Frances M. Brydon°, F 1862; William m Elizabeth Smither°, F 1806; Lawrence m Kitty Samuel°, F 1807, and they lived in what is now Anderson; Nimrod m Betsy Long, F 1813. Thomas Long m Bathsheba Moxley°. John Long m Betsy Martin°, W 1818.

Whittington: Isaac Whittington (son of Southy and Mary Fossett Whittington, and grandson of Col. William and Esther Littleton Whittington), of Maryland, m Elizabeth Wishart, and they had: 1, Hannah, m Henry Handy; 2, Ann, m William Cox°; 3, William (1759-1824), m Lucy Long°, W 1791. Since he was appointed in 1795 as one of the trustees of Versailles, it is possible that he lived there for some time, but he went later with his brother Littleton to the Clifton neighborhood. Their children were: a, Littleton, Jr., m Frances Glenn, W 1819, and they were the parents of: Tyre Glenn, m Julia Beaty (dau William), Shelby 1842; Thomas, and others. Littleton, Jr., went to Henry and then to Shelby. b, Southy; c, Mary, m James McCasland; d, Elizabeth Owen°; e, Anna Davis°; f, John; g, James; h, Rev. William Handy (1804-1855), a minister of the

Christian Church, lived near Farmdale. He is said to have organized Antioch Church in Franklin County, and he preached in the neighboring churches, including Grassy Spring, and to the dissenting members of the Forks of Elkhorn Church. He m first Susan Adelia Kavanaugh°, Anderson 1839, and they were the parents of Mary Adelia, who was Lady Principal of Daughters' College in Harrodsburg. He m second Ann M. Kavanaugh°, Anderson 1847, and they had Paul, Silas, and Ann Adelia, who died young; i, Atalanta Darnell°; j, Isaac, m Mary Edwards°, W 1834, and they had: Thomas; John Black; James Southy; Hervey; Lucy; Betty, m —— Pryor; Mary, m N. L. Curry, of Harrodsburg. Isaac lived at his father's home place at Clifton. k, Hannah, m Anderson Brown°; l, Samuel; m, Hervey, m Ann Storey in Missouri; n, Jemima Taylor°; o, Henry.

4, James, m Sarah Coulbourn; 5, Thomas, m Sarah Conner (W 1810?); 6, Joshua, m Mary Marshall°, W 1791. They lived near Pisgah until about 1812, when they are said to have gone to Missouri. The family record names their children as: a, Fanny; b, Thomas, m Lucy Brittenham, W 1819; c, Betty; d, Mary; e, Isaac; f, Jane; g, Anna; h, Charlotte; i, Humphrey, m Elizabeth Arnold, F 1840, and they had: Alonzo, m Sallie Hundley or Hundleigh (dau Morton Brinker Hundleigh: see Howe), W 1867, and lived on the Hanly Lane; Thomas; (Louis M.?); and it is possible that Joshua and Ellen Whittington, who were members of the forks Church in 1853, were also their children.

Another record states that the children of Joshua and Mary Marshall Whittington were: a, Charlotte, m W. H. Cummins; b, Kate, m James Dearing; c, Elizabeth; d, Ann; e, Isaac; f, ——, m —— Morrison, and had Catherine and Anna. One Joshua Whittington m Rachel Hancock, Mason 1814; Jane Whittington m Dr. Dorsey in Flemingsburg, 1826.

7, Littleton, m Sarah Hearn°, W 1795, and they were the parents of: a, Dr. William Wishart, who m Ann Handy, and lived near McKee's Crossroads. They had: Charlotte, m John L. Whittington; Robert, m Kate Hearn°; Maria, m Robert H. Berryman (s John H. and Jane Railey Berryman), W 1846, and they were grandparents of Mrs. J. A. Posey, of Frankfort; Hannah; Molly; Jennie. · b, Isaac, m Matilda Perry (dau Roderick and Susan Brown° Perry), W 1828; c, Milcah Smith°;

d, Jane, m Col. Samuel S. Graham°; e, James, m Margaret Lillard (dau John), Anderson 1831, and they were parents of John L., who m his cousin, Charlotte Whittington, W 1855; f, Caroline Taylor°; g, Edward Henry, m Sarah Cordelia Hawkins°, W 1833, and they had William L., who m Mary Elizabeth Gaines° and was the father of Miles Whittington, of Versailles; h, Betsy Hearn°; i, Nancy; j, Edna.

Loughborough—Betsy, to Frankfort 1816

Thomas Vangalen Loughborough (written also Loofburrow) m Betsy Samuel°, W 1801, and their children were: 1, John, m Jane Moore; 2, Preston, m first Nancy Haggin, W 1827, and second —— Yandell; 3, Charles; 4, Elizabeth Price°; 5, Isabella Gibson°.

The home of the Loughboroughs was in Frankfort, where the Rogers Funeral Home now stands, opposite the school on Second Street. Thomas Loughborough was one of the builders of the courthouse in Frankfort.

Alexander Loughborough was in Versailles, 1810, with a family of eight.

Lowry—Nancy, dis 1810

William Lowry m Nancy Fitzgerald°, F 1802. In 1810 they lived in Frankfort and had a family of six.

Stephen Lowry came from Pittsburgh, and was one of the party of explorers who built McClelland's Station (now Georgetown) in 1776. Stephen and John were in Fayette 1788.

Eliza Jane Lowry, who was born in Frankfort, 1803, went in 1809 to Natchez, Miss., where in 1818 she m Honore P. Morancy, and they were grandparents of Mrs. John R. McKee, of McKee's Crossroads.

The will of Patrick Lowry, Mercer 1796, mentions his wife and children: James, John, Melvin, Margaret, Hannah, Betty, Mary, Jane Todd. The will of Thomas Lowrie, F 1803, names Catherine Harris Shiell and Maria Knox Innes.

Lucas—Susan Peak, dis 1804

Thomas Lucas (1749-1833) came about 1765 from England to Virginia (probably to Orange County), where he m Lois

Singleton. They were in Scott County, Kentucky, in 1801. Their children were: 1, Richard, m Elizabeth Hackley, 1798; 2, William, m —— Higbee; 3, Elijah, m Margaret Moore; 4, Rev. John (1766-1848), was a member of the McConnell's Run Church. He began preaching about 1830, and his biographer says of him: "He was much loved by his brethren for his deep toned piety and earnest devotion to the cause of Christ."

It is interesting to note that to each of his nineteen children he gave "Peak" as a middle name. He m first Susan Peak°, 1804, and they had: a, Mary P., m Pierce Perry, 1849; b, Charity P., m Pierce Perry, 1827; c, Stephen P.; d, Singleton P., m Evaline Lucas (dau Elijah); e, Maria P.; f, Richard P., m Mary Bell, 1836; g, John P., m Catherine Bussard, and went to Illinois; h, Thomas P., m Minerva Neal, and went to Nebraska; i, Elijah P., m first Irene Lucas, and second Mrs. Jones, and went to Illinois; j, William P., m Margaret Parks, and went to Illinois; k, Elizabeth P., m Joseph Burt, 1834; l, Susan P., m Robert W. Raines, 1842; m, James F. M. P. (1828- ——), m Anna Schnebley, and went to Peoria, Ill.

Rev. John Lucas m second Caroline Peak, Gallatin 1831, and they had: n, Amanda P., m Robert H. Jones, 1851; o, Joseph T. P., m —— Butler; p, Huldah P.; q, Franky P.; r, Willis P., m Clara Ann Lucas, and lived in Georgetown; s, Sarah P., m Merritt Wayts.

5, Thomas, Jr., m Mary Williamson; 6, Stephen (1791- ——), m Maria Thomasson, and their son Le Grand, who m first Letitia Jones, F 1841, m second Mary Woollums (originally Wilhelms), W 1856, and they were the parents of Miss Dora Lucas, of Frankfort; 7, Elizabeth; 8, Polly.

Joanna Lucas had a family of three, F 1810.

McCANNA—Sister, 1790

McDANIEL—Mack, 1
        Lucy, 1

Mack McDaniel was living in Fayette in 1793, when he sold land in Woodford on South Elkhorn to John Martin. "Brother McDaniel's sons" are mentioned in connection with Jesse Cole in 1812.

In Woodford, George McDaniel had a family of nine. His dau Sally m Richard M. Young (s Col. Richard and Mary Moore Young), W 1803. Charles McDaniel m Hannah Campbell°, 1790; Charles m Eliza Thomasson, 1792. Susanna m Joshua Knap°; John m Mary Ann Walden°, 1814; James Rucker m first Sally McDaniel, and second Polly McDaniel; Betsy Long° m —— McDaniel. William McDaniel, who was an elder in Grassy Spring Church, m Catherine Garnett°. In 1839 he bought from Elizabeth Garnett a mill on Glen's Creek which he operated for many years.

In Franklin, Elisha McDaniel m Malinda Oliver°, 1830; Barnett McDaniel m Elizabeth Arnold, 1833, the bond signed by Simeon Arnold; Osborne McDaniel was the father of Ellen and Elizabeth Gravit°.

McGEE–Elizabeth, 1   Susanna, 1
          Mary, 1, dis 1807

Elizabeth McGee was on the tax list, W 1792, and Samuel was there on Clear Creek in 1810 with a family of six. John McGee was in Mercer in 1794, and Robert was there in 1800. William McGee was in Owen, 1819.

Carter T. McGee m Polly White, W 1815; Georgiann Brown McGee m Thomas Hawkins°, W 1828, the bond signed by Carter T. McGee. Also in Woodford were Betsy McGee Hiter° and Sarah McGee Mitchell°.

McGEHE–Susanna, 1

Elizabeth McGehee, dau Jacob and Ann McGehee, of Prince Edward County, Virginia, m Brackett Owen°.
Daniel McGehe m Mariam Shryock, W 1840.

McGRAW (McGrew?)–Anne, r 1805, dis 1812

Richard McGrow had a family of six, W 1810. William McGrew was in Woodford, 1792, and Charles was north of the river, F 1801. Alexander and John McGrew were in Shelby, 1796.

One record says that Louisa McClelland (dau Henry) m first —— McClelland, and second John McGrew; another says that John McGrew m N. McClelland (dau Henry), F 1815.

Elizabeth McGraw m Thomas M. Harrison°.

In the division of Alexander McGrew's estate, Henry 1822, are mentioned: John, Hannah, Molly, Moses, Margaret, James, Joseph, Nelly, Alexander, Rebecca Gullion°, Elizabeth.

MACEY—Reuben T., 1841-1842   Silas, 1841-1842

Alexander Macey came with his family from Virginia and settled on Elkhorn near Church's Grove, where in 1804 he built the brick house that was in later years the home of the Rev. Frank H. Hodges.

His will, F 1822, mentions his wife Penelope; a grandson, Leander Long; and these children: 1, Sally. One record says that Sally Macey (dau Alexander) m Reuben Long, while another record states that Sarah S. Macey (dau Alexander, deceased) m James M. Bryan°, F 1827, with the consent of her guardian, Leander Macey. The first Sarah died before 1807, and if these records are correct, it is possible that, when another daughter was born, the parents, in accordance with a frequent custom of that time, gave the new baby her deceased sister's name.

2, Leander (m Sophiah White, Fayette 1839?); 3, Jefferson. The will of Thomas J. Macey, F 1834, mentions his brother Leander. 4, Rev. Alexander R., who preached at South Benson and other neighboring churches. He was ordained in Frankfort, 1843, m Ellen E. Robson, F 1846, and afterward went South; 5, Mary Sullenger°; 6, Charles, who lived on Main Elkhorn. In his will, F 1828, he names his wife Polly (see Wilson) and children: a, Eliza Ann, m Morgan B. Chinn, F 1829; b, William M.; c, Alexander; d, Reuben T. A.; e, Silas N., and leaves an acre of land to the trustees of Bethel Meeting House. 7, Kitty Long°; 8, Gustavius S., m Frances M. Noel°, F 1818. Sarah A. Macey m George W. Henry, F 1838. Theodoric J. Macey m Sarah F. Gray, F 1847.

Several members of the family went to Woodford, where they intermarried with the Edwards, Railey, Gay families.

Bethel Baptist Church, on the Owenton road, has flourished since 1802, and it is said that in the congregation there has never been any dissension worthy of note. Rev. Frank H. Hodges was the pastor for more than fifty years.

MACKLIN—John, r 1841, dis 1842   A. W., r 1841
Eunice, r 1841, dis 1842

Robert and Richard Macklin were in Maryland about 1700. The Macklin family came from Ireland. Hugh Macklin was on Elkhorn, F 1801, and in 1810 had a family of nine, including: 1, Maria Ferguson°; 2, Polly, m William Copland, F 1813, and went to Jefferson County, Indiana; 3, Alexander W., m his cousin, Jane Macklin, F 1825, the bond being signed by John and Hugh Macklin. They lived near the Forks of Elkhorn, at the place originally occupied by George Smith, and later by the Rev. John Taylor.

Their children were: a, Alexander, m Anne Bedford°, and they were the parents of Bedford Macklin, who lives at the old homestead; b, Lydia, m Stephen Black, and they were the parents of Howard Black°, of "Silver Lake Farm"; c, Elizabeth Robb°; d, Maria Murphy°; e, Mary Frances, m J. J. Quilling, F 1855; f, George B., m Mary Caldwell (dau Thomas B. and Reubina Caldwell), Shelby 1859, and they were the parents of Mrs. J. W. Gayle, of Frankfort; g, Benoni, m Helen Harper, F 1855; h, William.

4, John, m Eunice (LeCompte?), and they lived near Woodlake and were the parents of: a, Mattie, m Demetrius Talbott, of Bourbon; b, Mary Jane, m John W. Cason, F 1851. John m second Elizabeth Black°, F 1846, and they had: c, Emma Blackburn°; d, Anna, m Rev. Thomas J. Stephenson; e, Charles; f, John Stephen; g, Sally, m ——— Stockton, of St. Louis; h, Betty.

Hugh Macklin m second Mrs. Susanna Scofield (widow Isaac Scofield, dau Hugh Alexander), F 1827. He died about 1831.

Bedford: Thomas Bedford (s Stephen and Elizabeth Flippen Bedford) m Mary Ligon Coleman, Cumberland County, Virginia, 1750. Three of their sons came to Bourbon County, Kentucky, and married daughters of Dr. Henry and Rachel Povall Clay: 1, Benjamin, m Tabitha Clay, and their son, John Franklin, m Sarah E. Bedinger (dau George) and went to Missouri. Ann Elizabeth (dau John F. and Sarah Bedford) m Frances Sterne Coleman, and they had Henrietta, who m Richard Edward Cobbs and was the mother of Mrs. B. T. Bedford, of Midway.

Benjamin F., another son of Benjamin and Tabitha Clay Bedford, m Eleanor Giles Buckner, and their son, Benjamin Thomas, m Mary Ellen Parker and had Sidney, who m Maytie Harper and was the father of B. T. Bedford, of Midway. 2, Littleberry, m Matty Clay.

3, Archibald, m Letitia Clay, Bourbon 1796, and they had: a, Henry C. m first Kitty Blanton°, Fayette 1821; m second Lucy Blanton°, Fayette 1822; m third Lucy C. Ware°, Bourbon 1829, and they had Sarah Catherine (m Samuel S. Clay) and William; b, Hillery Mosely, m Ann D. Chadwell, Fayette 1831. They came to Franklin and located at the Charles Patteson homestead on North Elkhorn. Their children were: Ryland T., m first Elizabeth Taylor, and second Mrs. Franklin Wilson°; Thomas, m Annie Harper, and they were the parents of Mrs. Maddox O'Nan, of Pleasureville; William, m Ida Allen, of Shelby, and went to Missouri; Hillery, m Maytie Harper in Providence Church, 1876. He bought the tract containing the old Forks meetinghouse, and built his home of the bricks; Mary Ellis; Anne Macklin°.

Major—John, Sr., 1	Betsy, 1
Elizabeth, 1	Patsy, 2
John, Jr., 1, dis 1817	John, dis to join a
Judith, 1789, dis 1817	Constitution 1801
Susanna, 1801, dis 1846	Betsy, r 1819
Olive, r 1811	Jane, r 1828
James, 2	Nancy, r 1828

From family records we learn that Richard and Jane Eyremongre Major came from England to New Kent County, Virginia, and from them descended George, who had several children, including John and Samuel.

John Major, Sr. (1740-1808) came with his family from Virginia and settled on a large tract of land on South Elkhorn and Dry Run. His first home was an old stone house which stands back of "Glen Airy," the home of Judge E. C. O'Rear—a building which is more than a landmark, for it was here that the Baptists of this section held their first meeting in January, 1788. His second home was on the site of "Weehawkin," now owned by E. R. Mills.

The wife of John Major, Sr., was Elizabeth Redd, and their children were: 1, William, died unmarried in New Orleans; 2, John, Jr., m Judith Trabue°, W 1789, and they built their home near the old stone house. Their children were: a, William, m Margaret Shipp°, Bourbon 1812; b, John, m Eliza Williams; c, Joseph, m —— Catlett; d, Benjamin, m Lucy Davenport°, 1820; e, Chastine, m Johanna Hopkins; f, Eliza Davenport°. After the death of his wife, John Major, Jr., went to Christian County, but most of his children went to Illinois.

3, Thomas, m Susanna Trabue, W 1793. Their children were: a, Olive T., m Nancy Gunnell°, and they had: Susan, m Thomas E. Gregory; Allen; Elizabeth, m George Fackler; Albert, m Martha Fackler; Thomas T., m first Rachel Lewis, and second Mattie Buckner; Margaret, m Charles Houston; John; Minor, m Sallie Thomson; Laura; Olivia, m Alexander Carlyle, 1863; Alva Curtis; b, John J., m Louisa Susanna Lewis; c, Elizabeth Gunnell°. Thomas Major built and occupied "Ingleside" (now the home of H. M. Collins), but afterward moved to Woodford and sold the property in 1829 to his son, Olive T. The family moved to Saline County, Missouri, about 1848.

4, James, m Elizabeth Minter (dau Rev. Joseph and Jane Trabue Minter). He bought land from Lewis Craig in 1797, but their home at Jett, now owned by Edmund Power and known as "Arrowhead," was not built until 1821. Their children were: a, Thomas; b, Benjamin, m Sally Leftwich; c, Joseph M., m Jane Boone° (dau William), Fayette 1825; d, James, m Kate Allen; e, Jane Branham°; f, William, m Amanda McCarty. This family also went to Missouri. 5, Lewis Redd, m Mildred Elvira Thomson°. They are said to have lived at "Weehawkin," but they owned "Silver Lake Farm," which they sold in 1833 to D. C. Freeman, and went to Missouri the following year. Their children were: a, Ann Redd (1824-1873), m William Gentry, 1840; b, Evelyn Elizabeth, m first Vincent Witcher, and second William Gentry; c, Vienna; d, John Thomson, m Mary Wood. 6, Susanna, m first Robert Wooldridge°, and second Ritchie Boulware°; 7, Frances Thomson°; 8, Elizabeth Price°; 9, Martha Sanford°; 10, Mildred Taylor Wooldridge°.

Samuel Major, of Middlesex County, Virginia, m Elizabeth Jones, and they had a large family, including two sons, John and Francis, who m two daughters of Thomas Porter°, of Culpeper, and came to Kentucky in 1786.

1, John Major (1755-1828), settled near Farmdale on the road leading from the old South Benson Church to Bridgeport. Several of the family tombstones may be seen at the old homestead, which is now occupied by —— O'Nan. John m first Elizabeth Porter°, and they had: a, Thomas Porter (1782-1851), who m first Mary Bennett, F 1805, and second Margaret Alexander, (dau Hugh), F 1814. His children were: Benjamin P., m Kate Foree, and went to Missouri; Walter, m —— Atkinson, and went to Texas; Nancy, m —— Smith, of Bourbon; Hugh, went to Missouri; Bettie, m —— Smith, of Scott; Porter.

John m second Euphrates Sleet, of Culpeper, and their children were: b, Rev. John Sleet (1789-1872), who was ordained at South Benson in 1830. On the death of William Hickman, Jr., he succeeded him at South Benson, where he preached until 1849, when he went to Clay County, Missouri. It was said of him, "His many excellent qualities much endeared him to his people." He m Lucinda Slaughter, Mercer 1817, and they had: Eliza Ann, m Joseph Flood, F 1839; John A. S., m Mary Bernard; Susan F., m J. C. Bernard; Rosanna, m first Johnson J. Yates, second Matthew Hodges, third Silas N. Hodges; Herman, m Mary Louise Swearingen, of Shelby 1850; Stephen, m Mary Elizabeth Cook, of Missouri; Lucinda Euphrates (Louise?), m Albert G. Davis, of Missouri; Sarah, m Wilson H. Smith. c, Weedon, m —— Overton; d, Rosanna, m Hezekiah Foree (originally Faure) of Shelby, F 1820; e, Elizabeth, m Dudley George, F 1837; f, Nancy, m Samuel B. Scofield, F 1824; g, Sarah C., m Francis Richardson°; h, Samuel Collier, m Elizabeth Daly, of Farmdale; i, Lucy Hawkins°; j, James, m Frances Bernard; k, Benjamin, m Emily F. Wilson (dau John T.), F 1829, and they had Sarah Jane, m Asa Foree; Col. John Crittenden; Elizabeth, m Patrick H. Parrent, F 1854; Susan, m Samuel E. Miles, F 1854.

2, Francis (1756-1835), m Margaret Porter, and was in Woodford in 1792. Family records state that they went to Bourbon, and later to Shelby. Their children were listed as: a, Ann, m Henry Buford; b, George, m Mary D. Bowman; c, Elizabeth, m William Pryor Foree, F 1807; d, Patrick, m Catherine Innes,

F 1823; e, Samuel Ire Monger (Americanized form of Eyre-mongre), m Martha Bohannan°, Fayette, 1821, and they had: Judge P. U.; William K.; Frances Ann; Col. S. I. M., who m Mary Scott°, and was the father of Lieut. Commander S. I. M. Major, of Frankfort; John B.; Alexander; Katherine, m Maj. Robert Call Williams, of Frankfort.

William B. Holeman m Margaret P. Major, F 1823.

MANIFIELD—Benjamin, r 1792

Benjamin Manifield was in Shelby, 1794. Alexander Manfield m Rachel Boone°, Jefferson 1787. George Manfield m Sarah Thomas, Fayette 1805.

MARSHALL—William, 1801, dis 1803
Elizabeth, 1801, dis 1803
William, r 1814, dis 1814
Elizabeth, r 1814, dis 1814

William and Elizabeth Marshall appear to have come with their family from Frederick County, Virginia, about 1793, and settled in Franklin on the Frankfort-Georgetown road. They went to Henry about 1803. Their children were: 1, William, m Elizabeth Edwards°, F 1811, and they were evidently in this neighborhood in 1814. They had a dau, Elizabeth C. Edwards°, and perhaps other children; 2, Thomas (1790-1854), probably the one who m Winna Dunaway, Henry 1821; 3, Polly; 4, Elizabeth Edwards°; 5, Sally.

Another William Marshall, of Henry, m Lucy ——, and they had: 1, John (m Molly Field, dau Lewis, Henry 1813?); 2, Sally, m Richard Anderson; 3, Polly, m William Webb, Henry 1801; 4, Anne C. Samuel°; 5, Frances, m Robert Tompkins.

John Marshall (1700-1752) of Westmoreland County, Virginia, m Elizabeth Markham, and among their children who came to Kentucky were: 1, Col. Thomas (1730-1802), m Mary Randolph Keith (dau Rev. James and Mary Isham Randolph Keith), 1754. They came to Woodford and settled at "Buck Pond," near Versailles, 1785, removing to Mason County about 1800. Some of their children were: a, Chief Justice John, of Virginia, m Mary Willis Ambler, 1783; b, Capt. Thomas, of Mason, m Frances Kennan (originally McKennon), 1790, and their dau, Lucy, m Col. Nicholas D. Coleman, of Cynthiana,

1826; c, Charles, who came to Fayette but eventually returned
to Virginia, m Lucy Pickett, and they had: Maria; Thomas;
Martin P., who m his cousin, Elizabeth Marshall, and their dau
Mary m Judge J. P. Foree; Charles, Jr.; Alexander; Jane; Lucy;
Susan; d, Alexander K., of Mason; e, Dr. Louis, who inherited
"Buck Pond," m Agatha Smith°, F 1800, and they had: Thomas
F., Edward C., and Agatha (Logan); f, Mary Ann, m Humphrey
Marshall.

2, John, m Jane Quisenberry°. They came to Woodford
with their children: a, Mary Whittington°; b, Elizabeth, m
Samuel January, W 1795, and they are said to have lived in
East Maysville; c, Jane; d, Nancy; e, Thomas; f, Senator
Humphrey (1757-1841), m his cousin, Mary Ann Marshall, and
they lived at "Glen Willis," near Frankfort. Their children
were: Judge John J., m Ann Reed Birney, Mercer 1809, and
evidently lived at what is known as the old Downey place, east
of Frankfort, where one of their children is buried; Thomas A.,
m Eliza Price (dau Susan), Fayette 1816; Eliza, died 1816;
g, James. One James lived on Clear Creek and had a family
of five, W 1810.

3, Rev. William (1735-1809) was one of the Baptist ministers
who came to Kentucky in 1779. He m Mary Ann Pickett (dau
William), 1766, and they came to Lincoln County, removing
later to Henry. Their children were: a, George, m Naomi
Vardeman, Bourbon 1796; b, Lewis, m Prudence Vardeman,
1789; c, William, m Rebecca Johnson°, and their farm was on
Bailey's Run, in Franklin County; d, Thomas, m Acton Penn, of
Bourbon, and they were ancestors of Miss Hattie Scott, of
Frankfort; e, Martin, m Matilda Taliaferro, and went to Augusta,
Ky.; f, Elizabeth Ballou°; g, Mary Ann, m Thomas Robinson
(Robertson?), Henry 1815; h, Susan, m Charles Masterson,
Henry 1810; i, Jane, m Frank Durrett, Henry 1808; j, Hettie
Ballou°; k, Lucy, m Edward Booker, Henry 1804. One William
Marshall m Martha Ballew° (dau Charles), Shelby 1814.

4, Abraham Markham, m Ann Bailey. They lived in Lincoln County, Kentucky, where he died about 1803. Their
children were: a, Ann Green°; b, John, m Frances Long°, W
1802; c, William (m Nancy Parks, Lincoln 1803?); d, Bailey;
e, Charles; f, James.

William Marshall, Sr., and William, Jr., were in Scott, 1801. Polly (dau William) m William Officer, Scott 1813.

The will of George Marshall, Harrison 1835, mentions his dau, Lucy Foster°, and other children. William Marshall, of Harrison, m Mrs. Lucy Foster, F 1848.

Charles Marshall m Adelaide Suter°, F 1834.

MARTIN—James	Betty, 1, dis 1803
Esther	Benjamin, 1801
William, r 1828	Patsy, dis 1812
Susan, r 1828	Elizabeth, r 1803
Henry, 1801	Peggy, 1
William, 1	Polly, 1
Thomas, 2	Betsy, dis 1808
Harry, dis 1813	
Molly, dis 1813	
Jacob	
Elijah, 2, dis 1803, ret letter 1805	

There were several Martin families here, and in some cases relationship is indicated only by their being grouped together in neighborhoods, or in the tax lists.

James H. Martain (now Martin) (1761-1811) was the son of Anthony and Sarah Holeman Martain, and the grandson of Pierre and Mary Ann Rapine Martain, Huguenot refugees to Virginia. He m first Esther Smith°, 1785, and their home was in Franklin County, immediately south of the Ed Ayres homestead near Duckers. Their children were: 1, Jean Bryan°; 2, dau m B. C. Stephens°; 3, Maj. William H., m first Susanna Smith Hale°, W 1820, and they had: a, Catherine Jane Viley°; b, Dr. Solon D., m Kate Pinkerton (dau William), W 1847; c, Ann Maria Peak°; d, Louis, m first Ann Dedman, m second Mrs. Nutter; e, James W., m first Betty Smith, m second Sue Taylor; f, Antoinette, m first Harvey Thompson, m second Warren Viley°. Maj. William H. m second Mrs. Sallie Nuckols True in Marion County, Missouri, and they lived in Scott County, Kentucky. 4, James S., m first Nancy Wilson°, F 1825, and second Mary Jane Gerard (dau William), F 1828. They sold their farm on South Elkhorn, and may have gone to Missouri with the Gerards. He was the father of eight children.

James H. Martain m second Sarah Davis°, F 1809, and they had: 5, Samuel D., died 1823; 6, Anthony R., never married. In 1834 he bought from his mother and her second husband a farm which was evidently the one owned later by C. T. Freeman.

In another group were: 1, Henry, listed in Mallory's Survey on the Kentucky River, who appears to have been the father of: a, Susanna Easterday°; b, Elizabeth Goldman°; c, William, m Jeanny Peak°, W 1793, and was in F 1797; d, Thomas, m Phoebe Gibson°, F 1799, and in 1810 they had a family of five, including Elizabeth and Sarah. They lived at "Wheatland," the Hanly homestead at Jett, which they sold in 1821 to Edmund Vaughan, Jr., and probably went to Gallatin.

Harry Martin had a family of two, F 1810.

The will of one John Martin, W 1832, indicates that he was either the father or a near relative of several brothers who came in 1779 to Fayette from Augusta County, Virginia. They are said to have been related to James H. Martain of Franklin. John Martin had a sister, Sally Williams°, and he may have been a brother of Samuel Martin, who was on Elkhorn, W 1810, with a family of ten, some of whom, it appears, were: Samuel, m Elizabeth —— ; Anna, m Elijah Tinder, W 1801; Abigail, m George Scroggin, W 1803; Nancy Graves°; Betsy Long°. John Martin's will mentions: 1, James (—— 1837) m Martha Elliott (dau Robert), W 1797, and they had: a, William, m Mary Alice Jones, W 1817; b, Elijah, m Sarah E. Goodloe, W 1834; c, Robert, m Italy Hammon (dau Ezra and Hannah Farra Hammon), W 1822, and went to Missouri; d, James, m Margaret Hammon; e, John, m Susan M. Vincent; f, Mary Alice, m —— Holeman; g, Martha; h, Jane, m James Cleland Martin (s James and Mary Rice Spilman Martin, of Muhlenberg), and they were grandparents of the Rev. Vernon P. Martin, Moderator of the Presbyterian Synod of Ohio, who furnished this record of his ancestor; (i, Henry, m Rebecca Taylor, W 1823?).

2, William, who settled on what is now the Big Sink pike in 1785. He m Letitia McClanahan, of Pendleton, W 1799, and they had: a, Agnes, m John Stogdell; b, William; c, Ann; d, Martha, m James Martin, 1841; e, Washington, m —— Offutt, of Scott; f, Hugh, m —— Graves; g, Joseph, m Talitha Martin; h, Jane. One record says she m her cousin, James McClanahan, another says James McAfee; i, Elijah, m Lou Allen Creason. He was the ancestor of E. L. Martin, of Lexington; j, John, m Mary Ann Alexander. James and William are buried in the Pisgah churchyard, where a reunion of their descendants is held every year.

3, Samuel, on Craig's Creek, had a family of ten. His will, W 1826, mentions his wife Susanna and children: a, Benjamin, on Griers Creek, was evidently the father of W. Holeman Martin, who m Susan Johnson°, W 1847; b, Elijah; c, Susanna, m Isaac Holeman, W 1804, and had Henry, Mahala, Caty, Nathaniel, Stephen; d, Married and unmarried daughters, probably including: Letty Martin, Aylse Taylor°, Polly Henton°. 4, Hugh, who apparently did not come to Woodford; 5, Nancy; 6, Nelly Maxwell. There were many intermarriages between the Martin and Williams families.

Also in Woodford was William Martin (s Thomas and Susanna Walker Martin, of Augusta County, Virginia). He m Jane Campbell and died before 1805, when his widow went to Muhlenberg. Of this family were Dabney, Hudson, and Henry Martin.

Thomas and Jacob Martin, listed in 1791, were on McConnell's Run in Scott. One Thomas m Elizabeth Vinzant, W 1791. Among Jacob's children were Susan, m John O'Bannon, W 1791; Jacob; Joel; Benjamin.

Of a different family was Samuel Martin (s Lewis and Elizabeth), who m Esther Morgan (dau Thomas and Margaret), and they came to Stafford County, Virginia (perhaps from Maryland), 1766-1767. Their son Lewis (1765-1816) m Frances ——, and they came to Kentucky in 1809, first to Woodford and later to Franklin, where they settled on Cedar Creek. Their children were: 1, James, Sr. (1789-1877), m first Polly Suter°, W 1811, and they had: a, Alexander; b, John Lewis, m Martha Hancock, 1839; c, James, Jr., who lived on the Georgetown pike opposite Black's pond (Silver Lake), m first Mary Prentice, 1837, and they were the parents of Samuel S., of Stedmantown (father of C. W. and T. E. Martin), and Ebenezer; he m second Mrs. Elizabeth Bradley, F 1850, and third Mary F. Harper, 1852; d, Isabella; e, William Harrison; f, George Washington; g, Caroline; h, Lafayette; i, Eliza J. Jackson; j, Andrew; k, Ann Maria, m John H. Martin, 1845.

2, Thomas (1792-1884), m Elizabeth Cole°, 1812. They lived near Midway, and were the parents of: a, Richard; b, James W., m Eliza McCoy (dau Daniel and Jennie), W 1839; c, Sarah, m Greenberry Moore; d, Mary, m John McKendrick; e, Eliza, m John Walston, of Louisville; f, Jesse, m Margaret Thornton (dau John), 1847, and they were the parents of Senator Henry L. Martin and Mrs. B. M. Hieatt, of Midway; g, John; h, Corda, m Alfred Conyer; i, Paulina, m Anthony Smith, W 1853, and went to St. Joseph, Mo.

3, William F., m Mrs. Anna Suter° Kring, F 1818; 4, George (m Fanny Penny, F 1818?); 5, Elizabeth; 6, Harriet, m James Shackleford, F 1826; 7, Robert (m Eliza Carter, F 1832?).

John L. and Russell Martin were early citizens of the western part of Franklin County. John L. went to Lexington, and Russell to Missouri.

In Franklin, Benjamin Martin m Patsy Robertson (dau John), 1798, the bond signed by Elijah; Polly (dau Elizabeth) m John Edwards°; Elijah m Elizabeth Hamilton, 1798; Thomas m Elizabeth Right, 1809. In Woodford, Joseph m ——' Salyers, 1794; Joseph m Rachel Shouse, 1798; Nancy (c Susanna) m James Campbell, 1800; Lyddy (dau Joel) m Jesse Hambrick, 1790; Caty m Henry Utterback, 1812; Rebecca m Archibald Maxwell, 1813; Hudson m America Jackson, 1814.

Viley: Capt. Willa J. Viley (1788-1865) was born in Montgomery County, Maryland, and in 1795 came to Scott County, Kentucky, with his parents, George and Martha Janes Viley. He m Lydia Smith° in 1813, and among their children were: 1, Maj. John R., m Mary S. Johnson, dau Elder John T. and Sophia Lewis Johnson, of Scott; 2, Warren (1817-1902), m first Catherine Jane Martin°, Scott 1838, and they had: a, George W.; b, John; c, Ann; d, Martha; e, Stoddard; f, Martinette, m Lister Witherspoon; g, J. Breckinridge, m first Flavilla Surles, and second Mary Philemon Parrish (dau Philemon Price and Margaret Magoffin Parrish).

In 1852 Warren Viley came to "Stonewall" on the Versailles-Midway pike. He m second Mrs. Mary Coleman Allen (see Coleman), who died in 1892, and third, Mrs. Antoinette Thompson, a sister of his first wife.

MASTIN—John, 1   Margaret, 1796
     Elizabeth, 1   Susanna, r 1814
     Frances, 1, 1800   Thomas

John Mastin had a farm on Elkhorn. His will, F 1808, mentions his wife Elizabeth and children: 1, Elizabeth Widner°; 2, Thomas; 3, Lucy McDowell; 4, John; 5, Mordecai; 6, Jenny Gravit°; 7, Phoebe Shepherd; 8, Lewis, m Margaret Cook°, and had Phoebe and Lewis. He was killed by the Indians in 1792. William Mastin lived on the river, F 1801. Elizabeth m Benjamin Adair°. The Franklin census of 1810 shows one John Mastin with a family of eight; another John with two; Thomas, Sr., with four; Thomas, Jr., with three.

No connection is indicated with the Mastin family of Woodford, who descend from John Gilbert Mastin (1793-1867, s John and Priscilla Hopkins Mastin, of Delaware) and his two wives, Sarah Hutton and Jane Miller.

MATTOCKS (Maddox)—Alfred, dis 1829

Thomas Mattox had seven in his family, W 1810, and Nathaniel had ten. Caty (dau Nathaniel) m Joshua Lindsay°. Thomas owned land on Lee's Branch and Dry Run, F 1812. Sherwood Mattox m America Jones, W 1820.

One Sherwood Maddox, of Goochland County, Virginia, m Elizabeth Ferguson in Cumberland County, Virginia, 1781, and they came later to Kentucky. His will, Owen 1840, mentions his wife and children: James; Jacob; Sherwood; Larkin; David; dau Elizabeth Rogers; dec dau Frances Noel.

Ralph Mattocks was in Lincoln, 1789, and Absalom was in Shelby, 1800.

MILES—Isaac, 1, left 1837, ret 1838
     Mary, 1
     John, r 1789, dis 1798

Isaac Miles m first Mary Curtis, in Virginia, and they were in Woodford in 1791. Though he owned land in Shelby, he lived in Millville, where he operated a mill.

In 1810 he had a family of ten, some of whom were: 1, Thomas, m Polly Henderson, W 1819, and went later to Morgan County, Indiana; 2, John Evans, m Malinda Brown, W 1818; 3, Jesse, who went to Indiana, m ——— , and their son Harmon m Catherine Henderson (dau Elizabeth Blackburn), W 1830; 4, Rachel, m Andrew Samples, W 1808; 5, Samuel, m Elizabeth Hawkins°, F 1825, and they had: a, John E., of Frankfort, m first Emily Payne, of Ohio, 1850, and they were the parents of James N., m Kate Franklin; Effie, m Rev. C. Q. Wright; Iva, m Guy N. Emmitt; and Samuel. John E. m second Annie Hawkins°, and they had Mary Keith, m Prof. A. M. Wilson; b, William J., m Susan Brassfield, and went to Missouri; c, Sarah Adelia, m Thaddeus Smith (s Bird and Elvira Price Smith); d, Mary Hannah, m John Taylor, of Midway; e, Samuel. Isaac Miles m second Mrs. Lucinda Tiller°, F 1827. Isaac Miles m Jane Maddux, F 1843.

One Isaac Miles m Jenny Bell (dau William), Lincoln 1803. Isaac, Jr. was on the tax list, W 1826. Margaret Miles was in Woodford, 1790. William Christie m Sarah Miles, W 1805, the bond signed by Isaac Miles. Reuben Carr m Susanna Miles, W 1807, the bond signed by Enos Miles, who owned land on Glen's Creek, W 1796, which he sold in 1809 to Aaron Darnell.

One John Miles and his wife Elizabeth probably built about 1796 the old house which stood on the site of the home of A. W. Lippert, near Duckers, and which they sold in 1803 to James Porter. One John m Peggy Abbett°, F 1803; William m Elizabeth Abbett, F 1804; William G. m Mary C. Brawner, F 1829. James was in Frankfort, 1810, and in Franklin County were John with a family of six, and William with five.

Samuel Miles m Eunice Cook, F 1797. Several of the family went to Shelby with the Cooks. John, Samuel, and James were in Shelby, 1802.

MITCHELL—Sally, 1801, dis 1807   Lucy, 1826

Rosanna Mitchell settled on Glen's Creek in the Millville neighborhood with her three sons: 1, Frederick, m Joanna Bohannon°, W 1801. His will, W 1847, names his children: a, George, m Lucy —— ; b, Frederick; c, William J., m Mahala Stucker (dau Sarah), F 1837; d, Abraham; e, Samuel G.; f, Permelia Brightwell°; g, Joanna B.; h, Margaret F. 2, John. One John died W 1842, leaving children: a, Rosanna, m William Stucker, W 1813; b, John L.; c, Elizabeth, m Lawson Self, W 1816; d, Susan Peters; e, David; f, Sarah Waldon°; g, Nancy Johnson°; h, Lucinda Green; i, Joannah Pepper; j, Paulina Dowden°; k,

Martha Beauchamp; 1, Franklin, m Nancy Miles, F 1830. 3, Michael, who lived on the river above the mouth of Glen's, m Elizabeth ——. His will, W 1833, mentions his wife and: a, Sarah, m John Stucker; b, Samuel; c, Polly, m Handy Tull, W 1814; d, Alexander, m his cousin, Joanna B. Mitchell, W 1827; e, John; f, David. One David m Mary ——, and their son George W., who m Jane Lewis, was the grandfather of Mrs. B. F. Fannin, Mrs. Edward V. Crutcher, and Mrs. Overton Parrent, of Frankfort; g, Eliza Jane Johnson°; h, William H.

Robert Mitchell lived on the river, and his will, W 1803, names his wife, Elizabeth, and children: John; William; Alexander; Rebecca Reed; Sarah; Elizabeth Suter°; Margaret; and three other sons, Robert, Samuel, and Thomas, at that time in Madison County, Kentucky. One John (son of Robert) m Patsy Suter°, F 1817.

Solomon Mitchell m Sally Bain°, W 1808. He had a family of three, W 1810, but went later to Shelby.

George Mitchell m Elizabeth Watts°, W 1790, and lived on Clear Creek. John Mitchell m Sarah McGee°, W 1792; John Mitchell m Sarah Mitchell, W 1794; Mary Mitchell m John Boyd, W 1795; John D. Mitchell m Maria Abbett°, W 1813; Edmund Mitchell m Elizabeth Gibson°, W 1820; George B. Mitchell m Mariam Morris, W 1828.

Capt. Joseph Mitchell, who evidently owned land south of the river in what is now Franklin County, died about 1789, leaving four sons: 1, Joseph F., m Rebecca Boyd, F 1795, and their dau, Rebecca, m Charles Scott Bibb, F 1822; 2, Samuel; 3, John A., m Peggy Pemberton°, F 1804; 4, Dr. Alexander J., m Elizabeth Allen (dau Capt. William), Fayette 1812, and their dau Martha m Oliver Frazer, F 1829.

John Mitchell m Milly Long°, F 1799; Thomas m Mildred A. Julian, F 1823; William m Frances Ann Lewis°, F 1836; Capt. David m Henrietta Scott°.

Bain: The Bain family of Scotch descent, settled in Woodford and what is now Anderson, in the vicinity of Clifton. George Bain, who is said to have m first —— Bush, m Betsy Blanton°, W 1795. They lived on what is now the Steele pike, a part of their land being sold in 1849 to Hezekiah Winn. George died W 1824. His children named in his will were: 1, Sally Mitchell°;

2, Jincy, m William Peacock, W 1810; 3, Nancy, m John B. Peyton, W 1811, and they had a son, Greenberry; 4, George (m Betty Updike?); 5, Joseph, m first Locky Sharp (dau Noah and Jane Dooly Sharp), F 1821; he m second Charlotte Updike, W 1841, and went later to Trimble.

George Bain, Sr., states in his will that he gave property to his first wife's children when they married. Patterson Bain, of Fayette, m Mary Theobald° (Scott?), 1835. Johnson Bain d Oldham 1831, leaving sons Lewis, Lindsey, Leroy; son-in-law Jesse Moreland; dau (Lena Clore?).

MONTGOMERY—William, 1801   Priscilla

Samuel Montgomery (s Robert), of Wythe County, Virginia, m Margaret (or Mary) Nichols, and they came to Kentucky in 1786. In 1791 Samuel bought land on Dry Run, at what is now Jett. He located on the tract now occupied by the old Graham Tavern, and sold to his son Robert the place now owned by Clarence Montague, and to his son William a tract on the north side of the Versailles-Frankfort pike opposite "Arrowhead." It is thought that the little house at the foot of the hill below the old schoolhouse was built by one of the Montgomerys.

Samuel died in 1797. His children were: 1, Robert (1762-1823), m first, Mary Love, and they had: a, Sallie, m Robert Montgomery, Jr., F 1806, and they went to Gallatin; b, John, m first Elizabeth Bohannon (dau John), 1813, and their son, Henry Partlow, was the father of Staiar Montgomery, of Frankfort. John m second, Priscilla Montgomery, 1847. Robert m second Rachel Bohannon°, W 1798, and they went to Gallatin in 1808. Their children were: c, Robert; d, Hugh, m Sallie Wilcoxon (dau Daniel), Shelby 1820, and they went to California; e, Mary, m William Woods; f, Margaret, m William Knox, 1821; g, Frances (or Mary), m Paschal Jackson, Gallatin 1824; h, Samuel, m first Susan Bacon, Gallatin 1836, second ——, and third, Mrs. —— (Owen) Walker, and went to Missouri; i, Elleanor, m Josiah Jackman. Robert m third Patsy Whitecotton, 1819, and they had: j, Joseph L.; k, Sarah Jane, m John Meek, 1838. Robert, Sr. died in Rush County, Indiana.

2, William. A Bible record indicates that his first wife was Mary ——, who died in 1800, and by whom he had: a, Margaret Graham°. William m second Priscilla Graham, F 1801, and their children were: b, Samuel C., m Mrs. Lydia Easterday°, and they lived in Gallatin; c, Jeptha Dudley, m Arabella H. Barrett (dau Eliza), F 1831, and they had several children, including Sallie Graham, m Rev. J. B. Tharp, 1858, and Arabella ("Belle Montgomery" who used to visit the Hearn family, and who united with the Forks Church about 1853), m Rev. Samuel P. Hogan, 1870; d, Francis G., m Ann Stites, and lived in Christian; e, James Harvey, m first Letitia Nation (dau Edward, Sr.), F 1824, and second, Louisa Trotter, Owen 1827; f, Priscilla Bryant°; g, Louisa Bacon°.

3, Lieut. James, while with the Lewis and Clark expedition was drowned in the Mississippi; 4, John, m Mary Oldham Thomas (see Christian), F 1795. They had a large family in Hopkins County; 5, Mary, who m Capt. Frederick Edwards, lived in Jefferson; 6, Elizabeth, m Lieut. John Crockett (one record states that she m Andrew Crockett); 7, Nancy, m Nathaniel Evans, and they settled in Woodford between Versailles and Lexington; 8, Samuel, who never married, evidently went to Gallatin; 9, Joseph, m Jean Sproule (dau James and Frances McCutcheon Sproule), F 1796, and they went first to Gallatin and later to Ripley County, Indiana. One of their sons was Commodore Joseph Edward, m first Clara Maria Jenison, 1840, and second, Rebecca P. Graham, 1845.

Rev. John Montgomery, the ancestor of James F. and Z. J. Montgomery, of Frankfort, was distantly related to Samuel Montgomery.

William Montgomery m Peggy Buntain (dau James), F 1812; William Montgomery m Paulina Oldham (dau Mary), F 1833; John Montgomery m Lydia Lucas (dau Abraham), Shelby 1796; Stephen Benson m Lydia Montgomery, F 1798.

Adam Montgomery m Mildred Guthrie°, W 1810. They lived on the Lexington-Leestown road, opposite the Harmony Church.

MURPHY—John, 1   Rachel, 1
John Murphy m Rachel Cook°. He was in Franklin, 1796, and one John Murphy was in Scott, 1806.

His will, Warren 1818, mentions his wife Rachel and: 1, William; 2, Hannah, m Thomas Ferguson°; 3, John; 4, Margaret Davidson; 5, Rachel Butler; 6, Isaac; 7, Hosea, m Sarah W. Haley, Warren 1819; 8, Joseph. In Warren, Elijah Davidson m

Nancy Murphy, 1825; John E. Murphy m Franky Doughety, 1827; John Murphy m Mary W. Vance, 1833.

William Murphy was in Woodford, 1792. William m Kitty Ware°, Shelby 1817. Anthony Cox m Nellie Murphy, F 1818.

Leander and Isaac Murphy were in Shelby, 1799; Joshua was in Scott, 1801.

The will of John Murphy, Scott 1829, mentions John and Charles Murphy, sons of Rachel Kyle, of Scott, and Laura and Jane Murphy, daus Peggy Daugherty, of Woodford.

NALL—Martin, 2
        Lucy, 1813, to Forks of Elkhorn 1818
        Elizabeth, dis 1806
        Nelley, dis 1814 to Glen's Creek

The will of Capt. Martin Nall, Culpeper County, Virginia, 1788, mentions his wife Isabel and children: William, Martin, Ann, Rachel, Winny, Clara James°, Milly, and granddaughter Caty Sparks°. His sons William and Martin evidently came to Woodford.

William m Eleanor ——— , and their children were: Charles Lewis, m Mourning Harrison°, W 1803, and they had two children who died in infancy; 2, William Henry, m Eleanor Yancey°, and they had: William; George, m Mildred Yancey, W 1834; Lewis Yancey; Nancy; Ellen Yancey°; Henrietta Davis°. 3, Gabriel J., m Frances Tutt°, and they had Gabriel and Henrietta; 4, Polly, m first L. Y. Tutt, and second John Matton; 5, Frances Bailey°; 6, Nancy Graves°; 7, Winnefred Graves; 8, Jane, m Lewis Nall; 9, Mildred Yancey°.

Martin settled in the part of Woodford that was afterward Scott, where he died about 1806. His wife was Ann ——— , and their children were: 1, Lewis, m Jane Nall, W 1791, and they had: Winnefred, Charles, Martin, William, Nancy, Elizabeth, Jane, Mildred; 2, Elizabeth, m John Nall; 3, Martin, m Lucy ——— , and they settled on Elkhorn in Franklin. They had a family of ten, among whom were: a, Elizabeth, m William G. Overton, F 1818; b, Cynthia, m Richard Quin, F 1824; c, Mary, m Nathaniel Shannon, F 1826; 4, James, who owned land in Washington County, Kentucky. One James m Susan Kendrick, Washington, 1804; 5, Nancy, m Thomas Thomas; 6, Milly Yancey°; 7, Mary; 8, Charles; 9, Ann James°.

William Nall m Mourning Harrison°, W 1828, and went to Clay County, Missouri; Martin m Margaret Wren (dau Nicholas), Mercer 1796; James m Amanda Boone°, Meade 1822.

Yancey: The Yancey family came from Wales. One account says that Capt. Lewis Davis Yancey, of Culpeper County, Virginia, m Mildred Kavanaugh° (dau Charles Sr.), but in Spotsylvania are deeds from Philemon Kavanaugh to his daughter Winifred, her husband, Lewis Davis Yancey, and their daughter Elizabeth, 1731-1732.

The will of Lewis Davis Yancey, Culpeper 1778, mentions his wife, Winifred, and: 1, Charles, m Elizabeth Powers, and one of their children was Keziah Freeman°; 2, Lewis, m Henrietta Faver. They had several children, including Ibby, who m Lewis Tutt, and George (b 1769), who settled in the Millville neighborhood. He died W 1857, leaving: a, Jane; b, Burkett, m Eleanor Nall, W 1828, and they were the parents of Mildred, m Dr. James Botts, of Millville; and Eleanor, m first Frank Taylor°, and second William W. Darnell°; c, William L.; d, Judith, m Anderson B. Johnson; e, Mildred, m George G. Nall; f, Henrietta, m George Tutt; 3, Richard; 4, John; 5, Philemon. One record says his wife was Unity ——— . Among his children were: a, Philemon (1753-1839), who came to Scott in 1814, and later to Franklin. His wife was Sarah ——— , and their son Alfred m Lucy ——— , and went to Minnesota; b, Mary Ann, m William Johnson, Culpeper 1806; 6, Ann Nall; 7, Winifred Nall; 8, James, said to have gone to South Carolina; 9, Capt. Robert, m Elizabeth Holloway, and they were in Woodford, 1810, with a family of eight.

Much confusion has arisen over this family because another Robert Yancey (s Jeremiah and Margaret Mullins Yancey, of Albemarle County, Virginia), m Phoebe Rozzelle, 1795, and settled with his family in Franklin near the borders of Scott and Woodford.

Capt. Robert and Elizabeth Holloway Yancey are said to have had these children: a, Katherine, m John Snyder; b, Martha S., m Robert (Augustin?) Campbell, W 1827, and they went to Mississippi; c, George; d, Nancy, m Capt. John Settle°; e, Mary Walker, who was reared by George Holloway, m Simeon Twyman°; f, Mildred; g, Charles, m Mary F. Bedford, and

went to Armstrong, Mo.; h, Robert. One Robert m Sarah Ann
Carter, F 1838.

Robert H. Yancey m Mildred Anderson°, F 1821, and they
went to Marion County, Indiana; Thomas Yancey m Sally Dixon°,
F 1814, and they were the parents of Edward, of Grant County,
Kentucky, and of Sophia, who m Lynn J. Fant, Owen 1830;
Charles Yancey m Jane Hancock°, F 1830; William Yancey m
Susan Combs (dau James), F 1820; Sarah Thornton Yancey m
John Edrington°.

Richard, Thomas, and Thornton Yancey came first to Scott,
and then to Franklin about 1816. George, Lewis, Philemon, and
William were in Scott about that same time. Bartlett or Buckham Yancey was in F 1815-1820.

Burkett G. Yancey m Mildred Menifee, Culpeper 1803. He
had a family of five, W 1810. Malinda Yancey m Philip Callen-
der°. The will of John Yancey, Todd 1825, mentions his wife,
Susan; his son, Gabriel; and grandchildren Maria Louise, Preston
I., and Robert. The will of James Yancey, Granville County,
North Carolina, 1779, names his children: Bartlett, Philip Thornton, Lewis, Thomas, Jenny Sanders, Nancy Baynes.

Tutt: James Tutt, of Culpeper County, Virginia, died 1786,
leaving his wife, Ann, and several children, including Lewis and
Hansford.

Lewis Tutt m Ibby Yancey, and they had a family of five,
W 1810, including Eleanor G. Williams°.

The name of the first wife of Hansford Tutt is not known, but
they had a family of nine, W 1810. In 1821 he m Mrs. Mourning Harrison Nall, widow of Charles. They lived on Beal's Run,
and were the proprietors of "Tutt's Tavern," an old log building
which stood until recently on the Lexington-Leestown road.
His tombstone is in the graveyard there.

His will, W 1827, mentions his wife (who died 1855) and
children: 1, William F.; 2, James D., m Elizabeth Rodgers°, W
1811. One James m Lucy Sargent°, W 1815. 3, Fanny Nall°;
4, Burkett G., m Henrietta Yancey, W 1816; 5, George H. One
George H. Tutt had a family of two, W 1810. George H. Tutt
m Mildred Rodgers°, W 1821. George Tutt m Henrietta Yancey°,
and they had: Elizabeth; Hansford; Charles; James; Mildred
Jane, m —— Robb; George W.; 6, The heirs of L. Y. Tutt.

Ann M. Tutt m William Smith, W 1819; Polly m John Milton, W 1821; William m Cordelia Goode°, W 1824; George G. m Elizabeth Williams°, W 1830; William H. m Cynthia Ann Johnson (dau Thomas and Betsy Warren Johnson), W 1836, and they were grandparents of E. B. Tutt, of Millville.

NEALE—Sally, r 1814, dis 1819
Sarah, r 1830, dis 1842   Robert, dis 1823

Robert Neale was in Franklin, 1806 to 1820, when he was listed for property on Owen. Thomas was on Elkhorn F 1806, Charles was in Franklin, 1808, and William in 1811. Margaret had a family of one, Stephen had six, and Rachel had five, F 1810.

John Neale m Elizabeth Marshall° (dau William), F 1821; Thompson K. m Fanny Abbett°; Jemima m Joseph Robinson°.

Daniel Neale (1735-1804), of Fairfax County, Virginia, m Jemima Kitchen (dau William and Margaret Ward Kitchen), and they came to Scott County, Kentucky. Their children were: 1, Daniel; 2, William; 3, Presley, who appears to have had by his first marriage: a, Almeda, m first James Penney, and second Elisha Beasley, 1835; b, Felicia, m Samuel Mason, F 1829. Presley m Nancy Calvert Grugin° (widow of Paul), F 1827; 4, John; 5, Thaddeus; 6, Rhodam; 7, Nancy Kelly°; 8, Jemima Leach m Henry Grimes, W 1792; 9, Penelope; 10, Susanna; 11, Mary.

Many with these names were in Westmoreland County, Virginia.

Penny (Penney): Rev. John Penny (1764?-1833), whom John Taylor calls "a respectable man from Virginia," was born in Hanover County, Virginia, and was converted under the preaching of Reuben Ford in 1785. He m Frances White, Hanover 1785, and they came to Franklin (now Anderson), where he became the first pastor of the Old Salt River Church.

He had a family of eleven, F 1810, some of whom were: 1, Thomas (m Elizabeth Allen, F 1813?); 2, Philip, m Margaret Burrus, Mercer 1825, and they had a dau, Sally; 3, Elizabeth, m first John Lillard, and had Fanny (Butts), Clement, and Elizabeth (Walker); she m second William James; 4, Polly Freeman°; 5, William W., m Mary —— ; 6, Rev. Eli, m Mary Burrus (dau Edmund), Mercer 1821. They went to Missouri, and their son,

James Cash, m Mary Frances Paxton (dau Col. Richard Paxton), and was the father of J. C. Penney; 7, James, m Almeda Neale, F 1821; 8, Capt. John, m Nancy Burrus (dau Nathaniel).

NEW—Jethro, 1, r 1794   Sarah, 1, r 1794

Jethro New was on the tax list, F 1795, but in 1799 was in Gallatin. One Jethro New m Agnes Thomas, Gallatin 1813.

A record states that George Wade New, of Woodford, Col. Anthony New, of Christian, and Johanna New, who m Chapman Taylor° were brothers and sister, their mother having been either a Wade or a Gregory.

George W. New, who was born in King William County, Virginia, 1764, had a family of six, W 1810. In 1822 the tax list showed George W., Anthony L., William, and John. Anthony New m Elizabeth Morrison (see Fox), W 1826. Patsy New m George Chambers, W 1816.

One record says the first wife of Col. Anthony New was Elizabeth Sthreshley, but another says she was Ann Anderson (dau Robert), of Hanover. He m second Nancy Wyatt (dau Richard and Amy Chiles Wyatt), Caroline County, Virginia, 1782.

David New was in Lincoln, 1795.

NOEL—Silas, r 1811, dis 1812   Maria, r 1811, dis 1812

Cornelius Noell, "borne in Holland, and professing ye Protestant Religion," was living in Virginia on the Rappahannock in 1686.

Family names indicate that the Noels of Essex County, Virginia, were closely connected with Noel Mercer, of Chester, England, whose grandson, John Mercer, m Grace Fenton in Dublin, Ireland, 1700, and was the father of John, who m Catherine Mason (dau Col. George), in Virginia.

Rev. Theodoric Noel was associated with Lewis Craig, John Taylor, and others in spreading the Baptist doctrines in Virginia. One record says he was born in Caroline about 1745, while another states that he was born in Essex, 1753. He preached in many places, chiefly in King and Queen and in Essex, and in 1812, the year before his death, he baptized 320 persons.

His children were: Silas; James; Theodoric; Robert; Fanny Macey°.

Rev. Silas Mercer Noel (1783-1839) was the son of Rev. Theodoric and —— Sullivan Noel. He was baptized by William Hickman in 1810, and in 1813 was ordained and took charge of the church at Big Spring. He preached the first sermon to the newly organized Baptist Church in Frankfort, where he afterward served as pastor for several years. It was at a time when doubts and divisions were rampant, and because he saw the need of a general organization through which the denomination could act in harmony, he not only promoted the Baptist State Convention and published religious periodicals of a timely nature, but was active in originating Georgetown College, and subscribed generously to its endowment. Spencer says, "The Baptists of Kentucky owe much, under God, to this good and great man."

He m Maria Waring (dau Robert Payne and Sally Upshaw Waring) in Maryland, 1805, and their children were: 1, Lawson F., m first Mary Long°, F 1849, and they had: a, John W., m first his cousin, Clara Noel (dau Silas), and second, Agnes Crouse; b, Robert, m Mattie Church; c, Laura, m William Quarles; d, Ellen, m Charles Gaines°; e, Elizabeth Ann, m John W. Gaines°. Lawson m second Elizabeth Hawkins°, W 1859, and they had: f, Fanny. 2, Robert P. W., m Adilla Suter° (dau James), F 1830; 3, John; 4, Florida, m Dr. John M. Franklin, of Tennessee, F 1842, and they had a dau Adele; 5, Anna Maria, m Williamson Bacon°; 6, Laura, m Rev. Frank H. Hodges, F 1834, and had: a, Ann Maria Forsee°; b, Silas N., m Rosanna Mary Major°; 7, Silas, m Nannie Davis, and their dau, Clara, m John W. Noel.

Theodoric W. Noel also came to Franklin County. He is mentioned in the will of Mildred Gregory, W 1820, and in the will of Susanna Sullivan, F 1820.

One Loftus Noel m Ann Espey, of Dumfries, Va., in Philadelphia, 1795. Loftus and *Roderick* Noel were on the tax list, F 1813.

The will of Scott Noel was probated in Essex County, Virginia, 1766. Mary Noel (dau Scott), m Berryman Brown°. The will of Bernard (Barnett, Barnard) Noel, Mercer 1802, names his wife Sally, and besides perhaps other children: 1, Elijah; 2, Scott, who with his family was in F 1797-1802; 3, William; 4, Polly; 5, grandson Philip — evidently the one who m Elizabeth Yeager (wid Fielding, and dau Richard Smart), F

1816, and went to Owen. There were many other Noels in Mercer and Owen.

Sally Noel m Stafford Pemberton°, the bond signed by Scott Brown. William M. McReynolds m Maria C. Noel, F 1830.

Upshaw: John Horace Upshaw, of Essex County, Virginia, m Mary Lafon, and their children, some of whom came to Kentucky, were: 1, Edwin; 2, Horace, m Lucy Baylor, 1809; 3, Dr. William; 4, Sally, m first Robert P. Waring, and second —— Bridges; 5, Lucy, m first Thomas R. Waring, and had: a, John U.; b, Robert W., c, Elizabeth, m James L. Berryman, Fayette 1811. Lucy m second Major William Sthreshley. 6, Maria, m Nicholas Lafon in Virginia, 1801. They lived for a time in Frankfort, and then went to "Spring Garden," on the Frankfort-Versailles road. Their children were: a, James, died 1823; b, Mary V. Jackson°; c, Lucy S. Jackson°; d, John U. 7, Hannah Price°; 8, Cordelia, m Chiles Terrell.

William Tennant m Lucy B. Upshaw, W 1838; John Cook m Agnes Lafon, W 1838.

Suter: The will of Andrew Suter, W 1807, names his children: 1, William m Elizabeth Mitchell°, W 1797, and in 1810 had a family of eight; 2, Ankey; 3, Jesse, m Rebecca Meek, W 1791. They settled on Elkhorn in Franklin, and had: a, Anna, m William Harris, F 1815; b, Andrew; c, Thomas, m Maria Clark, Owen 1829; d, Patsy Mitchell°; e, Sally; f, Polly; g, Ankey; h, Elizabeth (Finnell°?); i, Wesley, m Nancy McMinny (dau Sally), Owen 1832. 4, Rev. Thomas, "a good old brother," who in 1794 was living with William on what was then known as "the old Leestown road." He was ordained in 1834, and preached at Big Spring as late as 1844. 5, John, who had a family of eleven, W 1810, including: a, Polly Martin°; b, Ann, m first John Kring, W 1803, and second William F. Martin°. 6, Elizabeth Taylor; 7, Ann Bates; 8, Margaret Davis°; 9, Sarah Millett.

James Suter, of Woodford, bought land from William Martin, F 1817. He died about 1830, leaving his wife Ann, and: 1, Washington; 2, Elizabeth; 3, Adelaide Marshall; 4, Eliza Ann, m Horace H. Sullivan, F 1832; 5, Emily Jane; 6, Harrison; 7, Addella Noel°.

Catherine Robertson° (dau J. Suter) m George Hendricks°, the bond signed by James Suter.

NOLIN (Noland)—Betsy, 1802, left years before 1817

James Nolin was in Woodford, 1796, and Thomas in 1805. Resin Ricketts m Mary Nolin, W 1798.

Thomas Nolin had a family of eight, F 1810, and Matthias was in Frankfort with four. John R. Nowland m Eliza Lewis°, F 1817. John M. Noland m Emily Hall°, F 1823.

OLIVER—Morning, r 1816   Nancy, r 1816, dis 1816

John H., Mourning, and Peter Oliver were spoken of in 1816 as being "late of Virginia." Mourning m Mournin Hurt°. Three children of Mrs. Nancy Oliver were: 1, Willis, Jr., m Elizabeth Moore (dau Elnathan), F 1824; 2, Eliza, m John H. Oliver, F 1835; 3, Malinda McDaniel°.

John Oliver, brother of Thomas and William, was born in Spotsylvania County, Virginia, 1756. His will, F 1834, speaks of his (second?) wife Elizabeth (Mrs. Elizabeth Long, whom he m, F 1823), and children: 1, John E., m Lucy Prewitt, F 1812; 2, Willis; 3, Rice W., m Susan Church°, F 1816; 4, Catherine Church°.

The census of 1810 shows Benjamin with a family of four; Charles on North Elkhorn with thirteen; John on Elkhorn with five; Pleasant with three; Thomas, who afterward went to Owen, with seven; William with eight. John, in Woodford, had eight.

Nancy Oliver m Jonathan Abbett°; George W. m Mrs. Mary P. Hall°, F 1813; John m Ann Finney, F 1822, the bond signed by Benjamin Head; Daniel m Elizabeth Cox°, F 1821; William m Eliza Tiller°, F 1821; Benjamin m Polly Arbuckle, F 1807; Nancy (dau Presley) m Walker Rutherford°; one Presley m Jane Christian°, who was born 1790.

O'NEAL—James, 1801-1804   Robert, 1801

James, Robert, and John O'Neal were in Franklin, probably near Woodlake, 1801. Robert m Jemima Spicer, F 1812, and his will, F 1826, mentions his wife and his sister, Agnes Smith°. One John m Phoebe ——— , and went to Ripley County, Indiana.

William O'Neal m Mary Craig°, W 1790. Thomas P. O'Neal m Catherine Sanders°, F 1796 and bought land at the Forks of Elkhorn from Haden Edwards, 1802. John and William were in Shelby, 1799.

The will of Thomas O'Neal, Carroll 1844, mentions his heirs: Thomas, William, James, Robert, Polly Holladay, Nancy Garvey, Sally Ford°, Rosa Ford°, Catherine Sanders°, Agnes Ford°, Elizabeth Smither°.

Onion—William, 1803, 1810

The Onion family came from Staffordshire, England, to Maryland, and thence to Kentucky. They lived on South Elkhorn at what is now the home of Miss Georgia Crutcher, and later went to Indiana.

Charles and William evidently were brothers. Charles had: 1, Rebecca, m Andrew Kelly°; 2, Mary, m Tobias Kingerry, F 1803. Eli Onion m Polly Onion, F 1798. Elizabeth Onion m Reuben Crutcher°. Elias Onion was in Jefferson, 1809-1817.

Palmer—Anne, 1, dis 1812
Betsy (dau Anne), 1801, dis 1812
Isaac, 1, dis 1808   William, r 1812, dis 1816
Lewis, 1802, 1808   Charles, left 1824

Isaac and Thomas Palmer were on Elkhorn, F 1796. In 1810 Isaac had a family of six, and Thomas had nine. In 1825 Nancy and Elizabeth sold their interest in the estate of Thomas, Sr., to Isaac Wingate, and Nancy sold land in 1840 to William Triplett. Susan Palmer (dau Maryan) m John M. Worland, F 1824. Lucy Triplett° m —— Palmer.

Charles Palmer had a family of seven, W 1810. Charles and Isaac were in Scott, 1820; Henry was in Mercer, 1794; Richard was in Shelby, 1804. Lewis D. Palmer bought from Samuel and Esther Lewis, F 1809, land on South Elkhorn in the vicinity of what is now known as the old Freeman place.

Parks—Solomon, r 1812, dis 1813
Susanna, r 1812, dis 1813

Solomon Parks had a family of six, F 1810, and Robert had four. Solomon lived on the river in Mallory's survey. One Solomon Parks signed the marriage bond of John Herndon and Nancy Brasfield, W 1806.

Timothy Park was in Franklin, 1805. Solomon Park m Eliza Jerman, Madison 1829. Moses Park was on Bailey's Run, F 1803.

PARTLOW—David, 1805, dis 1809

John Partlow, who came from Wales, had three sons, John, Samuel, and David, who settled in Spotsylvania County, Virginia. David sold his land in 1786, and in 1789 gave slaves to his children, Nancy and Henry Brock Partlow. He was on Elkhorn, F 1805.

Nancy Partlow (dau David) m William Tandy, F 1806, and died in Carroll, 1857. One Nancy Partlow m Francis Graham°.

PATTERSON (Patteson)—Elizabeth, r 1828

One historian writes that this name is spelled *Patteson* by the family, but is usually copied *Patterson* by clerks.

Robert Patteson or Patterson (spelled both ways in records) petitioned the court for permission to build a gristmill on North Elkhorn, F 1795. In that same year he entered land for Charles Patteson, of Buckingham County, Virginia. Charles, according to tradition, was a nephew of Col. Robert Patterson, the founder of Lexington, who came from Pennsylvania and died in 1827.

Charles came shortly afterward, and was administrator of the estate of Robert Patteson, F 1801, besides having an interest in the estates of David, Thomas, Benjamin, Jonathan, and Peter Patteson, of Buckingham County, Virginia. He built the stone house on North Elkhorn which is now the home of George Brock, and a steep place in the road near by is still called "Patterson's Hill."

Charles died about 1805, leaving his wife Elizabeth and: 1, Martha; 2, Margaret Watts°; 3, Charles; 4, Elizabeth, m Robert McReynolds, F 1799, and had Charles and Mary; 5, Mary, m Caleb Worley, F 1803; 6, Jane, m William Letcher, F 1807; 7, Joyce, m Dr. Charles Mills, F 1807, and they had eleven children; 8, Anne Bacon°; 9, Frances, m William F. Gray, F 1812; 10, Henry. The Pattesons sold the homestead in 1847 to H. M. Bedford.

Alexander A. Patteson, of Buckingham County, Virginia, m Mary Jarrat. Whether he died before the family came to Kentucky is not known. They are said to have lived at the Mc-Cracken place at the Forks of Elkhorn, though Mary's tomb is at the Charles Patteson place. Alexander and Mary had: 1, Lucy, m William Ogelvie; 2, Elizabeth Lewis°; 3, Susan, m her cousin, Robert P. Mills; 4, Caroline, m Jacob Diuguid (who m second

Louisa Jett°), F 1837; 5, Maria Louisa, m Alexander Mills, and went to Mississippi; 6, Marion, who sold his woolen mill at the Forks of Elkhorn to Turner Stedman about 1857; 7, Dr. Alexander Augustus, m Jean Wood Lewis°, F 1841 or 1842, and went to Sangamon County, Illinois.

William Wiley m Polly Patterson (dau Joseph), F 1806. One Joseph Patterson m Susan E. Haggin, F 1849. Benjamin Mahoney m Patsy Patterson (dau Henry), F 1817; Thomas Noble m Sally Patterson (dau Henry), F 1821. These could not have been daughters of Henry Patteson, as he and his sister Frances were minors when their father died.

PEAK—William, 1
    William and wife, dis 1818
    Mary, 1, dis 1818

Betsy, 1	Susanna, 1800
Daniel, 2, dis 1822	James, 2
Mary, dis 1822	James and wife, dis 1803

William, Daniel, James, and Thomas Peak were early citizens here, and it was no doubt for one of this family that the village of Peak's Mill, on Elkhorn, was named. Thomas applied for a tavern license, F 1795, and William had a family of eight, F 1810.

Daniel and his wife, who was Mary Haldiman, lived on the old Frankfort-Versailles road, at what is now known as the Mc-Millan farm. Some of their children were: 1, Jeanny Martin°; 2, Thomas, m Catherine ——— ; 3, Charity, m Benjamin C. Chadwick; 4, Sarah, m William Bland, of Nelson, W 1794. In 1822 Daniel sold his farm to Peter Dudley, and went to Nelson. He died in 1834.

Jesse Peak m Sally Scandland°, W 1793. One Jesse and his wife Judith were in Gallatin, 1814.

The will of John Peak, Scott 1806, names his wife Jemima and children: 1, Isaac; 2, Presley. Presley B. Peak (1770-1821) m Judith ——— , and they had: a, James S.; b, Jordan J., m first Patsy Craig, m second Mary Hughes Watkins, m third Eliza Ann Bradley°, 1831; c, Polly; d, Leland W.; e, Paulina; f, Lavinia; g, Louisiana; h, Evalina; i, Madison; j, Dudley, m Ann Maria Martin°, Scott 1841; k, George, m Letitia Suggett°. 3, Spencer; 4, Constance Anderson°; 5, Milly Scott; 6, Ailsy Sanders°; 7, Ellen Cullin°; 8, Mally Mulberry; 9, Rachel Drake.

William Wilkins m Mary Peak (dau Mary Ann), F 1817.
Jemima Peak (dau Elizabeth), m Thomas Ferguson°. John
Peak was in Shelby, 1792; Benjamin was in Bourbon, 1797;
Nathan and John in Henry, 1800; Hezekiah in Scott, 1806.

PEMBERTON—Bennett, r 1801, dis 1813
Polly, r 1801, dis 1813

Charles Pemberton came from Caroline County, Virginia, to
Woodford, where he died 1792, leaving his wife Sarah and: 1,
Delphia, m first Larkin Garnett°, 1770, and second Henry Gate-
wood°; 2, Elizabeth Edwards°; 3, Nancy Owen°; 4, Bennett, m
Mary Tureman (dau Charles and Margaret Crutcher Tureman,
and granddaughter of Ignatius Tureman, who died in Spotsylvania County, Virginia, 1784).

Bennett and his wife probably lived opposite "Silver Lake
Farm" on the Georgetown road. They sold this property to
Samuel Moxley in 1803, and the tax list of that same year shows
them located on Benson. Bennett died about 1832, leaving: a,
William T., who in 1835 sold his share of the land to Austin
P. Cox; b, Peggy Mitchell°; c, Kitty, m first Christopher Hard-
wick, F 1826, and they had: John, William, Emily, Wilson; she
m second Henry Beckley, Shelby 1830; d, Mary, m Peter G.
Voorhies, F 1800; e, John T., m ——, and had Celia; John;
Amelia; Celistine; f, Susan Field; g, Elizabeth Bacon°; h,
Charles.

Richard Pemberton was on Elkhorn, F 1796, but in 1801 his
widow, Janette, was living on Benson. Their children were: 1,
Nancy Thomson°; 2, Henry, m Janey Baker°, F 1803, and some of
their children were: a, Nancy, m Richard Smart, F 1823; b,
Agatha, m Moses Shropshire, F 1823; 3, Stafford, m Sally Noel°,
F 1806; 4, Matilda James°; 5, Richard, m Rosanna Baker°, F
1817, 6, Peggy, m William Crockett, F 1807; 7, William, m Eliza
L. Richardson°, F 1822; 8, Malinda; 9, Edmund. Mrs. Janette
Pemberton m David Wilcox, F 1804. Dorinda Pemberton (dau
Sarah) m John J. Vaughan°; Kitty (dau Sarah) m James Dar-
lington, Shelby 1842, and they were parents of Bishop U. V.
W. Darlington.

William Pemberton m Jane Vaughan°, W 1813. They went
to Shelby, and their children were: Elizabeth, Nancy, John,

Polly, William. Martha Pemberton m Leonard Mahone, W 1822; Fanny Pemberton m Robert F. Gibbs°; Sarah Pemberton (dau John W.) m Simeon Watts°.

Reuben Pemberton m Elizabeth Crutcher°. They went to Shelby, and later to Henry, where their daughter Polly m Robert Bell, 1809. The will of Reuben, Oldham 1826, mentions all his children (not named); son John and his wife Margaret and his child Sarah Jane; son Thomas; son-in-law Reuben Sale.

Owen: William Owen m Nancy Pemberton, and they came from Virginia and settled on the river below Frankfort. Their children were: 1, Robert D., m Susan W. Adams (dau Susan), F 1815; 2, Capt. William, m Patsy Crutchfield (dau John), F 1813, and they had: a, Sarah Ann, m John Hawkins Wickersham, F 1828; b, Emily Wooldridge°; c, America, m John T. Dowdell, Jefferson 1821, and went to Missouri; d, Martha, m George Griffin; e, John W., m Lydia ——— ; f, James H., m Harriet ——— , and lived in Christian; g, George A. 3, Charles P., m Mary Ann ——— ; 4, Kathy Moss°; 5, Elizabeth, m first George C. Ashby, F 1812, second Samuel Adams, F 1818, third Bennett Edwards°.

Evidently related were Milly Haydon°; James Owen, m Polly Tureman (dau Thomas), W 1820; and Sanford Owen, who m Maria Sullenger°, W 1816, and went to Henry, where their family included: 1, Maria Louise, m William G. Connell, 1839; 2, Frances Guthrie°; 3, America, m C. Strother, 1847. One Sanford Owen m Elizabeth Whittington°, Henry 1841. Sanford P. Owen, of Henry, m Mrs. Sarah Guthrie°, Henry 1852, and Mrs. Mary Robb°, F 1855.

Brackett Owen, of Prince Edward County, Virginia, m Elizabeth McGehee°, and they came in 1785 to the part of Jefferson that is now Shelby, where they had a fort for the protection of the settlers. Brackett's will, Shelby 1802, mentions these children: 1, William; 2, Jesse; 3, Samuel; 4, Sally, m Robert Glass, Shelby 1796; 5, Jacob; 6, John; 7, Col. Abraham (1769-1811). For his heroism in the battle of Tippecanoe, when he gave his life for his commander, Gen. William Henry Harrison, by exchanging horses with him, the county of Owen was named for him. He m Martha Dupuy°, and their children lived in Newcastle, Ky., and in Texas.

8, David; 9, Joseph, m Dolly Darnell°, W 1794, and they went to Union County in 1810. They were the parents of Austin, m Catherine Runamus; and Abram, m Rachel F. Browder. 10, Robert; 11, Nancy.

William, David, and Thomas Owen were in F 1797; James and Thomas were in W 1801.

PILCHER—Lurana Jane (Pratts)   Anna, about 1840

William A. Gorham and Lysander Hord were guardians of Lurana Jane Pilcher (orphan of John), F 1840. Archibald Moore was guardian of Nancy, Albert A., and Henry Pilcher (orphans of John), F 1851.

Family records say that John Pilcher m —— Moore, and their son Harvey m first —— and had: 1, Louis; 2, Susan, m —— Wood; 3, dau m —— Sheehan; 4, dau m —— Stivers. Harvey m second America Bohannon° (dau John?), Shelby 1856, and their children were: 5, Robert, m Molly Moss°, and they were grandparents of Mrs. Otis Wood, of Frankfort; 6, William, m Alice Moss°, and they were the parents of Mrs. N. E. Stevens, of the Devil's Hollow pike; 7, Charles, m Amanda Burge, and lives on the old Lexington-Leestown road. Harriet Pilcher m Alexander Moss°.

One John Pilcher lived on Benson, and his will, F 1830, names his wife Sarah and: 1, Alexander S., m Lucy —— , and went to Fayette County, Illinois; 2, Samuel; 3, Elizabeth Rice; 4, Susan, went to Hendricks County, Indiana; 5, Frances, m John Holley, and went to Indiana; 6, Sarah Ann West°.

Shadrach and Fielding Pilcher were in Jessamine, 1799. Thomas Pilcher m Lucy Hackney, W 1842, and they had Sarah, America, and Georgiana. Reuben Young m America Pilcher, W 1844.

POE—Edmund, 1800, dis 1801

Edmund, Virgil, John, and Benjamin Poe were in F 1795, and in 1810 Edmund was on Elkhorn with a family of seven. One Edmund had a wife Nancy, and one m Mrs. Hannah Long (see Triplett). Listed as children of Edmund were: Maria Roberts°; Susan, m William Warner, F 1836; Martha, m Richard Taylor°, F 1851. Virgil Poe (1742-1840), who came from Caroline County, Virginia, had: 1, Rebecca, m Andrew Baldwin°; 2, Mary, m Robert Sacra, F 1802; 3, Elizabeth. John and Sally Poe had a family of twelve, including Catherine, m Reuben Smithers or Smothers, F 1813. William Poe m Charity Rogers°, F 1802; Virgil, Jr., m Keziah Taylor°, F 1807; Jesse (s Jesse) m Milly Dempsey, F 1810; John m Fanny Dempsey (dau Coleman), F 1825; Milly m Zachary Duvall, F 1831.

PORTER—Thomas, r 1797   Sister, r 1801

Thomas Porter, of Culpeper County, Virginia, was in Woodford 1792-1797. He went to Bourbon, and afterward to Shelby, where he died in 1817. His children were Peggy and Elizabeth Major°, a dau who m John Smith, and perhaps others. The wife of Thomas Wooldridge is thought to have been a Porter.

(Captain?) James Porter (once written James F. Porter) in 1796 bought from Lewis Craig a farm adjoining those of John Brown, Mrs. Sarah Gibson, and William Samuel. Somewhat back of the house near Duckers known as the old Porter place, now owned by B. M. Hieatt, were the remains of an old homestead and a graveyard that may have belonged to James Porter, who in 1820 sold a portion of his land to William Ducker and William Gibson.

The records are confusing, for the will of a James Porter, Shelby 1832, named his wife Elizabeth and all children; and in that same year the estate of James Porter was settled in Woodford, the heirs mentioned being: 1, John P. Mrs. Eliza Porter, wife of Capt. John P. Porter, d W 1821. John P. m Mrs. Sarah Martin°, W 1825. He was on Beal's Run and South Elkhorn, 1826-1838; 2, Nathaniel P. m Susan Singleton°, W 1851, and they lived for some time on the farm at Duckers; 3, William, who lived on Elkhorn; 4, Jeremiah; 5, Samuel T.; 6, Sally McCracken°; 7, Samuel D. Whitsell. Mrs. Margaret Porter, wife of James, d W 1823. Elizabeth Porter m George Singleton, W 1832, the bond signed by John P. Porter.

The last tombstone standing in the old churchyard in 1932 was that of William Porter (1784-1815).

William and Samuel Porter were in Lincoln, 1788. In 1793 William had a tanyard at Haydon's Station. A family record says that he was the son of William and Sarah Pierce Porter, of Maryland, and that he m Hannah Kennedy in Covington, Ky., about 1800. Some of his children were: 1, Thomas, m Geraldine Horton in Tennessee, 1824, and was the father of Gov. James D. and Thomas; 2, William, m Sarah Ware°, and they had: a, Betty, m Hon. J. D. C. Atkins; b, Diana; c, Annie, m —— Clark; 3, John C., m Sarah Ann Blanton°, and they had: a, John William (m Margaret, dau Robert P. Mills?); b, Willis; c, George; d, Thomas; e, Agnes Dorothy. 4, James D., m F 1823 Maria Rouzie (or Rowsey), (dau Agnes Rouzie by her first husband, Philemon Rouzie). Diana Porter, who m Thomas White, F 1816, and Sarah, who m George B. Wilcox, F 1820, may have been daughters of William and Hannah. Records show that William Porter, Sr., m Mrs. Agnes Rouzie (see Ware), F 1820, and they had: 5, Mary, m Jesse Cooper; 6, Rebecca, m Fleming Dawson. William, Sr., and some of his family went about 1822 to Henry County, Tennessee, where he and Samuel Porter were interested in the estates of Nathaniel and William.

Since the foregoing outline was written, there has been found a court record of 1822, stating that William Porter was guardian of Eliza K., Malinda K., and James D. Porter (see No. 4, above), infant heirs of William Porter. These may have been children of William and Hannah who remained in Kentucky when their father went to Tennessee.

In 1810 Nathaniel Porter was in Frankfort with two in his family, and William was there with seven. Out in the county another William had sixteen, and James had eight. One William Porter, Jr., m Mary Runyan°, F 1810. N. P. Porter m Martha Gwin, Shelby 1812. William and Mary, together with Nathaniel P. and his wife Martha, sold property in Frankfort, 1820. One Nathaniel, a hatter, was in Shelby, 1812.

An old house on the road between Duckers and the Leestown road (now the site of A. W. Lippert's home) was also known as the Porter house, and one of the very early citizens remembered being taken there in his childhood to the funeral of old Mr. Porter, the last Revolutionary soldier in that section.

In Woodford, William m Molly Cather, 1802; Catherine m Asa Butler, 1830; William m Elizabeth Wood, 1834. Some of the family lived in the vicinity of Clear Creek.

Nathan Porter m Catherine Kennedy, Mason 1797; William
Porter m Hannah Martin (dau Edmund), Mason 1806.

Singleton: Manoah Singleton m Sally Craig°. They lived in
Jessamine, and their children were: 1, Jeconiah (1776-1834), m
Jane Taylor (sister of Rev. John Taylor), and settled in Wood-
ford. They had: a, Lewis; b, John, whose daughters, Bettie
Robertson and Susan Porter°, were known as the characters in
"Tempest and Sunshine"; c, Elijah; d, Sally, m James Brown;
e, William; f, a granddaughter, Eliza Jane Rust. 2, Betsy, m
George O'Neal; 3, Sarah, m Moses Martin; 4, Mason, m Fannie
Garnett; 5, Hannah, m John Lancaster; 6, Anna, m James Hiter;
7, Mary, m —— Barkley; 8, Jane, m Samuel Barkley, Sr.; 9,
Martha, m Hawkins Craig°; 10, Joannah; 11, Susan, m Joseph
Hughes, Jr.

PRICE—Samuel, 1800, dis 1804, ret 1816, dis 1818
     Elizabeth, dis 1804
     John, 2, to Forks of Elkhorn 1818
     Susanna, 2, to Forks of Elkhorn 1818

There are several Price families connected with this congregation, but their relationship to each other is not known.

Col. Samuel Price (1740-1824) m Elizabeth Richardson°.
He was living north of the river, F 1796, and was at some time
a citizen of Fayette, but he died in Woodford. His children
were: 1, Ann, m Gen. William Russell, of Fayette, and their dau
Eliza m John Bradford; 2, Lucy, m Daniel Weisiger, Fayette
1791. They lived in Frankfort, and their children were: a,
Joseph; b, Daniel, m Mary H. Castleman°, F 1819; c, Samuel,
m Ann Elizabeth Cowan; d, Ann, m Col. George Adams, F 1811;
e, Lucy, m Judge William Roper; f, Elizabeth, m Robert Alexander, F 1814, and they were grandparents of Dr. A. J. A.
Alexander, of "Woodburn"; g, Emaline, m Jacob Swigert, F
1825; h, Mary Bell, m Col. John Slaughter, F 1819; i, Isabella,
m Thomas Noble Lindsey, F 1834, and they were grandparents
of Misses Maria, Isabel, Cordelia, Lilian, and Genevieve Lindsey,
of Frankfort.

3, Polly (Miriam?) Buck°; 4, Isabella, m William Samuel°;
5, Ruth Snowden, m Judge George Shannon, Fayette 1813;

6, Rebecca K.; 7, Mariam Buck°; 8, Maria, m —— Winter; 9, Capt. Richard, m first, Mary Waller°, and they had: a, Sally, m Lyddall Bacon Bowles, of Hanover County, Virginia; b, Eliza. He m second Hannah Upshaw°, and their children were: c, John, m Mary Helen O'Hara (dau Kean); d, Mary Cordelia, m first Lucas Brodhead, F 1832, and second Orlando Brown, Sr.; e, Anne, m Judge Lysander Hord, F 1839, and they were grandparents of Misses Annie and Mary Watts Brown, of Frankfort; f, Lieut. Richard; 10, Capt. Samuel, m Maria West (dau Edward), Fayette 1810, and their dau Samuella m Valerius Winchester, of Tennessee.

Elder John Price, who was born in Shenandoah County, Virginia, came to Kentucky, probably with the "Travelling Church," and with George S. Smith had charge of the congregation at Gilbert's Creek in 1785. He went later to Owen County, where in 1801 he was located at Twins, serving there and in the neighboring churches during the remainder of his life. It was noted that, "he was, while in Virginia, considered a man of weight in religious concerns. In Kentucky, likewise, he has been distinguished as a man of zeal and parts."

One Rev. John Price, of Jessamine, died 1822.

John Price, Jr., who is thought to have been a son of Elder John Price, lived in the Woodlake neighborhood. He m first Elizabeth Major°, and their dau Ann m first Col. James Innes (s Hugh), F 1811, and second, Caleb I. Sanders°, Fayette 1826. John Price m second Susan Gano°, F 1796, and their children were: 2, John G., m America Wilson°, F 1819, and they had: a, William; b, John; c, Lucy Mary; d, Susan, m (George W.?) Withers. Descendants of this family located in Missouri and Texas. 3, Dr. William H., m Elizabeth Haggin (dau Judge James and Hetty Humphreys Haggin), F 1824. He d 1836, leaving his wife and: a, William H., m Mary ——; b, James H.; c, Dr. John G., m Susan R. Lewis°; d, Hetty, m Alexander Cox, of Lexington; e, Daniel E. These heirs sold their farm to B. T. Bedford about 1851. 4, Margaret Sanders°; 5, Elizabeth, m William Hubbell°; 6, Evans; 7, Isaac E., m first Susan T. Haggin, F 1834, and second Elizabeth Loughborough°, F 1837, and they had: a, Florida Haren; b, Mary Belle Webb; c, Nannie; d, Harry; e, Elizabeth Richardson; f, Charles. This family went

to Ray County, Missouri. 8, Daniel C.; 9, Susan Mary, m Dr.
William M. Wilson, F 1834; 10, Richard M.; 11, Ezra.

John Mason Price m Sally Craig°, W 1796. They went to
Port William (Carrollton), where he died 1836. Their children
were: Silas; Cyrena Gex; Melissa Craig; Nannie Peak; Sarah
McCaslin; Elizabeth Shefer; Jane Brown; John M.; Esther
Lothrop.

Another Price family came from Chesterfield County, Vir-
ginia, and settled in Fayette, Scott, and Woodford. Philemon
Bird Price (1783-1835) m first Corrilla Mansell (dau George),
Fayette 1803. Their children were: 1, Theodore, who went to
Missouri; 2, Mortimer. P. B. Price m second Mary Dorsey
Wilmot (dau Col. Robert and Priscilla Dorsey Wilmot), Bourbon
1810, and they had: 3, Ann, m William Warren, 1827; 4,
Charles; 5, Dr. Williamson, m Margaret Theobald°, F 1835;
6, Andrew F., m Mary Regan; 7, Philemon B., m Elizabeth
Hurst, 1851, and they were the parents of Miss Mary Wilmot
Price, of Jacksonville, Ill.; 8, Robert; 9, Wickliffe; 10, Joel Scott,
m Susan Lampton, and they were the parents of Dr. J. Lampton
Price and Mrs. W. C. Herndon, of Frankfort. Several of these
families went to Illinois. Daniel Branch Price and Dr. Andrew
F. Price, of Woodford, were of this line.

Richardson: William Richardson (s Joseph and Sarah
Thomas Richardson) m Isabella Calmes (dau Marquis, Jr., and
Winnifred Waller Calmes), and their children were: 1, Eliza-
beth Price°; 2, Miriam (1748- ——), m John Buck°; 3, Sarah
Combs°; 4, Mary (1751-1828), m Charles Buck°; 5, John Croley,
m Sarah Bainbridge Hall; 6, Ann, m Thomas Buck°; 7, Samuel
Marquis Calmes, m Catherine B. Hall; 8, William, m ——
Pugh; 9, Marquis, m Henrietta Catlett. One Marquis Richard-
son was on North Elkhorn with a family of nine, F 1810. Capt.
Marquis D. Richardson (1789-1823), a native of Fayette, died
in Georgia.

Of another family was Turner Richardson, Jr., who m first
Ann Allen. They came from Fluvanna County, Virginia, about
1787, and settled near Haydon's Station. Five of their six children were: 1, James, who remained in Virginia; 2, Judge
Nathaniel, recorded as born in Goochland County, Virginia,

1768. He m first Ann Read°, 1791, and second Fanny Bullard°, Shelby 1821. He was in Woodford 1791, evidently in Frankfort, where about 1796 a lot was sold "next to Nathaniel Richardson's cabbin." He afterward lived on Big Benson, where in 1810 he had a family of eight, and in 1836 was in Lewis County, Missouri. His children were: a, Nathaniel, m Susanna Dupuy°, Shelby 1811; b, Mary Ann, m Charles Hall, F 1820; c, Eliza Pemberton°; d, William, m his cousin, Mary D. Richardson, 1825; e, Preston, m his cousin, Martha B. Richardson, 1834; f, John Carter, m Fanny Arbuckle; g, James A., m Mary Shannon (dau Rev. Samuel), F 1816; h, Francis R., m Sarah C. Major°, F 1826; i, Hiram, m Sally Scofield (dau John), F 1826.

3, Allen (1771-1818), m Elizabeth Payne, and they lived on South Benson. Their children were: a, Thomas, who went to Missouri; b, Lucy Ann, m John B. Foree, F 1834; c, Emerine or Evaline, m William Foree. 4, John Dorran (1774-1844), m Lucy H. Brown (dau Hezekiah and Ann Stubblefield Brown), 1802. They lived in Frankfort, 1810, and later on Cedar Run, and had several children, including Mary and Martha, who m sons of Judge Richardson; Eliza Jane Vaughan°; and James Allen, who m Elizabeth McCormack and was the father of Owen T., who m Sheffer Hayner, and Nathaniel F., who m Pinkie M. Stephens. 5, Polly Johnson°.

Mrs. Ann Allen Richardson died in 1794, and Turner, Jr., m second Catherine ——. He died in 1802.

Robert Richardson was in F, 1806, and Samuel had land on Benson in 1814 and thereafter. Turner, Jr., had a brother, Samuel.

PULLIAM—Zachariah, 1801   Sarah, 1, dis 1818
            Caty, 1

Zachariah Pulliam m Catherine Boulware° F 1796, and they lived at "Roselawn," in later years the home of Mrs. Sam South. Their children were: Ritchie B.; Elijah; Elisha; Mary, m —— Pulliam; Catherine; Alanson; Milton; Martha, m James Pulliam. The second wife of Zachariah Pulliam was Grace ——, and their children were: Thomas, Zachariah, George, Edward. Zachariah died in 1834, and Grace in 1844, after which, the records indicate, the family moved to Prestonsburg, Ky.

One Zachariah Pulliam m Sarah Black, and they were in Louisa County, Virginia, 1782.

John Pulliam (1783-1846) lived in the section of Franklin that is now Anderson. He m Elizabeth Blackwell°, F 1810, and their children were: 1, John; 2, Monroe, m Louisa Alexander (dau Robert), Mercer 1854, and they had Robert, John, and Graves; 3, Walker (m Minerva ——?); 4, America; 5, Martha, m —— Sanders; 6, Sallie, m —— Marshall;7, Nannie, m Richard Scott; 8, Betty, m —— Beddoe; 9, Mariam Gaines°.

Benjamin and Jennings Pulliam were in the tax list, F 1801.

RAMSEY—Seth, 2, to Glen's Creek 1801
      Lucy, to Glen's Creek 1801
      "Sister", dis 1836
      America, dis 1836
      Martha, dis 1836   Nancy, 1845
      Fielding, 1843   Seth, 1845

Seth Ramsey m Lucy Hiatt (dau William), Lincoln 1789. They lived near McKee's crossroads on a farm which they sold in 1824 to Richard Fox. Their children were: 1, Seth; 2, Enos, m Nancy George (dau Jeremiah Walker George, of Bourbon), F 1809. They lived on the Leestown (Cole's) road, on the farm now owned by B. J. Nickles, which was then called "Ramsey's Woods." Their children were: a, Jeremiah George Washington, m Mary —— and went to Shelby; b, Eliza Jane Crutcher°; c, Lucy Ann; d, America, m Louis Snowden, F 1836, and went to Illinois; e, Martha, m Madison Williams; f, Fielding, m Nancy Duvall, and went to Missouri; g, Cynthia Agnes, m William P. Robertson, F 1841; h, Madison; i, Seth Thomas; j, John T., m Mary E. Edrington, 1849, and went to Louisville; k, Martin D. Hardin, went to Missouri; l, Lewis Henry.

3, Joseph; 4, Sally, m Elijah Searcy, W 1815; 5, Martha; 6, Nancy, m Francis Norvil, W 1815; 7, Catherine Guthrie°; 8, Silas M. (1805-1887), who went to Missouri in 1824, m first Elizabeth Brown, 1835, and second Henrietta Baker (?), and his children were: John B., Martha, Robert, Samuel, Silas, James, Mary, Newton.

Polly Ramsey, who m Edmund Stephens°, may have been another daughter of Seth, as the bond was signed by him.

Esther Ramsey, who m Ritchie Boulware°, was closely related to Seth Ramsey.

RANSDELL (Ransdale)—Patsy, to Frankfort 1816

Christopher C. Ransdale was in Frankfort, 1810, with a family of two. Christopher Ransdale m Patsy Hickman°, F 1816, and they had: 1, Mary H., m Joseph H. Mayhall, F 1835; 2, Elizabeth; 3, Isabella. Christopher, Zachary, James, Nancy, and Benjamin Ransdale were in Franklin, 1820. The will of Zachariah, Owen 1864, mentions his wife Nancy and: John S.; William C.; Zerelda, m John McFeron, Owen 1838; Marne; Z. H.; Susan Snelson; Lewis A.

Presley Ransdell m Polly Shely, Fayette 1810.

REDDING—Brother

Rev. Joseph Redding (1750-1815), of Fauquier County, Virginia, m Ann Weakly and came to Kentucky. He was in Woodford, 1790, and was the pastor of the Great Crossings Church, in Scott, from 1793 to 1810. Joseph and Ann were the parents of Sarah Suggett° (b 1778) and perhaps other children. One Joseph m Nancy Banks (dau Sally), F 1818.

REDIFORD—see Rutherford

REED (Read)—Polly, 1801
Mrs. Mary, r 1812, dis 1814
Polly Wilson, 1841, 1850
Mary Brydon, 1842, 1850

Hankinson Read (s John and Winifred Favior Read), of Culpeper County, Virginia, m first Mary Slaughter (dau Edgecombe). Their children were: 1, Winnie Bledsoe°, b 1770; 2, Francis Slaughter, m first Hannah McKinley, 1804, and second Ann Waggener, of Danville; 3, Ann Richardson°. A family record says that Mary Slaughter Read died 1776, and Hankinson m second Mary ——. They had: 4, Elizabeth Ware°, b 1778; 5, Mary Allen°; 6, Hankinson, m Eleanor Shannon (dau Rev. Samuel), F 1809; 7, John; 8, Jemima Long°; 9, Lucy, m Robert Slaughter, W 1817; 10, Thornton, who was drowned in the Potomac River, 1814.

Hankinson was in Franklin County, 1796, and on Glen's Creek, W 1800. One Hankinson Reed m Susan Yotsler, Hardin 1799.

William Reed was in F 1801; Armistead was on Flat Creek, F 1820. Armistead had a family of six, James had five, and John had five, F 1810.

RENDOR (Randor)—Robert, 1   Sarah, 1

Robert Render, Sr., Robert, Jr., and George were in Woodford, 1799. Robert, George, and Joshua Render located in Ohio County, Kentucky, where they entered the Baptist ministry from the Beaver Dam Church. Robert died about 1861.

RENFREW (Rentfro)—James, 1

James Rentfro m Mrs. Mary Rucker Vawter°, who died in Versailles. He sold land on North Elkhorn to Achilles Stapp, W 1790, and to John B. Hodson, 1809, in Warren.

One James Rentfro m Margaret Jackson, W 1790, and one James was in Lincoln, 1801. Susanna Rentfro m Alexander Phillips, W 1795.

RENNIX (Rennick?)—Brother, 1803

Not certain that this man was a member of Forks Church.

John Rennick (———-1814) is said to have built his home— one record says in 1786, while another gives the date at 1791— on what is now High Street, in Frankfort. His wife was Mary ———, and their son, Alexander H. (1791-1871), m Letitia A. Lee (dau Willis and Mary McAfee Lee), F 1817. They lived at "Glen Willis," and their children were: 1, Todd; 2, Mary Willis, m first Thomas J. Todd°, F 1838, and second R. K. Woodson, F 1868; 3, Eliza C.; 4, Catherine Ann; 5, Allisonia Todd°; 6, Louisa, m William E. Milton, F 1849; 7, Henry; 8, Atwell.

Katherine Rennick m Rev. John Montgomery, of Harrodsburg, 1844.

William Rennick m Isabel Roberts°, F 1799.

James Rennick had a family of eight, W 1810, and Alexander had five. The will of Robert Rennick, W 1815, mentions his brother Alexander.

Samuel Underwood m Esther Rennick, W 1810.

RICHMOND—Ezra, r 1828
Eliza, r 1815, dis 1841
Polly, r 1828

Ezra Richmond m Elizabeth Carstaphron (dau Robert, of Fayette), F 1807. He was in Franklin County in 1805, his home at some time being what is known as the Duane Brown place, on South Elkhorn. The family went to Missouri in 1841. His dau Mary m Nathan Ayres°, and the settlement of his estate, F 1848, indicates that other heirs were: Ezra E.; John; Matilda P.; R. C.; Richard F., m Mrs. Edmonia Barton, F 1840.

ROBERTS—Edward, 1801   John, 1801, dis 1802
Eleanor, 1801   Elizabeth, dis 1802

Edward, Peter, and James Roberts were in F 1797. In 1810 Edward had a family of ten, including: 1, Susan, m James Benham, F 1806; 2, Elizabeth, m Benjamin Rosson, F 1812; 3, Sally, m John Rosson, F 1813; 4, Ruthy Lewis°.

John Roberts was here in 1802, but sold to Isaac Wilson in 1805, and apparently went to Henry, where the family married into the Baker, Marshall, and Haydon families.

One James, whose wife was Catherine, was in Frankfort with a family of nine, and one James in the country had eight. Patrick Henry Roberts (1758-1839) m Catherine Austin in Baltimore, 1810, and they came to Franklin County. They were the parents of John and Edmund A. N.

Dr. John Roberts (1744- ——) came to Frankfort from Virginia in 1804. An old newspaper clipping says he was a highly educated German exile who changed his name upon entering this country, and that the real name is not known. Whether his wife was living when he came is uncertain, but a deposition states that three of his children were of age in 1820. He was the father of: 1, Maria W.; 2, Susan; 3, Frederick, m Catherine Smith (dau Jesse), F 1832. They lived near Antioch Church, for which they deeded the lot in 1857, after the church had been built. 4, Dr. Joseph G., m Martha Ann Todd°, F 1824, and they were ancestors of Richard W. Knott, of Louisville; 5, John, m Mary ——, and went to Owensboro; 6, Lucy Lloyd°; 7, Elizabeth; 8, Henry B.

In Franklin, Polly Roberts (dau James) m Robert Black, 1795; Peggy (dau J——) m James Baker°; Isabel (dau Peter) m William Rennick°; Jacob m Sarah Moore (dau Elnathan), 1811; James R. m Elsey Egbert, 1815; John (s Edmund) m Elizabeth Bacon°, 1821; John m Maria F. Poe°, 1825; Edward W. m Mary Jane Thompson°, 1841.

Thomas J. Roberts sold to Enoch Fenwick, F 1811, and William Roberts sold to Benjamin Hickman, F 1819.

John Roberts m Dolly Dunn°, F 1798.

ROBERTSON—William P., r 1844, went West 1846
           Cynthia, r 1844, went West 1846

Charles Robertson had a family of four, F 1810, and Nathan had eight. The will of James Robertson, F 1846, mentions his wife Nancy and children (not named), and his brother George.

ROBINSON—James, 1805
           Polly Smither, dis 1809
           Nancy Abbett, dis 1811
           Jemimah, 2
           Owen, dis 1822

James Robinson m Polly Smither°, F 1804; Charles Robinson m Nancy Abbett°, W 1806; Jemima Robinson (dau William and Patsy, of Maryland) m Daniel Gano°; Joseph Robinson m Jemima Neale°, Scott, 1841.

Owen Robinson (1770-1833) was in Franklin County, 1795. He was living in Frankfort in 1810 when he m Sarah Gibson°, though they went later to Benson. Their children were: 1, Jeptha, m Bettie Williams°, 1827, and they were the parents of Misses Ruth and Hettie Robinson, of Frankfort; 2, Susan Tinsley°; 3, George, m first Mary E. Lawrence, F 1839, and second Mary Scofield (dau Marion and Ann Jenkins Scofield), and they were the parents of Dr. J. Owen, who m Lucy Brown°; 4, Jabez, m Mary Crutcher (dau William N.), F 1856; 5, James D.; 6, Owen, who went to California; 7, Elizabeth Pattie°; 8, Joseph, m Eliza Robb°, F 1852, and they had: Sarah, m Charles Newton, and Mary, m Benjamin T. Farmer°; 9, Benjamin, m Monica Hales (dau Corbin), F 1856, and went to one of the mountain counties; 10, John W.

Incomplete records indicate that south of the river in Franklin were four Robinson brothers and a sister: 1, Alex, d 1796; 2, Robert, who had a dau Polly; 3, William, had: a, Easter Thomson°; b, Rachel Settle°; 4, John, had: a, Alex; b, Patsy Martin°; 5, Rachel, m —— Campbell°. These same names are found in earlier Mercer records, sometimes spelled *Robinson* and sometimes *Robertson.*

John Robinson m Mary Ayres°, W 1823, and they went to Missouri.

Robinsons with families in the census of 1810 were: In Franklin, Benjamin, George, Isaac, two Johns, Robert, four Williams; in Woodford, Cornelius, George, Richard, Thomas.

Robb: Frederick Robb (s Michael and Elizabeth Markee Robb, who came from Alsace-Lorraine to Maryland), m first Mary Neat (dau John and Susan Neat). They were in Jessamine 1810, coming later to Bridgeport, in Franklin. Their children were: 1, Michael, m Polly Owen°; 2, George W., m Lizzie Macklin°, and they lived near Duckers at "Elm Grove," in recent years the home of J. D. Smith; 3, Susan, m Anthony Crockett, and they went to Hancock; 4, Eliza Robinson°; 5, Mary Ann Smith°; 6, Sallie, m Granville Crockett, and their dau, Susan, m Wilder Dupuy, and is the mother of Mrs. John Miles Emmitt, of Frankfort; 7, Martha, m H. H. Tilford, and they went to Texas; 8, William N., m first Molly Kelly°, and second Letitia Dallam, Fayette 1850; 9, Jonas, m first Fanny Crockett, F 1850, and second Lucy Foster; 10, James, m Julia Beauchamp, of Hancock; 11, Joseph. Mary Robb d 1855, and Frederick Robb m second Julia A. ——, and died in Shelby, 1861.

Michael Robb m Mary S. McBride, F 1837. Mrs. Mary J. Robb m Sanford P. Owen°.

ROBISON—James, 1801   Patsy, 1801
Mary, 1   (See Robinson)

RODGERS—Elizabeth, 1843

Probably from Culpeper County, Virginia, was Turner H. C Rodgers or Rogers (1766-1812?), who in 1798 bought land from his brother-in-law, Abraham Gregory. He lived near Big Spring Church, and his tombstone may yet be seen in an old graveyard on the Woodburn estate. He m Eleanor Watts°, and in 1810 had a family of eight, including: 1, Elizabeth Tutt°; 2, Mildred Tutt°; 3, Christian Sargent°; 4, Permelia (?) Sargent°; 5, Perlina (?) Sargent°. Others who may have been his children were: (6?), David, m Elizabeth Sargent°, W 1817; (7?), John T., m Elizabeth Elliott°, W 1825, and they had Lewis and John. They sold their land to D. C. Humphreys, W 1835, and bought a farm on Dry Run from Ezra Richmond, F 1841. They went later to Bullitt, and sold their farm in 1857 to G. W. Hancock.

Elliott: Rev. James Elliott (s —— and Martha Elliott) probably came from Augusta County, Virginia. He settled on a large tract of land on the Leestown road in the vicinity of Spring Station, W 1813. He died before 1832, leaving his wife, Mary T., and children: 1, Elizabeth B. Rodgers°; 2, Ann Louisa, m Benjamin Elliott, W 1815, and they had: Cordelia, Benjamin, Thomas; 3, Martha Temple, m first Dr. John T. Moore, W 1822, and second —— Guthrie°. In a deed, F 1851, her children are listed as: a, James E. Moore; b, Margaret T., wife of Dudley Davis°; c, Benjamin Moore; d, Joseph Moore; f, John Moore. 4, James, m first Sarah G. Peart, F 1812 (and second Mrs. Jane E. Plummer (see Taylor), F 1827, and went to Springfield, Ill.?). His children are mentioned as: a, William B.; b, John James; c, Temple; d, Lewis. One James Elliott m Prudence ——. 5, Cordelia; 6, Virginia Hickman°; 7, Lucy C., m —— Hart. Also mentioned in the will of Mary T. Elliott, W 1840, were: Elizabeth, Agnes, Lucy Ann, and John Baylor Elliott, and Margaret and Lucy Davis°.

The similarity of names suggests a relationship with the family of William Gayle°, in Scott.

ROGERS—Andrew, dis to North Fork Elkhorn 1801
      Elijah, 2, dis to North Fork Elkhorn 1801
      Charity, 2, dis to North Fork Elkhorn 1801
      Jesse, 2

Andrew Rogers m Polly Kennedy (dau Mrs. Elizabeth McGaughey), F 1803. In 1810 he had a family of six, includ-

ing: a, Nancy, m Lewis Thacker, Owen 1828; b, Mary Grugin°.
He was in Owen 1819. Elizabeth Rogers had a family of four,
F 1810, and Elijah had five, including: Perlina, m Jackson
Hewlett, F 1837; Elijah, m Permelia Pilcher°, F 1856. John
Rogers was the father of Charity Poe°. The association of this
family with the North Fork Church indicates that they may have
been connected with the Rogers family in Scott.

The records show that Joseph Rogers (s Peter), of Culpeper
County, Virginia, m Lucy (Burgess?), and among their children
who came to Kentucky were: 1, William, m Nancy Johnson°,
1764, and they came to Scott with their children: Joseph, William, Martha, Betty, Mildred, Sally. 2, John, who died in Scott,
1829 (?). His wife was Susan, and they were the parents of
Elizabeth Pitts°. 3, Betsy, m John Garnett°, 1771.

Valentine Rogers m Elizabeth Kelly°, and their son, Joseph
Johnson, m Cordelia Ann Boulware°. Jacob Stucker m Betsy
Rogers, W 1789. One Elijah Rogers m Judith Buford°, Barren
1800, and died Fayette 1834.

Pitts: Fragmentary records show that Younger Pitts, Sr.,
died in Scott about 1793, leaving: 1, Younger, Jr., who m Elizabeth Todd Rogers°, died about 1822. Their infant heirs were:
a, (Rev.) Younger R. (1812-1871), who m Eleen Hawkins°
(dau Elijah), Scott 1834. He was ordained at Great Crossings
in 1841, and preached there and in the neighboring churches
until 1860, when he went to Missouri. He had: Sophia E.,
Denney°, and Elizabeth, m James F. Barkley. b, Elizabeth M.
The records indicate that two other children of Younger, Jr.,
were: c, Albert; d, Permelia (?), m William Nutter, Scott 1830,
and they had Y. P. Nutter. Others who may have been his children were: e, William C.; f, Malissa, m William C. Offutt, Scott
1820. 2, Phoebe.

Josiah Pitts was in Woodford, 1791, and on Elkhorn, Scott
1802. He m Lucy Craig°, and they had five children, including
Margaret Gayle°, Phoebe Woolfolk°, and possibly Julia Elliott°.
He died in 1815.

In Scott, John Pitts m first Cynthia Swetnam°, and second
Malvina Swetnam°. Thomas Pitts m Fanny Swetnam°, and
they had: George Henry; William Thomas, James H. Nancy
Pitts m William S. Swetnam°.

Joseph Pitts m Sally Daniel°, Caroline County, Virginia, 1792, and they came to Franklin and settled on Big Benson. Their children were: 1, Burkin or Burden, m first Sarah Arnold, F 1829, and second Nancy Parrent, F 1837; 2, Robert G., went to Indiana; 3, Agnes, m James Lovett, F 1823; 4, Lucy, m John Woods, F 1824 or 1827; 5, Polly, m George Reading, F 1813.

James R. Roberts m Susan Pitts, F 1830. John A. Pitts m Sarah R. McDowell, Mercer 1827. Thomas Pitts was in Woodford, 1826.

Rose—Reuben B., r 1829
Nancy, r 1829

John Rose was on Salt River, Lincoln 1796, and Lewis and Charles were in Mercer, 1801. The will of Charles, W 1809, names sons William, James, and Thornton, and daughter Betsy. Elizabeth Rose m William W. Gaines°.

Benjamin Rose m Susanna Rutherford°, Garrard 1816, and they had a son George.

Ross—Zachary, 1801, 1804
Sally (Brown), 1801

Zachary Ross (1761- ——), son of Jonathan Ross, of New Jersey, came to Kentucky in 1789. He m Elizabeth Cushenberry (Quisenberry°), Bourbon 1793 or 1795, the bond being signed by Nicholas Ross. In F 1799 he and Vachel Lindsay were joint owners of a tract of land on the east bank of the Kentucky River. He had a family of ten, F 1810, including: 1, Susan, m Samuel Shelton, F 1818; 2, Sally Anderson°; 3, Marcel, m David Parish, Owen 1825. Zachary died in Owen.

Vincent Ross, Sr., had a family of six, W 1810; Andrew had three; while Vincent, Jr., was in Versailles with six. One Vincent Ross m Elizabeth Florence, W 1809.

Rout—Catherine, r 1827

Harvey Rout and his wife Catherine bought from Horace Shely, F 1828, a farm near Woodlake, which they sold in 1834 to William French.

Rhodam Rout m Phoebe Blanton°, W 1794. They lived in Versailles, and in 1810 had a family of eleven. His will, W 1838, mentions his children; Jane, Eliza, Sophronia, Paulina Lewis°, Thomas, Henry L.

William and Byrom (or Hyrom) Rout were in Bourbon, 1787; Charles was in Lincoln, 1795; George in Clark, 1796. George Routt m Catherine Hendrix°, Bourbon 1797. John Rout was in Woodford, 1791, and William in Anderson, 1827.

ROWLET—William, 1, dis to Mouth of Elkhorn 1801, r 1802, dis 1807

Jemima, 1, dis to Mouth of Elkhorn 1801, r 1802, dis 1807

William, Jr., r 1802, dis 1807

Nancy, r 1802, dis 1807

Daniel, 2

Nancy, 2

The will of Jesse Owen°, Prince Edward County, Virginia, 1794, mentions daus Jemima and Nancy Rowlett.

William Rowlett lived on Cedar Creek, and in 1810 had a family of eight. His dau Nancy m George Smoote, F 1805. Jacob Reasor m Franky Rowlett (dau William, Jr.) F 1813. Daniel Rowlett m Nancy Ellis°, F 1807, and in 1810 had a family of three. William Woodsides m Polly Rowlett, F 1809.

In Owen were Susan Rowlett Smither° and Eliza Rowlett Clemens°. Richard J. Minnish m Louisa Rowlett, Owen 1839.

The will of William Jackson°, W 1795, mentions a dau, Eady Rowlett.

RUTHERFORD (Rediford)—John, 1800, 1802

Dinah, 1801, 1802

Elizabeth, 1801

John Rutherford was in F 1796, and had a family of ten, 1810. Polly Rudford (dau John) m John Cook°, Shelby 1815. Walker Rutherford m Nancy Oliver, F 1814. He had a tavern somewhere on the Frankfort-Lexington road.

Hugh Rutherford m Elizabeth Blanton°, W 1816. Archibald Rutherford was in Jessamine, 1799.

SAMUEL—John, 1800, dis 1806   Peter, 1790
         Betsey, 1800, dis 1806   Susanna, 1, dis 1813
         Giles, 2   Fanny, r 1812
         Patsy, 1801, dis 1818   Lucy, 2
         William, 2   Nancy, 2, dis 1818
         Isabella, r 1818   Sally, 2

All the Samuels in this section probably descend from Anthony Samuel, Jr., who m Mary Ann Rogers (b 1690, dau Giles and Rachel Eastham Rogers, who came from England to New Kent County, Virginia, 1670). Their children were: Anthony, James, Peter, Giles, John, Thomas, William, Elizabeth, Easter, and Margaret Samuel.

An old record says that three Samuel brothers, Reuben, Charles, and Anthony, came from England, and that those who came from Virginia to Franklin County were descended from Reuben. One Reuben Samuel is known to have had five sons: William; Giles; Reuben; John; Robert; and a daughter Sarah Ware° who settled near the church. One family record includes a son, Nicholas, and a dau who m —— Sullenger°.

1, William (1770-1833), m first Ann Samuel (dau Peter and Susanna), W 1793. Their children were: a, Matilda Forsee°; b, Nancy; c, Churchill, m Juliet Talbot (dau Isham and Margaret Garrard° Talbot), 1828, and they had: Talbot; Edwin, m Rebecca Triplett°; William Russell, m first Mrs. Adelaide Williams, second Anna Mcgowan, third Mrs. Mary Jane Smith; Florence, m Stephen A. Scearce; d, Jamison, m Sarah ——, and they had Ann Perry and Jamison. One Jamison Samuel had a dau m —— Lounsberry, and they had Louise, who m William Hudson, of Frankfort. A Jamison Samuel m Margaret Kinkead, Mercer 1787.

William Samuel m second Isabella Price°, Fayette 1812, and they had: e, Elizabeth Ann Blanton°; f, William Price, m Sarah L. Shannon, 1838, and they went to Missouri; g, Isabella; h, Miriam, m —— Doom, and had Elizabeth (Wood), William, and Benjamin; i, Sarah Rebecca; j, Richard Parker.

In 1794 William Samuel bought from Benjamin Craig a tract of 29 acres "five miles from Frankfort, including the cross roads where said Samuel now lives." This was probably at the intersection of the Steele's Ferry and the old Lexington road. In 1809 he bought from Richard Taylor 162 acres, including the little house at the foot of the hill below the school at Jett.

2, Reuben, Jr., m Polly Letcher (dau Stephen G. and Betsy Perkins Letcher), W 1794. They lived on North Elkhorn near Stamping Ground, and were the parents of: a, Willis; b, Charles Patterson; c, Stephen; d, Robert L., m Martha Overton and went to Missouri; e, Fielding; f, Riley Grandison, m first his cousin —— Welch, and second Mary Davidson; g, Reuben; h, Betsy, m William B. Sinclair, F 1813; i, Jane, m Joshua Burdett, F 1829; j, Catherine, m —— Deering; k, America, m Nelson Burdett, F 1819.

3, John, who lived at what is known as the Gibson homestead, at Duckers. This was the original "Woodburne," but after the Alexanders chose the same name for their home, its use here was discontinued. John d 1798, leaving his widow, Lucy Woolfolk Samuel, and: a, Spilsbe; b, Betsy Loughborough°; c, John. One record states that John never married, but another says that he m Mary Elinor Welch (daughter of his brother-in-law, William Welch, by an earlier marriage to Mary Underwood), and went to Columbia, Mo.; d, Frances Gibson°, (1786-1871); e, Larkin, Jr., m Catherine Graham° 1810, and their children were: Catherine Coleman°; Larkin Robinson; Mariam, m —— Smith, near Eminence; Lucy; f, Wyatt; g, Kitty, m John Wood, F 1816; h, Lucinda, m William Gibson Welch, F 1826, and their son, Gibson, m Annie Fogg° (dau Elijah and Ann Ware Fogg) and was the father of W. G. Welch, of Frankfort; i, Richard, m ——, and died before 1838, leaving an infant orphan John.

In 1819 William Gibson bought from the other heirs of John Samuel their interest in his estate.

4, Giles, the court records indicate, lived at the old stone inn, where the Steele's Ferry road crosses the Leestown pike. He m Martha Slaughter (who was evidently his second wife), W 1791. His children were: a, William; b, Giles; c, Jesse; d, Edgecombe, m Virginia Carter (dau Abram), F 1817; e, Betsy; f, James; g, Presley; h, Francis; i, Sarah Bacon°; j, Malinda Sullenger°. Giles died about 1817, and his heirs sold the farm to Martin D. Hardin, and left the neighborhood.

5, Robert, who lived on North Elkhorn, died before 1814. His wife was Catherine ——, and their children were: a, Jesse; b, John; c, Betsy (m Peirson Douthit, F 1823?); d, Patsy; e, Nellie Triplett°; f, Robert, Jr., m Ellen Anderson°, F 1816.

Others who probably were closely related were: Jesse Samuel, d before 1794, leaving sons Larkin and Peter; Betsy, m Sullenger°; Peter d 1797, leaving his wife Susanna (who bought a farm adjoining John Samuel's on the north), and children: 1, Ann, m William Samuel; 2, John (m Betsy Hancock°, W 1798?); 3, Reuben (m Nancy Ware°, 1802?). William Samuel m Susan Ware°, F 1806, and they went to Shelby. John T. Samuel m Maria Douthit, F 1831.

William Samuel, Sr., son of Mrs. Sarah Colquit°, came to Henry County, Kentucky, where he was one of the trustees of Newcastle. His will, Henry 1807, names his wife Frances (who may have been the dau of Daniel Goodwin, who died in Gallatin, 1805), and children: 1, Sarah Vaughan°; 2, Elizabeth Pemberton°; 3, Fanny, m —— Goodwin; 4, Agatha (m first —— Branham; second William Bullard°; third Benjamin Towles, Shelby 1814?); 5, Phoebe, m William Mountjoy, Henry 1800; 6, Reuben, m Patsy Bartlett°, Henry 1802; 7, John (m Elizabeth Moody, Henry 1802?); 8, William, Jr., m first Judith Dupuy°, W 1795, and they had: a, Washington, who lived near Georgetown, m Nancy F. Gray, Gallatin 1825, and their children, according to a family record, were: Richard, m his cousin, Anne Gray; Eleanor, m Marcellus Polk, Scott 1854; a dau m Col. Richard West; Hazael, m Sallie Worthington; Washington, Jr., m Mary Graves° (dau Caswell and Jane McFall Graves), 1872; Joel; James, m Puggie Patterson; William. Another record adds Benjamin and Edmund to the list. b, Mary Suggett°. William, Jr., m second Ann C. Marshall°, Henry 1800, and they had: c, William (m Eliza Bartlett°, Henry 1841?); d, Eliza, m James Pryor, Henry 1831; e, Nancy, m Samuel Pryor, Henry 1824.

Anthony Samuel was in Woodford, 1811. His dau, Sarah, m Lewis Sublette°, and in his will, W 1813, he makes bequests to his grandson, Samuel Sublett, and to Henry Samuel. One Henry A. W. Samuel m Louisa Gayle° (dau Judith), W 1833, and records show that their son, Augustin S., died in Owen 1852.

One Anthony Samuel, of Fayette, located in Jessamine, 1803, and in 1826 he and his wife Margaret sold their farm and evidently left the county. Lucy Samuel m Philip Collins, Jessamine 1821. Anthony Samuel m Sarah Johnson, Madison 1838.

Thomas Samuel, on Benson, had a family of four, F 1810, and one Thomas Samuel was in Scott, 1805-1820. John Samuel, of Scott, m Caty Freeman°, W 1808. Several members of the Samuel family lived in Anderson.

SANDERS—Nathaniel, 1	Sally, r 1810
Sarah, 1	Sally Hancock
James	Peggy, r 1812, dis 1814

Since "Nathaniel" was a favorite name in the Sanders family, the records are most confusing. Hugh Sanders (son of Nathaniel, and brother of the Rev. Nathaniel, of Virginia), died in Spotsylvania County, Virginia, 1781, leaving his wife Catherine and these children: 1, Elizabeth Craig°; 2, Sarah Gatewood°; 3, Mildred Jones; 4, Nathaniel (1742-1826), m Sarah Pattie°, who died in 1814. They lived at the Forks of Elkhorn, and old deeds mention Sanders' tavern and fish dam, while the road from the Forks to the Frankfort-Versailles road was known as "Sanders' Mill and Steele's Ferry Road." Nathaniel spent his last years in Gallatin.

The records make it appear that Nathaniel and Sarah had these children: a, Hugh (——— 1844), m Nancy Moxley°, F 1800, and they had: Sally Settle°; William; James; Nathaniel; Samuel L.; Emerald, m William D. McBride, F 1833; Elizabeth Tyler; Catherine Suter°; Nancy Graham°; Mary Thomas°. b, Catherine O'Neal°. c, James, who was in Owen, 1826. The will of one James Sanders, Owen 1834, names his wife Elizabeth and children: Ophelia, Isabel, Jeremiah, Napoleon. d, (Reubie, m Nathaniel Sanders, F 1796?); e, Robert, in Owen 1826. One Robert m Nancy Blanton°, Gallatin 1815. f, John, in Owen 1826. One John m Nancy Samuel°, W 1800; g, George W., in Owen 1826. h, Nathaniel whose heirs, F 1818, were: Lewis, Jr., m Margaret H. Price°, F 1821. They lived near the Forks on land which they sold to William D. Hubbell in 1823, and in 1848 were in Natchez, Miss. Their children were: Eliza Jane, m James B. Haggin, 1846; Susan, m Lloyd Tevis; Edith Hunter°; Laura, m

first George Vorhies, and second J. P. Amsden; Ezza, m Isham
Railey, Jr. Other heirs of Nathaniel, F 1818, were: Lemuel G.,
m Sarah Winslow, Fayette 1821; Nathaniel (H.?), who was in
Owen 1826, and in Gallatin 1828; Isaac Smith (m Polly Myer,
Fayette 1818?); Brazilla; Bennett P., m Eleanor Stephens, Fay-
ette 1825. i, Sarah (Smith?), born 1781.

    5, Robert, in Woodford 1790. The will of Robert Sanders,
Scott 1805, mentions his children: a, Toliver (Valentine?), who
went to Owen; b, Benjamin; c, Thomas. One Thomas m Alice
Peak°, W 1791, and was in Gallatin 1822; d, Walker, who went
to Shelby; e, Nancy (Ann T. Bartlett°); 6, Charles, in Franklin
1798; 7, Mary Lee; 8, Ann Tally; 9, Catherine; 10, Rosey; 11,
Abigail; 12, John, m Jane Craig°. The record says their children
were: a, John; b, Lewis; c, Nathaniel; d, Polly; e, Betsy; f, Lydia.
John was in Scott 1794; John Sr. and John Jr. were in Gallatin
1801, and one John lived on Cedar Creek and had a family of
eight, F 1810. John P. Sanders m Betsy Moxley°, F 1820. John
P. Sanders, Jr., was guardian of Sarah C., Nancy C., Mary E., and
Louisa B. Sanders, orphans of John P. Sanders, Sr., F. 1834.

    A family record states that John Sanders m Sarah Alsop,
Caroline County, Virginia, and their son James m Phoebe Bart-
lett°, W 1795. They lived on South Benson, and his will, F 1854,
names his children: 1, Nancy (m Joel Medley, F 1817?); 2, John;
3, James; 4, Henry Bartlett, m Jane Crockett, 1830; 5, Franky;
6, Betsy; 7, Alice; 8, Leanor; 9, Reuben; 10, Edward; 11, Guilford. Another record adds: 12, William. One James m Jane
Hardin°, F 1813; James m Sally Moxley°, F 1819 and went to
Gallatin; Thomas m Jemima Byrne, F 1807; Nathaniel m Maria
Brewer, F 1815. Also in F were Polly Ware°; Lucy Gale°; Betsy
Smith°. One Philemon Sanders, Sr., who was 78 in 1840, went
from Franklin County to Barren.

    Henry Sanders was in Woodford 1790, and Richard was
there in 1810, with a family of six. William Sanders m Elizabeth
Bullard°, W 1794; one William m Azubah Wright Sisk°, W 1827.

    In F 1810, Thomas Sanders had a family of four, and William
had four.

    Moxley: Samuel Moxley was in Woodford 1791, and on Elk-
horn, F 1796. He bought the land opposite "Silver Lake Farm"
from Bennett Pemberton in 1803, and died about 1817. His

wife was Agnes Cox°, and their children were: 1, Nancy
Sanders°; 2, Bathsheba Long°; 3, Polly Gore°; 4, Joseph, m Grace
Head°, F 1820, and went to Gallatin. Benjamin T. Head was
guardian for Agnes and Mildred Moxley, F 1829. 5, Kitty, m
James Welch; 6, William, m Nancy Welch, F 1815; 7, Sally
Sanders; 8, Louisa or Levisa Cox°; 9, Betsy Sanders; 10, Jeptha
D., m Elizabeth Clinton (dau Moses) F ——— . Bennett Moxley
m Mary P. Forsee°, F 1817.

Daniel Moxley was in Shelby 1799.

SANFORD—Patsy, dis 1826

Capt. Daniel Sanford came from Virginia to Bourbon County,
Kentucky, 1798. He afterward went to Henry, where his will,
1824, mentions his children: 1, Daniel, Jr.; 2, Charles, m Martha
Major°, 1823. They lived in Newcastle, and were grandparents
of Mrs. John D. Carroll, of Frankfort; 3, Henry; 4, Rebecca
Blincoes; 5, Lawrence S.; 6, Elizabeth, m first Joseph Foree,
Henry 1809, and second William B. Foree, Henry 1821; 7, Hannah
Webb; 8, Susanna Speer; 9, late dau Nancy Owens (one record
says Capt. Daniel's dau Nancy m Jesse Combs, Henry 1832, and
was the mother of William Pryor Combs); 10, Penelope Dawson,
dec'd.; 11, Kitty Fuller, dec'd.; 12, Fanny, m John Minor, Henry
1809.

It is said that there are two separate families of Sanfords in
Franklin County, but their names do not appear in the early
records. Sarah A. Sanford m Nat Hardin°; Presley A. Sanford
m Matilda Tracy (dau Jeremiah and Elizabeth), F 1835, and
their dau, Lucy Jane, m Charles T. Pierce, and was the grandmother of Mrs. A. F. Peters, of Frankfort. In Woodford were
Thomas and James, 1828, and Eliza Green°. John Sanford was
in Mercer 1795, and Richard died in Scott 1795.

SCANDLAND—Robert, 1, 1800   Sally, 1

Robert Scandland was in F 1796, but in 1799 and thereafter
was in Gallatin. He was the father of Sally Peak°, and he
appears to have had two sons, Robert, Jr., and Reuben.

Edmund Scandland m Anna Hawkins°, F 1796. They lived
near Farmdale at "Scandland's Springs," now the site of the
Stewart Home. His will, F 1851, mentions his children: 1,

Edmund; 2, G. Wash; 3, John, m Amanda Hawkins, and their
children were: Byron S., O. A. C., John W., Sally I., Ann Mary,
Betty Miles°; 4, Azubah Hawkins°; 5, O. H. P.; 6, Sarah
Crutcher°.

James M. J. Scandland m Eleanor Long°, F 1816. William
R. Scandland signed the marriage bond of Elisha Hawkins and
Rachel Scandland.

Hawkins: Though there were many branches of the Hawkins
family in this section, space can be given to only a few of the
most widely connected. The early records show Elisha, Reuben,
Moses, Arculous, Thomas, and so many Williams that they were
designated as, "Black Head Billy," "Red Head Billy," "Cooper
Billy," "Green River Billy," and "Post and Rail Billy."

William W. Hawkins (s Jehu) m Azubah Scandland°, F 1832,
and they went to Woodford, where he bought from William
Wood the place on the Frankfort-Versailles road that is still the
home of his granddaughter, Mrs. Allie Hawkins Elmore.

Elisha Hawkins, Sr. (1752-1833), of Orange County, Virginia,
m Elizabeth Edwards°. He was on Dry Run, F 1796, and had
a family of four in 1810. One Elisha m Rachel Scandland°,
F 1820, and one m Sarah Steele (dau Robert), F 1819, and they
were the parents of Elizabeth Noel°. Reuben Hawkins m Rebecca Edwards°, and their dau Elizabeth m Moses Hawkins,
F 1814.

William Hawkins, Sr., m first Mary ———, and second Anne
B. Smith, Culpeper County, Virginia, 1785. His will, F 1818,
mentions his wife Anne, and children: 1, John Dyer; 2, Tabitha
Foster; 3, William: It has been suggested that this was William
B. Hawkins, who m Mary Crockett (dau Anthony and Mary
Robertson Crockett), F 1802. His will, F 1845, names his wife
and children: a, Samuel F.; b, Mary Blanton°; c, Rebecca, m
James G. Wright, F 1825; d, Martha, m John Clark; e, Anthony
C.; f, Elisha Obed; g, William Granville; h, Katherine Farmer°;
i, Sarah, m Samuel McKee; j, Elizabeth, m William H. Wright,
F 1823. 4, Azubah Long°; 5, Anne Scandland°; 6, John Scott;
7, Smith; 8, Moses; 9, Elisha, m Sally Crockett (dau Anthony),
F 1807. The records indicate that this was Elisha C., whose
will, F 1861, mentions his wife Sally C., a son, Samuel S., and
a daughter Alice. Another record says he was the father of

Fountain P. Hawkins, who m first Priscilla K. Taylor, F 1834, and second Marinda Branham. 10, Juretta Wallace°; 11, Joseph F., m Mary Ann Hancock°, F 1824; 12, heirs of deceased son ——; 13, Lucinda Bartlett°; 14, Sally Haydon°; 15, Agnes, m Moses Hawkins, Jr., F 1815.

William R. Hawkins (1776-1854) lived on the farm on the Frankfort-Lawrenceburg road recently owned by Frank Moore. He m Hannah Clemens°, F 1799, and their children were: 1, Fielding, m —— Coons, and went to Missouri; 2, Elizabeth Miles°; 3, Mary B., m Daniel Epperson, F 1825; 4, Amanda Scandland°; 5, Emerine, m John Julian, and they were the parents of Rev. Epaphroditus Julian; 6, Julia Ann, m William W. Wright, and they were the parents of Rev. Carroll Q. Wright (1856-1924), a chaplain in the U. S. Navy; 7, Thomas Jefferson, went to Missouri; 8, Ruth Ann Gaines°; 9, James C.; 10, William H.; 11, Smith.

Capt. Moses Hawkins, of Orange County, Virginia, m Susanna Strother, 1770, and their sons were: 1, William Strother, m Katherine Keith (dau Capt. Isham and Charlotte Ashmore Keith), W 1802, and they were the parents of Isham K. Hawkins, who lived opposite "The Old Stone Church." He m first Lucy Major°, and they were the parents of Katherine Darnell°; he m second Sarah Hall°, F 1838, and among their children were Mrs. John E. Miles, of Frankfort, and Mrs. R. J. Fogg°, of Jett; 2, Moses, Jr., who had a mill on Glen's Creek. He m Sarah Castleman°, who after his death went with her children to Missouri.

Of another family was Dr. James Russell Hawkins (1805-1897), son of Joseph L. and Ann Parker Robinson Hawkins, of Spotsylvania County, Virginia. He practiced at Bridgeport, and was the grandfather of Miss Addie Hawkins, of that vicinity.

Scott—John, r 1798, dis 1802	John R., r 1840
Jane, 1800, dis 1802	Sidney Jane, r 1840
Joel, r 1834	Robert W., r 1840
Deborah, r 1834	Eliza W., r 1840

Rev. John Scott was born, 1767, in Londonderry, Ireland. He came to Pennsylvania in 1788, and to Kentucky in 1789. Originally a Presbyterian, he joined the Town Fork Baptist Church, near Lexington, and was baptized by Joseph Redding. In 1802, at the Forks of Elkhorn Church, he was ordained to the ministry by William Hickman and George Smith. He is said to have been the first preacher in Owen County, where he preached at New Liberty 1802-1833. In 1825 he moved to Carroll, where he had charge of the church at Ghent.

He m first Jane Sneed°, 1795, and their children were: 1, Samuel; 2, Harriet, m William Bond, 1819, and they had: Samuel; John C.; James; Frank; Robert; Jane; Julia; 3, Robert Miller, m Polly Garvey, and they had: Samuel; Calvin; John; Elizabeth; 4, Elizabeth, m John Orr, and had: Judge John James; Richard; Eliza Jane; 5, John Taylor (1805-1839) m Elizabeth Bond (dau John and Mary Sale Bond), and they had: a, Mary Jane, m Albert Tilton, and their son, Silas Gex Tilton, m Emma Crouch, and was the father of Mrs. A. C. Brooks, of Frankfort; b, Eliza Blanton; c, Richard; 6, William Alfred; 7, Miriam (1809-1854) m John Lindsay°; 8, Melissa; 9, James Blanton; 10, Benjamin Sneed.

Jane Sneed Scott died 1832, and John Scott m Mrs. Mary Adams Bailey (Whitehead). Their children were: 11, Edward Spencer, b 1835, m Sophia Duvall, and they had four sons; 12, Lyman Martin; 13, Mary E., m John Howard, and they had: Dr. Scott; Hallie; Gertrude; Ulie J.; Hubert.

Mary Bailey Scott d 1840, and John Scott m Marcia Alexander, 1842. He died in 1847, and his widow m Berdett A. Blanton°.

John Scott (1748-1815) s Thomas and —— Coleman Scott, of that part of Culpeper which is now Madison Co., Va., m 1770 Hannah Early, who is said in one record to have been the daughter of Jeremiah and Elizabeth Buford Early, while another states that she was the daughter of Joshua Early. They came to Kentucky in 1785, locating near Great Crossings in Scott.

Their children were: 1, Elizabeth; 2, Early, who lived on Elkhorn, and had a family of five, F 1810. A portion of his will, Scott 1836, mentions his wife, Susanna, and John and Sanford Scott; 3, Mary Brooking°; 4, Eleanor Branham°; 5, Thomas, m —— Parker, and had John and Parker; 6, Joel (1781-1860), m first Rebecca Ridgeley Wilmot (dau Lieut. Robert and Priscilla

Dorsey Wilmot, who came from Maryland to Bourbon County, Kentucky) in 1805, and they had: a, John R. (1806-1871), m Sidney Jones°, F 1837, and they lived first at the W. B. Allen place (now owned by —— Mitchell), and then at "Valley Farm." They had: Rebecca Freeman°; Joel Early, m Elenora Allen (dau Rev. —— Allen, of Fayette); Thomas Winn, a stanch pillar of the Forks of Elkhorn Church, who married Martha Ayres°. He inherited "Valley Farm," and was the grandfather of Scott and Robert Thompson, of Frankfort, and George Sager, of Louisville; Sidney Jane Lewis°; b, Robert W., who bought the Martin D. Hardin homestead and built the house which now stands there. He named the place "Locust Hill," and it was so called during his lifetime, but in recent years the name has been changed to "Scotland." He m Elizabeth Watts Brown°, F 1831, and their children were: Dr. Preston B., m Jane E. Campbell; Joel; Dr. John O., m Ellen Melville; Mary Major°; Ella, m Lafayette Green; Henrietta Mitchell°; Elizabeth; Louisa, m first E. Rumsey Wing, second Col. W. C. P. Breckinridge.

Some time after the death of his first wife, Joel Scott m Mrs. Deborah Gano (dau Daniel Winter°, and widow of Gen. R. M. Gano°), F 1821. After serving as warden of the penitentiary for seven years, he moved to the country near Duckers and built his home, the original "Scotland," at what is known as the Freeman place.

7, Ezekiel, m Dorothy Hawkins, of Madison County, and they went to Missouri in 1820. Their children were: Samuel, William, Dorothea, Huldah, John, Hester, Joel. 8, John; 9, Sarah. John Scott's will mentions also a grandson, Samuel Birch.

Another branch of the Scott family which was indirectly connected with the Forks Church was that of John Scott, of Pennsylvania. He had: 1, Matthew, whose son, Matthew T., came to Fayette and was the grandfather of Miss Mary Mason Scott, of Frankfort; 2, Moses, who came to Clark, and whose descendants intermarried with the Straughans°, in Shelby; 3, Dr. John Mitchell (1764-1812), who came to Frankfort and m CatherineWare°.

Freeman: George D. Freeman (1763-1831) m Keziah Yancey°, Culpeper County, Virginia, 1781, and about 1800 they came with their family to Kentucky, where they lived, it seems, in three different counties. The family tradition is that they settled first in Woodford, on land that is now a part of the "Woodburn" estate, and went later to Anderson. Here, the records state, they built a log house in 1804, but the Woodford census shows that George Freeman was there in 1810 with a family of eight. In 1819 he transferred his membership from the Fox Creek Church (now in Anderson) to Frankfort.

The records indicate that they had these children: 1, Caty Samuel°; 2, Elizabeth Kavanaugh°; 3, Yancey, m Polly Penny°, F 1817, and among their children was John, who m Nancy Todd, of Shelby, and was the father of Prof. C. C. Freeman, of Lexington; 4, Dandridge Claibourne (1794-1866), m Martha Fox°, 1825. Their home was at "Silver Lake Farm," which they bought in 1833 from Lewis R. Major. D. C. Freeman and his wife joined the Forks Church in 1851.

Their children were: a, Mary Jane, m Rev. Robert H. Thurman, of Bardstown; b, Col. D. C., Jr., m first Mary Ann Giltner, Bourbon 1854, and second Mary E. Robison, 1869; c, Capt. George R., m Mary F. Rust; d, Newton; e, Capt. Charles Thomas, m Rebecca Willmott Scott°, and they lived at the original "Scotland," which she inherited from her father. They were the parents of Mrs. Martha Shackleford and Mrs. Elizabeth Farmer, of Louisville, and T. W. Freeman, of Raleigh, N. C.; f, Maj. Terah M., m first Alice (Samuel) Beckwith, and second Mary O. Shaw; g, Elizabeth Eloise, m Lucius P. Little, of Owensboro. Several members of this family went to Texas.

5, George W., m Susan Hough° (dau John and Sally Witherspoon Hough°?), F 1837; 6, Eloise Hall°; 7, Thomas Major, m Sarah Bell Pattie°, F 1839, and they had: a, Mary Lucy, m Dr. Chambers; b, Sarah, m Oscar Farmer; c, John; d, Eloise, m —— Coleman, of Owensboro. There may have been a son of George and Keziah Freeman who m —— Lillard, and perhaps other children. Moses Freeman m Patsy Huff, Mercer 1815.

SETTLE—Thomas, 1808   Bennet
      Milly, 1   Nancy, 1811

The Settles came from Yorkshire, England. George Settle (s Isaac and Charity Browne Settle) of Fauquier County, Virginia, m Mary Morgan (dau William and Mary Duncan Morgan) and came to Warren County, Kentucky, where he died in 1820. His children were: 1, Thomas. Family records say that Thomas m first Molly Price, and their children were: a, John, m Betsy Yancey°, F 1812, and went to Missouri. One John m Amanda Edrington°, F 1831 (the bond signed by Charles L. D. Yancey), and they sold land on Elkhorn to Richard Church, F 1834; b, Sally Brown°; c, Bennett P., m Delilah Jefferson (dau of his stepmother, Priscilla), F 1816; d, Cooper, m Sally Connell; e, Nancy. Thomas m second Polly Brown°, F 1803, and they had: f, George; g, William; h, Elizabeth, m Elliott West; i, Jephthah; j, Lucy, m Bluford Phillips; k, Isaac; l, Joseph, m Sally Sanders°, F 1822, and they were grandparents of Hon. Evan E. Settle, of Owenton. Thomas m third Mrs. Priscilla Jefferson, W 1814, the bond signed by Cornelius Robinson. (Family records say that she was the daughter of George Jefferson and the widow of Benjamin Jefferson). They had: m, Mary Ann Thomas, m John Butler, of Jessamine, 1834. Thomas Settle lived at "Hicklin Hill," on a farm which his heirs sold to William Gerard, F 1818.

2, Hannah Willis; 3, Betsy, m Nimrod Young; 4, William (1770-1808), m Elizabeth Huffman. They came to Barren County, Kentucky, and were ancestors of Judge Warner E. Settle, of Frankfort, and of Simon DeWitt Settle, of Bowling Green, the family historian from whom much of this data came. 5, Molly Smith; 6, John Morgan, m Rebecca Edrington°, F 1799, and settled on Big Benson now in Anderson. Their children were: a, Mary, m Peter Miller, F 1818; b, James M., m Elizabeth Riley; c, Margaret, m Daniel Riley, F 1823; d, Jane Hancock°; e, William, m Julianna Yates°; f, Elizabeth Hancock°; g, Malinda, m Ambrose Medley, F 1822; h, Joseph E.; i, Benjamin E., m Mary Riley, Anderson 1842. 7, Dr. Isaac; 8, Dr. Simon; 9, Dr. Charles.

Priscilla Jefferson had another daughter, Caroline, m George Sanford, whose descendants live in Tennessee. Priscilla m third Gen. John E. King (s William and Elizabeth Edwards King), F 1818, and went to Cumberland County, Kentucky.

Alexander Settle m Rachel Robinson°, F 1800.

SHACKLEFORD—John, 1808   Ryland, 1801

Some of the Shackleford family came in with the "Travelling Church." The Rev. John Shackleford (1750-1829), of Caroline

County, Virginia, was one of the ministers imprisoned in the Essex jail for preaching the Baptist doctrines. He came to Kentucky, and preached at South Elkhorn Church for many years.

Samuel, Thomas, John, and Zachariah Shackleford were in Lincoln about 1791, and John was in Jessamine after 1799. In Franklin, Ryland and Carter were living north of the river in 1801.

Green Shackleford m Nancy James°, F 1818; James Shackleford m Harriet Martin°, F 1826.

SHADDOA—Sally, 1811, dis 1812

It is possible that she was a member of the Chaudoin family of this vicinity, who pronounce their name *Shad'-do-in.*

SHADRICK—Elizabeth, 1, r 1796, dis 1809

John Shadrick m Elizabeth Sanders° in Orange County, Virginia, 1789. One John was in Lincoln 1789, and in 1797 was living north of the river in Franklin. John Shadrick m Rebecca Penn (dau Benjamin), F 1817. In Woodford, Benjamin Johnson° m Peggy Shadrick, 1809.

Thomas Shadwick m Sary Sanders°, Orange County, Virginia, 1795.

SHAW—Nancy Smither, dis 1809

Thomas Shaw, who lived north of the river, m Nancy Smither°, F 1806.

There were many Shaws among the early settlers. In Lincoln were Matthias, Daniel, Thomas, William; in Fayette, Samuel; in Woodford, Thomas, James, Nancy, William, John; in Jessamine, David, Elizabeth; in Shelby, Jacob; in Henry, William, John, Michael. Archibald was in Frankfort, 1810, and in 1820 Archibald and William were in Christian.

John Robert Shaw, an Englishman, came to Lexington about 1791, and to each child in his large family he gave as a middle name his own name, Robert. One son, James Robert Shaw, m Margaret McQueen (dau Joshua), Madison 1824, and they were the ancestors of the Shaws now living in this vicinity, some of their children being: 1, John R. ("Mack"), m Sallie Ann Giltner, (dau David and Nancy Shaw Giltner). They lived at the Isaac Crutcher homestead between Jett and Millville, and were grandparents of Misses Stella and Gertrude Shaw, of Frankfort; 2,

Harrison, m Pattie South (dau Col. Jeremiah and Mary Cockerell South); 3, Armilda Shipp°.

In Franklin, John P. Shaw m Jane Graham° (dau Elizabeth), 1819; John Robert Shaw m Nancy Bell, 1820; William Shaw m —— Bell about that same time.

SHEETS—Charles, 1828   Maria, 1828
Sally, 1828

Benjamin Sheets had a family of thirteen, W 1810, but he came to Franklin and settled on Big Benson.

His will, F 1842, mentions his wife Lena and indicates that they had: 1, Charles, m first Sarah Edrington°, F 1821, and second Malinda Rupe, F 1835; 2, Granville, m Martha Crutcher°, F 1835; 3, Samuel; 4, John, m Betsy —— ; 5, Benjamin, m Sally —— ; 6, Martin, m Malinda Watson, F 1830; 7, (Joel?) Henry; 8, Rebecca Ford°; 9, Rachel Moss°; 10, Essey, m Hiram G. Crutcher°, F 1829; 11, Maria Swepston°. Walter Sheets m Judith A. Brown°, F 1835; Martin, Jr., m Mrs. Eliza Brown°, F 1836, the bond signed by James D. Brown. Joseph Sheets m Lena Moss°, F 1844.

Henry and Martin Sheets were in Woodford, 1801, but in 1810 they were in Franklin, each with a family of nine. Two of Henry's daughters were: 1, Elizabeth Hardin°; 2, Mahala, m William D. Clark, Owen 1820. Mary Ann Sheets (dau Martin) m William Vaughan°.

William Sheets had a family of ten, W 1810, and probably lived between Versailles and Clifton. He may have been the father of Nancy Hunter°, and of John Sheets, who m Elizabeth Reardon (dau Nancy Waldon°), W 1817.

SHIPP—Elizabeth, r 1801
Richard and wife, to Glen's Creek 1801

Richard Shipp (1747-1828?) lived in Caroline County, Virginia. He is said to have been a brother of Lemuel Shipp, who remained in Caroline; Edmund, who came to Jefferson County, Kentucky; and of Mrs. Ann Garnett°, Mrs. Lucy Ford°, and Mrs. Fanny Sullenger°, of Woodford. There is a tradition that they descend from Pocahontas.

Richard and his wife, Elizabeth Doniphan Shipp, came to Woodford with their family, 1792-1793. The records state that they settled at the site of an ancient mound near the present town of Midway, the place being first called "Lovedale," then "Old Fort," and now "Sunny Slope Farm." The present house, which is occupied by the family of Van de Graaf Shipp, Jr., was built by John G. Shipp in 1820.

Unauthenticated records indicate that Richard and Elizabeth Shipp had these children: 1, Richard Doniphan (1779-1852), m Sarah McCracken°, F 1802, and records from various sources name their children as: a, Polly W. (m Elijah E. Thomas, W 1837?); b, Merritt L., m Julian Davis°, W 1837; c, Olivia, m Joseph M. Violett, W 1825; d, William, m Alice (Lewis?); e, Margaret, m James Parrish (s James and Tabitha Parrish), W 1830, and they were the parents of Richard D. Parrish, of Duckers; f, Seneca (1815-1895); g, Richard D., m Jane —— ; h, John G. (1820-1846); i, Sarah, m, W 1842, Rev. Lyman W. Seely, of Scott, who was considered one of the best Greek scholars of the country. He was ordained in 1842 at Mt. Vernon, where he was pastor for ten years before extending his work in Maryland and Virginia. They were the parents of Dr. Richard Seely, of Midway. j, Thomas H., m Mary H. Van de Graaf, W 1857, and they had Van de Graaf, Sr., Cornia, and others.

2, Narcissa Edwards°; 3, Elizabeth Doniphan Fogg°; 4, John G.; 5, Mary, m John Shephard, W 1813 (see McCracken); 6, Sophia, m Laban Sebree, Shelby 1804, and they had a family of five, W 1810, one child being Sallie, who m first —— Connell, and second Rev. —— Harding, of Trimble; 7, Emey Grant (1787- ——), m William Truman, of Shelby, W 1808, and they lived near Bagdad. Their son, Anderson S. Truman, who m Mary Jane Holmes, Shelby 1846, and went to Missouri, was the grandfather of President Harry S. Truman. 8, Edmund, m Polly Thomson°, W 1813, and they lived at McKee's Crossroads. Some of their children were: a, Ulysses, m Rebecca C. Forbes, and their son, James Henry, m Mary Clay Finnie°, who lives in Midway; b, Ann Ophelia Finnie°; c, David Richard, m Armilda Shaw°, and continued living at McKee's Crossroads; d, Apphia Edwards, m George Jackson, of Frankfort. 9, Anderson, m Elizabeth Blanton°, W 1816, and they were the parents of: a, Benjamin Blanton; b, Ann Robinson. Anderson D. Shipp was in Scott 1820-1821, but his estate was appraised, W 1829, and his widow sold land on Glen's Creek to Lewis Crutcher in 1831.

Another family of Shipps, children of John and Sally Johnson Shipp, of Fauquier County, Virginia, came with the Travelling Church and settled in this section. In this group were: 1, Richard Wyatt, m Elizabeth Turner, 1778. He came to Scott, where he died in 1793, leaving: a, Polly (1779-1833), m Martin Hawkins, of Fayette, about 1800; b, Sally (m Dr. John Stites?); c, William; d, Richard Turner; e, Dudley, m first his cousin, Polly Ellis, Fayette 1815, and second Eliza Buckner, Fayette 1832.

2, Laban (1748-1828), m first Sally Johnson° (dau William and Elizabeth Cave Johnson), Orange County, Virginia, 1780, and they had: a, John; b, Betsy C., m Hanley Haydon, Bourbon 1804. One Laban Shipp m Rebecca Turner, Fauquier 1786. Laban m next Elizabeth Allen, and they had: c, Sally Garrard°; d, Margaret Major° (1792-1882). Laban was in Fayette 1790, in Bourbon 1797, and later in Christian. He had several other children. 3, Colby, m Sally Elley (dau Henry and Sarah Burbridge Elley), W 1789. He lived in Scott, but some time after his wife's death he went to Owen. Records indicate that his children were: a, Richard Wyatt, m Sarah —— ; b, Edward E., m Mary —— ; c, Henry (R. H.?); d, George; e, Sarah, d 1844; f, John (m Harriet Swetman°?); g, William.

4, Elizabeth. The records say that Elizabeth Shipp (sister of Richard W., Laban, and Colby) m first Capt. William Ellis, Jr., and second Jesse Bryant°, 1803, and died near Lexington, 1833. One Elizabeth Shipp (—— 1805) m James Kay, W 1789. They lived in Scott, where he was guardian of the orphans of Richard W. Shipp.

Mary Shipp m George Earlywine, Bourbon 1787; Joseph was in Bourbon, 1795; Joseph, James, Elijah, and John Shipp were in Clark 1815; Samuel Shipp was in Woodford 1796. Richard Shipp m Mary Copeland (dau James), Mercer 1788.

Elizabeth Shipp m Ignatius Byrnes, F 1819. Susan Shipp m Henry Crutcher°. In her will, F 1854, she leaves property to James Shipp's children in Virginia.

Fogg: Obadiah Fogg (s John Fogg, of Essex County, Virginia?) m Elizabeth Doniphan Shipp°, W 1799, and they were the parents of Capt. Elijah Fogg (1803-1881), who m Ann Richardson Ware°, 1833. Captain Fogg and his family lived first on the Steele's Ferry road near Duckers, and later at "Spring Garden." Their children were: 1, Betty, m Anderson Chenault; 2, Samuel, m Fannie Gaines°, and they were the parents of Misses Annie Belle, Jennie, and Mary Fogg, Mrs. John Church, and Mrs. C. E. Lawson, of Frankfort; 3, Agnes, m Capt. Thomas Steele; 4, Anna, m Capt. W. G. Welch; 5, Richard J., m Susan Hawkins°; 6, Virginia Thompson°.

James Fogg petitioned the court for a road from Fogg's ferry to Castleman's mill, W 1799. In that same year he m Elizabeth Dupuy°, and they were the parents of Mary M. Taylor°. His estate was settled, F 1802.

SHOCKLEY—Ann, dis 1841

Thomas Shockley (s Benjamin and Sarah Shockley) m Ann Stephens°, F 1818, and their dau Judith Abbott° was the grandmother of Mrs. E. B. Weitzel, of Frankfort.

SIMONUS (Semones)—Jean, to Glen's Creek 1801

Thomas Semones was in Mercer 1795; one William in Franklin 1796, and one in Woodford 1800; Samuel, John, and William were in Henry 1811. John m Delilah Moore, W 1800, and one John had a family of six, F 1810.

Melton Semones m Mahala Moore (dau Gersham), F 1823; Basil Semones m Deby Fowler, F 1827.

SISK—Pluright, r 1798, withdrew 1807
Ruth, r 1798, dis 1822

Pluright Sisk m Ruth Boone in Culpeper County, Virginia, 1790, and they came to Woodford and settled near Thomas Henton, from whom they bought land. Some of their children were: 1, Hannah Henton°; 2, Betsy Hardin°; 3, Deborah; 4, Azubah Sanders°; 5, Ruhemah (Thompson?).

In 1828 Pluright and his wife sold their property to Elijah Pepper, and evidently left the neighborhood.

Martin Sisk was in Scott 1803; Barnett was in W 1816, and in Scott 1820.

Boone: The Boone family is difficult to trace, since it is widely scattered, and the same family names are used repeatedly.

The records state that Josiah Boone, Sr., son of George, was born in Pennsylvania 1726, and settled on Glen's Creek, W 1794, where he died in 1814, leaving seven heirs. He m first, Hannah, —— , 1750, and they had: 1, George, who sold his farm to Elijah Pepper, W 1828; 2, Noah, died young; 3, Josiah, Jr., who appears to have married first Persis Hinton and second Ellenor Boone, 1815. The settlement of his estate, Shelby 1826, names these heirs: wife Elenor; a, Leah, m Christopher Kearns, Shelby 1808; b, Hannah, m James Barnhill, Shelby 1804; c, Deborah, m George Teague, Shelby 1800; d, Persis, m Abner Stark, Shelby 1811; e, —— , m Caleb Starke; f, Ruth, m William Barnhill, Shelby 1810; g, Telitha; h, Charity (i, Edward?). 4, Jeremiah, m Joyce Nevil (dau James and Sarah Joyce Nevil), Lincoln 1787. They went later to Indiana.

Josiah, Sr., m second, Hannah Hite, 1766, and they had: 5, Ruth Sisk; 6, Deborah, twin of Ruth, who lived in Henry after her father's death; 7, Ruhamah Thompson°; 8, Allison, died young; (9, Hannah, m George Barger, Culpeper 1789?).

Hezekiah Boone was in Woodford 1806-1816. He had a family of six, of whom some appear to have been: 1, Elizabeth, m Richard Haynes, W 1813; 2, Moses, m Elizabeth Cunningham°, W 1819. They lived on Clear Creek, and their children were: a, Hezekiah; b, John; c, Hamilton; d, Elmira; e, Jane; f, Melvina; g, Julia; h, Molly Morris°; i, James; j, William.

Isaiah Boone m Elizabeth Brown° (dau Dawson and Sarah Brown), W 1815. They appear to have lived in Mortonsville, and their children were: 1, Eliza Jane, m Warner Dodd, W 1846; 2, Mary Susan; 3, Thomas H.; 4, William; 5, George W.; 6, Daniel; 7, Elizabeth, m Cornelius Haynes, W 1850; 8, Pamela, m George Boone, W 1846. Solomon Boone, who had a family of twelve, was in Woodford 1809-1817. Mark Hammond m Julia Ann Boone, W 1836; John D. Boone m Margaret McLane, W 1851.

Enoch M. Boone (1777-1852, s Rev. Squire and Sarah Morgan Boone), m Lucy Gouldman°, Shelby 1797 or 1798. Enoch and Lucy sold land on Elkhorn to Elizabeth Gouldman, F 1825. They lived in Meade, where they had a large family, including Amanda, m James Nall°, 1822.

George Boone (s Isaac), m Lucy Green° (dau William), Henry 1803; Isaiah Boone m Elizabeth Green (dau William), Henry 1804. Samuel Boone, of Jefferson, was the father of Rachel Manfield°.

SMITH—Catherine, 1, to Big Spring 1812

Gabriel, r 1828	Agnes, 1800, dis 1811
Elizabeth, r 1828	Sukey Hancock, dis 1805
Gabriella, dis 1850	George, 1806

Much of the land in this section was owned by members of the Smith family, Charles Smith sold land on Glen's Creek to Giles Samuel and Carter Blanton. Francis Smith m Ann Preston (dau John and Elizabeth Preston) in Virginia, and they came to Kentucky, where he died W 1817. Their children were: 1, Elizabeth, m James Blair, of Frankfort; 2, Col. John, m in Lincoln 1797 a daughter of Capt. Nathaniel Hart, who, because she was thought to be the first white child born in Kentucky, was given the Indian name for Kentucky, "Chenoe" or "Chinoe." They built the front part of the stone house at Valley Farm, and lived there with their children until 1831, when they sold the place to Joel Scott and went to Henderson. John Smith had extensive land grants on Elkhorn, and sold farms to Simeon Deering, Henry and Reuben Crutcher, D. C. Humphreys, James and Samuel Davis, James Brown, and others. 3, Susan, m William Trigg; 4, Jane Madison; 5, Capt. William Preston; 6, Agatha Marshall°.

The will of Joel Smith, W 1840, mentions his wife Catherine, and: 1, Gabriel, m Elizabeth Frawner (dau John and Mary Guthrie° Frawner), W 1817. In 1842 they bought from William H. Martin the old Ayres place, now the home of John Lewis Thomas. Gabriella Smith, evidently their daughter, m Robert Wilmot, W 1849. Thomas S. Ragland m Mary M. Smith, F 1835, with the bond signed by Gabriel Smith. 2, William; 3, Joel, m Dorcas Tureman (dau Thomas), W 1825; 4, Guthrie; 5, Mary, m John Guin or Gwyn, W 1820; 6, Elizabeth, m Caleb Guthrie°; 7, Frances Guthrie°; 8, Phoebe, m —— Wells, and had Elizabeth and Gilbertson.

Records indicate that Thomas Smith, of Franklin, m first Agnes O'Neal° and second Sally Anderson°, F 1828, and went to Marion County, Missouri.

In Virginia, George Smith m Ann Bailey, and they had: 1, James; 2, Mildred Waller°; 3, Thomas (1719-1786) of Powhatan County, m first Mary Ann Rapine, and they had: a, Rev. George (1747-1820), who came to Kentucky and settled at what is now the home of Bedford Macklin, across the creek from his good friend, William Hickman, whose views on anti-slavery he shared to such an extent that in 1798 he emancipated nine of his own slaves. He m first, Judith Guerrant, and their children were: Mary Ann Forsee° and Esther Martin°. Rev. George m second, Sally Heydon°, and they had George Rappeen, who m Melita Ann Thomson° and went to Georgetown, Mo. He m third Mrs. Elizabeth Dupuy Fogg (widow James Fogg and dau Bartholomew Dupuy), 1805; b, Judith, m Peter Guerrant.

Thomas Smith m second Frances Stovall, and they had: c, Rev. George Stovall, who settled at Gilbert's Creek, in Jessamine. Spencer called him "much of a doctrinal preacher," and said, "Simplicity and plainness attended his whole course." He m Frances Sandifer (dau Abraham), and they had a large family, including James, the grandfather of Miss Lockett Smith, of Frankfort; d, Elizabeth, m —— Gatch. Thomas m third Magdalen Guerrant, and they had: e, James, m Elizabeth Porter, and went to Ohio; f, Martha, m Peter Sublett° in Virginia.

William Smith m Deborah Hearn, W 1793. In 1815 he bought a farm on Big Benson, where he died about 1840. His children were: 1, Jacob, m Amanda Todd°, and they had: a, Paschal H., m Martha Mothershead, Owen 1856; b, Elizabeth; c, Mary; d, Amanda. 2, Icephine or Josephine, m Thomas Hopkins, Owen 1842; 3, Jane, m —— Orr; 4, James, m Milcah Whittington°, W 1835, and they were the parents of James and Cordie, of Versailles; 5, Polly Hearn°; 6, Malinda Todd°; 7, Elizabeth F. (?).

William Smith m Obedience Brown°, F 1800, and they had: 1, Milton; 2, Matilda; 3, Sarah, m Henry Hays, F 1831. William died in 1816, and his heirs sold land in the vicinity of "Valley Farm" to Ezra Richmond, F 1835.

One William Smith, of Louisa County, Virginia, m Mary Rodes in 1762, and they came later to Fayette. Among their children were Nancy Ferguson°, and Rhodes (1766-1845), who m Eunice Thomson° and was the father of Lydia Viley°.

Francis Smith m Fanny Graves°, F 1827. In W, Philip m Mary Berry, 1806; John m Rachel Berry°, 1808; John m Betsy Hall, 1815; Bird m Elnore Price° (dau Mary), 1826. In F 1810 were George, John, Thomas, William; in W, Alex, George, Henry, Humphrey, Joel, John, Joseph, Samuel Smith.

Madison: Governor George Madison (1766-1816) was the son of John and Agatha Strother Madison, of Augusta County, Virginia. He m Jane Smith°, F 1796, and their home was at what was later known as the Joe Scott place ("Redstone Hall"), at Woodlake. In 1810 he had a family of ten, of whom some were: 1, John; 2, Agatha; 3, William; 4, Myra, m Andrew J. Alexander, W 1822, and they lived at the Daniel Swigert farm, now owned by the James Williams family, at Spring Station. Their children were: a, Apoline Agatha, m first Gen. Francis P. Blair, and went to Missouri; she m second Franklin Dick; b, Myra; c, Gen. A. J.; d, George Madison; e, William. 5, George.

SMEATHERS—see Smither

SMITHE—James, dis 1816

SMITHER—John, 1801, dis 1811	Esther, 1, dis 1809
Betsy, 1801, dis 1811	James
Polly, 1801, dis 1811	Nancy, 2, dis 1815
William, 1, dis 1809	

No connected record of the Smither family in Franklin County has been obtained. They lived on Elkhorn and court records show that one William had three children, and perhaps more: 1, Polly Robinson°; 2, Nancy Shaw°; 3, Noel, m Nancy Smoot (dau William R.), F 1817, and died in Owen, 1840. William and Esther Smither were mentioned, W 1790, among the heirs of Joseph Noel, of Essex County, Virginia.

In F 1810 were James with eight, John with five, Leonard with six, Polly with three, and William with four. John Smither m Sally Head°, F 1804; Leonard m Elizabeth Sparks°, F 1800; Lucy (dau William and Mary) m John Dodd, F 1805; William m Ann S. Wilson° (dau Taylor), F 1809; Sarah m Armstead Wilson°; Elizabeth m William Long°; Polly m Reason West°; Anthony m Araminta J. Cox°, F 1828; Benjamin m Susan Ann Haydon°, F 1840; William m Jane Penn, F 1834.

Many of the family went to Owen. Robert m Catherine Wilson, F 1810, and his will, Owen 1853, mentions his wife and children: Robert, John, William, Amanda, James Taylor, children of his daughter-in-law, Jane Bourn. William (s James and Nancy) d Owen 1852.

In Woodford the records are even more confusing, for both the Smither and the Smithey families lived there, and the difference in spelling has not always been observed. William Smither was on the tax list, 1790. In 1810 there were two Williams, John, Samuel, and Benjamin. Dorothy Smither (dau William) m Benjamin Stepp°; John m Polly Taylor, W 1810; Benjamin m Sally Whiting, W 1819; Emaline m Robert D. Johnson, W 1836; William m Permelia Johnson°, and they had: 1, William; 2, Breck; 3, Fauntley; 4, James; 5, Eliza; 6, Julia, m Alonzo E. Burke, and they were the parents of Mrs. R. I. Johnstone, of Frankfort.

The will of William Smither, W 1857, names his children: Clark; Mary McTive; Alexander, m Sarah C. Whittington°, W 1845; Lucy Garnett; William; Fanny; Newton; Juliana or Paulina; Reuben; Ann (?).

Reuben, Thomas, and William Smithey are said to have come from Caroline County, Virginia. Robert, Robert, Jr., James, and William were in W 1792, and Reuben in 1800. Samuel Smithey m Anna Williams°, W 1808; William m Margaret Eaton (dau Joseph), W 1810; Richard (s William) m Nancy (dau William, Sr.), W 1811; Thomas m Isabella Gravitt°, W 1820; John m Virginia Kennedy, W 1839.

SNEED (Snead)—Betsy, dis 1819
Polly, r 1798, dis 1815

The two Sneed families represented here were probably related, but the connection is not known.

Israel Sneed m Mary Crutcher°, dau Thomas Crutcher, of Caroline County, Virginia. There is a tradition among their descendants that they came from North Carolina, and records show that one Israel Sneed (s Major Samuel), was in Anson County, North Carolina, 1775, and was a trustee chosen to establish an academy in Richmond County, North Carolina, 1788.

Several of the children of Israel and Mary came to Mercer, including: 1, William (——-1827); 2, Landon (1770-1847), who lived in the Bridgeport neighborhood, m first, Nancy Eidson°, F 1807, and their children were: a, James L., m Mary Ann Clark (dau Joseph and Harriet Julian Clark), and they were the parents of Mrs. Mary Sneed Lewis°, of Frankfort, and Lewis (1847-1874), who m Ann Mary Stephens° (dau Walker), and they had James Mitchum, of California; b, Henry; c, Dr. William C., m Sarah Russell, Shelby 1841, and they had Russell, of Frankfort, and others who went to Missouri; d, Dr. Lewis, m Susan C. Russell, F 1836, and they were the parents of Judge W. H. Sneed, of Frankfort; e, Elizabeth. Landon m second Elizabeth Gibson°, F 1823, and their children were: f, John G., m Sarah Taylor Coleman°, and they were the parents of Coleman H., of Louisville, who m Bina Guthrie°, and is the grandfather of J. Snead Yager, of Frankfort; g, Thomas, m Susan Blanton°, and went to Missouri about 1850; h, Dr. Achilles F., m Lavinia Blanton°, and went to Boone County, Missouri; i, Sarah Ann, m Preston Pattie°.

3, Achilles (1772-1825), who also came to Franklin, m Sally Stewart°, F 1800, and their children were: a, Eliza, m Dr. Luke Munsell, of Louisville, F 1822; b, Maria H., m first Richard Blanton°, and second A. Churchill; c, Louisa, m Dr. Bryan R. Young, of Elizabethtown, F 1824; d, Sarah Ann, m first Orville B. Martin, of Lexington, F 1826, and second —— ——; e, Julia, m Richard H. Southgate, F 1829 and they went to Covington; f, Thomas; g, William; 4, Thomas, m Sarah ——, and died Mercer 1804. One Sarah Sneed, possibly the widow of Thomas, m Edmund Bartlett°. 5, John, d Mercer 1825, leaving his wife, Patsy, and: a, Lucy, m William Long; b, Betsy, m John S. Newton, Mercer 1812; 6, Elizabeth; 7, Fielding, who probably died en route to Mercer. His will, W 1794, mentions his wife, Elizabeth (Crutcher?), who returned to Virginia, and was in Stafford, 1809.

A letter written by Harrison Blanton, of Frankfort, states that his grandmother, the wife of Richard Blanton, was a Sneed, being the aunt of Achilles, Landon, and William Sneed, and of Thomas Redd, of Franklin County, and Samuel Redd, of Lexington. The record of Miss Kate Payne, of Lexington, says that the wife of Richard Blanton was Nancy Sneed, sister of: 1, Alexander, whose will, Mercer 1818, mentions his wife Susanna (dau James and Nancy Broaddus Daniel°, of Trigg County, Kentucky?), and: a, Thomas; b, Patsy Munday; c, Sally Brown°; 2, Ruth, m first Edmund Munday, and they had: a, Harrison, m Patsy Sneed (dau Alexander), Caroline County, Virginia, 1797; b, Thomas, who operated the ferry at Munday's Landing. He m Susan Slaughter and they had: Edmund, Vardeman, Robert, Gabriel, Lucy, Polly, Reuben; c, William; d, James, m Joyce Chenault, 1813, and probably went to Owen or Carroll; e, Reuben; f, Lucy Brown°, g, Elizabeth; h, Sally; i, Polly; j, Nancy, m Christopher Chinn. Ruth m second Robert Slaughter, Mercer 1804; 3, Mollie, m Charles Brown°; 4, Lucy, m Benjamin Newton.

The other Sneeds descend from Benjamin Sneed, of Caroline County, Virginia, who died in Virginia. His widow, Mary (Coleman?) Sneed, who m second Thomas Ayers (see Ayres), came to Kentucky with her children: 1, Susanna, m Carter Blanton°; 2, Jane, m Rev. John Scott°; 3, Samuel Coleman, m Polly Daniel°, Caroline County, Virginia, 1797. They came to Franklin, where they lived for a few years before settling in that part of Gallatin which was afterward in Owen. He died about 1823, leaving his wife and: a, Fanny (m James Chrisman, Owen 1821?); b, Jane, m James Snape, Gallatin 1818; c, Betsy, m Francis Moore, Owen 1824; d, William (m Nancy Munday?); e, James; f, Susan. 4, Mary, m Thomas Daniel°; 5, Elizabeth, m Samuel Sale, and they settled in the section of Mercer that is now in Anderson. Their children were: Stephen, James, Ira, Samuel, William D., Lucy, Mary, Nancy. 6, Nancy, m John Elliston, and they went to Gallatin. Their children were: Maria Garvey, Elizabeth Sale, Polly, Susan Knox, James T., Ben S., Catherine Scruggs, John G., Robert M.

Probably related to these families was John Sneed (1755-1855, s Benjamin, who came to Danville about 1816, and d 1819), who was born in Albemarle County, Virginia, and died a hundred years later at the home of his son, Alexander, in Danville. He m Sally Johnson, and they came to Mercer. He is recorded as having ten children, some of who were: 1, Cynthia Mims, b 1784, m Joseph Wilson, Mercer 1810; 2, Alexander, b 1786, (father of Sally, m Senator G. G. Vest, of Missouri,

1854?); 3, John H., b 1792; 4, Matilda, m William Hughes; 5, Polly, m Thomas Harrison, Mercer 1811.

Patrick Sneed, who is said to have lived near Richmond, Va., was in Henry 1820, and in Oldham 1823. His children were: 1, Jane Wingate°; 2, William G.; 3, Lavinia, m Asa Clark, Shelby 1818; 4, Ann, m Francis Woolfolk°, Oldham 1827; 5, Nancy, m Cyrus Turk, Oldham 1831; 6, Patrick D., m Nancy W. Maddox° (dau Nelson), Shelby 1831; 7, Dabney; 8, Obadiah; 9, Sarah; 10, America.

Richard Sneed was in Fayette 1795-1796; James was in Jefferson 1791; Jane was in Owen 1821.

Pattie (originally Patche); Thomas Patty (s Thomas, who came to Virginia in 1619) was the father of Silvester, who m Sarah ——, and they had two sons: James, of Caroline County, who m Sarah ——, and two of their children were: Sally Sanders°, and John, who m Ann Sanders°, and came to Bracken in a party with George Rogers Clark and Philip Buckner. William, the other son of Silvester, was the father of John, who m Lucy ——, and had 1, William, m (Frances?) Vaughan°; 2, Lucy, m John Yeatman, Caroline 1792. They came to Kentucky and settled on "Yeatman's Branch," a mile above Frankfort, where he died in 1822. Their sons, Thomas, John, Walker, Preston, Robinson, Henry, are thought to have gone to Tennessee.

3, John (1768-1833), m Lucy Daniel°, Caroline County, Virginia, 1794. They came first to Maysville, and then to Farmdale, where they located near what was afterward the Kentucky Military Institute. Their children were: a, Mary Hall°; b, Daniel, m Margaret Campbell, 1819; c, Mahala, m William Payne, F 1818, and they were grandparents of George L. Payne, of Frankfort; d, Samuel, m Tabitha Buntain, F 1823; e, Elizabeth, m first James Monks, F 1824, and they had a son James; she m second Edmund Vaughan°, Sr.; f, John, died 1829; g, Lucy Ann, m William Adams, F 1826; h, William, m Mary Jane Smart (dau Henry and Phenton Daniel° Smart), 1835. They lived at Farmdale, and were the parents of Dr. Coleman D. Pattie, of Richmond, Ky., and of Miss Lucy Pattie, who had the distinction of being the only woman member of the Sigma Alpha Epsilon fraternity. When, at the beginning of the War Between

the States, all the members of the chapter at the K. M. I. went
to fight for the South, they entrusted their records to the care
of Miss Lucy, who was then a young girl. So well did she
guard the secret that, on their return, they elected her an
honored member of their fraternity, and throughout her long
life they paid tribute to her fidelity. i, Thornton, m Juliet
Cooper, and lived at Hawesville, Ky.; j, Henry, m Mary Lyons,
of New Orleans; k, James S., m first Mary Whip (dau John),
Anderson 1837, and second Elizabeth Portman; l, Sarah Bell
Freeman°; m, Preston, m first Sarah Ann Sneed°, and they had
James and John; he m second Elizabeth Robinson°, F 1851, and
they went to Texas, where they had a large family, including
Hugh, who m Lucille Gibson°.

SNELL—Robert, r 1820

John Snell m Elizabeth Watts° in Virginia, and they came
to Scott County, Kentucky, where he died about 1820. Varying
records list their children as: 1, John, m first Polly Burton,
W 1789, and second Barbara Roth. He went to Missouri, and
is said to have had twenty-six children. 2, Willis, m Jane
Herndon, and went to Missouri; 3, Robert, who bought from
Samuel and Elizabeth Lewis a tract near Cedar Cove Spring,
F 1820. He m first Polly Blanton°, F 1812, and they had: a,
Dr. Carter; b, Susan or Louisa, m 1848 her cousin, Loudon
Snell, and they had: Victor, Loudon, William, Henry. c, (one
record lists Mary E., m Andrew J. Briscoe, Scott 1845). Robert
m second Mrs. Elizabeth Simpson, Scott 1837. 4, William, m
Ann Bates, Scott 1794, and they went to Missouri; 5, Joseph,
whose children were: a, Elizabeth; b, Ann; c, Lucinda; d,
Susanna; e, Margaret, m —— Branham°. 6, Anna, m ——
Owen; 7, Cumberland; 8, Loudon, m Judy ——; 9, ——, m
—— West; 10, Frances, m —— Wells; (11, Frank?).

Armistead F. Fant m first Harriet Snell, 1836, and second
Susan H. Snell, 1843. Members of the family named as heirs
of Carter Blanton, F 1842, were: Albert, Louisa, Carter B.,
Susan, Henry, Dupey, and Frances Snell; Armistead F. Fant
and wife Harriet; William and Juliet Trotter.

William Grimes m Rebecca Snell, Fayette 1814; Lucretia
Snell (dau John) m William Tompkins, Owen 1819.

SPARKS—Milly, Sr., 1801, dis 1818

    Milly, Jr., dis 1818   Isabella, 1802

The Sparks family came from Culpeper County, Virginia. Humphrey Sparks m Milly Nall°, and they were in Scott County, Kentucky, 1795, removing later to Owen. Their children were: 1, Caty, born before 1783; 2, Maria, who died in Henry, 1859; 3, Fanny, m Madison Sparks; 4, Martin, m Caty Middleton, W 1801; 5, Isabella Ballard°; 6, Milly Smither°; 7, Humphrey, m Eliza Ann Calvert°, F 1836. Sarah Palmer°, niece of Martin Sparks, m R. F. Oliver°, Owen 1847.

Henry Sparks (1753-1836) m Lucy ——, Culpeper 1776. They came to Franklin in 1795, and lived on the river in the northern part of the county, going afterward to what is now Owen. They had: 1, Elizabeth Smither°; 2, James, who had a family of five, F 1810; 3, Anthony, who also had five, F 1810; 4, William, m Kitty Peel, F 1813; 5, Thomas; 6, Mary, m Joshua Wilhoit, F 1808; 7, Reuben; 8, Madison, m Fanny Sparks, W 1818; 9, Henry, m Sally Smither°, Owen 1830; 10, John; 11, Alexander Ivason, m Mary Calvert°, F 1829; 12, Rhoda Hill°. One record mentions a dau, Franky Woolfolk°, and his will speaks of a granddaughter, Kitty.

Nancy Sparks, contemporary with Humphrey and Henry, m Jesse Cole°. James Sparks m Rachel Petty, W 1804; Archibald Sparks m Elizabeth Carter, W 1814. Robert Sparks was in Woodford, 1836.

STEPHENS—John, 2

Martha, 2, dis 1836	Sally, dis 1820
Benjamin, 1801, 1804	Leroy, dis 1836
Benjamin and wife, dis	Elizabeth, dis 1810
Lewis, 1801, 1804	Sarah, dis 1843

John Stephens (1763-1842) came from Orange County, Virginia, to Franklin County, Kentucky. In 1785 he m Martha Faulkner (dau John and Joyce Craig° Faulkner), and they settled on the Lexington-Leestown road about six miles from Frankfort. Their children were: 1, Benjamin C. One Benjamin Stephens m Nancy Jackson° (dau John C.), F 1805; Benjamin m Polly Williams; records indicate that Benjamin C. m a dau of James Martin°; Benjamin m Sally Ware°, F 1816, and went to Shelby. 2, Lewis, m ——, and they had William Henry. Lewis F. m Mrs. Frances B. Lewis°, F 1819. 3, Ann Shockley°; 4, John; 5, Daniel H., m Nancy ——; 6, Jane Stout°; 7, Sally W.; 8, Leroy D.; 9, Verinette Lafayette Lewis°; 10, Artimasia Wallace°.

One John Stephens m Nancy Jackson° (dau John), 1792; John m Frances Faulcner (dau Joseph), Fayette 1809; William m Catherine Clemens°, F 1805. Sally Neal°, who died F 1838, was an aunt of Jane Stout.

Another Stephens family in the vicinity appears to have been connected with the Mitcham and Beasley families in Spotsylvania County, Virginia. James Stephens was in Mercer 1795, and in 1805 was on Glen's Creek in Woodford. Among his children are recalled: 1, Mary R. Hall°; 2, William W., m Mrs. Margaret Guthrie°, F 1828. They lived at the old "Stephens Tavern" on the Frankfort-Versailles pike, and their children were: a, Richard, m Margaret Ellen Egbert (dau Oliver and Margaret White Egbert), and they were the parents of Miss Ella Stephens and Mrs. Harry Rogers, of Frankfort; b, Robert; c, Mary Wilson°; d, Jennie Brown°. 3, James Mitcham (1804-1852), m Mrs. Eliza Oliver°, F 1827. One record says he m also a dau of William R. Combs°. He lived at "Roselawn" on the Frankfort-Versailles pike (recently owned by Dr. John G. South), and his children were: a, Mary Ann Bailey°; b, John m Agnes White, and they were grandparents of Mrs. Charles Morris and Judge Leslie W. Morris, of Frankfort; c, Edmund, m —— Gorham; d, Walker, m Barbara Ann Sargent° (dau James P.).

Edmund Stephens (s Edmund) m Polly Ramsey°, W 1817.

Tiller: The will of John Tiller, F 1822, mentions his wife Lucinda (see Miles), and children: 1, Polly Bridgeford°; 2, Margaret, m first John Guthrie°, and second William W. Stephens°; 3, Eliza, m first William Oliver°, and second J. M. Stephens°; 4, Nancy; 5, William; 6, Thomas.

STEPP—Dorothy, 1801

Benjamin Stepp m Dorothy Smythy (see Smither), W 1794, and they were living south of the river, F 1796.

The name is sometimes written *Stepp*, and sometimes *Stapp*, though evidently applied to the same family.

Stapp: James, Reuben, Joshua, and Achilles Stapp came from Orange County, Virginia, to Woodford. Achilles Stapp m Margaret Vawter°, Orange County, Virginia, 1782, and bought land on North Elkhorn from James Rentfro, W 1790. He sold land on Elkhorn to Joshua Stapp and his wife Hannah in 1790, and to Joseph Anderson in 1792. He was in Scott, 1821. Two of his children were: 1, Mary Branham°; 2, Elijah M., who lived near Frankfort and went to Texas in 1828. His children are given as: a, Elijah, Jr., who lived at Newport, Ky.; b, Preston; c, Darwin M., born F 1808; d, Oliver. Nancy and Milton Stapp also married Branhams, but their connection is not known. Elias and Susan Branham were on Elkhorn, 1817. Major Elijah Stapp was in Georgetown, 1820.

James and Sally Stapp lived near McKee's Crossroads, and had a family of ten, W 1810, including Milly Berry°.

Polly Stapp m Henry Jenkins, W 1791; Levi m Nancy Jones Carlisle, W 1811; Achilles m Anne ——— , 1813. Reuben and Wyatt Stapp were also in Woodford.

The Stapps in Madison County, Kentucky, were connected with the Burbridge family.

STOCKDELL—Hannah, dis 1850

Thomas R. Stockdell in Hannah H. Hurt°, W 1831, the bond signed by Reuben Anderson, Jr.

The family is said to have come from Orange County, Virginia. Jediah Stogdel was in Fayette, 1788; William Stockdell was on North Elkhorn, Scott 1799-1811, and perhaps later; John R. Stockdale was in Woodford, 1827. W. H. Stockdell, of Georgetown, m Rachel Kincaid, Madison 1826.

STOUT—Elijah, 1, r 1799, dis 1802   Polly, dis 1806
        Sister, 1, r 1799, dis 1802

The Stouts descend from Richard Stout, who came from Nottinghamshire, England, to America about 1634, and married Penelope Van Princin.

One record says that Elijah Stout, Sr. (s Joseph) m Mary Matthews, and their son, Elijah, Jr., m Elizabeth Turnham in

Culpeper County, Virginia, 1791, and died in Shelby County, Kentucky, 1846. Elijah, Sr., was in Woodford, 1800, and Elijah, Jr., on Craig's Creek at the same time, and both were in Shelby, 1806. Elijah and Ann sold land on the river, W 1808. The will of Elijah Stout (Jr?), Shelby 1846, names sons: 1, David; 2, Elijah, m Mrs. Nancy Rice Cave (wid Hiram Cave), W 1826, and died in Owen 1845; 3, William; 4, Clagit, m Mary Utterback, W 1836; 5, Milton G., m Susan Utterback, W 1839; 6, John I. or J.

Sarah Stout (dau Elijah) m Joseph Hainds, W 1799. One Elijah was in Scott, 1801-1820.

Another branch of the family in Woodford descends from Amos Stout, who came from New Jersey and m Olivia Hicks (dau William and Bettie Harris Hicks), W 1817. They lived near Mt. Vernon Church, and their children were: 1, John, m Susan Bohannon°, W 1844; 2, William, m Judith Jameson, W 1848(?); 3, Robert Hicks, m Fannie Gillespie, 1853, and they were the parents of Judge Robert Lee Stout; 4, Amos, Jr.

Samuel Stout m Martha Hancock°, W 1800, and was in Henry, 1814; Randolph m Lucy Dale (dau Abraham), W 1807; Philemon m Penelope Anderson° (the bond signed by Andrew W. Anderson), W 1810, and was in Scott 1820. Also in Woodford were James, Joseph, David, and Nehemiah Stout.

Daniel Stout (s Jonathan and Hannah Jewell Stout) m Elizabeth ——— , about 1775. After some years they left West Virginia and traveled until they reached the Kentucky River, when they built a raft and floated with their family and possessions until they reached Hammond's Creek, a short distance above Frankfort. Here they owned a farm in 1806, and lived for several years. They took a trip to southeastern Missouri, where one of their daughters was married, but they returned to Franklin County, and in 1820 moved to Jefferson County, Indiana. Some of their children were: 1, Jonathan m Agnes ——— ; 2, Hezekiah, m Nancy McGuire, F 1809; 3, Hannah Edwards°; 4, Mary, m Joseph Lambert, 1811; 5, Daniel, m Elizabeth McGuire, 1811; 6, Penelope, m Ezekiel Randol; 7, Thankful, m Medad Randal in Scott County, Missouri.

David Stout was in F 1795, and one David (s Judiah) m Sally Stone, Fayette 1812. David m Nancy Buckley°, F 1819, and it was perhaps his will, F 1873, which mentions: 1, son, John T.; 2, granddaughter, Sally Johnson; 3, Paulina, m —— Roberts; 4, Eliza Jane, m Wyatt H. Stone, F 1835; 5, Frances Mary, m George Mountjoy; 6, Susan, m —— Miller; 7, Sarah, m Thomas Mountjoy, F 1837; 8, Minerva, m Jacob Gudgell, 1857. Armetta Stout (dau David) m William F. P. Wilson, 1837; Mary Ann m Cyrian Clay, 1833. W. Mountjoy m H. Stout F 1843. There was some connection, possibly in New Jersey, between the Stouts and the Andersons. David Stout and his wife Rachel, of Fayette, sold land on South Elkhorn to Andrew Anderson in 1801. Charles Anderson signed the bond of Richard K. Stout, who m Jane Stephens°, F 1821, and was the father of Cornelia Roberts°; Louisa Cannon; John S. Stout; Sarah Luckett.

Several members of the Stout family, including Elijah, sold land on South Benson to William Hodges, F 1842.

Sutphin Stout was in Scott, 1799-1801, and James was there in 1801.

STRAUGHAN—John, 1, 1789, dis 1798
Mary, 1, 1789, dis 1798

John Straughan m Mary Sanders°, Orange County, Virginia, 1783. They were in Woodford 1790, and south of the river, F 1796, but were in Shelby 1799.

In Shelby, John Straughan m Obedience Scott° (dau Moses), 1808; John m Jane Scott (dau Arthur), 1815; James m Teny Scott (dau Arthur), 1814; Sally (dau Polly) m Moses Scott, Jr., 1815; Nathaniel m Teeni Martin° (dau Nimrod), 1815; Nathaniel S. m Mary Brewer (dau Daniel), 1830; Nancy (dau John) m Moses Scott, 1823.

Sally Straughan was in Shelby 1808. Mary died about 1824, and her estate was settled by Moses Scott.

SULLENGER—Thomas, 1
Fanny, 1

This name has been thought to be a form of the English name St. Leger.

The Sullengers probably came to Kentucky with their relatives, the Samuels. Thomas Sullenger, who lived on Glen's Creek, died W 1795, leaving his mother, Mary, who had a family of four, W 1810; his wife, who was Fanny Shipp°; and children: 1, Reuben, m Polly Baxter, W 1805; 2, Gabriel, m Polly Macey°, F 1804. In 1835 they sold their farm on Elkhorn to James Sullivan and went to Warren, where he died that same year, leaving, besides his wife: a, Polly Moss°; b, Catherine; c, Anna Maria; d, Gustavus; e, Reuben; f, Gabriel; g, Penelope, m Harry B. Innes, F 1827. 3, Thomas, m first Ruthy Haydon°, F 1805, and second Elizabeth Bell (dau James), W 1808; 4, Betsy, m Robert Langford, W 1804.

5, Capt. John, m Elizabeth H. Pepper (dau Elijah and Sarah Neville O'Bannon Pepper), W 1818. They lived for some time in Madison, but eventually returned to Woodford and settled on what is known as the Nat Harris farm, south of Grassy Spring Church. Their children were: a, Dr. John, m Eliza King (dau Dr. Archibald and Martha Trabue° King), and they were the parents of Martha, m Hiram Perham. Dr. Sullenger built the house now occupied by his granddaughter, Mrs. Charles Moorman, and practiced in the Jett neighborhood for many years; b, Oscar; c, Thomas, went to Missouri; d, Amelia Clay, m —— Long or —— Gillespie, and went to Missouri; e, Edna, m first Martin D. Field, Madison 1836, and second Edward P. Bowman, Madison 1843. By the second marriage was a dau, Laura, m —— Bright; f, Sallie Ann, m John H. Estill (s Wallace and Elizabeth Rodes Estill), Madison 1839, and went to Missouri; g, Alice C., m Talma Breden, W 1858, and went to Missouri. Capt. Sullenger's heirs sold the farm in 1858 to T. N. Lindsey, of Frankfort.

6, Nancy Edwards°; 7, Maria Owen°. Mrs. Fanny Sullenger m second George Turpin°.

Betsy Samuel° m a Sullenger, possibly James, Robert, or Larkin, who were in W 1791, and in Shelby 1799. One James m his cousin, Malinda Samuel°, Shelby 1821. They went to Boone County, Missouri, where he died in 1833, leaving his wife and children: 1, Giles; 2, James; 3, Martha Frances, m Dr. Allison and had James, Giles, Martha, and Linnie. In 1843 Malinda Sullenger, who was still in Missouri, sold her farm in Franklin County, Kentucky, to Jesse Sinclair.

The will of Robert Sullenger, Henry 1831, names his children: 1, Betsy, m Reuben McEndre, Henry 1800; 2, Nancy, m Lawrence

Johnson°, Henry 1801; 3, Robert, m Jane Johnston (dau Larkin), Henry 1811; 4, William. One William m Mary Jane Frank (dau Polly), Henry 1835. 5, Thomas, m Susan Collayer (dau Jacob), Henry 1808; 6, Larkin. John Sullenger m Lucinda Berry° (dau Thomas), Henry 1820; Reuben m Polly Shepherd (dau Christopher), Henry 1822; Jesse m Jane Berry° (dau John L.), Henry 1826. James, Sr., James, Jr., and Gabriel Sullenger were also in Henry.

Brockman White m Sally Sullenger, Scott 1809; Solomon Jones° m Mary Sullenger, Gallatin 1815; Reuben Long° m Patsy Sullenger, Caroline County, Virginia, 1807.

Moss: The will of Francis Moss, F 1824, names his wife Peggy and children: 1, Elizabeth Cox°, who was born in Buckingham County, Virginia, 1793; 2, Cate; 3, Polly Church°; 4, James; 5, William Stephen, m Nancy ——— , and they had: a, William T.; b, Elizabeth; c, Mary Ellen; d, John Jesse; e, Robert F.; f, Aletha Anna; 6, Nancy; 7, Daniel Perry, m Polly Sullenger°, F 1826; 8, Samuel, m Catherine Owens°, F 1824; 9, Jesse, m Eliza Edwards°, F 1834; 10, John.

Alexander Moss m Rachel Sheets°, W 1813, and they had: Rachel, m William M. Walston, F 1848; Polly, m John W. Russell. One Alexander Moss m Martha Bohannon°, F 1824, and his will, F 1851, mentions sons Benjamin and Alexander; daus Lena Sheets° and Rachel Moss; and his wife Martha and her children, William F., Elizabeth M., Austin A., and Malinda Ann. Alexander Moss m Harriet Pilcher°, F 1848. Whether this family was related to the Moss family in Woodford is not known.

SWEPSTON—Maria, dis 1832

Thomas Swepston m Maria Sheets°, F 1829. In 1857 Maria sold land on Big Benson to William M. Crutcher.

SWOOPE—Catherine, r 1826, dis 1827

The records indicate that Francis Jackson° had a dau Catherine, who m George Swoope or Swope. One George was in Lincoln 1788-1796. He sold land in Woodford to Daniel Trabue, and in 1823 sold stock to Francis Jackson, Sr., the deed being recorded in Franklin. He witnessed the will of George Smith,

F 1820, and the marriage of W. H. Patterson, W 1818. He was in Gallatin 1833. In Rockbridge County, Virginia, was one George Swoope (s Peter), who was born in Pennsylvania, 1776.

The Swopes descend from Yost Swope, who came from Germany to Lancaster County, Pennsylvania, 1720. Rev. Benedict Swope, of Baltimore, came very early to Kentucky and was at Logan's Fort. He went back to Baltimore for a time, and was there in 1784, when he assisted in the ordination of his friend, Bishop Asbury. He returned to Lincoln, and it was his wife, Susanna Welker Swope, who was so highly commended in the early records for her hospitality and aid to the pioneer preachers.

They were ancestors of Judge King Swope, of Lexington, and of William M. Swope, who m Martha Gay, of Woodford.

George Swope, Sr., and George, Jr., were in Shelby 1816. William, Henry, and Joseph were also there.

TATE—James

The Tate family came from Augusta County, Virginia. James Tate m Mary Lloyd°, and they were living on Elkhorn, probably between the Forks and Woodlake, F 1796. Their children were: 1, Elizabeth M. Cox°; 2, Thomas L. One Thomas Tate is listed in the F 1810 census with a family of six. He may have been the father of: Eliza, m Samuel Luckett, F 1827, and of Juliana Tate Cox°. Thomas L. Tate m Mrs. Nancy Taylor° Gray, F 1829, and they were the parents of James, who m Lucy J. Hawkins°, W 1856; 3, Araminta Julian Cox°; 4, Sally; 5, Martha.

William Tate was in Lincoln 1797; Benjamin was in Henry 1811.

Lloyd: The will of Thomas Lloyd, F 1795, mentions his wife, Araminta Julianna Lloyd; his daughter Mary Tate°; granddaughter Martha Lloyd Cox°; and Thomas Cox°.

Dr. Francis Lloyd, from England, m Lucy Roberts°, F 1821. He conducted a school for girls on the site of the present Feeble Minded Institute. They had: a, Ann Maria Frances, m George Stealey, F 1843; b, Dr. John (1830-1852), who had a drug business on Main Street and afterward taught music; and perhaps other children. Rhodes Lloyd was an early citizen of Franklin County, owning land on Benson, 1820.

TAYLOR—Laura, dis 1847

There were three Taylor families in the vicinity, and perhaps more.

Rev. John Taylor (1752-1835), affectionately known in his late years as "Daddy Taylor," was the son of Lazarus and Anna Bradford Taylor. He m Elizabeth Kavanaugh°, Orange County, Virginia, 1782, and the next year they came to Kentucky. They stayed at Gilbert's Creek for a few months, and then went to Clear Creek, in Woodford. After preaching in that neighborhood for several years, he went to Boone County, Kentucky, and labored in that territory until 1816, when he came to Frankfort. He finally settled at the Forks of Elkhorn, where he bought from George Smith a large tract of land on which he built homes for his daughters.

In 1824 he wrote of his pastoral experiences in his famous book, *A History of Ten Churches*.

John and Elizabeth Taylor had: 1, Benjamin, evidently the one who m Elizabeth Cotton (dau John and Susanna Adams Cotton?), W 1827. They were in Fayette, 1835. 2, Rev. Joseph (1786-1845), was ordained in 1829, and went with his family to Illinois in 1834. He m Mary M. Fogg°, W 1817, and they had: John, Elizabeth, Benjamin, Joel, Dione, Lucy, Joseph. 3, Nancy (1788-1847), m first John D. Gray, and they had: a, Mary Jane, m Rice Smith°, F 1831; b, Elizabeth Forsee°; c, Sally Ann Forsee°. Mrs. Nancy Gray m second Thomas L. Tate°. 4, Polly, m Capt. William French (s James), 1808. They lived near Woodlake and had: a, William, m Martha Wingate°, and they were the parents of Miss Laura French, of Frankfort; b, James; c, Joseph L.; d, Sidney; e, Stephen; f, Richard C.; g, Benjamin; h, Catherine Ford; i, Jane, m LeGrand Buford°, F 1828 j, Sarah Ann, m Rev. B. T. Quinn; k, John W., m Amanda Chinn (dau Franklin and Mary Scott Chinn). 5, Sallie, m Joseph Smith°, F 1822, and they lived at "Llangollen," near Woodlake; 6, Jane E., m first William Plummer, and they were the parents of Ophelia Triplett°; she m second James Elliott°; 7, John W., m Mary ——.

Elizabeth Kavanaugh Taylor died 1832, and Rev. John m Mary Nash, W 1833.

Commodore Richard Taylor (1749-1825), a son of Col. George
and Rachel Gibson Taylor, m Catherine Davis, an English girl,
in King George County, Virginia, 1771. Some of his children
were: 1, Col. Richard ("Hopping Dick," so-called because he was
crippled while trying to rescue a friend from the Indians), m
Mrs. Mary Ann (Martin) Buckner, and they lived at the "Mansion House" in Frankfort; 2, Richard, Jr. ("Black Dick"), m his
cousin, Mary Taylor, and they were the parents of John Eastin,
m 1827 Rebecca Edrington°, and had Col. Edmund H. who m
Elizabeth Fall°, 1861, and was the father of Mrs. Jouett Taylor
Cannon, of Frankfort. 3, Colby Harrison, b Caroline County,
Virginia, 1780, m first Elizabeth McGuire. He m second Lucy
Taylor (dau Hubbard and Clarissa Minor Taylor), and their son
Hubbard, who m Catherine Taylor (dau Reuben and Mary
Thornton Taylor), lived at "Sunnyside" (later the site of Ex-
celsior Institute), and was the father of: Reubenia; Sallie; and
Colby Harrison, who m, 1860, Sarah Addison Brown°, and they
lived with their family at the old Head place, now the home of
Quarles Thompson.

Richard Taylor, whose will was probated in Orange County,
Virginia, 1779, left these children: 1, Chapman (—— -1830)
m Johanna New. They lived on the Shryock's Ferry road, and
their children were: a, Richard (m Laura Kirtley, dau Rebecca
Bohannon° Kirtley, W 1813? or m Mary Brooking°, W 1822?); b,
Daniel, m Cordelia B. Giltner (dau Bernard and Fanny Edwards
Giltner), W 1839; c, Patsy; d, Polly, m her cousin, James Cole-
man°; e, Sally, also m James Coleman. 2, Capt. Richard (1756-
1822), m Sally Blanton°, W 1794, and they had: a, Nancy R., m
William H. Hawkins°, W 1813, and they had Dr. Taylor Hawkins;
b, Polly Wade, m first, William Ballard°, and second Anderson
Garnett°; c, Elizabeth Strother, m Horatio Lynn, W 1824, and
they had: James; Harvey; Elmira, m C. E. Carter, and was the
mother of Lillard H. Carter, of Anderson; Rev. Horace Thomp-
son; d, Richard Samuel Hopkins, m first Caroline Whittington°,
W 1833, and they had: John; Sarah Jane Darnell°; Peggy
Whittington°; Richard. He m second Jemima Whittington°,
Henry 1842, and they went to Missouri, where they had: Lewis,
Molly Pryor, Frank, Atlanta Glass, Hannah Dunn, Florence; e,
Willis, m Elizabeth Buck; f, James; g, Horace; h, Benjamin

Franklin, m Ellen Yancey° and they had Mildred Johnson°, and Burkett. 3, Sarah Coleman°; 4, Mary Brooking°.

Brooking Taylor m Ann Gayle° (King and Queen County, Virginia?), 1806. They came to Kentucky and settled on South Benson near Bridgeport, F 1811. They were the parents of Sally Cunningham°. The family went to Henderson, Ky., in 1806. Ezekiel Taylor m Aylse Martin°, W 1824.

Kavanaugh (Cavanaugh): Philemon Cavanaugh came from Ireland in 1705, and settled in Orange County, Virginia, where he died in 1744. He m Sarah Williams° (dau William and Jael Harrison Williams), and among their children were: Winifred Yancey°; Philemon, m Ann Cave°, and was the father of Elizabeth Taylor; Charles, m Ann Coleman°, and they came to Madison County, Kentucky. Their son William m Hannah Woods, and was the father of William, m Betsy Freeman°. William and Betsy lived in Anderson, and were the parents of: 1, Ann Mariah Whittington°; 2, Hon. George W.; 3, Susan Adelia Whittington°; 4, Araminta; 5, Charles Nicholas, m Lucy E. Lillard, and their dau Aileen m Dr. J. W. Gilbert; 6, Dandridge Whitfield; 7, Hubbard Hines; 8, Thomas Archibald.

Brooking: Samuel Brooking m Mary Taylor° in Orange County, Virginia, 1785. They settled in Woodford near McKee's Crossroads. His will, W 1816, names his wife Mary and: 1, John W., m Polly Long°, W 1808; 2, Sally Shely°; 3, Fanny; 4, Polly; 5, Patsy Branham°; 6, Pameley, m Alvin Brooking; 7, Harriet Hickman°; 8, Juliana Hickman°; 9, Martilla. He named his brother, John Brooking, and Anderson Garnett as executors.

John Brooking m Mary Scott°, W 1789. One account says they lived for some time in Scott, and went later to Hart County, Kentucky. The will of one John Brooking, Scott 1817, mentions his wife Levina, and children: 1, Samuel Scott; 2, Alvin, m Pameley Brooking, W 1817; 3, Matilda Branham°; 4, Vivian; 5, Robert; 6, Polly; 7, Cyrene.

John C. Chiles m Mary T. Brooking, 1827, and they were the parents of Judith Coleman°. Samuel T. Brooking, of Woodford, m Eunice Branham°, Scott 1835. John C. Brooking was in Henry, 1820.

THEOBALDS—James 1, r 1791, dis 1794   Mary, 1

James Theobald lived in the Millville neighborhood, on a farm which he and Mary sold to Isaac Miles, W 1795.

James F. Theobald m Patsy Arnold° (dau John), F 1817. Frederick Theobald m Sarah Clarke, F 1819, the bond signed by Elijah Clarke.

Samuel, Clement, and William Theobald were in Bourbon, 1789, and in 1790 Thomas was there also.

Samuel Theobald, said by some historians to be a lawyer from Frankfort, and by others to be a physician from Lexington, was one of Kentucky's heroes. At the battle of the Thames, he was one of twenty men, the "Forlorn Hope," who volunteered to advance into the woods and receive the fire of the hidden savages, whereupon their comrades would charge upon the Indians before they could reload. Samuel Theobald was the only one to escape unhurt from this sacrificial ordeal, of which Col. Bennett H. Young wrote:

"The 'forlorn hope' had been annihilated. On this fateful field it had won imperishable renown and carved out fadeless glory. It had been destroyed, but its members had magnified Kentucky manhood and written in the life-blood of three-fourths of its members a story of courage and patriotic sacrifice which would live forever."

One Samuel Theobald m Nancy D. Warfield, Fayette 1816. Dr. Samuel Theobald, of Lexington, m Mrs. Harriet B. Blanton°, F 1841, and they were living in Frankfort when his dau, Ruth Ann Theobald, m B. B. Sayre, 1844. They went later to Greenville, Miss., where Mrs. Theobald is said to have given the land on which the town is built. Dr. Theobald was living in Frankfort, 1865.

Thomas S. Theobald was born in Bourbon, but he lived in Scott before coming to Frankfort about 1835. He m Sarah Keene, 1813, and they had a large family, among whom were: 1, Mary Bain°; 2, Margaret Price°; 3, Harriet, m George W. Craddock, of Hart, F 1841, and they were the parents of Mrs. James Blackburn°, of Frankfort; 4, Edwin S. Thomas A. Theobald, of Frankfort, m Susan Moffet, of Trimble, 1845.

Arnold: Capt. John Arnold in 1783 built Arnold's Station near the point at which the Frankfort-Lawrenceburg road crosses

Little Benson. It was described as being at that time the extreme frontier, since all the other stations were up nearer the settlements. Captain Arnold was the commandant of a company of spies who ranged the country as far down as Drennan's Lick.

He was the son of James Arnold, who came later and built a log house opposite the mouth of Glen's Creek. James Arnold was the ancestor of the Frankfort historian, L. F. Johnson.

THOMAS—Philip (Philemon?), 1	Jean, 1
Richard, 1	Mary, 1
John, 1, dis 1794	Isabelle, 1
Wife, 1	Ruthana, 1

Soon after the Forks Church was organized, Philemon Thomas, who is referred to as a statesman, and his brother Richard were baptized, and in 1789 it was agreed that they should be "at liberty to use their gifts as suits them." Arrangements were made for the ordination of Richard Thomas in 1794, and he became the minister of the Flat Lick Church, in Bourbon. Spencer says of him: "He was a young minister of some sprightliness, and might have been useful, but for his union with the Licking Association of Anti-missionaries."

Philemon Thomas was in Fayette, 1788, with three tithables; John had two; and William one. Gen. Philemon Thomas m Fanny Hawkins° (dau John and Sarah Johnson Hawkins).

Tapley and Richard M. Thomas were in Woodford 1800. The will of Richard M. Thomas, W 1825, mentions his wife and children: 1, Betsy; 2, John W.; 3, Sally, m John Haydon, W 1819, and had Thomas, Eliza Jane, and Thompson Ann; 4, James.

In Franklin, Henry W. Thomas (s Thomas Thomas) m Mary Nall°, 1810; Richard m Nancy Ellison (dau Jacob), 1821; John m Anny or Amy Buntain (dau Elizabeth), 1823.

Elisha Thomas (s Henry) m Polly Sanders° (dau Nancy), W. 1791; Elijah E. Thomas m Maria Louisa Shipp°, W 1837.

One Richard Thomas was the father of Isabella Bledsoe°.

James Pendleton Thomas m Martha Green°, F 1854, and they were grandparents of Mrs. J. L. Cox of Frankfort.

THOMPSON—Ruhamah, 1800, dis 1812

Ruhamah Boone° m William Thompson, and they came to Woodford, where in 1810 their family numbered six. They went afterward to Henry, where he died in 1816. Amasa Thompson m Ruhamah Sisk°, W 1828.

Another family was that of William R. Thompson (1776-1860), who came from Island and taught with Louis Marshall at Buck Pond. His wife was Margaret McCulloch, and their son, Dr. Robert J., m Barbara Wilson°, W 1833, and was the father of: 1, William, m Virginia Campbell (dau Alexander Campbell, leader of the great Church movement, and his second wife, Selina H. Bakewell); 2, Dr. Benjamin Wilson, m Fannie Goodwin (see Gibson) 1868; 3, Rebecca; 4, Dr. Robert J., Jr., m Maxey Ayres°, and went to Missouri; 5, Katherine, m J. Tilford Brown; 6, Enna; 7, Oakley, m Jennie Fogg°. They lived on the Frankfort-Versailles pike east of the old Steele's Ferry road, and were parents of Mrs. Oakley Brown, of the Louisville pike, and others.

Dr. Robert Thompson, Sr., and his son, Dr. B. W. Thompson, lived in the Duckers neighborhood.

THOMSON—Anthony, 1789   Nathaniel, dis 1807
　　　　　 Ann, 1   　　　　　Betsy, r 1818
　　　　　 Mary 1,

Anthony Thomson, Sr. (――― -1794) was the son of Robert and Susanna Thomson, of New Kent County, Virginia, and the grandson of Robert and Judith Thomson. He came from Louisa County, Virginia, with his family in 1784, and lived first at the Lafayette Crutcher place on the Frankfort-Versailles road, and later at "Thomson's Manor," (also called "Thomson's Castle" and "Thomson's Fort"), a large stone house which he built on a high point opposite the Henton residence.

His wife was Ann Bibb (dau Henry and Eleanor Fleming Bibb, of King William County, Virginia), and their children were: 1, Robert, remained in Virginia: 2, Judith, m Thomas Bell (s Thomas and Elizabeth Ware Bell), of Woodford, and they went to Ohio County, where they had: a, Thomson; b, John; c, Samuel; d, Thomas; e, Robert; f, Jefferson; 3, Eleanor (1759-1810), m David Thomson (s Waddy and Elizabeth Anderson Thompson), who was a Baptist minister in Virginia, and they lived at the Alex Wright farm (afterward "Hereford"). Their children were: a, Anthony (b 1782), m Sarah Thomas; b, Anderson; c, Waddy, m Cynthia Thomas, of Greenup, and their children were: William; David; Nancy; Parthenia; and Robert Thomas, who m Mildred Henton°, W 1840, and lived near Duckers on the farm now owned by B. M. Hieatt, where they had: Mary Eliza, m Thomas Lewis, of Shelby; Lucy; Ella, m Virgil Lewis; Thomas, m Mary Quarles (dau Dr. Archibald and Mary F. Quarles), and they were the parents of Quarles Thompson, of Duckers, and Mrs. Mervin Parrent, of Frankfort; Cynthia, m S. J. Gibson°; William; Elizabeth, m Thomas Shaw, and they were the parents of Mrs. Clarence Burke, of Versailles; John; Parthenia; James, m Martha Scott° and they were the parents of Scott and Robert Thompson, of Frankfort; Lewis.

d, Elizabeth Blanton°; e, Louisa, m Joel Thomasson; f, Mary Shipp°; g, Ann Bibb, m Robert Adams, W 1817, and had David Thomson and Virginia; h, William, m Eliza Peters; i, David, m Eliza Beatty, 1827, and they had Judge Robert Alexander, m Lavinia Wingate, F 1851, and was the grandfather of Mrs. Henrietta Callis and Miss Lucy Thomson, of Frankfort. 4, Susanna Vaughan°; 5, Anthony, Jr., m first Ann Pemberton°, F 1797, and they had: a, Richard P.; b, Anthony; c, Ann Bibb, m Francis R. Black, W 1826; d, Margaret, m Thomas Berryman; e, Mary, m —— McDonald. Anthony, Jr., m second, Katherine Mason, their children: f, Katherine, m William Hines; g, Henry Bibb.

6, Nathaniel, m Frances Major°, 1795. They lived at "Thomson's Manor" and had: a, Elizabeth Hicklin°; b, Ann Dillon°; c, Martha Crutcher°; d, John; e, Maria, m Maurice English; f, Zoraida E. Crutcher; g, Henry; h, Paulina V., m G. W. Thomson; h, Mary Louise Crutcher. 7, Mary, m Samuel Waddy, of Shelby; 8, Henry; 9, Elizabeth; 10, Sarah.

One Anthony Thompson m Sarah Williams° (dau William), 1828; William Thompson m Peggy Hambleton, 1789; Roger Tomson m Easter Robinson°, F 1800.

Mrs. Ann Rodes Thomson, widow of William Thomson, of Louisa County, Virginia, came to Scott with her children, among whom were Eunice Smith° and Gen. David Thomson, who m Betsy Suggett°, and had a large family, including Mildred Elvira Major°, Melita Ann Smith, and Marion Wallace Gunnell°. In 1833 General Thomson and several members of his family went to Pettis County, Missouri, where the city of Sedalia was named for one of his granddaughters.

Wingate: Two brothers, Joseph and Smith Wingate, who lived near Wilmington, Del., came to Kentucky, Joseph settling in Lexington, and Smith in Franklin County, where he died shortly after his arrival.

Smith m Susanna Capes, and they had a daughter and four sons: 1, Thomas S., m Betsy Woolridge°, F 1805. They lived in Owen, and had: a, Smith (m Mary C. Todd?); b, John W., who went to Hickman, Ky.; 2, Cyrus, m Milly Spicer (dau Elizabeth), F 1808. They also lived in Owen, and had fourteen children. 3, Isaac (1791-1876), who lived at Woodlake, m Jane N. Sneed°, Shelby 1816. They had a large family, including: a, Isaac, m, Betty Bailey, and their dau, Desdemona, m Isaac W. Parrish, of Midway; b, Martha French; c, Lavinia Thomson; d, Mary, m Lee Watkins; e, Laura, m W. S. Dehoney; f, Susan, m Benjamin T. Quinn; 4, Henry (1795-1862), m Penelope Hart Anderson (dau Reuben), F 1819, and they had: a, Lucien, m Elizabeth Knight; b, Maria Louise, m first Russell McRery, 1842, and second Rev. Duncan Campbell, 1848; c, Reuben A., m Sarah Graham, of Shelby; d, Sarah Hart, m George R. McKee, 1843; e, Susan Mary; f, Robert; g, Henry; h, Ellen, m Dr. Nathaniel J. Sawyier, F 1861, and they were the parents of Paul Sawyier, of Frankfort.

TINDER, ——

This was among the names of women who joined the Church after 1840.

TINSLEY—Mary, 1

The Tinsleys were connected with the Dupuy, Samuel, and Vaughan families. William Tinsley was in Woodford 1791, and Jonathan and Archibald were there in 1794. Archibald owned land on the river, F 1801. He m Polly Yeates° (dau Enoch), F 1822, and his dau Sarah Ann m William S. Bayes, Anderson 1846. Samuel Tinsley, Jr., m Betsy Vaughan°, F 1813, and Ira Vaughan m Elizabeth Tinsley. Abram B. Tinsley m Rachel Gaines°, Anderson 1836.

In Lincoln, George Tinsley m Polly Gaines°, 1786; James m Mary Graham, 1794; William m Mrs. Agnes Logan, 1798; David m Sarah Oliver (dau William), 1803.

In Franklin, Henry Tinsley had: Eliza, m Buford Rice, 1828; Judith m James Rice, 1829. Henry T. Wright m Rebecca Tinsley, F 1882, and Peache Tinsley, 1832. Jeptha D. Shields m Frances Tinsley, F 1831; James Tinsley m Susan Robinson°, F 1839.

TODD—Betsy, dis 1822

In this vicinity were two Todd families, one from Ireland and one from England. A Scotch laird (one record gives his name as John Todd, and another as Robert) went to Ireland, and his descendants came first to Pennsylvania, and then scattered to Virginia and other sections. Of this family is said to have been Richard Todd (1768-1858), who came, probably from Spotsylvania, and lived first in Scott and later in Owen. He m Elizabeth Hickman°, F 1802, and their children were: 1, Mary C. Wingate°; 2, Amanda M. Smith; 3, Rev. Paschal H., who was licensed to preach in Owenton, 1837, and was ordained in 1841. He was a city missionary in Louisville, and it was said that his superior gift of exhortation rendered him a valuable workman. He m Malinda Smith°, Owen 1828, and at some period they lived in Frankfort in a house opposite the old Governors' Mansion. Three of their children were: Robert S.; Icephena D.; Lura, m Rev. Lewis M. Thompson (s Capt. Ed Porter Thompson, historian of the Confederacy), and they were parents of Ed Porter Thompson, of Frankfort, who m Emily Hickman Coleman° and went to Oklahoma.

Also descended from the Scotch laird was Samuel Todd, of that part of Botetourt that is now Rockbridge County, Virginia. He m Jane Lowry, and about 1808 they came to Clay County, Kentucky. In 1812 they removed to that section of Jefferson which is now Oldham, where his will was probated in that same year. Some of their children were: 1, "Parson John," a Presbyterian minister in Oldham; 2, Jane, Kentucky's heroine of pioneer surgery, m Thomas Crawford, 1794, and they lived in Greensburg, Ky.; 3, Alice Craig°; 4, Judge Samuel, who came to Gallatin about 1811, and later to Frankfort, where he purchased the property in Bellepoint which is still occupied by his descendants. He m first Charity Dabney, and they had: a, William; b, Louisa; c, Mary. He m second Monarchia Fenwick (dau William), F 1824, and their children were: d, Judge Dabney, who m Mary Bosworth, and was the father of Miss Ellen Todd and Mrs. T. H. Locke, of Frankfort; e, Dr. Lewis, m Kate Lancaster, of Lebanon, Ky.

Robert S. Todd, of Lexington, a son of the old Indian fighter, Col. Levi Todd, was also from the Scotch-Irish family. His first wife was Eliza Parker, and their dau Mary was the wife of Abraham Lincoln. He m second Eliza L. Humphreys (dau Dr. Alexander and Mary Brown° Humphreys), F 1826, and for a number of years the family used "Buena Vista" as their summer home.

Richard Todd, of English descent, m Elizabeth Richards, and they lived in King and Queen County, Virginia. Their children were: 1, William (1750-1815). One record says he m first Phoebe Ferguson, Halifax County, Virginia, 1770, and another says she was Phoebe Ramel. He m second Jane Shelton (dau Crispen), Pittsylvania County, Virginia, 1774. He came to Woodford with his family, among whom were: a, George, m Mary Ellis Montague°, F 1806. They lived for a time in a log house at "Spring Garden," his uncle's place, coming later to Frankfort. They were ancestors of the McClure, Lewis, and Hodges families, of Frankfort. b, Letitia, m William F. Haslett, W 1810. They lived in Anderson, and from them are descended the Egberts and Saffells, of Frankfort. 2, Mildred, m Thomas Tunstall, and came to Frankfort; 3, Richard, m Mary Lankford (dau Benjamin), Pittsylvania County, Virginia, 1780. He died in 1795, and his widow and children came to Kentucky and made their home with Justice Thomas Todd. The children were: a, Thomas, who evidently went to Jefferson with some of the Tunstall relatives; b, Benjamin L., m Elizabeth Green°, W 1813; c, Mildred, m first John Green°, and second John Louderback, F 1818; d, Richard. 4, Justice Thomas (1765-1826) came to Danville in 1783 with the family of his relative, Judge Harry Innes, but he came to Frankfort, and in 1803 was living in Woodford at "Spring Garden," in the brick house which he is said to have built in 1795. In 1813 he sold this property to William Duncan, of Philadelphia, who in 1816 sold it to Nicholas Lafon. Thomas Todd removed to Frankfort, where he lived in the house on Wapping Street that was in recent years the home of H. P. Mason, Jr.

He m first Elizabeth Harris (see Stewart), 1788, and their children were: a, Harry; b, Col. Charles S., m Letitia Shelby (dau Gov. Isaac Shelby), F 1816, and they went to Shelby; c, John Harris, m Maria Knox Innes (dau Judge Harry and Ann Harris Shiell Innes), F 1817; d, Elizabeth, m John H. Hanna, W 1811; e, Ann Maria, m Edmund Starling, F 1817. Justice Todd m second Mrs. Lucy Payne Washington (widow of George Steptoe Washington), 1812, and they had: g, James Madison, m Allisonia Rennick°, F 1847; h, Dolly Madisonia, m Charles Quin, Jefferson County, Virginia, 1839; i, William Johnston. One account says his wife was ––––– Swain, though persons who remember the family think that he died when quite young.

An old newspaper mentions Thomas Todd's daughter, Milicent, who died at the age of eighteen and was buried at "Spring Garden." Thomas Todd was buried in the old Innes graveyard on Elkhorn, but in 1891 his remains were reinterred in the Frankfort cemetery. One Johnston Todd m Mary Hanna (dau Martha), Shelby 1835.

Trabue–Olympia, r 1800

The Trabues descend from Anthony Trabue (1667-1724), a Huguenot who came to King William Parish, Virginia, 1701. His wife was Magdalen, dau Jacob Flournoy, and their children were: Anthony; Jacob; John James, who m Olympia Dupuy°; Judith m Stephen Watkins; Magdalene, who m Peter Guerrant, and was the mother of Judith Smith°.

John James and Olympia Trabue came to Woodford and settled with their relatives west of Versailles near the river. Their children were: 1, James (1746-1803), m Jane, dau Robert Porter, and some of their children were: a, Elizabeth, m Chastain Trabue; b, Martha, m Archibald King, and was the mother of Mrs. John Sullenger°; c, James, of Ruddle's Mill, in Bourbon, m first Judith Wooldridge°, and second Lucy Cosby°, W 1848; 2, Magdalen, m Edward Clay (uncle of Henry Clay), and went to North Carolina or Alabama; 3, Phoebe; 4, Jane, m Rev. Joseph Minter (s Joseph Anthony Minter), and had besides other children: a, Elizabeth Major°; b, Sarah Cosby°. 5, John, m ––––– Pearce; 6, William, m Elizabeth Haskins (dau Col. Robert and Betsy Hill Haskins); 7, Mary (1758-1792), m Lewis Sublette°; 8, Capt. Daniel, m Mary Haskins (dau Col. Robert), and settled on Griers Creek; 9, Martha Wooldridge°.

10, Col. Edward, lived on Griers Creek. His first wife was Martha Haskins (dau Col. Robert), and they had among other children, Ann, who m Asa Pittman and was the mother of Martha Crutcher° and of Ann, who m Rev. Z. F. Smith, the historian. Edward m second Jane Clay, 1797. Many of his descendants went to Missouri. 11, Stephen, m Jane Haskins (dau Col. Robert). Their oldest son, Chastain (1786-1852), preached the doctrines of Alexander Campbell to the dissenting group in the Forks of Elkhorn Church. He married his cousin, Elizabeth Trabue, and they lived at "Weehawken" and were parents of Stephen Fitz James, and others. 12, Elizabeth, m W 1794, Fenelon R. Willson, an Englishman. Their son, Rev. John Slater Willson, was pastor of the First Baptist Church of Louisville. 13, Samuel; 14, Susanna Major° (1772-1862); 15, Judith Major°.

Dupuy: John James Dupuy was the son of Count Bartholomew Dupuy and his wife, Countess Susanna Lavillon Dupuy, Huguenots who escaped from France after many exciting adventures. He m Susanna Levilain, and their children were: 1, Olympia Trabue° (1729-1822); 2, Bartholomew, m Mary Mottley and came from Amelia County, Virginia, to Woodford. Their children were: a, Achsah, m Benjamin Davis; b, Susanna; c, Joel, m Lucy Craig°. They lived on Grier's Creek, where they built their home, "Stony Lonesome" (now owned by Mr. and Mrs. Gordon Wilder, of Lexington), which is considered an outstanding example of the architecture of that period. d, Elizabeth, m first James Fogg°, second George Smith°; e, John; f, Judith Samuel°; g, James; h, Nancy McClure; i, Martha Owen°; j, Joseph, m Nancy Peay, and they lived in Henry; k, Sallie, m Poindexter Thomasson, and they had Dr. John James, of Trimble, who m Sarah E. Coleman°; 3, Susanna, m James Lockett.

4, Mary, m Benjamin Hatcher; 5, Rev. John (1738-1831), was pastor at "Dupuy's Meeting House" in Powhatan County, Virginia. He came in 1784, and was affiliated with the Clear Creek Church. He went to Oldham in 1801, and later to Shelbyville. His wife was Elizabeth Minter, and many ministers of the Gospel are among their descendants. 6, Elizabeth, m Thomas Atkinson; 7, Rev. James (1745-1837), was also a member at Clear Creek, going afterward to Shelby. He m Anne Starke (dau Maj. John

Starke, of Virginia), and they were the parents of a large family, including: a, Rev. Starke Dupuy, who in 1812 edited in Frankfort "The Kentucky Missionary and Theologian," the first religious periodical published west of the Alleghenies, and was the compiler of "Dupuy's Hymns," of which it is said more than 100,000 copies were printed. He m ―――― Webber, Shelby, 1805. b, Susanna Richardson°.

Sublette: The Sublettes descend from Abraham and Susanna Soblet, Huguenots who came to Virginia. One record states that his wife was Susanna Dupuy°, while another says she was Susanna Chastaine. Their son, Pierre Louis, m Marte Martain (dau Jean and Marie Martain), and their son, Louis, who m Frances Magruder, was the father of Lewis who m Mary Trabue° in 1779.

Lewis Sublette (1759-1830) came with his family from Chesterfield County, Virginia, and settled in Woodford opposite Tyrone, where he established Sublette's ferry (now Shryock's) across the river. The children of Lewis and Mary were: a, William, m Mrs. Nancy Sanders° (widow of John and dau Thomas Samuel), W 1806; b, James, m Susan Edzard (dau William), F 1807, the bond being signed by Jane T. Sublett; c, Lewis, m Susan Coleman° (dau Thomas and Susanna Strother Hawkins Coleman), 1808, and they were the parents of Miss Susie Sublette, of Lexington; d, John; e, Frances Vaughan°.

Lewis Sublette m second Sarah Samuel°, W 1794. Their children were: f, Abraham; g, Samuel, m Fannie Aynes (dau James), W 1824, and they were grandparents of Dr. S. O. Sublette and Judge Robert S. Hawkins, of Woodford, Mrs. John Trumbo, and Keene McGinnis of Frankfort, and many others; h, Elizabeth, the second wife of William A. Cotton (s John and Susanna Adams Cotton), who had: John Lewis (1838-1919?), m Emma Moss; William, m Mary Stockton, and they had: Augusta; Stockton; Robert; Louie, m J. F. Waddell. The family went to Sedalia, Mo.; Abram Randolph, m Henrietta Anderson°, and they were parents of William and Dunlap, of Woodford; Dunlap, Sr. i, Ann Mariah (1808-1836), m William A. Cotton, W 1829 (his first wife), and their children were: Elizabeth (1830-1848); Susan Frances Darnell° (1832-1893); Martha Ann, m

James Sublette°, and they were the parents of Misses Willie and Fannie Sublette, of Versailles; Mary Lewis.

TRIPLETT—James, 1811, dis 1813
Nancy, to Forks of Elkhorn 1815

Charles Triplett was in F 1816.

One record states that Hedgman (or Hedgeman) Triplett (1760-1838?), son of John and —— Popham Triplett, of Culpeper County, Virginia, came to Kentucky about 1792 and died in Bourbon. Another record says that Hedgman Triplett m M. McClanahan (dau Rev. William and Mary Marshall McClanahan), Culpeper 1788.

Hedgman Triplett was in Scott 1801, and had a family of eight, F 1810. Disconnected records indicate that his children were: 1, Polly Clements°. She is said to have married second —— Palmer, and to have gone to Warren; 2, Hedgman, m Peggy Eddins°, F 1814, and they had: H. H.; John E.; George C.; Alex H.; and Thomas W., who sold land to the Duvalls in 1846; 3, Mildred, m Abner Wright, F 1815; 4, John, m Polly Finnell°, F 1814, and John H., m Nelly T. Samuel°, F 1828. He is said to have gone to New Orleans. 5, Francis, who went to Memphis; 6, Capt. William, m Dianna Ballow°, Shelby 1827. They lived on Elkhorn, and in 1842 sold their land to John Peak; 7, Hannah, who may have married first —— Long, m Edmund Poe°; 8, Elizabeth Gravit°; 9, George W., m Pamela Head°, F 1827, and they went to Daviess in 1833. Their son, Robert S. (b Scott 1830), m Louisa Vest (dau John J. and Harriet Graham° Vest), F 1851, and was the father of George V., who m Nannie Beckham. In 1828 it was announced in the *Frankfort Commonwealth* that Robert Triplett would remove "to the Yellow Banks" (Owensboro). Robert S. Triplett m second Helen H. Brown°, W 1857, and they were parents of Mrs. Willard Winter, of Frankfort. Another record lists: 10, Lucy, m —— Palmer°, and was dead in 1837.

Thomas Triplett (s Thomas and Elizabeth Hedgman Triplett), who was a cousin of Hedgman Triplett, is said to have come also to Bourbon, where he died 1833. His children are recorded as: 1, Francis; 2, Thomas, m Rebecca Wagner, Bath 1815. He died, F 1836, leaving his wife and: a, George W., m first Ophelia Plummer (dau Mrs. Jane Taylor° Elliott), F 1836, and they had Ophelia, m Dr. —— Samuel, and went to Kansas. George W. m second Mary Elizabeth Spotts (dau Capt. Samuel and Mary Hanna Spotts), and they had John H. (father of Eugene Triplett and Mrs. Frank Moore of Frankfort), and George, Samuel, Louis, Annie, and Minnie, who went West; b, Mary E., m Francis H. Moffett, F 1839, and their dau Rebecca m Dr. James Ely, of Frankfort; c, Rebecca Samuel°. 3, Hedgman, who went to Arkansas; 4, William; 5, Hannah; 6, Elizabeth; 7, Eloise, m Andrew Trumbo, of Bath, and they were the parents of John, Robert, and Frank Trumbo, who lived at "Big Eddy," southeast of Frankfort; 8, Mary, m William Warner, Bath 1818.

Reuben and Francis Triplett were in Lincoln 1792, and Frederick was in Mercer 1799, and in Woodford 1802. Charles Triplett was on Elkhorn, F 1817, and on Dry Run in 1820.

Ballou (Ballew, Ballow): The Ballews are said to have come from Scotland. In the family of Diana Triplett° and her sister Catherine Gayle° (1798-1872) is a tradition of descent from Pocahontas.

Solomon Ballow was in Woodford 1791, and later in Scott. Also in Scott were James; Henry; Elijah; Richard; John; and Mary, who lived on North Elkhorn, and may have gone to Breckinridge after 1820.

Charles Ballew m Elizabeth Marshall°, Lincoln 1787. In 1797 he was in Shelby, where he died 1818, leaving his wife and: Charles; America; Elizabeth (m Samuel Barnes, Shelby 1818?); Martha, m William Marshall°, Shelby 1814, and others. Edward Ballew, in Shelby 1800, m Hethe Marshall°, 1804. Others of the name lived in Madison.

Turpin—Fanny, to Glen's Creek 1801

George Turpin m Mrs. Fanny Sullenger°, W 1798, and in W 1810 he had a family of eight, including: 1, Frances, m John A. Markley, W 1818, and they had: a, Margaret; b, Apphia, m W. T. Lowe; c, John, m Susan Stapp°. John A. Markley m second Virginia Darnell°. 2, America, m Alexander Hugley, W 1824; 3, Affiah, m William H. Pepper, W 1823, and they were grandparents of Mrs. Arthur Crutcher, of Versailles. George Turpin went with his family to Henry, where he died in 1833.

TWYMAN—George, 1 to Glen's Creek, dis 1816

George Twyman (s William and Winifred Cowherd Twyman, of Madison County, Virginia), came to Kentucky about 1781. He made his home with his brother, Capt. Reuben Twyman, who lived on the Midway-Versailles road opposite "Bosque Bonita."

Capt. Reuben Twyman m Margaret Griffin, and their children were: 1, Elizabeth Buford° (1789-1877); 2, Mildred, m Buford Twyman; 3, Simeon, m Mary Walker Yancey°, W 1822; 4, Joel, m Margaret Buford°, went to Glasgow, Mo.; 5, George, m Eliza Crutcher; 6, Colby, m Eliza Stone.

One George Twyman (s George and Catherine Montague° Twyman) m Agatha Buford°, 1724, and their son George m Mary Walker and was the father of Agatha Deering°.

VANMETRE—Rebecca, r 1811, dis 1811

The Van Meters are said to descend from the Dutch Jacob Van Meteren, who assisted Miles Coverdale in printing the first English Bible.

Jacob and Letitia Strode Van Meter, who came from Frederick County, Virginia, to Hardin County, Kentucky, had a dau Rebecca, born 1746. One Jacob Vanmetre m Rebecca Rawlings, Hardin 1793. Many of the Van Meters settled in Clark.

VAUGHAN—Susanna, r 1813   Sythy, r 1820
Edmund, Jr., r 1820   William, r 1828, dis 1830

Cornelius Vaughan (1729-1785) was sent by George II to America as a solicitor. He m in Virginia, 1745, Franky —— , and their children were: Elizabeth, Milly, Mary, Sally, Fanny, Edmund, Phoebe, Nancy, Peggy. One account mentions another son, Thomas, who is said to have gone to South Carolina. One Thomas Vaughan was in Fayette, 1791.

Edmund Vaughan, Sr. (1760-1823) was married in 1784 to Sally Samuel°, who, according to the Bible record, was barely eleven years old at the time. They lived in the Jett neighborhood, where their home, known as the old Haydon place, is still in good condition. Their children were: 1, William, m Frances Sublette°, F 1808, and they went to Shelby. Though one record says they had no children, one Nancy Vaughan (dau William) m Joseph Green°, Shelby 1825. 2, Nancy; 3, John; 4, Edmund, Jr. (1790-1857), m first Sythy Blanton°, Fayette 1815. They lived at "Wheatland," the home of the Hanlys at Jett, and their children were: a, Sarah Frances; b, Edmund Carter; c, Harrison Blanton; d, James Orville; e, Benjamin, who went to Missouri; f, Lucy Catherine, m Samuel B. Scearce. They lived on Glen's Creek, and had Edmund and Blanton, who went to Missouri, and Elizabeth, who m Willis Berryman, of Versailles. g, Ira. One record says his wife was his second cousin, Lizzie Tinsley°, whose mother was a Vaughan; another says he m Elizabeth Underwood, Shelby 1856. They are said to have lived in Shelby, where they had several children, including: Sally, m A. D. Middleton, of Shelby; Mettie, m Lee Long, of Bagdad; Lucy, m Roger Bryan, of Winchester. h, Elizabeth Sarah (1833-1917) m Hezekiah Winn, 1865, and they were parents of Miss Lucy Winn, of Versailles; i, John. Edmund Jr. m second Mrs. Elizabeth Monks (dau John Pattie° and widow James Monks), F 1839, and they had: j, William Walker; k, Henry. Edmund Jr. m third Mrs. Ellen Clarke Fox (dau Joseph Clarke and widow George F. Fox).

5, Walker, m Fannie Blackwell°, F 1824, and they had: a, William P., m Susan S. Harper, and went to Saline County, Missouri; b, Dr. Robert, who practiced in Louisville and Versailles, m —— Culver, and had William and Millard; c, Mollie F., m Daniel C. Hitt; d, Sallie, m —— Fletcher, and went to Missouri; e, Edmund, also went to Missouri; f, John M., m ——, and had R. S. and Ellen M. 6, Elizabeth Tinsley°; 7, Thomas, m Mary Hughes°, F 1817; 8, Reuben.

In W 1801 Edmund Vaughan, Sr., m Susanna Thomson°, and their children were: 9, James, m Charlotte Ashmore Hawkins°, W 1827, and they had Edward and William; 10, Mary Ann, m Dandridge S. Crockett (s Col. Anthony and Mary Wilson Crockett), Shelby 1820. They lived on a farm on the Lawrenceburg road which is now owned by Mrs. Leslie Morris, and their children were: a, Susan, m Dr. John Hickman°, of Clay Village in Shelby, who went afterward to Cynthiana. They were the parents of George, m Hallie Hockensmith, and Pickett. b George, m Elizabeth Ellison (dau James Hiter and Dolly E. T Foree Ellison), and they were the parents of Hiter Crockett, o

Frankfort; c, William Overton, the teacher, m Margaret Dillon; d, Florence, m Alfred Stedman; e, Edmund, m Mary Holton, and they were the parents of Mrs. Fanny Frazier, of Frankfort; f, James G., of whom the statue was made for the monument to the Confederate soldiers in the Franklin cemetery; g, Dandridge; h, Emma, m Dr. Coleman D. Pattie°.

John Vaughan lived in the Bridgeport neighborhood, and had a family of ten. He died F 1814, leaving his wife, Elizabeth, and children. Lucy L. Vaughan (dau Elizabeth), m Stith M. Hawkins°, F 1825; Elizabeth Vaughan (dau Elizabeth), m Owsy Daniel°. Others in that vicinity were: John Vaughan, m Elizabeth Newberry, F 1813; John H. (1800 or 1803-1876) m first Almira Payne (dau Col. Samuel and Nancy Blackwell° Payne), F 1829, and second Eliza Jane Richardson°, 1841. James Vaughan m Maria Motts, F 1821; James m Catherine Jackson°, F 1830; and the infant heirs of one James Vaughan, F 1847, were James F., Amanda, Ellen, Emily, Martha, Elizabeth. Nelson Vaughan m Sally Jackson°, and died F 1814, leaving a son, John J., who m Dorinda Pemberton°, F 1837, and they went to Shelby. They were ancestors of Mrs. Ada Darlington, of Frankfort. Winston Vaughan (1798-1885) m first Polly Gale°, F 1821, and they had several children; he m second Sally Richardson (dau John Scofield and wid Hiram Richardson), F 1839.

Philip Vaughan m Margaret Blanton° in Virginia, and they had William, who was of age in 1807, another son, and two daughters. It is not known whether these children came to Kentucky or not. One Philip Vaughan m Sarah Fleming Bates, Halifax County, Virginia, 1790. The will of Philip Vaughan, Green County, Kentucky, 1827, names his wife Judith, son John, dau Sarah Fryer, granddau Judith B. Clark.

John Vaughan was in Woodford, 1790. He lived on Clear Creek, and was the father of: 1, Ellen, m John Dale, W 1808, and went to Shelby; 2, Jane, m first William Pemberton°, and second John Dale, Shelby 1838; 3, Alpheus, who died 1828, leaving his wife (Louisa?), and son, Andrew T.; 4, James, of Shelby. David and Daniel Vaughan were in W 1797. Daniel m Polly Covenhoven, W 1797, and had a family of eight, W 1810. James A. Vaughan m Sallie E. Lewis°, W 1856. William Vaughan m Mary Christie, W 1824. Cornelius Vaughan (s James) m Franky

Webster, Fayette 1806; Cornelius m Emily Fitzpatrick, Fayette 1850.

Blackwell: Robert Blackwell (1758-1856) m Mary White. They came from Orange County, Virginia, and settled in that part of Franklin that is now Anderson. Some of their children were: 1, Patsy (1789-1861), m Andrew McBrayer, F 1805; 2, Elizabeth Pulliam°; 3, Nancy, m Col. Samuel Payne, F 1810; 4, Sally, m Gen. Christopher Lillard, F 1818; 5, John F., m Mrs. Rachel Russell (dau William Lawrence), F 1822; 6, Fannie Vaughan°; 7, Robert Preston, m Susanna Crutcher°, W 1826. Their home was at the southeast corner of the intersection of the Versailles-Frankfort and Grassy Spring pikes, nearly opposite the Lafayette Crutcher homestead. Tombstones in the Grassy Spring churchyard indicate that their children were: a, Mary Ann, m Dr. Bradford C. Snedaker, and they had: Alonzo; Preston, who went to Texas; Joseph; William; Laura, m Rev. Ross Lloyd; b, Isaac R.; c, Martha F., m I. R. Blackwell.

VAWTER–Jesse, 1803

David Vawter, of Orange County, Virginia, went to Orange, where he m Mary Rucker. After his death, his widow m James Rentfrow°. David and Mary Vawter had: 1, Rev. Jesse (1755- ——), m Elizabeth Watts°, Culpeper 1781, and their children were: a, Rev. John, who preached first at Long Lick, in Scott, going later to Vernon, Ind. He m first Polly Smith, 1805; second Jane Smith; third Ruth Minton; fourth Mrs. Martha Pearce. b, William, m his cousin, Frances Vawter, Gallatin 1809; c, James, m Sarah B. Watts°, 1816; d, Frances Branham°; e, Mary Branham°; f, Sarah, m Thomas T. Stribling, F 1806; g, Julia, m Matthew Wise; h, Achilles, m Martha Smith; i, Ann, m Abner Moncrief.

In 1803 Rev. Jesse was licensed to preach at North Fork, where he served for several years before going to Dearborn County, Indiana. He was described as "a good preacher, an easy, fluent speaker, and an excellent singer," and eventually was known and loved throughout a wide territory.

2, Rev. Philemon, m his cousin, Ann Vawter (dau Beverly), 1779. Their children were: a, Richard, of Lexington, m Sarah

Snelling, 1802; b, Elliott, m Anna Gray, 1804, and lived in Todd; c, Frances, m her cousin, William Vawter; d, Nancy, m Alexander Lewis; e, Jesse, m Frances Ann Watts°, and lived in Oldham; f, Beverly, m Elizabeth Crawford; g, Lucy, m James Crawford; h, Elizabeth, m James Glover; i, David, m Lucinda Glover. In 1792 Philemon came with his family to Woodford, where he became a member of the Clear Creek Church. He went to Boone County in 1795, thence to Trimble, and to Indiana in 1808. He was ordained in 1797, and "was much loved by the people, and exerted all his influence for good."

3, William, m Mary Rucker, Orange County, Virginia, 1784, and came to Versailles, where in 1810 he had a family of nine. He afterward went to Boone. 4, Winifred; 5, Margaret Stapp°; 6, Mary.

Also in Versailles, 1810, were Edmund F. Vawter with a family of three, and Jesse with four. Maria Vawter m George W. Rucker, W 1809; Daniel Vawter m Harriet Rucker, W 1812. William Vawter m Ann Bullard°, Orange County, Virginia, 1774. One William was in W 1791, listed afterward as owning land on Glen's and Griers creeks.

WALDON—Walden, Philip, 1
Joseph and wife, to Glen's Creek 1801

The Waldens apparently came from Pittsylvania County, Virginia. John Walden was in Woodford 1790. Elijah Walden m Martha Nowlin°, Garrard 1800, and in W 1810 one Elijah had a family of five, and Joseph had nine, including Mary Ann, m John McDonald or McDaniel°. One Joseph m Nancy Davenport° (dau Richard), W 1812; Joseph m Mrs. Nancy Reardon, W 1815; William m Sally Mitchell°, W 1817; Polly m John *Debenport* (Davenport?), F 1820.

Edmund Walden sold land on Glen's Creek to William Brightwell about 1839.

WALLACE—Artimesia, dis 1843

John Wallace m Artimesia Stephens°. Thomas Wallace m Juretta Hawkins°, F 1831. One Thomas was the father of Dollie Ann Haydon°. Thomas sold land below Leestown to John McClelland, F 1810.

Samuel McDowell Wallace (s Judge Caleb Wallace) m Matilda Lee (dau Maj. John and Elizabeth Bell Lee), W 1816 or 1817, and their son Thomas m Frances Taylor, of Beaufort, S. C., and was the father of Louise Lewis°.

Fannie Wallace (wife of Reuben) bought land on the Peak's Mill pike from Andrew Webster°, F 1878.

WALLER—Benjamin, 1788

The notes on the Waller family have been gathered from many sources, and their connection is not always easy to understand.

The name of Benjamin Waller was dropped from the list in 1792 because of his long absence. One Benjamin Waller was in Gallatin, 1822.

John Waller (1673-1754), a son of Col. John and Mary Key Waller, of Spotsylvania County, Virginia, m Dorothy King, and among their children were: Mary, m Zachary Lewis°; Benjamin, m Martha Hall, 1746, and had a son, Benjamin Carter, who m Catherine Page; Col. Edmund, who m Mary Pendleton (dau Philip and Martha Pendleton), and they had: 1, Rev. John (1741-1802?), was one of the jury in Virginia that, about 1765, indicted Lewis Craig for preaching the forbidden doctrine, but afterward was so much impressed by Lewis Craig's preaching that he was converted, and in 1768 he himself was imprisoned for preaching. He became one of the most distinguished Baptist ministers of his generation.

He came to Kentucky with the "Travelling Church," and appears to have been in Bourbon for some time, after which, according to one account, he had a gristmill in Washington County, Kentucky, where his dau Mary m Nehemiah Webb, 1799. One John Waller was in Washington 1794-1805, and Thomas was there 1795-1805. John Waller m Garner Routt (dau William), Bourbon 1786; Thomas m Polly Vaughan, Washington 1793; Dempsey m Sally Slack (dau John), Washington 1804.

2, Rev. William Edmund (1747-1830), m Mildred Smith (dau Stephen), and they also came with the Traveling Church. He was first in Garrard, and then was in the neighborhood of

Bryan's Station in Fayette for about twelve years, and though not a pastor of any church during that time, was "a useful co-laborer with the pioneer preachers of that early period in building up the cause of the Redeemer in the wilderness."

About 1799 he went to Shelby, where he organized Buck Creek Church (Finchville), of which he was pastor for four years. In 1803 he returned to Virginia, where he married the second time. His children were: a, Stephen. One Stephen m Tabitha Prewitt (dau Elisha), Shelby 1799, and a Stephen m Sally McLure, Shelby 1816. He is said to have been the father of: Edmund, m Elizabeth Johnston (dau Thomas), of Barren; George, m Angelina F. Lewis, Barren 1834; and William, m Sarah Ann Johnson (dau Thomas). Abraham Vanzant m Jane Waller, Barren 1820. b, Sarah; c, Mary Price°; d, Rev. Edmund (1775-1843), m first Ann Durrett, and second Elizabeth Lightfoot (dau John), F 1800. They went to Anderson, where in 1801 they joined the Salt River Church under John Penny. In Franklin, 1802, Edmund was granted credentials to celebrate the rites of matrimony. He preached at Bluestone, in Shelby, about five years, and then went to Woodford, where he had charge of the Hillsboro and Glen's Creek churches. He spent his last years in Jessamine. He was considered one of the most influential ministers of his time, having baptized about 1,500 converts.

He had a family of seven, W 1810, one of his children being Rev. John Lightfoot Waller (1809-1854), the brilliant orator and writer, who was ordained in 1840, and three years later succeeded his father at Glen's Creek. He was for several years editor of *The Baptist Banner*, the name of which was afterward changed to *The Western Recorder*. In 1849, in order to debate with Thomas F. Marshall on his convictions concerning slavery, he became a candidate for delegate to the Constitutional Convention, and so compelling were his arguments that he was elected over his opponent by a majority of 219 votes. It was said that his speech in opposition to the adoption of an article in the Constitution making a minister of the Gospel ineligible to a seat in the Legislature was pronounced the ablest of the session.

He lived at one time in an old house on the site which was later used for the home of Dr. John Sullenger.

Rev. Napoleon B. Waller (1826-1855), a brother of John Lightfoot, was born in Jessamine. He was educated at Georgetown College, and was licensed to preach about 1849, but as he was about to accept a pastorate, he was stricken with cholera and died.

e, Rev. George (1777-1860), succeeded his father at Buck Creek. He was described as "a man of enlarged public spirit, prominent in all the general enterprises of his denomination." He m Polly Ware° (dau Reuben), and they had: A. D., the father of Rev. William Edmund, Jr. (1845-1878), who was ordained in 1868, and served as a missionary in Jefferson, Bullitt, Shelby, and Franklin; and Lucinda B., m Chesterfield Overstreet, 1829.

f, Lucy, m —— Smith; g, Richard; h, William Smith, m Catherine Breckinridge, W 1810. They lived in Frankfort, in the house now occupied by Mrs. H. P. Mason, and had seven children, including Catherine, m James G. Carson, F 1835. In that same year the family went to Lexington, but there is evidence that his will was probated in Carroll, 1849. i, Nancy Jane.

3, Benjamin (1749-1835), m Jean Custis.

William Brannum m Phoebe Waller (dau Benjamin, deceased), Henry 1828.

WARE—	
James, 1789	Sally, 1789
Nicholas, 1801, dis 1805	Agnes, 1800
Polly, 1801, dis 1805	Sally, r 1811
Iverson, 1801	Rebecca, 1801, dis 1840
Reuben, r 1801	Edmund, 1789
Nancy, r 1801	Susanna, 1789
John, 1801-1809, to Shelby	
James, Jr., 1801-1815	
William, 1795	

James Ware (1714-1796) and his wife Agnes, of Gloucester County, Virginia, were in Caroline 1777, and came afterward to Kentucky, locating at "Wareland" (the Bedford place, now owned by the Hay family, at the intersection of the Frankfort-

Versailles and Shady Lane pikes). Their children were: 1, John (1736- ——), m Ann Harrison (dau Andrew), of Goochland County, Virginia; 2, Nicholas, d before 1796, leaving some children. One Nicholas m Polly Sanders, F 1798, the bond being signed by James and Charles Sanders°. His will, Shelby 1837, mentions his wife Mary and: a, James; b, Susanna, m Archibald Collins, Shelby 1828; c, Jeptha; d, Robert; e, Nancy; f, Catherine Murphy°; g, Eliza Jane; h, Nicholas. Iverson Ware m Anne Hansbrough, Shelby 1811, and his will, Shelby 1822, mentions his wife Anne, and children, John and Louisianny.

3, Dr. James (1741-1820), m Virginia Catherine Todd° (dau Dr. James Todd), 1764, and they came to Fayette. Their children were: a, George; b, James; c, Charles, m Fanny ——, and lived in Woodford; d, Thompson, m Sally Conn (dau Thomas), and they had: Lucy Bedford°; Kitty Todd°; Davidella; e, Lucy, m Capt. Isaac Webb; f, Polly, m Charles Webb; g, Kitty Scott°. 4, Richard; 5, Clara, m —— Sale; 6, William, m Sarah Samuel°, and they lived at "Wareland." Their children were: a, Elizabeth Bacon°; b, James; c, Agnes, m first Philemon Rowsey, F 1805, and had Maria; she m second William Porter°; d, Rebecca Blanton°; e, Sarah Porter°; f, Samuel, m first, Elizabeth Read°, W 1801, and had: Hankinson; Agnes, m Major Thomas Bullock, and went to Illinois; Ann Richardson Fogg°; James R.; William S. He m second Mrs. Elizabeth Redd (dau James and Anne Waller Bullock, and widow of Thomas M. Redd), W 1823, and they had Elizabeth, m J. B. Utterback; he m third Mrs. Mary Ann Jennings, F 1834, the bond being signed by Elias B. Meyers.

7, Edmund (1753-1814), m Susanna ——, and they probably built the original house at "Scotland," now owned by the Hay family. Their children were: a, Nathaniel; b, Elizabeth Blanton°; c, Nancy Samuel°; d, Agnes Jeffreys°; e, Susan Samuel°; f, James; g, Sally Stephens°; h, Lewis; i, Kitty; j, Edmund.

Reuben Ware, who evidently went to Shelby, was the father of Polly Waller°.

George Ware m Nancy Ferguson° (dau Abraham), Fayette 1812; James Ware m Joannah Parrish (dau James and Tabitha Parrish), W 1810. Isaac Ware was in Fayette 1788.

WEBSTER—Polly, r 1818

Andrew Webster m Usilla Smither°, Orange County, Virginia, 1788. The estate of one Andrew was inventoried, F 1808.

Andrew, the father of Mary Haydon° and the grandfather of Ira Webster and Mrs. Bowman Gaines, of Frankfort, came from Virginia in an ox-cart, and died F (1893?) at the age of 104 years.

Andrew Webster bought land on Main Elkhorn from W. R. Graham, F 1860. One Andrew, in Owen, sold land in Franklin County to Dollie Ann Haydon°, 1864.

John Webster was the father of Fanny Cullen°. Achilles Webster m Elizabeth Peckham, W 1812; Arden Webster m Milly Smither°, W 1821, the bond signed by John Smither.

WEST—James, 2

The will of Edward West, W 1792, mentions his wife Elizabeth and children: Edward, William, John, Thomas, Lewis, James, Betsy, Polly, Peggy, Sally. William West m Sally McCracken°, W 1804.

In the Franklin census, John had a family of eight; Jeremiah, who lived on Elkhorn, had seven; Reuben had eight; Reason, who lived on Cedar Creek in the section that was afterward a part of Owen, had eight; and three Williams had respectively six, two, and two. One Reason West m Polly Smither, F 1812, and Harriet (dau Reason) m Benjamin Berry, F 1800. James West m Judith Pate Bacon° (dau Elizabeth Barrett), F 1815, and went to Elizabethtown. Jacob West m Rebecca Anderson° (dau Joseph), F 1824, and went to Marion County, Missouri, where they had: Joseph, Sanford, Spencer, Adiline, Thomas Franklin. William W. West m Sarah Pilcher°, F 1833, and they went to Hendricks County, Indiana. William P. West m Sarah Blanton°, Owen, 1830.

WESTERN—Betsy, r 1820

James Weston (or Western) m Elizabeth C. Gale°, F 1801, and in 1810 they had a family of seven. Samuel Western was in Henry 1818.

WIDNER–Elizabeth, r 1814

George Widner m Elizabeth Mastin°, W 1792, and they had a daughter Sally, m Willis Sharpe, F 1812. Though he lived north of the river in Franklin, he owned land on South Benson in 1801, and in 1810 had a family of three. In 1816 he was living on Eagle Creek in Gallatin.

WILLIAMS–Sally, r 1811, dis 1815
George M., 1843

Sarah Hicks, dau William Randolph and Mary Elizabeth Harris Hicks, m Daniel Jackson Williams. He was the son of Capt. Daniel and Mary Jackson Williams, who came from Virginia and settled on the farm on the Mt. Vernon-Pisgah pike now owned by their great-grandson, Claude S. Williams. Daniel Jackson, who taught a high school in Woodford, was also a surveyor and a farmer. He and his wife lived at "Pleasant Lawn," and had: 1, Daniel Jackson (1821-1881), who lived on the Big Sink pike and was a member of Glen's Creek Church, m first Amanda Weathers, Fayette 1851, and their dau Bettie m John O. Rogers. He m second Susan McClure, Anderson 1857; 2, John Hicks.

John Williams, designated in the tax list as "Irish," lived on Elkhorn. His will, W 1802, names his wife Agnes and children: William, John, Moses, Mary Martin°, Elizabeth Beard, Nancy, Jane Brady, Becca, Peggy, Sally Ann. His heirs sold his farm to Thomas Redd, W 1813.

John Williams, Sr., lived on Sinking Creek (Big Sink). His will, W 1825, mentions his wife Sarah; brother Andrew, of Franklin County; children: Andrew, William, John, Sarah, Thomas, Mary, Henry, James. His heirs sold the property to —— Martin in 1830.

Another John Williams, on Glen's Creek, died W 1811, leaving his wife Sarah, and: William, Betsy Usselton, Abigail Holeman, Polly Latta, Sally Flora, Rachel Harrison, Pheby Delaney; grandson William McCracken°; granddaughter Sarah Ship°. This farm was sold to Abraham Hammon, W 1844.

Josiah Williams (s John Williams, of Philadelphia), m Nancy Finnie°, W 1801, and had a family of eight, W 1810. They were on Elkhorn in 1812, but went afterward to Union.

William Williams, who lived on the river, died W 1805, leaving his wife Keziah and sons George, Urbane, Ezra, Zepheniah. The will of one George Williams, F 1844, mentions his wife Elizabeth, his children (not named), and his brother-in-law John P. Reading.

Elias ᴍM. Williams m Elizabeth Dixon°, Owen 1828. They lived near Switzer, and their children were: 1, Cyrus, m ——, and their dau Rebecca m —— Jenkins; 2, Merit, m Mary J. Crutcher°; 3, Mattie, m William Seay°; 4, Mary, m —— O'Nan.

John Williams m Kitty Eddins°, W 1818; John m Martha McCracken°, W 1822; Joseph m Adeline Sparks°, W 1828; James m Julian Martin°, W 1832.

One John Williams m Winnefred Howard in Richmond County, Virginia, 1781. They came to Woodford in 1785 and settled on Clear Creek. Two of their children were Polly Edwards° and Nancy Davenport°.

There were many intermarriages among the Williams, Harrison, and Tutt families.

WILSON—Isaac, dis to Forks of Elkhorn 1818, r 1841
               Lucy, r 1804, dis to Forks of Elkhorn 1818
               John, r 1841
               Polly, r 1841
               Jane, dis 1845
               Sally, r 1811, left years before 1817

The name "Isaac" was a favorite in the Wilson family. Records of Culpeper County, Virginia, show that Isaac Wilson m Eliza Cook, 1793; Isaac Wilson m Anna Garnett, 1798. Isaac Wilson came from Philadelphia to Fayette in 1787 and established the Lexington Grammar School. Isaac m Sarah Neal, Fayette 1808; one Isaac m Nancy Clark, Fayette 1818.

One Isaac was in Woodford 1791. John Taylor speaks of the illness of "Old Man Wilson"—possibly the Isaac whose inventory was recorded in Jessamine, 1801. The will of one Isaac was probated in Nelson, 1844.

In Woodford, one Isaac had land on Glen's Creek, and one on Craig's Creek. Jeremiah was on Craig's Creek; Thomas and

John on Clear Creek; Joseph on Elkhorn. One Isaac m Lydia Ashford, W 1831.

The records indicate that one Isaac was the son of Joseph Wilson, of Wilkes County, North Carolina, whose widow m John Whitaker.

In 1800 Isaac Wilson bought land at Woodlake from the Rev. John Taylor, and he m first Lucy Morton (dau Jeremiah), W 1801. Their children were: 1, America Price°; 2, Eliza Ann, m Capt. Thomas Steele, Jr., F 1829, and they had William and Dr. Theophilus; 3, Jane; 4, Benjamin Franklin, m Martha Wilson, and they had: a, Franklin, m Elizabeth Taylor (who afterward m Ryland Bedford°), and they were the parents of Mrs. Lelia Scott, of Georgetown; b, Lucian, m Elizabeth Rankin; c, Dr. J. William, m Mamie Erdman; d, Mattie; e, Mary Miller Gibson°; f, Robert, m Bettie McKee; g, Alice, m Rev. William Williams. 5, Isaac, Jr., m in Texas; 6, John, m Laura Dillon; 7, Nancy Martin°. Isaac Wilson, Sr., m second Mrs. Polly Macey°, F 1831, and they had: 8, Robert A., m Annie Bell (dau James Franklin and Mary Wilson Bell). The will of Isaac, Sr., F 1863, mentions a grandson, John Wilson, and a granddaughter, Nancy Caldwell.

Benjamin Wilson m Barbara Bullock (dau James and Rebecca Wingfield Bullock). They lived on the Versailles-Midway road, and were the parents of Barbara Thompson°.

WOOLDRIDGE—Robert, 1
  Thomas, 1, 1800, dis 1806
  Sally, 1, 1800, dis 1806

Thomas and Edmund Wooldridge, according to the statement of William Hickman, were in the party who in 1776 started with him for Kentucky.

Thomas, who was a minister, went from Franklin to Shelby, and in 1811 was living in Henry. His wife was Sally (Porter?), and the will of their son, John B., F 1822, mentions his two sisters, Polly Hall° and Betsy Wingate°, and his father.

Edmund m Elizabeth Watkins (dau John and Phoebe Hancock Watkins), and their children were: 1, Edmund (1776-——), went to Mississippi; 2, Samuel C., went to Texas; 3,

Phoebe, m Philip Watkins (s Samuel), W 1798; 4, Nancy, m Stewart Wilkins, W 1798; 5, John W., m Eliza M. Jeffries° and in 1822, after selling his farm to William Samuel and Samuel Ware, he settled near Hopkinsville. His dau, Mary Elizabeth, was under the guardianship of Henry and Samuel Moss, F 1840. 6, Powhatan, m Mildred Major°, F 1815, and they were in Christian in 1820, going later to Missouri, though some of the family afterward returned to Woodford. Edmund, Sr., died in Woodford about 1791, and his widow m John Moss, W 1792.

Robert, who was in Fayette 1787, m Susanna Major°, and their children, who went to Christian, were: 1, Merrite; 2, Thomas, m Eliza Cates; 3, John; 4, Elizabeth Redd Jeffries°. Robert died after 1796, and Susanna m Ritchie Boulware°. Robert's farm, which adjoined that of John Major, was sold in 1814 to Lewis R. Major.

In 1800 Josiah Wooldridge was living on Griers Creek in Woodford, but in 1820 he was in Henry. He m Martha Trabue°, and they had: 1, Seth, m Mary Ewing°; 2, Daniel, m Lucy Thurman; 3, Samuel; 4, Martha, m Major Cheatham, W 1808, and went to Illinois; 5, Mary, m Joseph B. White, W 1808; 6, Claiborne, m Frances Trabue°, 1838; 7, Stephen, m Mary Williams°; 8, Josiah, m Elizabeth Hill; 9, Judith, m James Trabue°; 10, Levi, m Henrietta Phelps; 11, Livingston.

Elisha Wooldridge was in W 1791, and in 1810 he had a family of seven.

William Wooldridge, of Clark, whose dau m Mordecai Boulware°, was evidently of this family, as the bond was signed by Robert Wooldridge, and the marriage witnessed by Edmund Wooldridge.

LeGrand F. Rucker m Caroline Wooldridge, W 1813.

Leroy Wooldridge m Emily Owen°, 1837, and they lived at the Owen Tavern in Benson Valley, northwest of Frankfort.

YESTERDAY (Easterday)—Susannah, 1

This is a significant word with which to conclude a Church history, for though we look at Yesterday, we must always see— Easter Day.

INDEX

In this index, family groups are marked with °, and those included in them, unless for special reasons, are not indexed elsewhere. Listed under the same names are other persons apparently not connected.

Rouzie, Rowsey, 228, 300
Row, Rowe, 2, 140
Rowan, 184
Rowland, 64
Rowlett, 242°
Royster, 144
Rozzelle, 214
Rucker, 196, 235, 295, 296, 305
Runamus, 226
Runyan, 153°
Rupe, 256
Rush, 131
Russell, 88, 169, 229, 243, 265, 275, 295
Rust, 134, 229, 253
Ruth, 157
Rutherford, Rediford, 242°
Ryland, 97

Sacra, 107, 113, 227
Saffell, 88, 286
Sager, 252
Sale, 66, 113, 159, 225, 251, 266, 300
Salley, 28
Salyers, 102, 207
Samonis, 27
Sampey, 48, 51, 52, 55, 56, 57
Samples, 89, 169, 182, 209
Samuel, 243°, 291
Sanders, 140, 233, 246°
Sanderson, 171
Sandifer, 262
Sanford, 127, 156, 248°, 254
Santa Anna, 7
Sargent, 161°
Satterwhite, 68, 93, 117
Saunders, 80
Sawyier, 284
Sayre, 280
Scandland, 248°
Scearce, 114, 155, 171, 243, 293
Scofield, 198, 201, 232, 237, 294
Schnebley, 195
Scholl, 19
Schools, 29, 45
Scott, 60, 110, 119, 123, 155, 203, 233, 250°, 277, 304
Scroggin, 105
Scrogin, 90
Scruggs, 74, 188, 266
Sea, 136
Searcy, 28, 126, 129, 158, 233
Seay, 115°
Sebree, 88, 158, 169
Seely, 257
Self, 209
Settle, 253°

Shackleford, 67, 173, 174, 207, 253, 254°
Shaddoa, 255°
Shadrick, 255°
Shannon, 11, 117, 213, 229, 232, 234, 243
Sharp, 211
Sharpe, 302
Shaw, 130, 167, 253, 255°, 283
Sheehan, 226
Sheets, 256°
Shefer, 231
Shelburn, 123
Shelby, 97, 174, 286
Shelton, 81, 98, 139, 241, 286
Shely, 85°, 234, 241
Shepard, Shephard, 28, 131, 257
Shepherd, 208, 275
Sheridan, 168
Sherman, 109
Shields, 285
Shiell, 178, 194, 287
Shiloh Meetinghouse, 14
Shipman, 165
Shipp, 256°
Shockley, 259°
Shoole, 192
Short, 144
Shortridge, 70
Shouse, 207
Shrewsbury, 124
Shroff, 106
Shropshire, 86, 224
Shryock, 57, 67, 89, 114, 196
Shumate, 53
Simcox, 147
Simmons, 92
Simonus, 259°
Simpson, 70, 78, 114, 123, 268
Sinclair, 74, 244
Singleton, 79, 195, 227, 229°
Sisk, 259°
Skinner, 143
Slack, 119, 177, 297
Slaughter, 28, 201, 229, 234, 244, 265
Sleet, 201
Smart, 117, 218, 224, 267
Smeathers, 263°
Smith, 86, 105, 117, 119, 141, 143, 153, 157, 158, 165, 169, 178, 181, 191, 261°, 288, 295, 297
Smithe, 263°
Smither, 227, 263°, 301
Smoot, 242
Smothers, 227
Smythy, 270
Snape, 102, 266
Snedaker, 295